HITLER'S FINAL FORTRESS

The Stackpole Military History Series

THE AMERICAN CIVIL WAR

Cavalry Raids of the Civil War
Ghost, Thunderbolt, and Wizard
In the Lion's Mouth
Witness to Gettysburg

WORLD WAR I

Doughboy War

WORLD WAR II

After D-Day
Airborne Combat
Armor Battles of the Waffen-SS, 1943–45
Armoured Guardsmen
Army of the West
Arnhem 1944
The B-24 in China
Backwater War
The Battalion
Battle of Paoli
The Battle of France
The Battle of Sicily
Battle of the Bulge, Vol. 1
Battle of the Bulge, Vol. 2
Battle of the Bulge, Vol. 3
Beyond the Beachhead
Beyond Stalingrad
The Black Bull
Blitzkrieg Unleashed
Blossoming Silk Against the Rising Sun
Bodenplatte
The Breaking Point
The Brigade
The Canadian Army and the Normandy
    Campaign
Coast Watching in World War II
Colossal Cracks
Condor
A Dangerous Assignment
D-Day Bombers
D-Day Deception
D-Day to Berlin
Decision in the Ukraine
The Defense of Moscow 1941
Destination Normandy
Dive Bomber!
A Drop Too Many
Eager Eagles
Eagles of the Third Reich
The Early Battles of Eighth Army
Eastern Front Combat
Europe in Flames
Exit Rommel
The Face of Courage
Fatal Decisions
Fist from the Sky
Flying American Combat Aircraft of World
    War II, Vol. 1
Flying American Combat Aircraft of World
    War II, Vol. 2
For Europe
Forging the Thunderbolt
For the Homeland
Fortress France

The German Defeat in the East, 1944–45
German Order of Battle, Vol. 1
German Order of Battle, Vol. 2
German Order of Battle, Vol. 3
The Germans in Normandy
Germany's Panzer Arm in World War II
GI Ingenuity
Goodbye, Transylvania
Goodwood
The Great Ships
Grenadiers
Guns Against the Reich
Hitler's Final Fortress
Hitler's Nemesis
Hitler's Spanish Legion
Hold the Westwall
Infantry Aces
In the Fire of the Eastern Front
Iron Arm
Iron Knights
Japanese Army Fighter Aces
Japanese Naval Fighter Aces
JG 26 Luftwaffe Fighter Wing War Diary,
    Vol. 1
JG 26 Luftwaffe Fighter Wing War Diary,
    Vol. 2
Kampfgruppe Peiper at the Battle of
    the Bulge
The Key to the Bulge
Kursk
Luftwaffe Aces
Luftwaffe Fighter Ace
Luftwaffe Fighter-Bombers over Britain
Luftwaffe Fighters and Bombers
Massacre at Tobruk
Mechanized Juggernaut or Military
    Anachronism?
Messerschmitts over Sicily
Michael Wittmann, Vol. 1
Michael Wittmann, Vol. 2
Mission 85
Mission 376
Mountain Warriors
The Nazi Rocketeers
Night Flyer / Mosquito Pathfinder
No Holding Back
On the Canal
Operation Mercury
Panzer Aces
Panzer Aces II
Panzer Aces III
Panzer Commanders of the Western Front
Panzergrenadier Aces
Panzer Gunner
The Panzer Legions
Panzers in Normandy
Panzers in Winter
Panzer Wedge, Vol. 1
Panzer Wedge, Vol. 2
The Path to Blitzkrieg
Penalty Strike
Poland Betrayed
Prince of Aces
Red Road from Stalingrad

Red Star Under the Baltic
Retreat to the Reich
Rommel Reconsidered
Rommel's Desert Commanders
Rommel's Desert War
Rommel's Lieutenants
The Savage Sky
The Seeds of Disaster
Ship-Busters
The Siege of Brest, 1941
The Siege of Küstrin
The Siegfried Line
A Soldier in the Cockpit
Soviet Blitzkrieg
Spitfires and Yellow Tail Mustangs
Stalin's Keys to Victory
Surviving Bataan and Beyond
T-34 in Action
Tank Tactics
Tigers in the Mud
Triumphant Fox
The 12th SS, Vol. 1
The 12th SS, Vol. 2
Twilight of the Gods
Typhoon Attack
The War Against Rommel's Supply Lines
War in the Aegean
War of the White Death
Warsaw 1944
Winter Storm
The Winter War
Wolfpack Warriors
Zhukov at the Oder

THE COLD WAR / VIETNAM

Cyclops in the Jungle
Expendable Warriors
Fighting in Vietnam
Flying American Combat Aircraft:
    The Cold War
Here There Are Tigers
Land with No Sun
Phantom Reflections
Street without Joy
Through the Valley
Tours of Duty
Two One Pony

WARS OF AFRICA AND THE MIDDLE EAST

The Rhodesian War

GENERAL MILITARY HISTORY

Carriers in Combat
Cavalry from Hoof to Track
Desert Battles
Guerrilla Warfare
The Philadelphia Campaign, Vol. 1
Ranger Dawn
Sieges
The Spartan Army

HITLER'S FINAL FORTRESS

Breslau 1945

Richard Hargreaves

STACKPOLE
BOOKS

Published in paperback in the U.S. in 2015 by
STACKPOLE BOOKS
5067 Ritter Road
Mechanicsburg, PA 17055
www.stackpolebooks.com

Printed in the United States of America

10 9 8 7 6 5 4 3 2 1

Cover design by Wendy Reynolds

Library of Congress Cataloging-in-Publication Data

Hargreaves, Richard, 1972–
   Hitler's final fortress : Breslau 1945 / Richard Hargreaves.
      pages cm. — (Stackpole military history series)
   First published in the United Kingdom in 2011 by Pen & Sword Military.
   Includes bibliographical references and index.
   ISBN 978-0-8117-1551-5
1. Hitler, Adolf, 1889–1945. 2. World War, 1939–1945—Campaigns—Poland—Wroclaw. 3. World War, 1939–1945—Campaigns—Germany. 4. World War, 1939–1945—Campaigns—Soviet Union. 5. Wroclaw (Poland)—History—Siege, 1945. 6. Twierdza Wroclaw (Wroclaw, Poland) I. Title.
   D765.2.W7H37 2015
   940.54'213852—dc23
                                      2014040825

CONTENTS

Introduction

On a summer's day in Wrocław, take a stroll along *Ulica* Marie Curie Sklodowskiej – Marie Curie Sklodowskiej Street. Modern 'bendy buses' with TV screens and electronic ticket machines vie for room on the suburban boulevard with clapped-out yellow coaches and trams which trundle east and west at regular intervals. After ten or so minutes you will cross the *Most Zwierzyniecki* – Zwierzyniecki bridge – which spans one of the countless arms of the Oder. It has stood here since 1897 – there is an inscription celebrating the toil of the men who spent two years building it. But like all traces of the city's Germanic past, the plaque above the dateline has gone. Less easy to erase are the traces of battle; as with many of Wrocław's Oder crossings, Most Zwierzyniecki, is scarred by the bullets which struck it in the spring of 1945. Across the bridge you enter a district of avenues lined by trees. Ulica Marie Curie Sklodowskiej becomes Ulica Zygmunta Wróblewskiego – the fourth title it has enjoyed in a century. On your right are the zoological gardens, on your left Ulica Adama Mickiewicza. Follow it for 150 yards until the trees part, revealing an alley leading to one of Wrocław's jewels: *Hala Ludowa* – the People's Hall – Max Berg's imposing colosseum of concrete and steel, built in 1913 to celebrate the 100th anniversary of the German people breaking the shackles of Napoleonic rule. Tall columns, their plinths empty, lead down a sprawling concourse, dominated by a gigantic metallic spike or spire, the *Iglica*, erected in 1948 to celebrate Silesia's 'return' to Poland. To the left is a four-domed exhibition hall, latterly home to the *Wytwórnia Filmów Fabularnych* – the factory of feature films. Four concrete modernist statues stand guard in front of it. The entrances are barred, the doors obliterated by Polish graffiti. The portico's cracked tile floor is covered with leaves, cigarette ends, sweet wrappers and other detritus. At one end of this seemingly forgotten porch is a huge tablet in a wretched state of repair, honouring the deeds of Polish soldiers who marched westwards with Soviet troops in 1944 and 1945 from the Bug to the Vistula, through Warsaw, through Pomerania, across the Oder and Neisse, and finally into Berlin. Turn around and you will find another huge stone inscription. A helmet adorned with a Red Star sits on a laurel wreath, chipped and discoloured, stained by more than six decades' exposure to the elements. Beneath it a litany of Red Army victories: Moscow, Stalingrad, Kursk, Leningrad, the Ukraine, Byelorussia, Warsaw, Budapest and Bucharest, Belgrade, Vienna, Prague, and Berlin among them, plus the name of this city, Wrocław. Like every monument, memorial and grave for the fallen of 1945, the gigantic tablets in the grounds of the Hala Ludowa are crumbling, decaying, overgrown, unloved, forgotten.

For once a terrible battle raged for this city. The siege of Breslau – as it was then – lasted longer than the battle for any other German city in 1945. The city was encircled for longer than Berlin (ten days), Budapest (sixty days), even Stalingrad (seventy-three days). It is a struggle which came to naught for the defenders. It achieved nothing, save to reduce a city, which was barely touched by war as 1945 began, to a ruin by the time it surrendered on May 6th. The devastation wrought was greater than in the German capital, greater than in Dresden – that byword for destruction in World War 2 – and as great as in Hamburg, another metropolis laid waste by Allied bombers.* At least 18,000 of Breslau's population died in less than one week, fleeing the advancing Red Army in the depths of winter. A further 25,000 people – soldiers, civilians, foreign labourers, prisoners – were killed during the twelve-week struggle for Breslau. Nor does the story – or the suffering – end with the city's fall. For the German survivors, bitter fates awaited: for the soldiers, prison camps in the Soviet Union; for civilians, rape, plunder and starvation, and finally expulsion from their homes as Silesia became Polish and Breslau became Wrocław. For Polish settlers – many driven from their homeland like the Germans they displaced – there were decades of toil and hardship as they struggled to rebuild the Silesian capital.

They succeeded. Today Wrocław is a flourishing city once more, the fourth largest in Poland, its war-scarred landscape cleared, its battle-scarred buildings restored and rebuilt. It is a seat of learning, the heart of Poland's electronics and rail industries, a centre of banking and finance, a destination for hundreds of thousands of tourists every year. Most of these visitors are oblivious to the bitter struggle for Breslau.

The actors may be bit-part players compared with those at the fall of Berlin, the stakes not as high as at Stalingrad, the suffering not as protracted as in Leningrad, but the siege of Breslau is terrible, if compelling, drama. For the sake of the men and women involved on all sides it is a story which deserves to be told.

Gosport, November 2010

---

* Around one in five buildings in Berlin was destroyed during the war; the figure in Dresden was double that; some two in every three homes in Hamburg and Breslau were uninhabitable; the heart of Aachen lost four out of five homes; and in Cologne, an estimated ninety-five per cent of the old town was destroyed.

Acknowledgements

No-one can embark upon researching the fall of Breslau without consulting two seminal works. Horst Gleiss's monumental *Breslauer Apokalypse* and the thousands of documents and testimonies it contains is a project unique in the history of World War II; it forms the kernel of this book. Similarly, Norman Davies and Roger Moorhouse's *Microcosm* is a wonderful biography of Breslau/Wrocław, which is as balanced as it is illuminating. Jan-Hendrik Wendler deserves special mention for providing documents relating to Schörner's Army Group and obscure German unit histories. Elsewhere, the staff of the Bundesarchiv in Freiburg proved as helpful as ever, as did the staff of the Department of Documents at the Imperial War Museum, London; the Public Record Office, Kew; the following libraries: University of Nottingham, University of Manchester, University of Sussex, University of Portsmouth, University of Warwick, and Lancashire, Portsmouth, and Nottinghamshire; New York Public Libraries; British Newspaper Library. I would also like to thank: Jason Pipes and his colleagues at www.feldgrau.net; Michael Miller for his help with Karl Hanke's biography; Howard Davies for his inestimable knowledge of the German language; Matt Abicht for rare aerial photographs of the battle; Andy Brady for the maps; Tom Houlihan, Bill Russ, Yan Mann, Darren Beck, for proofreading, advice, and occasional moral support. The book which follows is all the richer for their input. For any mistakes, I alone bear responsibility.

Abbreviations Used in References

AOK	*Armeeoberkommando* – staff of an army in the field
BA-MA	*Bundesarchiv-Militär Archiv* – Bundesarchiv Military Archive, Freiburg
Div	Division
DDRZW	*Das Deutsche Reich und der Zweite Weltkrieg*
Documenty	*Festung Breslau: Documenty Oblezenia 16/2-6/5/45*
HGr	*Heeresgruppe* – Army Group
IMT	International Military Tribunal
IWM	Imperial War Museum, London
Kdo	Kommando – command
KTB	*Kriegstagebuch* – war diary
NA	National Archives, Kew
NMT	Nuremberg Military Tribunal
OKH	*Oberkommando des Heeres* – German Army High Command
OKW	*Oberkommando der Wehrmacht* – German Armed Forces High Command
Pz	Panzer
SD Meldung	*Sicherheitsdienst* – SS Security Service – report
TB Cohn	Diary of Willi Cohn
TB Goebbels	Diary of Joseph Goebbels
TB Oven	Diary of Wilfred von Oven
Vertreibung	Dokumentation der Vertreibung der Deutschen aus Ost-Mitteleuropa I, *Die Vertreibung der deutschen Bevölkerung aus den Gebieten östlich der Oder-Neisse*

Author's note

German ranks throughout, with the exception of *Generalfeldmarschall* (field marshal), have been left in their original language. An explanation of the comparative ranks can be found in the appendix. The names of towns, villages, streets and buildings in Silesia retain their German names for events prior to their becoming Polish; thereafter they revert to their post-1945 Polish names.

Map 1

1. Kreuzkirche
2. Cathedral
3. Sandinsel
4. Sandkirche
5. University
6. River Oder
7. Elisabethkirche
8. Oberpräsidium
   (Hanke's headquarters)
9. Sparkasse
10. Ring
11. Rathaus
12. St Maria Magdalena
13. Freiburger Bahnhof
14. Stadtgraben
15. Schlossplatz
16. Dorotheenkirche
17. Stadttheater
18. Liebichshöhe
    (Siege headquarters)
19. Tauentzienplatz
20. Hauptbahnhof
21. St Mauritiuskirche
    (Paul Peikert's church)
22. Lessingbrücke

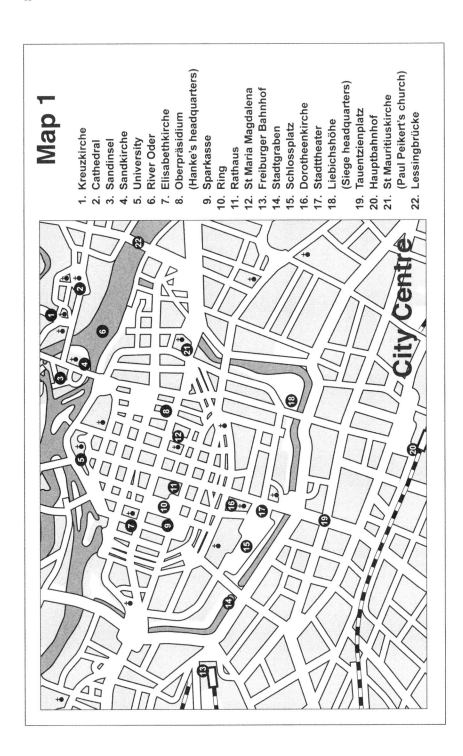

City Centre

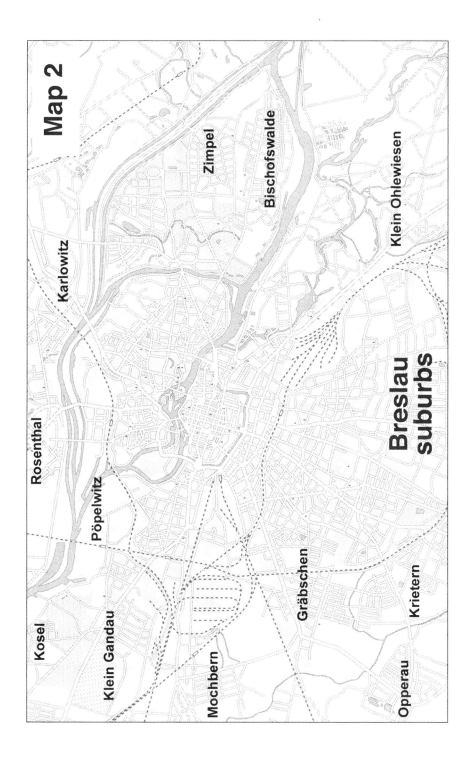

Map 2

Breslau suburbs

Zimpel

Bischofswalde

Klein Ohlewiesen

Karlowitz

Rosenthal

Pöpelwitz

Kosel

Klein Gandau

Mochbern

Gräbschen

Krietern

Opperau

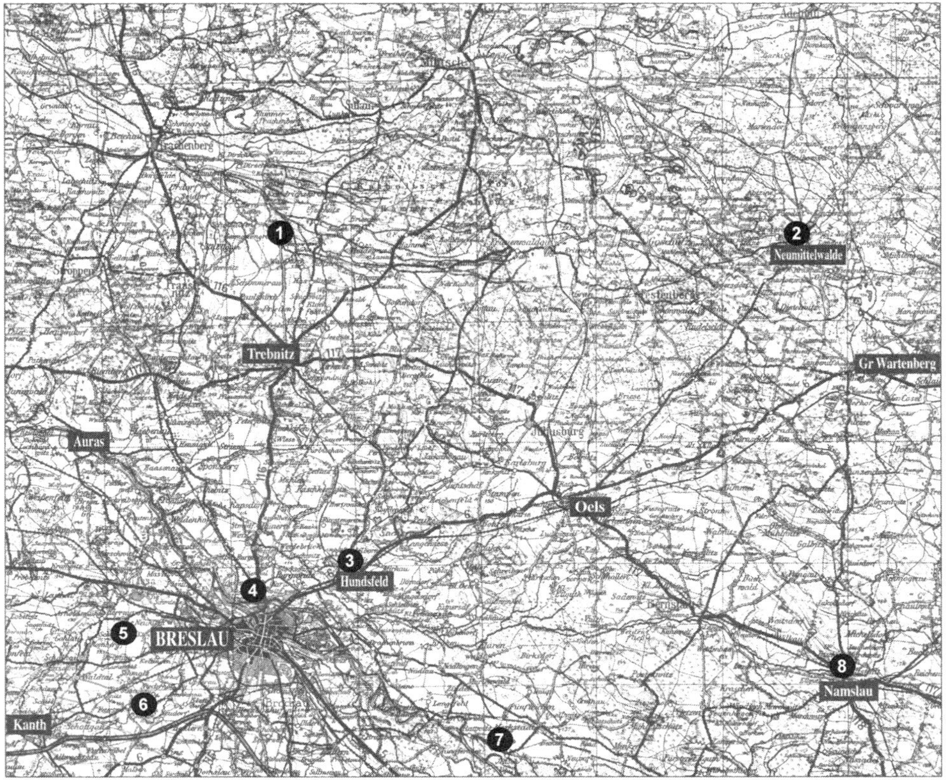

Map 3

1. Ulrich Frodien/
   Germanengrund
2. Peter Bannert
3. Herbert Rühlemann/
   Rheinmetall works
4. I-Werk 41
5. Hugo Hartung/
   Schöngarten airfield
6. Kanth Death March/
   Vera Eckle/
   Lucia Kusche/
   Frau Hanisch
7. Krupp Berthawerk
8. Karl Hanke's speech
   August 1944

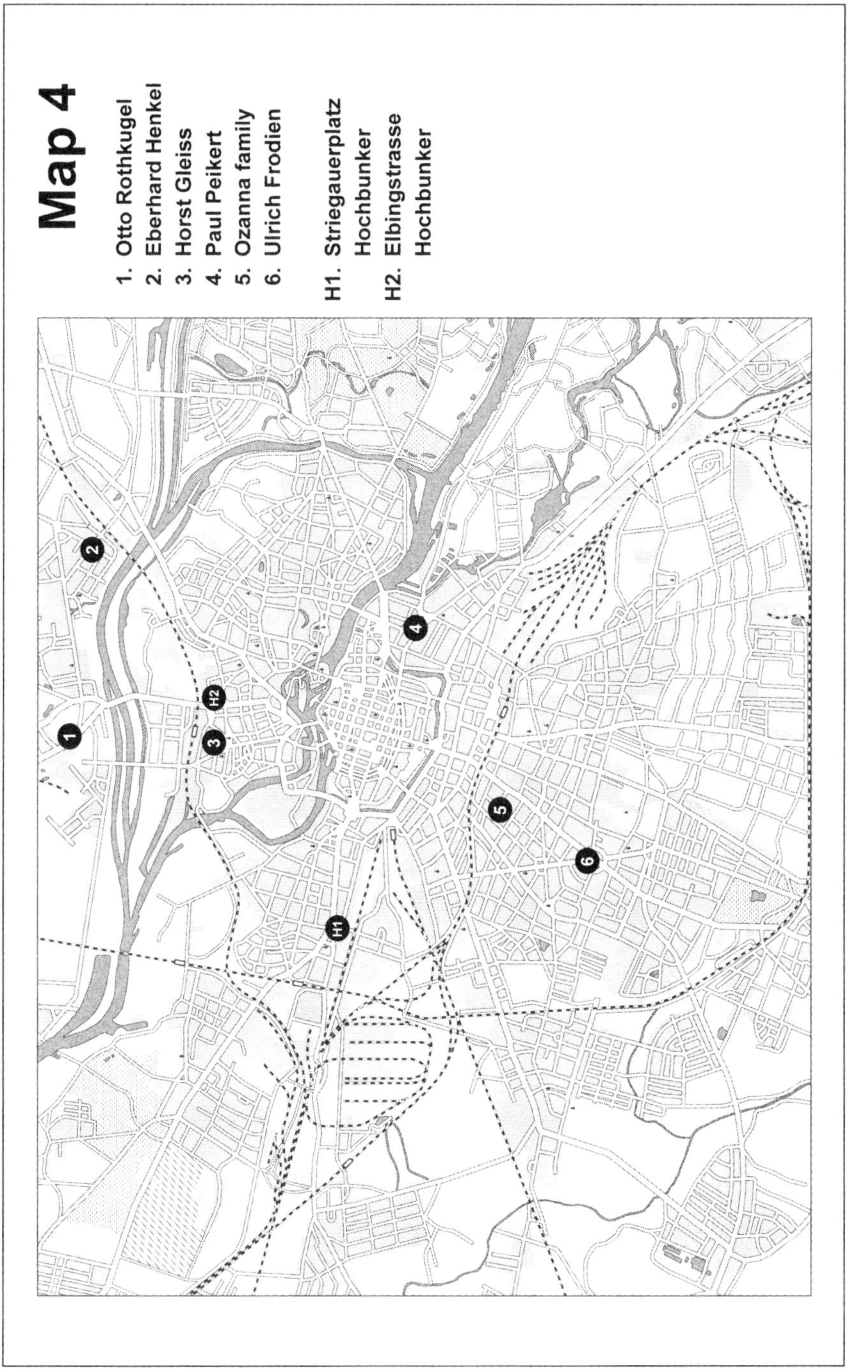

Map 4

1. Otto Rothkugel
2. Eberhard Henkel
3. Horst Gleiss
4. Paul Peikert
5. Ozanna family
6. Ulrich Frodien

H1. Striegauerplatz
    Hochbunker
H2. Elbingstrasse
    Hochbunker

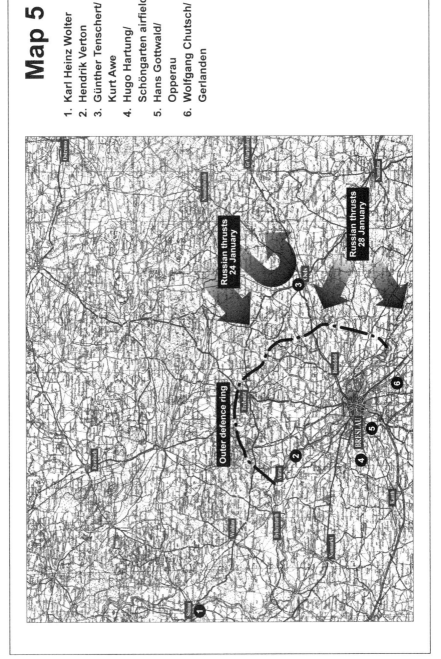

Map 5

1. Karl Heinz Wolter
2. Hendrik Verton
3. Günther Tenschert/
   Kurt Awe
4. Hugo Hartung/
   Schöngarten airfield
5. Hans Gottwald/
   Opperau
6. Wolfgang Chutsch/
   Gerlanden

Map 6

1. Hauptmann Heinz/
   Dyhernfurth
2. Paul Arnhold
3. Hendrik Verton
   Günther Tenschert/
4. Werner Zillich/
   Brockau
5. Domslau – ring of
   encirclement closes
   here on February 13

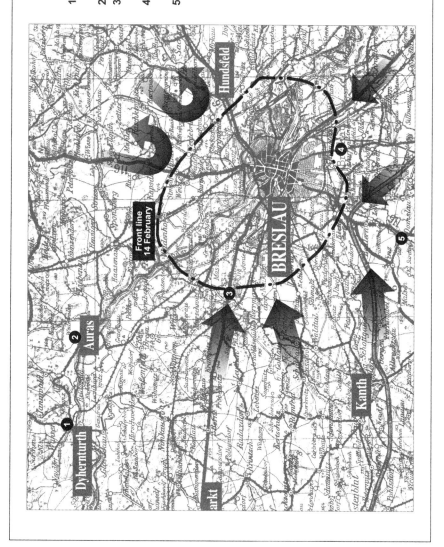

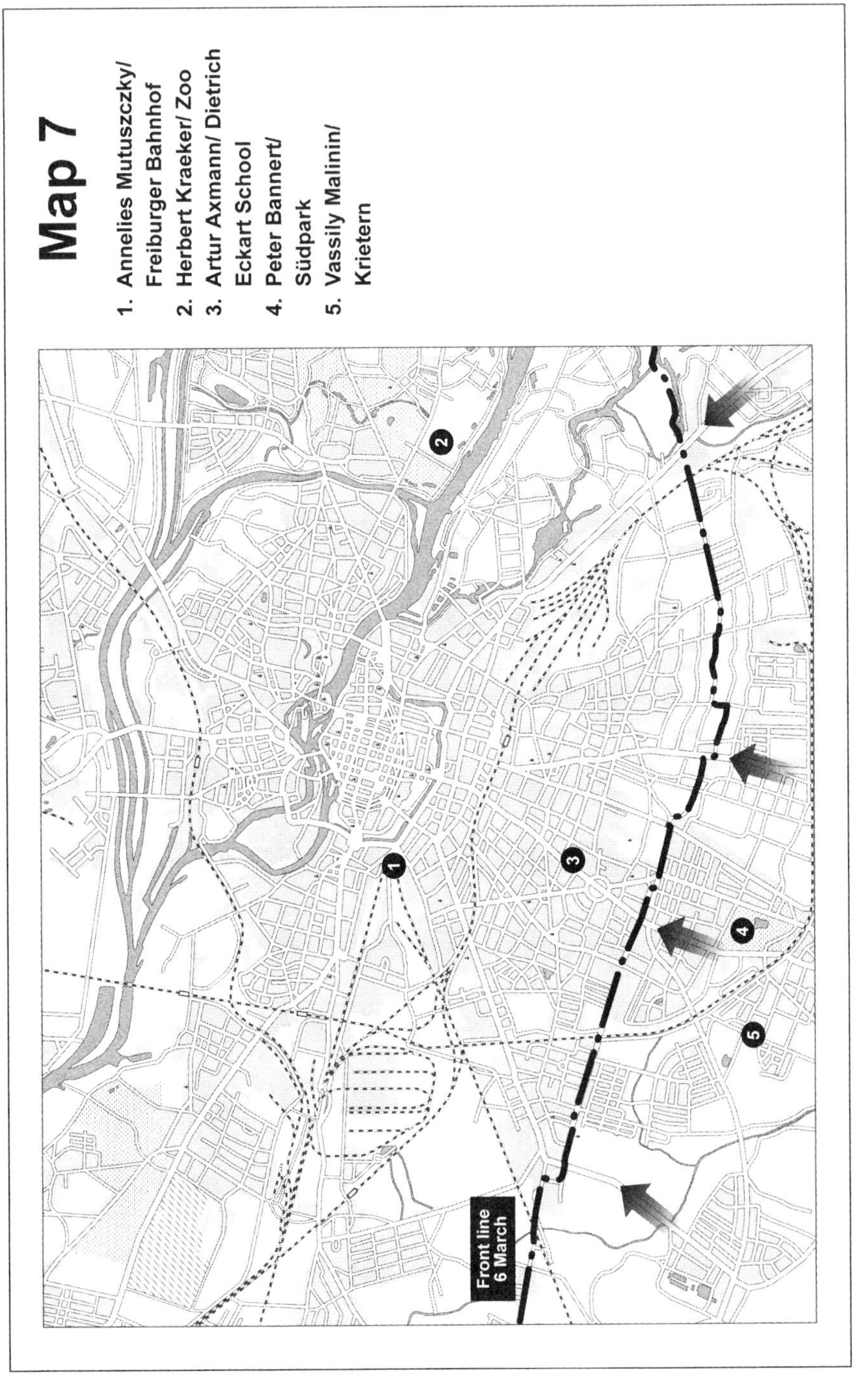

Map 7

1. Annelies Mutuszczky/
   Freiburger Bahnhof
2. Herbert Kraeker/ Zoo
3. Artur Axmann/ Dietrich
   Eckart School
4. Peter Bannert/
   Südpark
5. Vassily Malinin/
   Krietern

Front line
6 March

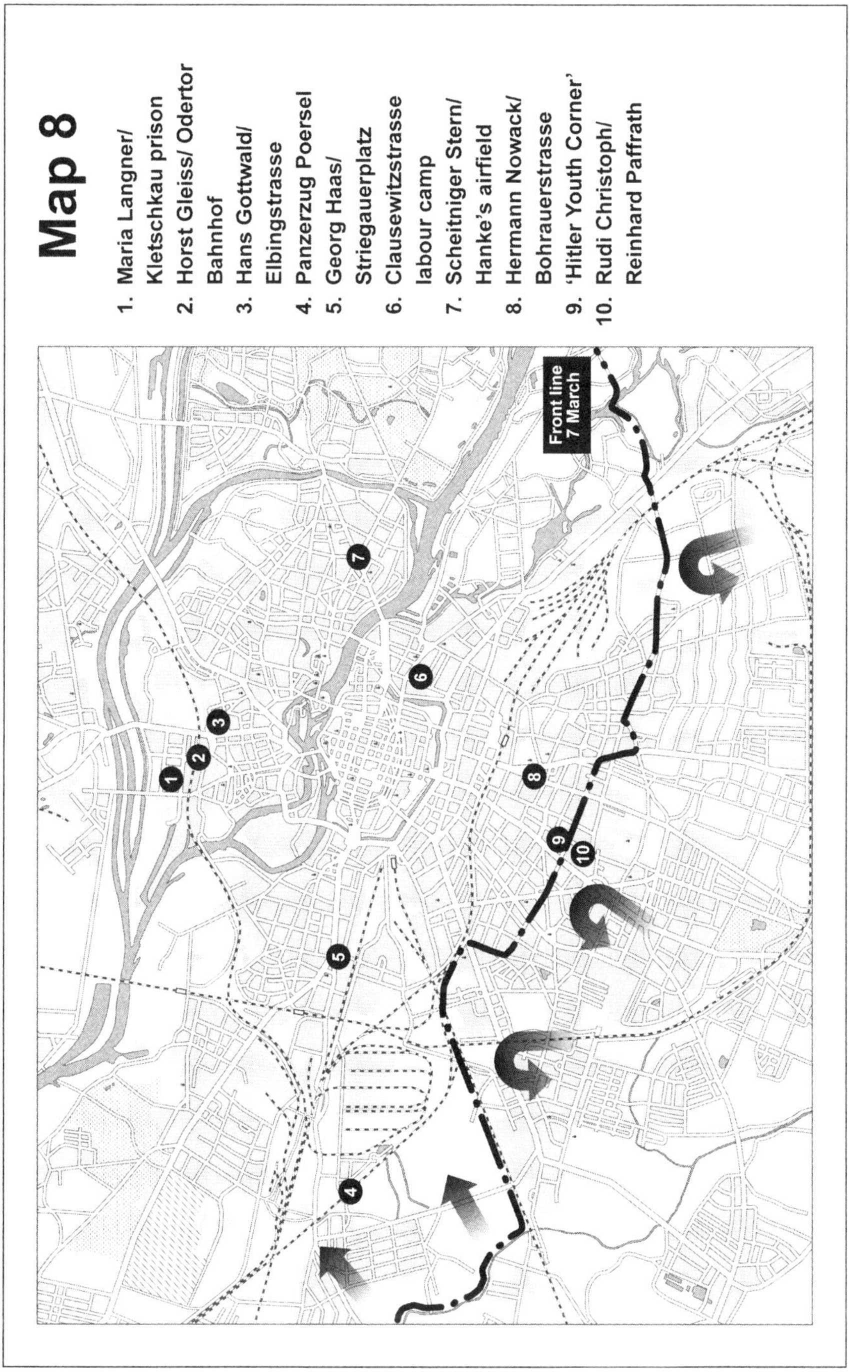

Map 8

1. Maria Langner/ Kletschkau prison
2. Horst Gleiss/ Odertor Bahnhof
3. Hans Gottwald/ Elbingstrasse
4. Panzerzug Poersel
5. Georg Haas/ Striegauerplatz
6. Clausewitzstrasse labour camp
7. Scheitniger Stern/ Hanke's airfield
8. Hermann Nowack/ Bohrauerstrasse
9. 'Hitler Youth Corner'
10. Rudi Christoph/ Reinhard Paffrath

Front line 7 March

Map 9

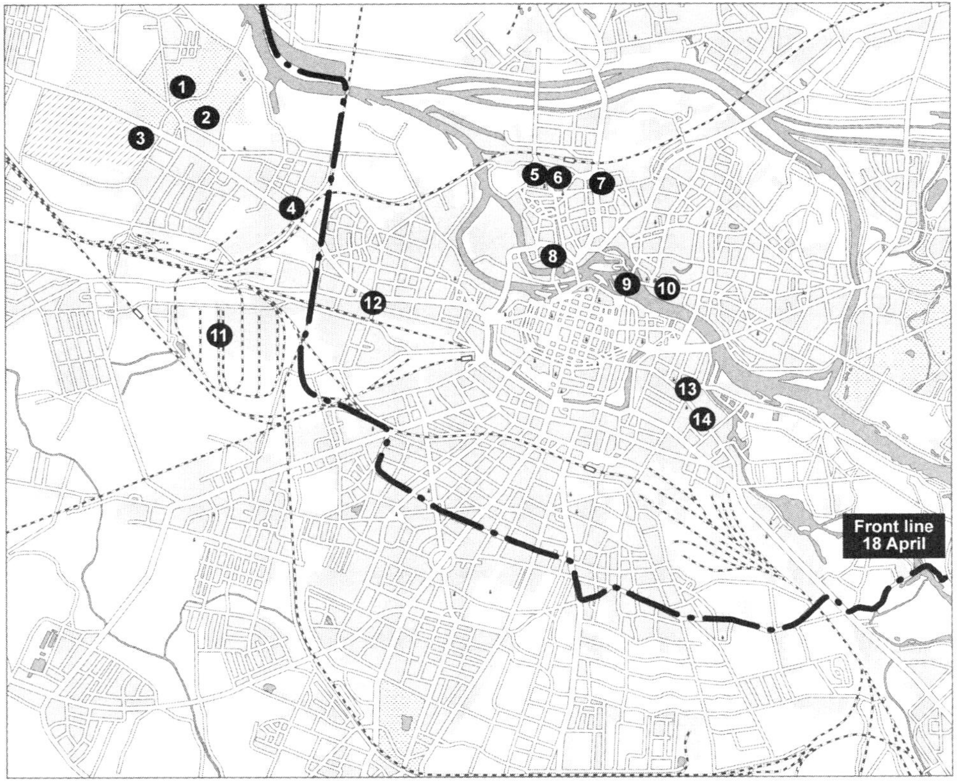

1. Leo Hartmann/ Westpark
2. Max Baselt/
   Blind Institute
3. Peter Bannert/ Rudi
   Christoph/ Gandau
4. Willy Merkert/ abattoir
5. Horst Gleiss/
   Belltafelstrasse
6. Wilhelm Saffe/
   Benderplatz
7. Hans Gottwald/
   Elbingstrasse
8. Hugo Hartung/
   Matthiasplatz
9. Friedrich Grieger/
   Sandinsel
10. Walter Lassman/
    Dominsel
11. Klaus Franke/ Linke
    Hofmann works
12. Gustav Paneck/
    Striegauerplatz
13. Gertrud Hassenbach/
    Mauritiusplatz
14. Georg Haas/
    Klosterstrasse

Front line
18 April

Map 10

1. Horst Gleiss/ Benderplatz
2. Horst Vieth/ Friedrich Karl Strasse
3. Niehoff's headquarters/ Sandinsel
4. St Maria Magdalena
5. Hendrik Verton/ Hotel Monopol
6. Peter Bannert/ Hauptbahnhof
7. Gluzdovski's headquarters/ Villa Colonia

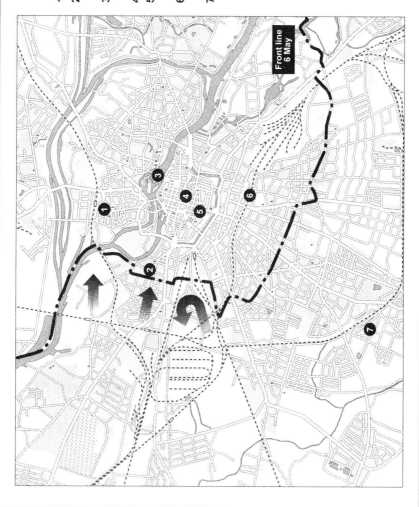

Front line 6 May

Map 11

1. First Polish administration/ Blücherstrasse
2. 'Szaberplac'/ Scheitniger Stern
3. Joanna Konopińska/ Heinzelmannchenweg
4. Cemetery for Red Army soldiers
5. Cemetery for Red Army officers

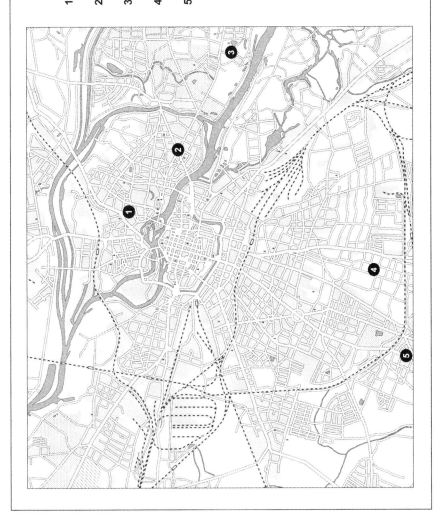

The Square

Every front had always seemed a world away
Gefreiter Ulrich Frodien

T
he standard-bearers appeared first. Like every one of the 150,000 participants, they had arisen with the first rays of light this Sunday morning, mustering in streets and squares across the city. In the north, men and women from Bavaria, Württemberg, East Prussia and from native soil, from Silesia. In the east, the boys of the *Hitlerjugend* and girls of its female counterpart, the *Bund Deutscher Mädel*, formed up alongside ethnic Germans from the Sudetenland, just over the Czech border. In the south, athletes from Franconia and the Ostmark – Austria, the newest addition to the Greater German Reich. Berliners held high the city's coat of arms, a bear. Danzigers raised shields. There were the red banners of the *Reichsbund für Leibesübungen*, the Nazi sporting organisation, and the black and red flags of the Sudeten Germans. From the north of the Reich, track-and-field athletes dressed in red shirts and white shorts clasped their running shoes in their hands. There were ethnic Germans from Romania, the men in embroidered white shirts, the women in bright dresses with long ribbons fluttering from their headdresses, carrying colourful bouquets of wild flowers. Men of the labour service, the *Reichsarbeitsdienst*, shouldered their spades.

The thunder of three cannon echoed across the sandy parade ground, bidding the thousands of spectators take their seats on the seventy-feet-high temporary stands erected around the square, the *Schlossplatz*. One thousand feet long, the square was bordered on its narrower west side by the *Landeshaus*, the government building, to the south by trees which lined the banks of the old city moat, and on its broader west side by the ninety-seven-year-old *Stadttheater* where the works of Lorking and Wagner had been performed this past week. On the north side stood the building which gave the square its name, the Schloss or palace. The rather austere stone façade belied the grandeur which lay within – the fine rococo-style state rooms, the sprawling ballroom with its fine chandeliers. Here Frederick the Great had assembled a library to match that at his palace of Sanssouci in Potsdam, here he had governed, here he had pondered, here he had composed music. Here Frederick William III had awarded the first Iron Cross and issued his legendary appeal '*An mein Volk*' (to my people) calling on them to cast off the Napoleonic

1

yoke. "There is no other way out," the king told his subjects, "than peace with honour or glorious defeat."

Today there would be no speeches, no appeals in the Schlossplatz, just a carefully-choreographed procession by 150,000 athletes as the week-long *Deutsche Turn und Sportfest* (German athletics and sports festival) reached its climax. From 7am until almost 10 pm each day, sportsmen and women from every *Gau* (district) of the Reich had locked horns at the newly-renamed *Hermann Göring Sportfeld*, a sprawling complex of football stadia, athletics tracks, tennis courts, hockey pitches, a boxing ring, swimming baths, and a vast open arena surrounded by grandstands, all built a decade earlier three miles east of the city centre. Gerd Hornberger had upset the form book in the hundred-metre sprint, crossing the line in ten and a half seconds, a fraction ahead of his Eintracht Frankfurt teammate Manfred Kersch and thirty-three-year-old favourite Erich Borchmeyer, victor at four of the past five German championships. In the women's events, Käthe Krauss added gold in the hundred-metre and two-hundred-metre dash to her Olympic bronze medal, while world and Olympic record holder Gisela Mauermeyer proved unbeatable once more in the discus – and took gold in the shot putt as well. The hosts' few triumphs had come in the water: Hartmann in the hundred-metre breaststroke, the men's hundred-metre crawl and backstroke relays, the coxless fours, the folding canoes.

The Sportfest was a triumph of Aryan strength and Nazi organization. Every minute of every day, every procession and parade, every performance of dance and gymnastics was minutely choreographed and arranged. A town of tents – more than 100 each housing forty boys as well as 170 wigwams for a dozen girls apiece – grew up around the sports ground, a sea of streamers, banners and flags fluttered in the east wind. Seemingly every hour special trains had pulled into the main railway station, the *Hauptbahnhof*, on the southern edge of the city centre, carrying guest athletes from throughout the Reich and beyond. Early on Tuesday, July 26, 800 *Volksdeutsche* – ethnic Germans – from Estonia and Latvia arrived. From Hungary fifty, from Romania 400, from Memel 100, from overseas – Argentina, Chile, Brazil, South West Africa, Venezuela, Canada, the United States – 450. And at the classical-styled *Freiburger Bahnhof* on the western edge of the historic city centre, the never-ending arrival of Sudeten Germans. "Breslau is like a giant magnet," the Nazi Party organ *Völkischer Beobachter* proclaimed. "With magical power it draws all Germans under its spell. They come here from all over, driven by the calling of their blood and their heart."[1]

The Sudeten Germans – perhaps 30,000 in all – had indeed been called, but not by their blood and their heart. They had been called by Joseph Goebbels.[2] Outwardly, the *Deutsche Turn und Sportfest* appeared to be a celebration of the human body and physical achievement. In reality, it was the latest act in a propaganda campaign carefully orchestrated by Berlin to demonstrate solidarity with the 'oppressed' ethnic Germans who inhabited the mountainous Sudeten region just a few miles south of Breslau. The Silesian capital was festooned with the black flags of the Sudeten Germans. Cries of 'Sieg Heil!' echoed through the narrow alleys, across the squares decorated with swastika banners and green garlands. "It's as if all the hardship has suddenly ended," the *Völkischer Beobachter* gushed. "Joy – a silent joy which springs from the depths of the heart – is etched on the faces of men and women."[3] Wherever visitors to the *Sportfest* went, they were reminded of Sudeten Germans' suffering and sacrifices. At the sporting exhibition in the four-domed pavilion in Schneitniger Park, one and a half miles from the sports ground, there was the usual Nazi art – statues of naked wrestlers, a bare-chested Aryan swinging a mighty hammer. There were also two halls of honour: one dedicated to the 236,000 German athletes who fell in the world war – plus thirty-eight 'heroes' who had been executed for their part in the failed Nazi coup in Austria in 1934 – and a second devoted to the Sudeten 'fallen'. Black flags hung over two golden basins commemorating Niklas Böhm and Georg Hofmann, Sudeten Germans shot on May 21 1938. "See our flags wave," the words of Nazi poet and journalist Kurt Eggers exhorted, "black like death. We must go forwards through night and hardship." The propaganda onslaught reached its zenith after dark on Friday, July 29. The grandstands in the Schlossplatz were filled as the audience watched more than a thousand flags – the standards of more than a thousand groups of ethnic Germans from beyond the borders of the Reich – march on. Sudeten Germans lined all four sides of the square, carrying torches to create a 'fiery border'. They heard their bespectacled leader, Konrad Henlein, a former junior officer, bank clerk, gymnastics instructor, and belated convert to the National Socialist cause. Henlein was not a great orator – there was no spontaneity, he read his speech. His reception was rapturous nevertheless, as he declared there was now "one united, one great, one proud German people". He continued:

> We will return from here to our homeland proud that destiny has given us a special and difficult task: to faithfully protect German soil and German blood and to help the German people safeguard peace.
> As the spokesman of the largest German ethnic group in Europe I proclaim to every German living beyond the borders of the Reich: We are all inseparable parts of the great German people![4]

Joseph Goebbels *was* a great orator. And tonight, the propaganda minister smugly noted in his diary, he was "on top form", filling his speech with jokes and sarcastic comments. "These past few days, tens of thousands of our German brothers and sisters from abroad have poured into this Reich," he told his audience. "Do not believe . . ." The applause drowned out Goebbels' words. "Do not believe that we do not understand your feelings. I can well imagine that all of you crossed the German border with a shudder of emotion." The minister paused once more as cries of 'Heil' reverberated around the square. In the past these ethnic Germans had returned to their adopted homes "with a feeling of shame in their hearts about their native land". Today, however, every German, every *Volksdeutsche* could be proud of his nation and his people – thanks to the achievements of one man, "an unknown

Gefreiter from the world war who directs the fate of the Reich". To cries, cheering, chanting and applause, Goebbels closed his address:

> From his face, you will draw fresh faith and fresh hope, which you need more than anyone else, which will take with you in your difficult daily struggle for the greatness of our people and the honour of our blood.[5]

And now on Sunday morning, July 31, 1938, they would see his face. And they would draw strength from it. As the thunder of the cannon faded, the bombastic strains of Hitler's favourite piece of music, the *Badenweiler March*, performed by the combined band of the German Army and Navy which had entertained thousands the previous evening, announced the Führer's arrival. It did not need to. A roar, growing ever louder, deafening, terrifying, intoxicating, steamrollered through the Breslau streets towards the Schlossplatz. Dressed in his brown Party uniform, the German leader shook hands with local Nazi dignitaries before striding across the square accompanied by the slavish Martin Bormann, a weary Goebbels, SS leader Himmler, Henlein, Silesian *Gauleiter* Josef Wagner with his copycat Hitler moustache, to a specially constructed rostrum opposite the Stadttheater. A small balcony, carpeted in red, adorned with a huge swastika and surrounded by a sea of colourful hydrangeas, had been erected at the front of the rostrum for the Führer and his closest entourage. As Hitler took his seat, his SS *Leibstandarte* bodyguard, each man dressed in black, each wearing a black steel helmet, each at least five feet ten inches tall, closed ranks in front of the tribune. Standard-bearers marched into the Schlossplatz, filing past both sides of the theatre, following ropes which marked out the huge square and guided their route around it. Athletes from Bavaria, the cradle of Nazism, were the first to parade past the tribune, yodelling as they did. There were four German mountaineers who had recently scaled the north face of the Eiger – the 'face of death' – fencers whose foils glinted in the morning sun, Austrians from the Tyrol in their bright national costumes, East Prussians, Danzigers. The cacophony of cries, shouts, cheers and applause reached their deafening peak as the Sudeten Germans, six rows deep, dressed in grey with Tyrolean hats, led by their black flags, entered the square.

A little over one hundred yards away, twelve-year-old Ulrich Frodien clung to the flagstaff he proudly held, bearing the black standard of the *Deutsche Jungvolk*, the younger arm of the *Hitlerjugend*. Like everyone else in the Schlossplatz, the schoolboy was excited. He had never seen 'him' before. Now, he observed Hitler's every move, every expression. Sometimes tense, sometimes smiling, sometimes standing with his hands on his hips, sometimes turning to Henlein, so far the Führer had appeared somewhat subdued. It was all an act. As the first Sudeten standard-bearers marched past the rostrum, Hitler stood up, stepped forward to the balustrade, raised his right arm and saluted the 'oppressed' athletes. "I felt the entire square and the hundreds of thousands of people in it explode like a bomb," Frodien recalled. "If the roar had been almost unbearable so far, now it reached a level which

I would never have thought possible." The schoolboy was carried away by the enthusiasm, by the mass hysteria. He yelled for all he was worth. "I wanted to be part of it, to feel I was part of this great, magnificent community," he admitted. Suddenly, out of the tumult, the indescribable, indistinguishable roar, a sharp, staccato sound became apparent. "I couldn't make it out at first, but it spread like wildfire around the entire square, passing from mouth to mouth." The crowd swayed backwards and forwards feverishly. "*Ein Volk, ein Reich, ein Führer!*" the spectators yelled in unison. One people, one empire, one leader. Repeatedly. Ever louder. "In my long life," Frodien wrote six decades later, "I have experienced nothing comparable." He continued:

> This euphoria took people away from their daily existence, it gave them an uplifting feeling: they were part of one great, admirable community, invincible, strong, powerful. For a few moments, it promised the impossible, a touch of immortality.

All order, all discipline collapsed. A fair-haired boy darted out of the procession and rushed up to Hitler's dais. He offered his hand to his Führer, who leaned over the edge and pressed it strongly. Young Sudeten girls and women in traditional dirndl dresses broke ranks and swarmed around the foot of the platform, pushing the *Leibstandarte* bodyguards aside. It was, Joseph Goebbels observed, as if "a wave of fanaticism and belief breaks in front of the tribune". Himmler stretched far over the parapet and urged his men to close ranks and move the women on. It was pointless. A mother carried her five-year-old daughter on her shoulders, raising her up to show Hitler. With tears streaming down their faces, crying 'Heil, heil!' the Sudetenlanders stretched out their arms. Again the Führer obliged. Smiling, he shook hand after hand offered to him.

It took several minutes for the procession to re-form, to move on. Ethnic Germans from Belgium, Denmark, Estonia, Latvia, Lithuania, Poland, Romanians. Athletes from overseas, Argentina, Chile, Brazil, South West Africa, the USA, *Volksdeutsche* from the Netherlands. Again they frequently broke ranks and shook the Führer's hand. A procession which should have ended after three hours dragged on for nearly four. As the last marching athlete left the square, the audience left their seats in the stands and spilled across the sandy parade ground, rallying around the dignitaries' platform. Once again there was a surging wave of outstretched hands, hysterical women, screaming girls. The band's podium was the sole island of calm and order amid a raging sea of enthusiasm. Only reluctantly did the throng disperse and Hitler step down from his tribune. He shook hands with a row of disabled veterans in wheelchairs then climbed into his black open-topped 1937 Mercedes-Benz 770. Adolf Hitler left the Schlossplatz "deeply moved". He was, his club-footed propaganda minister observed, "the great hope of Germany" and "a symbol of our national awakening". It was, Goebbels decided, "an honour to be permitted to serve him".[6]

On a bitingly cold January morning, Ulrich Frodien stood once more before the Schlossplatz. The city moat was frozen. The sand was hidden beneath a blanket of snow. Military vehicles, guns, a few panzers were mustered on the parade ground – on the exact spot where Hitler's tribune once stood.

A week before he had been hunting with his father in the village of Germanengrund, two dozen miles north of Breslau. The now eighteen-year-old panzer grenadier was convalescing, recovering from an artillery strike on the Eastern Front the previous autumn which smashed his thigh, and left shrapnel in his head and chest. Frodien still clung to the slight hope that the war might end in Germany's favour. His father, a doctor, could only scoff at – and feel pity for – Ulrich's naïve optimism. War had not touched this rural idyll, save for the death notices which filled the papers each day. To the villagers of Germanengrund "every front had always seemed a world away". But now there was talk of a new Russian offensive, an attack from the bridgehead on the Vistula at Baranow, a little over 200 miles to the east. The armed forces communiqué mentioned the Soviet spearhead passing the famous monastery of Łysa Góra, near Kielce. The news seemed to galvanize Frodien's father. He decided to return to Breslau immediately.

Now, this Tuesday, 23 January, 1945, the teenager headed for the centre of Breslau. For three days Breslau's railway stations had been under siege, ever since an alarming, electrifying broadcast from the 1,000 loudspeakers, erected throughout the Silesian capital shortly before the *Sportfest*, once clarions of Nazi triumphs. "Women and children leave the city on foot in the direction of Opperau-Kanth," the tinny voice urged, adding comfortingly. "There is no reason for alarm and panic."[7] Their men would not join them. Breslau had been declared a *Festung* – fortress, a fortress which would be 'defended to the last'.

But not by the Frodiens. Ulrich's mother and younger brother Michael had already fled Breslau. His father had every intention of joining them and sent the young *Gefreiter* into the city centre to see whether there was a chance of fleeing the city via the Freiburger Bahnhof. He left the family's comfortable third-floor apartment in Kaiser Wilhelm Strasse – renamed Strasse der SA in honour of the Nazi brownshirts. He passed beneath the railway bridge where two elderly militia stood guard, shouldering *Panzerfaust* anti-tank weapons. He crossed Tauentzienplatz, past the Ufa Palast, the city's largest cinema. The hoarding over the entrance still spelled out the title of the last film shown, *Opfergang* – The Great Sacrifice – an *Agfacolor* melodrama, the story of a Hamburg politician's son who becomes infatuated with a young woman. Frodien passed the Wertheim department store, again the city's largest, now known as AWAG after being appropriated from its Jewish owners. He skirted the edge of an empty square where once Breslau's new synagogue had stood and came to the frozen moat, staring across at the Schlossplatz, recalling that Sunday in 1938. "I was seized by a profound feeling of sadness and despair at the thought that perhaps it had all been utterly pointless, our belief in Germany, our belief in the ideals of National Socialism, the endless sacrifices and the many fallen comrades," he wrote. For a moment he considered reporting to the nearest barracks, joining one of the hastily-formed *Festungskompanien* – fortress companies – and manning a machine gun, determined to go down with his home. Reality quickly made him change his mind. Pain from his shattered thigh, his bandaged head, his scarred chest, pulsed through his body. Ulrich Frodien, just eighteen years old, was, he realized, "a wreck, utterly unsuited to any heroic fantasy of going under".[8]

Ulrich Frodien and his father would escape the besieged Silesian capital. Thousands more would die trying. And thousands more still would die fulfilling the promise to defend the city 'to the last'. They were as good as their word. *Festung* Breslau would hold out longer than Königsberg, longer than Danzig, longer than Vienna, longer even than the capital of the Reich itself. But Breslau and Breslauers would pay a terrible price for their obstinacy. At least 6,000 soldiers were killed and another 23,000 wounded defending the fortress on the Oder. The toll among civilians was far graver. Perhaps as many as 80,000 died. The city they knew, the city they had grown up with, the city where they had fêted Hitler and his cabal, the city which had been virtually untouched by war before 1945, would be no more. Two-thirds of all industry was destroyed. Seven out of ten high schools lay in ruins. Two in every three homes were uninhabitable. Nearly 200 miles of roadway were impassable – more than 600 million cubic feet of ash and rubble were lying in them. Eighty per cent of the railway and tram network was wrecked. All electricity lines and seventy per cent of the telephone lines were down.

The end of war would offer no salvation. Breslau's German inhabitants would be driven out of their homes, driven out of their city, driven westwards. Their city would rise again, rebuilt not by Germans but by Poles, rebuilt not as Breslau but as Wrocław.

Such was the price demanded of Hitler's last fortress.

Notes

1. *Völkischer Beobachter*, 27/7/38.
2. TB Goebbels, 23/4/38.
3. *Völkischer Beobachter*, 26/7/38.
4. Lukas, Oskar, *Breslau: Bekenntnis zu Deutschland*, pp.43-4.
5. *Völkischer Beobachter*, 30/8/38 and TB Goebbels, 30/7/38.
6. Frodien, pp.134-7, TB Goebbels, 1/8/38 and *Völkischer Beobachter*, 1/8/38.
7. Gleiss, *Breslauer Apokalypse*, i, p.204. Hereafter cited as Gleiss.
8. Frodien, pp.134, 138.

CHAPTER 1

The Happy Fusion

*The war on the Eastern Front only interests me when
the first Russians appear before Namslau*
Gauleiter Karl Hanke

The passing of the old year and the start of the new had always been a cause for celebration for Breslauers. In the final hour, its residents converged on the Ring, at first a trickle, then a deluge, waiting tensely for the clock on the Rathaus to strike twelve. And when it did, the square reverberated to cries of "*Prosit Neujahr*". A choral fanfare sounded from the tower of the town hall. In the distance, the deep chimes of the bells of St Elisabeth and St Maria Magdalena churches could be heard. For fifteen minutes or so the crowd milled around, then began to drift away down the maze of alleys and streets leading from the square, bound for the suburbs. A few called in at Breslau's restaurants or bierkellers, but most went home.

Breslauers had celebrated *Silvesternacht*, as Germans call New Year's Eve, like this for as long as any of them could remember. But the final day of 1944 was different. Inhabitants stayed at home. They waited tensely for midnight, not to hear the chimes of St Elisabeth or Maria Magdalene, but to hear the words of their leader. At the end of this darkest of years for the Reich, perhaps he might offer hope, even assurances.

Fifteen-year-old Peter Bannert sat down to a festive meal with his newly acquired friends in a former school on the edge of the city centre. Bannert had arrived in the Silesian capital in the first days of December, summoned from the small town of Habelschwerdt, sixty miles away, by the regional *Hitlerjugend* leadership. They gave him the grandiose title *Kriegseinsatzführer* – war service leader. The reality was rather less grand: making a tally of uniforms and equipment in warehouses across Silesia. He was one of eighteen schoolboys billeted in the old Andersenstrasse school, now makeshift quarters for youths called up to serve the Reich. A twenty-year-old blonde, "who embodied the ideal of an Aryan woman" with her flaxen hair neatly plaited in buns, looked after the boys, providing meals and keeping an eye on the accommodation. Tonight she laid on a substantial spread to mark 1944's passing.

At his villa on the edge of Lake Bogensee, two dozen miles north of Berlin, Joseph Goebbels struggled valiantly to carve the roast goose on his plate into edible pieces. There was an awkward silence around the dinner table as the Propaganda Minister's guests, his secretary Wilfried von Oven, the wife of the Nazis' favourite stage and fashion designer Benno von Arent, and Breslau *Gauleiter* Karl Hanke played with their tough slices of goose. Finally, the master of the house broke the silence. "Tell me, my dear, is your goose leg as incredibly tough as mine?" Lively discussion ensued. It was, Hanke said, a good sign of Germany's food supplies that in the sixth year of war such an old goose could have survived to be served.

Later, hosts and guests retired to the hall and sat in front of an open fire. Joseph Goebbels was glad to see the back of 1944 – "the worst year of my entire life. I hope Fate will spare us having to endure another year like it." Karl Hanke assured him it would. He had mobilised all of his *Gau*, Lower Silesia, to dig an intricate network of fortifications – trenches and anti-tank ditches. "People in the East are convinced that we will succeed in holding the Soviets at bay in their impending offensive." As the clock approached midnight, the radio was turned up to full volume, while servants brought in several bottles of champagne. Through the receiver came the voice of veteran character actor Heinrich George reading Clausewitz's political will. As George came to the final sentence – "I would only feel happy if I found a glorious end in a magnificent struggle for the freedom and dignity of the Fatherland" – his words merged with the strains of the national anthem played on a violin. Twelve strokes brought 1944 to a close. With the final stroke, the iron clang of the Rhine bell in Cologne cathedral began and a choir sang *O, Deutschland hoch in Ehren*. Goebbels and his guests stood up. Frau Goebbels began to cry. Everyone raised their glasses and toasted each other.

Satiated by his meal, Peter Bannert listened to the evening's entertainment – stirring speeches by the boyfriend of his young maid, a senior *Hitlerjugend* leader. The youth read some Nietzsche, a few extracts from *Mein Kampf*. "I did not understand the content, but the rousing words left me awestruck." The small group downed several glasses of wine. Suddenly, the leader leapt up, pulled out his pistol and yelled: "I will defend my girlfriend and myself against the Russians with this weapon!" No one said a word. The silence was broken by the clocks of Breslau's churches striking midnight.[1]

The radio's speaker reverberated to the sound of Hitler's beloved *Badenweiler Marsch*, before, at five minutes after twelve, the Führer himself spoke. For the next half hour it was a rather subdued – Goebbels preferred to call it "a firm and certain" – Adolf Hitler who addressed his nation. He offered his people no certainties, no specifics, no hopes of 'wonder weapons'. Germany, he assured them, *would* not lose the war because it *could* not lose the war. "A people which achieves so many incredible things at the front and at home, a people which suffers and endures so many terrible things, can never go under."[2]

Adolf Hitler was right. The German people would not go under in 1945. But many of their cities would: in Berlin, one fifth of all buildings – one in every two in the city centre – were destroyed; in Dresden, a byword for devastation, two out of every five homes had been reduced to ruins; the figure in Hamburg was three out of five. And in one city, seven out of ten homes were devastated. That city was Breslau.

The name is thought to come from Vratislav I, but people lived there long before the Bohemians laid claim to the city. They settled there because the river which cut through the land was passable, fragmenting into rivulets which created a dozen islands, where two ancient trade routes intersected, the Amber Road from the Baltic to the Adriatic and the *Via Regia* from the Rhineland to Silesia. Vratislav either built or bolstered a small fortress on an island on the right bank of the Oder. By the beginning of the first millennium Bohemian rule had been usurped by Polish, and Wrotizla, as it was known, had grown beyond the original fortress to hold a population of around 1,000, including the city's first bishop. Wrotizla would fall under the rule of first the Poles, then the Piast dynasty for the next three centuries; but for Nazi historians the defining moment in Breslau's early history came in the year 1241 when the Mongols invaded. Inhabitants either fled west or withdrew to the fortified islands, razing the rest of the city. The Mongols invested Wrotizla briefly, then continued into the heart of Europe where they met the armies of Heinrich II – 'The Pious' – the city's Piast ruler, on the battlefield at Wahlstatt, three dozen miles west of Wrotizla. The battle and Heinrich's stand would enter Nazi mythology – they would frequently draw parallels between the Mongols and the 'Asiatic hordes' of 1945 – but the truth was that Heinrich's armies were slaughtered, their leader decapitated. The Mongols advanced no farther westwards, however; internal politics rather than Heinrich the Pious and his knights led the invaders from the steppe to return to the east.

In 1241 Wrotizla was destroyed and reborn. To the Nazis, 1241 was the year Breslau was born – they would celebrate its 700th birthday in 1941. In the wake of the Mongol invasion, Third Reich histories proclaimed, "Breslau was built anew by German settlers as a German city and has remained so until the present day."[3] Latin and German became the sole official languages. The heart of Wrotizla – also known as Presslau, Bressslau and, for the first time, Breslau – shifted from the right bank of the Oder to the left. A large market square, the Ring, became the focal point of the new city; a new cathedral, or Dom, began to grow on the site of the old city, giving name to the land around it, *Dominsel* – cathedral island.* As Breslau flourished thanks to trade between East and West, and goods from the Netherlands, Hungary, Russia, southern Germany, Prussia and Poland were exchanged at its markets, it earned the trappings of a great city and gained the title *die Blume Europas* – the flower of Europe – courtesy of the seventeenth-century Silesian historian Nicolaus Henel von Hennenfeld. The flower possessed a myriad of churches – the twin-towered present-day cathedral, built between the fourteenth and sixteenth centuries, the Elisabethkirche with the highest steeple in the city, the Gothic St Maria on the Sand on Sandinsel, the imposing Kreuzkirche with its steep roof and three naves; there was a university, a library holding maps, manuscripts and the oldest printed volume in the city, *Statuta synodalia episcoporum*

---

* The arm of the Oder which flowed around the island to the north was filled in by the Prussians, but the name Dominsel stuck.

Vratislaviensium; and in the Ring, the city's defining image, the Rathaus – the city hall. Built over a period of more than 200 years, the red-brick landmark is regarded as one of the finest examples of late Gothic architecture with a particularly ornate eastern gable featuring an astronomical clock and numerous pinnacles. On the south-facing façade stand two bays depicting life in the city in the fifteenth century, while the western gable is dominated by the 200ft tower. Below ground, in the Rathaus' great vaults, Breslau's most famous hostelry, the Schweidnitzer Keller, thrived.

While Breslau prospered, the city changed rulers frequently: Bohemia until the early sixteenth Century, the Habsburgs for the next 200 or so years, Prussia from 1741 until the formation of Germany 130 years later. Prussian rule began largely peacefully, but twice the city fell into the hands of invaders, first to the Austrians during the Seven Years' War, then to Napoleon's armies in early 1807 after a brief but bloody siege which saw much of the suburbs destroyed. Determined that Breslau would never again offer resistance to an invader, the French had the city's ramparts and fortifications pulled down. Walls can be broken, but not a spirit. Six years later, with Napoleon tottering after his mauling in Russia, Breslau was the wellspring of revolt. The city's university was the heart of the uprising. Volunteers who took up arms gave rise to Germany's national colours – black, red and gold. And in the Schloss, Friedrich Wilhelm III, issued a legendary appeal, '*An mein Volk*' – to my people – which captured the mood of the 1813 perfectly. "This is the final decisive struggle for our existence, our independence, our prosperity," the king told his subjects. "There is no alternative than an honourable peace or heroic destruction."

At the time of Friedrich Wilhelm III's appeal, the city counted 70,000 inhabitants – and was growing rapidly. With the ramparts gone, Breslau began to expand beyond its former limits. Wide promenades, public gardens and fine houses dominated the suburb of Schweidnitz, south of the old town, while "high chimneys and the howl of machines"[4] dominated Nikolai to the west. Even before the railways came to the city in the 1840s (the imposing *Hauptbahnhof* – central station – was built a decade later on what was then the southern edge of Breslau), Gottfried Linke was building his first hundred railway carriages. There was a thriving woollen industry. There were firms producing steam engines, powered by Silesia's rich seams of coal, mills, breweries, oil refineries, gas works, a fledgling chemical industry; there were firms producing clothes (more than thirty firms producing straw hats alone) and furniture, and paper mills on the banks of the Oder. The railways and industrialisation led to an influx of people from the countryside. By 1840, the city's population had topped 100,000. It doubled in the next three decades and more than doubled again by the turn of the twentieth century. It was a reasonably cosmopolitan population: a large Jewish populace and three Poles for every hundred Germans. They were educated at a growing network of public schools and, from 1910, a technical university. They travelled on an extensive tram network which spanned the Oder on a flurry of new bridges. They were treated at numerous new hospitals, while spiritual needs were catered for by a host of new churches – the neo-Gothic Lutherkirche which dominated the suburb of Scheitnig with its 300ft spire, or the rather less forbidding St John the Baptist in Kleinburg in the south of the city.

Breslauers could survey their metropolis by climbing some of these church steeples, or from the top of the 140ft water tower in the south of the city and the Kaiser Wilhelm Memorial in the north. There was entertainment for the few – opera at the new Stadttheater, singing festivals, museums, sprawling public parks; and for the masses – the variety theatres such as the Viktoria, the circus, the zoo, and, by 1900, the first cinemas. Such distractions perhaps took the minds of the working classes off their wretched lives in the city's slums where conditions were fearful – and would persist as such well into the 1930s. Breslau's wealthy and poor united in 1913, as they did throughout the Reich, to celebrate the centennial of throwing off the Napoleonic yoke. They did so at a huge new exhibition ground on the north-east of the city centre. There were pavilions, gardens, a lake with a pergola, and at the heart of the site, the largest reinforced concrete building in the world at the time, the huge domed *Jahrhunderthalle* – Century Hall. Here up to 10,000 people at a time could watch sport or theatre, industry could stage trade fairs, and politicians could – and would – stage rallies.

Six thousand people attended the hall's opening ceremony. Some 100,000 would visit the inaugural exhibition. But the hopes of prosperity the Jahrhunderthalle embodied would be dashed within eighteen months as Germany went to war. In peace, the city had been the home of VI Corps. In the summer of 1914, the troops marched through northern Luxembourg then wheeled left to bear down on the Marne with Germany's Fourth Army. Those who fell in the march on Paris were the first of around 10,000 men of Breslau to fall at the front, but the European conflagration demanded equally great sacrifices at home. Over the next four years, prices rose as much as 400 per cent. More than half Breslau's schools were commandeered for military use. Gottfried Linke's locomotive works – now renamed Linke-Hofmann – focused its efforts not on the railways but on aircraft, building scouts, fighters and finally four-engined leviathans, thanks not least to the work of prisoners of war, a practice it would repeat a generation later. By the war's end, Breslauers were expected to survive on fewer than two ounces of meat a week, a solitary pint of milk, five pounds of potatoes, four ounces of green vegetables and half a pound of flour. Those were the official figures; they were rarely met in Breslau. Nearly half the city's population relied on soup kitchens. Weakened by an inadequate diet, the populace succumbed to starvation, to tuberculosis and, in the closing weeks of 1918, the global influenza pandemic which killed 1,000 of Breslau's inhabitants in a single month at its peak.

Even before the Armistice in 1918, Breslauers threw off the vestiges of Wilhemine rule. Authority collapsed. Troops fuelled the popular uprising rather than quelling it. On the same day that the Kaiser abdicated, a people's council of Socialists and Liberals took charge in Breslau in what their leader, Paul Löbe, called, "a quiet revolution. No human life had been sacrificed and no damage had been done."[5]

If the revolution of November 1918 was bloodless, the years which followed were not – and Upper Silesia was the flashpoint. It was one of the industrial powerhouses of Germany, responsible for a quarter of all its coal, eighty per cent of its zinc, one third of its lead. But two out of three of its inhabitants were Poles, not Germans, and they wished to join the re-born Polish state. Allied leaders in Paris suggested a plebiscite to determine Upper Silesia's fate, but its Polish populace was not prepared to wait that long. In August 1919, a general strike turned into a widespread uprising. It lasted only a week. More than 20,000 German soldiers were dispatched to put it down – which they did, brutally. As many as 2,500 Poles were executed in the aftermath of the revolt. They rose up again twelve months later – and again were put down. Only in March 1921 were Silesians able to go to the polls. A gerrymandered result ensured that Upper Silesia remained German. After six weeks of tension, Upper Silesia exploded again. The third uprising was the largest, longest and most brutal. Some 70,000 Polish 'volunteers' seized eastern Upper Silesia. In response, some 25,000 German 'volunteers' marched against them. In pitched battles, notably on the dominating heights of Annaberg, 1,000ft above the right bank of the Oder forty miles north-west of Katowice, the German volunteers prevailed. The Allies intervened before the German troops could press home their advantage, finally forcing an uneasy peace upon Upper Silesia in the summer of 1921.

Breslauers did not take kindly to the Polish uprisings. In the summer of 1920 they smashed the Polish consulate, a Polish school and a Polish library, among other buildings. Three out of four of the city's Polish inhabitants fled Breslau. There was unrest too when nationalists seized power in Berlin in March 1920. The workers of Breslau went on strike. Troops appeared in the streets accompanied by armoured cars, ostensibly to maintain order (which included arresting the city's police chief). The regional president, Wolfgang Jaenicke, appealed for calm. "Any drop of blood which is spilled here by Germans fighting against Germans is spilled unnecessarily."[6] Despite Jaenicke's plea, some blood was spilled in Breslau during the revolt – known to history as the Kapp Putsch – but in Silesia, as in Berlin, the coup collapsed in less than a week.

Breslau of the 1920s was a city of contrasts. There was the unrest and upheaval of revolt and riots, yet the Linke-Hofmann works was producing 4,000 locomotives and carriages every year. Hyperinflation crippled the city's economy. As September 1923 began, a single American Dollar could buy ten million marks. By the month's end that had risen to 160 million marks. German currency lost value by the hour. Riots erupted once more. And yet at the same time, the face of Breslau was changing: huge new headquarters were erected for the police and the post office savings bank. A sprawling sports complex was laid out on the north-eastern edge of the city. The exhibition grounds around the Jahrhunderthalle hosted trade fairs and '*WuWa*', a display of modernist architecture and fittings for the home and office. The city trebled in size as it incorporated outlying villages or sprouted new suburbs, such as 'new town' of Zimpel, the workers' quarters of Pöpelwitz and Westend. As well as creating a new Breslau, the city's ruling Socialists – supported by one in two voters in 1921 – tried to erase traces of the old Breslau. Kaiserbrücke was renamed Freiheitsbrücke. Kaiser Wilhelm Platz became Reichspräsidentenplatz. Platz der Republik replaced Schlossplatz, while one of the founding fathers of this new republic, Friedrich Ebert, had Tiergartenstrasse named in his honour.[7] The names would be in place barely a decade.

On the afternoon of Monday, 30 January, 1933, six-year-old Ulrich Frodien sat with his mother on the edge of his bed and watched two workers struggle to raise a huge flag on the pole of the post office in Kaiser Wilhelmstrasse. A breeze suddenly stirred and the swastika banner billowed in the wind. Frodien's mother hugged him. "This is a wonderful day," she told her son with tears in her eyes. "A day you must always remember, for from today a new, much better era begins for Germany. Hardship and misery for so many people will finally end. Justice will reign once more. A wonderful future is in store for you – all of us, together."[8]

Only five years before, just one in every hundred Breslauers had supported the National Socialists. But Breslau suffered more than most towns and cities in Germany during the economic crises of the late 1920s and early 1930s. Wages were lower. Unemployment was higher – it trebled in the second half of the decade. By January 1933, one in ten Silesians was out of work. The Frodiens had fared better than many fellow Breslauers – the master of the house was a doctor. Yet the effects of the worldwide depression were not lost on young Ulrich. "The illusion of the 'roaring twenties' cultivated within recent decades only applies to an extremely small group in the witch's cauldron of Berlin," he recalled. Almost half Frodien's classmates attended school barefoot "until the first snow fell," many were undernourished and to most owning a bicycle was but a dream. The six-year-old became friends with a boy from an unemployed family who lived in a Breslau cellar 'apartment'. There were no windows – the only light came through a grill; four children shared a single bed – and a single threadbare blanket. Such conditions were commonplace; nearly one fifth of all apartments in the city comprised a single room. The Nazis courted them – "Our last hope, Adolf Hitler!" exhorted bill posters of a haggard, unemployed family, pasted around Breslau in the autumn of 1932 – and the Nazis succeeded. In the spring of 1933, more than half of Breslauers voted National Socialist.[9]

The Nazis set about putting their stamp on the city immediately. Civic posts, such as the regional president and mayors, were quickly filled with Party members, but the tentacles of National Socialism soon extended into every sinew of city life. In civic administration, in the post office, in the university, where lecturers extolled the virtues of Aryan art and literature and students greedily tossed ten thousand "dirty and disgraceful volumes" on to a pyre, "eradicating the un-German spirit" and destroying books "which poison the soul of the German people" in the process.[10] School lessons began and ended with the *Hitlergruss* – the Nazi salute – the holy cross was replaced with portraits of the Führer and pupils learned the history of the swastika through five millennia. Every anniversary, every National Socialist milestone was commemorated: the death of the nationalist Leo Schlageter, the anniversary of Frederick William III's appeal in 1813 to rise up against Napoleon – never commemorated in the 120 years before the Nazis seized power – there was a memorial day for Silesia's SA, and, of course, Hitler's birthday on 20 April and the failed putsch in Munich each 8 November. A propaganda office was established and, in time, 1,000 loudspeaker columns carrying the *Drahtfunk* public address system would announce every triumph, every victory with a fanfare from Liszt's *Les Preludes*.

The *Sturmabteilung* relished their new-found importance. These youths in uniform swaggered around the city, posing, stamping their feet, showing off the machine pistols, revolvers, truncheons hanging off their belts. They held tattoos, torchlight processions, they paraded by night through the Platz der Republik – soon to regain its former name of Schlossplatz. Other streets and squares would revert to their pre-1919 titles, or earn new ones: now it was Horst Wessel Strasse running past the Jahrhunderthalle with Adolf Hitler Strasse leading off it, while the main artery leading out of the city to the south became the Strasse der SA. Honorary citizenship was granted to Nazi grandees – Göring in October 1935, Goebbels in August 1937, and Adolf Hitler, naturally, as early as March 1933.

Hitler was an infrequent visitor to the Silesian capital, especially after he came to power, and his appearance in Breslau was always attended by a higher goal. The 1938 *Sportfest* highlighted the plight of the 'repressed' Sudeten Germans, one year earlier it was the 'enchained' Austrians fêted at the annual festival of German singers when Breslau, Joseph Goebbels noted was "swimming in a sea of joy".[11] The city was in equally festive mood in late September 1936 when the 1,000th kilometre of Autobahn – 'the roads of Adolf Hitler' – was ceremoniously opened by the Führer. The road, so the Nazi Party organ, the *Völkischer Beobachter* opined, "gives Silesians fresh assistance in the struggle against poverty in this ancient German land."[12] The reality, as Jewish teacher Willy Cohn perceived, was that the Autobahn was actually "an instrument for preparations for war, propelling the world even more quickly towards a terrible catastrophe". The masses, Cohn sighed, "do not see that".[13]

Breslau had the largest Jewish community in Germany outside Berlin – not, Ulrich Frodien remembered, "those unpopular stereotype Eastern European Jews with their kaftans and sidelocks" but men and women fully integrated into the city's society. Fewer than half were practising – but that did not spare them from Nazi repression and persecution. Almost immediately after the seizure of power, Breslau's Jewish stores were boycotted. There were burnings of 'Jewish-Marxist' books. Jews were forced to salute the swastika flag of every passing SA troop marching through the streets. Hitler Youths filed through the city singing "Set fire to the synagogues". They were driven from professions and public service. Relations between Jews and non-Jews were forbidden. "Many Jews had belonged to my parents' circle of friends, something so normal and everyday in middle-class society in Breslau that it was considered natural." But now, Frodien observed, "people distanced themselves. Friendships and relationship were discreetly ended." The Frodiens too began to disown their Jewish friends, "submitting to the *Zeitgeist*".[14]

Occasionally, however, their consciences were pricked, never more so than on the morning of 10 November 1938 – the day after *Kristallnacht*, 'the night of broken glass'. As 'retribution' for the assassination of a German diplomat in Paris by a Jew, a pogrom was unleashed across Germany by the authorities. Heading to school near the Freiburger Bahnhof, Ulrich Frodien frequently had to climb off his bike to avoid the broken glass strewn across the streets from smashed shop windows. "The shops were wrecked, all their wares smashed, scattered, trampled upon." The New Synagogue in Wallstrasse, a fine, imposing building with a Romanesque dome, was ablaze. "The fire-fighters were standing around doing nothing," Frodien observed. "It struck me that they were restricting their efforts to protecting the surrounding houses; they let the synagogue burn." By the time Walter Tausk, a veteran of the Great War and a Jewish convert to Buddhism, arrived in Wallstrasse, the synagogue was "nothing but a smoking ruin," its dome had already collapsing. Tausk was shocked. "The closer I got to the centre, the more desolate the scenes of senseless destruction: cigar stores robbed, their contents smashed and tossed all over the place." When items in furniture stores could not be wrecked, they were scratched using shards of glass. The streets filled with curious Breslauers. Police formed cordons, but only to protect them from being struck by things being flung out of the ransacked businesses. A few in the crowd muttered their disapproval, only to be taken away. Nearly 2,500 Jews in Breslau suffered the same fate on 9 and 10 November, arrested by the police, SA, SS or Gestapo. By the time the 'retribution' ended, one synagogue had been burned down, two more demolished, some 500 Jewish shops and three dozen Jewish-owned businesses wrecked. Yet, as Jewish teacher and historian Willy Cohn observed, "We are still not at the end and there are surely even worse things to come."

"Breslau gets even with the Jews," screamed the *Schlesische Tageszeitung*, the Party's mouthpiece in the city. "Their synagogues are nothing but heaps of rubble." Many of the city's residents felt deep unease, even anger at the events of *Kristallnacht*. Ulrich Frodien's father flew into frequent fits of rage. "But like everyone else, he did nothing, he remained a Party member and only clenched his fist in his pocket," his son observed. As for Ulrich, he continued to faithfully serve the *Deutsche Jungvolk*, the junior wing of the Hitler Youth, as "a brainless twelve-year-old, showing no sympathy, bone-headed and naive," parading through the streets of his home city singing "the most horrible rabble-rousing anti-Semitic slogans". It was, Ulrich Frodien realized years later, the ideal way to "educate the 'manpower' which it would need for the coming war." [15]

Breslau's road to war did not end with preparing the mind, of course. Just four days after the stretch of Autobahn was opened, a new military unit was formed in Breslau, 28th Infantry Division. The city was the headquarters of *Wehrkreis* VIII – Military District VIII – the administrative centre responsible for training and equipping divisions raised in Silesia such as 18th Infantry in Liegnitz, 5th Panzer in Oppeln, as well as the 28th and 221st Infantry and a myriad of supply, training, replacement, signals and other units in the *Gau* capital. After the fallow 1920s, work in the city's principal industries picked up to meet the demands of rearmament. The workforce of the Archimedes steel works trebled. The world-famous Linke-Hofmann factory produced locomotives and railway carriages, while its former motor vehicle wing, now the *Fahrzeug und Motoren Werke* – Vehicle and Motor Works or FAMO to everyone in the city – produced tank chassis as well as tractors, trucks and other road vehicles. Rearmament, conscription, huge public construction projects. All helped to eradicate the spectre of unemployment for all but a handful of the 600,000-plus Breslauers by the end of the decade.

And so on the eve of war, this metropolis on the Oder was vibrant once more. During the spring and summer, the promenades along the river were a popular destination for thousands of Breslauers, especially on Sundays. The cafes, restaurants and beer gardens along the river buzzed with conversation and music. "In that respect," one proud resident recalled, "Breslau competed with Vienna."[16] Breslauers enjoyed some of the finest sports facilities in Europe courtesy of the Hermann Göring Sportfeld, even if the city's sporting teams were rather second-rate. They might visit an exhibition or watch a circus performance in the Jahrhunderthalle, or perhaps stroll around the zoological gardens opposite. In the evening, the Ring remained the focal point of city life with its restaurants and bierkellers. The 1,300-seat Stadttheater and even larger Schauspielhaus offered opera and high-brow entertainment, while the masses could catch a film at one of more than three dozen cinemas.

To visitors, the *Baedeker* tourist guide enthused, Breslau presented "a happy fusion of historic, attractive ancient culture and Silesian down-to-earth nature with the vibrant features of a big city". The guide particularly recommended the Monopol in the old town with its forty *en suite* rooms for up to 10 Reichsmarks a night, or the Savoy, close to the Hauptbahnhof, offering the same facilities for a similar price. Budget travellers could find a room for the night in one of Breslau's hostels for a little over 2 Reichsmarks. Most would come by train – the express would bring them from the capital in a little over three hours for just short of 18 Reichsmarks. The wealthy might come by Autobahn – or even by air. There were two flights a day to the capital in summer, one every weekday in winter, from Gandau airfield, four miles west of the city centre, as well as services to Warsaw, Stettin, Berlin, Prague, Dresden and beyond. The old airport building which resembled a village hall had been replaced with a huge brick structure, five-storey tower and a hangar large enough to accommodate the four-engined Junkers G38 airliners of the day. Despite such improvements, the field itself still needed 250 sheep to keep the grass short.

But like everywhere else in the Reich, the inhabitants of 'happy fusion' had surrendered their freedoms. Every facet of this life was either controlled or monitored by the arms of the Nazi Party from the regional leader, the *Gauleiter*, to the *Kreisleiter* – responsible for a town or parish; the *Ortsgruppe*, overseeing Party affairs for up to 3,000 households – there were more than 90 such offices in Breslau; *Zellenleiter*, responsible for up to eight city blocks; and finally, the *Blockleiter*, whose domain covered between forty and sixty homes. Boys aged ten and above were compulsory members of the *Deutsche Jungvolk* and from the age of fourteen moved into the *Hitlerjugend*, while girls joined the *Jungmädel* and *Bund Deutscher Mädel* respectively. Workers joined the sole trade union, the *Deutsche Arbeitsfront* – German Labour Front – and enjoyed excursions, holidays and other activities through the Nazis' leisure organisation *Kraft durch Freude* – Strength Through Joy – which even ran Breslau's Gerhart Hauptmann Theatre. On top of the *Party* apparatus, there was the *state* apparatus, the *Sicherheitsdienst* security service who monitored public opinion among other duties, or the secret police, the Gestapo. The latter arrested Joachim Konrad, priest of St Elisabethkirche near the Ring, on at least three occasions, and even banned him from speaking throughout the Reich. He was regularly summoned to the Gestapo headquarters in Berlin, where officials showed him the thick file they had compiled, listing "all my 'sins' against the Third Reich". The ban would eventually be lifted and Konrad allowed to return to his home city; he would serve it, and its people, through its most bitter days.[17]

War came to Breslau inevitably, if reluctantly. In the closing days of August 1939, a constant stream of vehicles and troops moved through the city, bound for the Polish frontier barely twenty-five miles away where men of the labour service erected barbed-wire fences in the face of the Polish 'threat'. The soldiers marched silently, no songs accompanied the thud of boot upon tarmac. "We had to tear ourselves away from what we clung on to with all our strength: family, job, home," remembered Breslau student and reservist artillery officer Hans Thieme, recalled to the colours. "The days which followed were possibly the most challenging of the entire war emotionally."[18] Breslauers watched the soldiers march past without saying a word. Diarists Walter Tausk and Willy Cohn could find no appetite for war among the citizens of Breslau. "There's none of the patriotic enthusiasm of August 1914," Cohn noted. "It's more a silent despair." Shops filled with hoarders desperate to fill their pantries before rationing took effect. Police moved through the city handing out instructions telling residents to maintain a black out at night and keep buckets filled with water handy. Women on the trams talked openly about fleeing the city for the safety of the countryside and withdrew their savings from the banks. Tausk bumped into drunk soldiers on a final fling before heading off to the front. Their boisterous behaviour was too much even for Breslau's ladies of the night who disappeared into their apartments and locked the doors. The troops, Tausk observed, "are depressed, morose, show no enthusiasm for war, and rage inside against Adolf. In the barracks at Karlowitz, young men as well as the old reservists say: 'He can pick up his things and go, we've had enough of it.'"[19]

Silesia served as the springboard for the thrust on Warsaw. The staff of Army Group South could be found in Neisse, forty-five miles south of Breslau, the specialist dive-bomber unit of Wolfram von Richthofen seventy miles to the east near Rosenberg, and in the city itself, the headquarters of Eighth Army. "If war is necessary now," its chief-of-staff Hans Felber enthused, "then let's grit our teeth and take a leap into uncertainty!"[20] If Breslauers did not necessarily share his enthusiasm, few shed a tear for Poland's demise. Still smarting from defeat in the World War, "most Silesians did not like this new hostile neighbour in the East, this Polish state," Ulrich Frodien remembered.[21]

War with Poland was brutally swift – the first troops began to return from the front before the end of September. The following summer, the city's own 221st Infantry Division was welcomed home after victory over France. It had played a minuscule role in the triumph, but it still marched through the streets of Breslau where it was "showered with flowers and gifts. Every street and the buildings on them were decorated with garlands and flags. There was not a single soldier, not a single vehicle without a floral decoration. Everywhere the men were welcomed by cries of '*Heil*' from the populace, which frequently chanted rousing choruses such as 'We thank you.'"[22] But for boys like ten-year-old Peter Bannert, the war had been a huge let-down. "We were in a high spirits, but we were soon disappointed," he recalled. "Life seemed to go on as normal and no enemy aircraft could be seen in the sky."[23]

And so it would be for the next five years, more or less. Breslau was not untouched by war – nowhere in Germany was – but beyond the range of enemy bombers, the city was less affected than almost any other in the Reich. There were restrictions – on travel, on food, on personal liberties – but otherwise life went on as it did in peacetime. On Sundays, the *Hitlerjugend* would parade through the streets singing anti-Jewish songs before marching into the Jahrhunderthalle to the sound of tympani and fanfares. Each Wednesday and Saturday, Ulrich Frodien pulled on the uniform of the *Jungvolk*, and from the age of fourteen, the *Hitlerjugend*. He was "always in uniform, always in a column". Some boys found it a chore, some spellbinding, but putting on that uniform invariably made Breslau's youths slightly cocky. Riding home on the tram to Karlowitz, three miles from the city centre, Hans Henkel watched a group of boisterous Hitler Youths climb on board. One youth stared through the glass partition at the passengers, most of them elderly. "That's right," the boy yelled. "The cemetery fodder sit down while Germany's future stands." There was an awkward silence in the carriage, then an elderly gentleman stood up, approached the cock-sure youngster and slapped him in the face. Striking a *Hitlerjugend* in uniform was a criminal offence, but no one intervened.[24]

The lively nightlife for which Breslau was renowned continued, although the strict black-out meant that trams and cars drove through the streets with their lights dimmed and the streetlamps were out; Breslauers wore luminescent badges to avoid bumping into each other in the dark. The restaurants, the theatres, the bars, the cinemas remained open. Most weeks, Ulrich Frodien headed into town to catch a film. He particularly enjoyed historical dramas, of which there were many: *Ritt in die Freiheit*, the story of a 19th-Century Polish uprising against the Russians, *Der Grosse König*, an award-winning biography of Frederick the Great, or *Ohm Krüger*, an account of the Boer War laden with anti-British vitriol. And before each main feature, the *Wochenschau*, the weekly newsreel, a pot pourri of events at home – engineers at work in Silesia's steel mills, large-scale Nazi ceremonies, submariners skiing in the Alps – and events at the front – the bombardment of Warsaw, mountain troops in Narvik, the fall of Paris. Frodien watched the newsreels avidly, but it was only years later that he realized how sanitized a picture of war they presented. There were shots of "carefully-erected birch crosses with a steel helmet on top, pretty nurses and recuperating soldiers in the hospitals," or graveside ceremonies with heroic speeches and guards of honour. But of the dead themselves, nothing. "No shot-up panzers, no shot-down aircraft, no bombed flak position," he recalled.[25] What propaganda tried to hide, life could not. Willy Cohn was struck by the large number of women walking around Breslau, their faces covered by black veils. "All widowed by the war – most of them not reported in the newspaper," he observed in his diary.[26] And occasionally, there were direct reminders of the war raging across Europe. In mid-November 1941, Breslau was bombed in broad daylight. The sum total of seven bombs fell on the city (one of those was a dud), but ten people were killed. The *Schlesische Tageszeitung* immediately branded the Soviet attack a 'terror raid' aimed at defenceless civilians. "In fact, the attack was aimed at the Hauptbahnhof – and struck very close to it," Willy Cohn noted. At least one bomb landed in the station, tearing both legs off a woman. "War always affects the innocent but this air raid is also proof that the enemy is now catching up."[27]

The enemy was not catching up quickly enough for Willy Cohn. One week after that entry in his journal, he was arrested with his wife and two children. They joined a train carrying another 1,000 Breslau Jews to Kaunas in Lithuania. Before November was out, the Cohn family had been exterminated. Walter Tausk too. He was also shipped to Lithuania with the first transports. Over the coming eighteen months, trains would leave for camps at Auschwitz, Majdanek, Sobibor, Belzec in Poland and Theresienstadt in Czechoslovakia under what was cynically called the 'Jewish Resettlement Action'. By the summer of 1943, the authorities could proclaim Breslau *Judenrein* – cleansed of Jews.[28]

It wasn't merely the deportation of the Jews which changed the demographics of Breslau as the war progressed. By the spring of 1944, nearly half a million Germans had been relocated from western and central Germany to Silesia, which quickly earned the nickname *Luftschutzkeller Deutschlands* – Germany's air raid shelter. With the people came industry which also sought to escape the grasp of Allied bombers. Despite the Nazi's much-trumpeted *Volksgemeinschaft* – national community – Breslau's womenfolk did not welcome the influx of refugees, not least because they quickly emptied shops and stores of underwear and bedding.[29] What Breslauers resented more, however, was the influx of foreign labourers – French, Russian, Polish prisoners of war, Czechs, concentration camp inmates – needed to fill the gaps left by Breslau's men leaving for the front. There was no hiding these new arrivals: Poles wore armbands branded 'P' and carried identity cards with a pig stamped on the reverse; White Russians wore a badge on their upper left arm bearing their national colours, white, red, white; Ukrainians a blue-yellow badge with a trident, the coat of arms of the ancient state of Kiev under Vladimir the Great; and Russians were marked by a white-blue-red badge featuring the cross of St Andrew.[30] None was the equal of a German – as Breslauers constantly reminded these captive peoples. They were infuriated when prisoners of war marching to and from camp did not make way for them in the streets. They were even more infuriated when they watched Russian labourers hanging around for fifteen minutes or more at a time doing nothing.[31] Poles, Ulrich Frodien observed, were "treated worse than farm dogs. They had become fair game, whipping boys for every thug in the village police, worked until every last ounce of strength had been squeezed out of them, and despised even more than the lowliest German village idiot."[32] Foreign drivers on the trams – also branded by armbands – grew rather too close to the young Breslau women serving as conductors for the liking of many.[33] Fraternisation with these foreigners was not merely frowned upon – it was a criminal offence; girls could be fined 10 Reichsmarks merely for drinking and dancing with Polish prisoners in a bar.[34] A twenty-three-year-old housewife who befriended and then had an affair with an English prisoner, helping him escape, was jailed for four years, while a labourer who passed letters between a captured Soviet soldier and a female Russian worker – letters which were "hostile to the state" – was sentenced to two years in prison.[35] The penalties for foreign labourers who transgressed were far more severe, however. Twenty-year-old Marian Kaczmarek laid track for the *Reichsbahn*, the state railway. After repeated beatings by his German foreman, Kaczmarek struck out. His temper cost him an additional six years of hard labour. The punishment was too mild for Breslau's chief prosecutor; he imposed the death penalty.

Working on farms, on the trams, on the railways, all demanded forced or foreign labourers, but never in the numbers required by the armaments industry. A dozen forced labour and concentration camps grew on the periphery of the city to meet the demands not just of Breslau firms such as Linke-Hofmann and FAMO – producing parts for the V2 rockets and panzers, respectively – but other industry which began relocating to the area as the bombing of the industrial heartland of the Ruhr intensified. Three slave camps fed the Rheinmetall-Borsig ammunition works at Hundsfeld, five miles north-east of the city centre, which churned out three million electric fuses for bombs in 1943, as well as ten million rounds of 20, 30 and 37mm shells and some 6,000 electrical gun sights. Three decades later and living in the USA, the works' director, Herbert Rühlemann composed a long-winded and rather self-satisfied memoir, *Father Tells Daughter*. Father did not tell daughter *everything*, however. Less-than-honestly, Rühlemann referred to the bulk of his workforce as *Gastarbeiter* – guest workers. Some were, but 2,000 were concentration camp prisoners, half of them women.[36]

Rheinmetall's demand for labour paled compared with one armaments factory which began to take shape from the spring of 1942. The Berthawerk – named after the matriarch of the Krupp family – at Markstädt, sixteen miles south-east of Breslau, would produce up to 600 field howitzers and anti-tank guns every month, employing upwards of 12,000 people. One of its directors, Eberhard Franke, painted an almost idyllic picture of a true 'workers community': it was renowned throughout Lower Silesia for the quality of its food; its football team won the local league over four successive seasons; there were boxing matches at which the legendary fighter Max Schmeling officiated; there were libraries, musical instruments, films, radios provided for workers who formed theatre groups and staged variety shows for colleagues.[37]

The reality was far less idyllic. Nearly half of the Berthawerk's employees were concentration camp inmates. After being woken at 4.30am, they trudged for fifty minutes each morning from the nearby camp at Fünfteichen, usually in broken clogs or with rags wrapped around their feet, then worked for twelve hours. There was no breakfast, no evening meal, just a bowl of soup at mid-day. If they pushed too forcefully for their daily meal, they were beaten with a rifle butt by a guard. They were beaten too if their work did not come up to scratch – usually with a whip of iron and rubber. When there were air raids, Germans sought refuge in the air raid shelters; forced labourers remained at their posts. "We were not slaves, our status was much lower," recalled Tadeusz Goldsztajn, a Polish Jew who was sixteen when he arrived at the Krupp works. "The equipment in the shop was well maintained. We, on the other hand, were like a piece of sandpaper which, rubbed once or twice, becomes useless and is thrown away to be burned with the waste."[38]

Given such treatment, it was hardly surprising hatred welled up in the *Ostarbeiter* – eastern worker. The security service intercepted one letter from a Ukrainian. "I submit to these Fascists, I have become their servant," the writer sighed. "Oh, damn these years! I want my liberty, I want to fill my lungs with the fresh Russian air." Each morning he bowed, humbly offered his hand to his masters and greeted them repeatedly. He longed for the day when the Red Army neared. "I'll be one of the first to join the partisans or fight at the front," he vowed. "I will be the first to shoot at their merciless hearts, those who laugh about the hardships faced by the Russian people. And all this will happen – sooner or later."[39]

In the broiling heat, the sweat streamed down the faces of the several dozen standard bearers, holding their banners high between a sea of outstretched hands. As the bearers took their place on the stage, Joseph Goebbels entered the Jahrhunderthalle, followed by the luminaries of the Nazi Party in Silesia and senior Wehrmacht officers. The Propaganda Minister had spent the afternoon of 7 July 1944 visiting his wife Magda in a Breslau clinic, where she was recovering from an operation on her jaw. Otherwise, he found himself frustrated away from the capital. It was nearly impossible to obtain news from the Eastern Front. No news, he reasoned, would be good news.

As Goebbels fretted, the halls and assembly rooms of Breslau began to fill this Friday evening. All 12,000 seats in the Jahrhunderthalle itself. A sizeable crowd gathered outside in Scheitniger Park. The loudspeakers he'd had erected six years earlier would carry the minister's words outside the confines of the huge domed building to other halls throughout the Silesian capital. State radio would carry them across the Reich – and beyond.

It was one of the Goebbels' more measured performances. He looked relaxed, leaned with one hand of the podium, put his hands on his hips, his gesticulations were less frantic than usual. He left his audience in no doubt about the gravity of Germany's plight. The enemy had launched a general offensive in the East and West with overwhelming superiority. "If we do not throw them back now, our enemies will wipe Germany – and everything German – from the face of the earth," he told his audience bluntly. "The German people are in danger!"

Mention of the "aerial criminals", the Anglo-American bomber crews with names such as Murder Incorporated who were "turning German cities to rubble and ash", was drowned out by boos. "There will be retribution," he promised, "and when it comes, not one tear will be shed in Germany." The 12,000-strong audience rose from their seats, shouted, applauded, stamped their feet. It was several minutes before the uproar subsided and the minister could continue. When he did, he urged the German people to summon their strength for one final push. "The hour demands a total war effort by every individual and the entire nation, using all our spiritual and material reserves." He continued:

We National Socialists have endured and overcome so many crises and hard tests in the history of our movement and the Reich that we have never doubted our success for a moment.

The best guarantee of victory is the Führer himself. We look to him with religious faith. He will lead the nation through all dangers and tests with a sure hand. His pledge is the same as ours: a struggle which a nation stands behind with utter fanaticism can never end in anything but victory.

The organ began to play the national anthem. Inside and outside the Jahrhunderthalle, Breslauers stretched their arms out again and sang with gusto. "There's probably no one in the crowd who's not carried away deep down in their heart and filled with belief in a positive end to this difficult struggle," Goebbels' secretary Wilfred von Oven wrote fawningly.[40]

Despite Goebbels' assurances and von Oven's observations, Breslauers were beginning to doubt the war would end in Germany's favour. Outwardly, life in the city went on as usual. Every date in the Nazi calendar was still marked extravagantly with some form of rally or demonstration. There were the 'Day of Duty for Youth' and 'Day of the Wehrmacht' in March, the anniversaries of the Nazis' flying and welfare organisations in April, there was a celebration of the tenth anniversary of the Nazi seizure of power in the Jahrhunderthalle, each Heldengedenktag – Heroes' Memorial Day – was commemorated on the fifth Sunday before Easter with guards of honour standing in front of Breslau's war memorials while Wehrmacht and Party leaders laid wreaths and soldiers formed up on the Schlossplatz to listen to a speech by the city's ranking general, Rudolf Koch-Erpach. April 20, Hitler's birthday, was celebrated of course, but by 1944 it had become a normal working day. In kindergartens, teachers still put garlands on portraits of the Führer and lit 'Hitler candles', however, while children sang hymns of praise and listened to stories from the life of their leader. Flags flew in the streets, pictures and busts of Hitler were displayed in shop windows and in the evening, the *Ortsgruppen* celebrated as 13,000 Hitler Youths marched through the city's streets, while there was a performance of Beethoven's *Symphony No.9* in honour of wounded soldiers and workers in the armaments industry. With the arrival of summer, the outdoor swimming pools opened daily from 7am until dusk for bathers.[41] The Cologne Radio Orchestra performed marches, dances and songs from the silver screen on the promenade by the Oder. The Liebich, Breslau's famous variety theatre, offered *Melody of Love*, a quick-fire sketch show, while at the Circus Busch comedian Harry Zimmo entertained a 3,000-strong audience. At the Wappenhof, Germany's largest open-air theatre by the banks of the Oder, patrons enjoyed a new drink, a honey-yellow apple pomace with a frothy head which tasted sweet and sour. It was particularly popular at Gandau airfield, so locals dubbed it *Fliegerbier* – airmen's beer.[42] As it had done the previous two years, the Nazi Party leadership organised the *Verwundetenfahrt* – trip for the wounded – to the historic town of Trebnitz, a dozen miles north of the city. There the famous Flying Trebnitzer light trains, festooned with cartoons and caricatures drawn by students of a local art school, took the men for a day out.[43] In spite of the frivolity of the event with its marching bands and smiling girls, there was no hiding the cost of the war to Breslau. That same day the *Schlesische Tageszeitung* published thirty death notices of men killed in action: twenty-four-year-old *Unteroffizier* Gerhard Weiss, a soldier for five years, killed in Normandy; *Oberwachtmeister* Helmut Czembor, holder of the Iron Cross, killed in Italy during the battles south of Rome; twenty-one-year-old *Obergefreiter* Günter Kochner, killed in an air raid. "Anyone who knew him will understand our pain," his grandparents eulogized.[44] But most of the fallen listed in Breslau's Nazi Party mouthpiece were killed on the Eastern Front – a front which was beginning to draw ever closer to the borders of the Reich. In mid-June, the German Army still held Byelorussia – Minsk, Vitebsk, Grodno. Six weeks later, the Red Army was at the gates of Warsaw and had crossed the Vistula upstream of the Polish capital at Pulawy and Baranow, less than 250 miles from Breslau. The collapse of the Eastern Front provoked alarm. "The Russians haven't far to go now to the German frontier," one Breslau housewife wrote. "If it gets very bad, there will be nothing left for us but the gas tap. We won't let ourselves be deported." She was, she said, not alone. "Many are of my opinion."[45] All manner of rumours circulated. Entire regiments had deserted. (They hadn't.) Hitler had visited the front and sacked several generals on the spot. (He didn't.) Some generals had not been killed in battle but had been executed. (They had not been.) Officers had fled the battlefield with their Polish or Russian mistresses. (They had.) Weary soldiers struggled back to German lines barefoot, without belts, tattered and torn, undisciplined. (They had.) "This retreat," one person was overheard to say, "is one of the darkest chapters in German history."[46] Even the *Schlesische Tageszeitung*, conceded there was an "obvious crisis in the East".[47] *Gauleiter* Karl Hanke still exuded confidence. On a visit to the historic town of Namslau, three dozen miles east of Breslau, he told the populace: "The war on the Eastern Front only interests me when the first Russians appear before Namslau."[48] As he spoke, thousands of Silesians were already preparing for the defence of their native soil.

At the beginning of August 1944, children in the picturesque town of Habelschwerdt were enjoying summer at the foot of the Sudeten Mountains, among them Peter Bannert. Bannert had taken advantage of the school break to spend a few days in Prague. Proudly wearing his *Hitlerjugend* badge, he visited the church where the assassins of Reinhard Heydrich had committed suicide when surrounded – the walls were pockmarked with bullet holes. On his return to Habelschwerdt, the schoolboy found posters plastered around the town, signed by the local *Hitlerjugend* leader: boys born in 1928 and 1929 had been called up to support the war effort. Townsfolk protested. Their complaints were brushed aside. Their sons packed rucksacks and headed for the railway station, where a fanfare from *Hitlerjugend* trumpeters bade them farewell. The squeal of the wheels drowned out the final words of advice from mothers on the platform. The boys waved furiously, "torn between an awful feeling and a curious thirst for adventure," Bannert recalled. The train moved slowly through the Silesian countryside, through Glatz, through Oels. Around midnight it came to a halt in Neumittelwalde, thirty-five miles north-east of Breslau. The boys marched in darkness to a large field on the edge of the town where a sea of tents awaited them. They threw down straw mattresses, put their rucksacks under their heads and tried to settle down under canvas. "We fought for every centimetre," Peter Bannert recalled – there were sixty-five to seventy men in every tent. "When sleeping, the legs of my opposite number reached as high as my stomach." The Hitler Youths were woken at 6am. They ran a mile to a dirty pond where they washed, then grabbed a breakfast of cold malt coffee, bread, a little fat. There was an hour of cleaning kit and tents, then the boys marched out of the town and headed east.
    Peter Bannert was one of more than 100,000 people – German men and women, Hitler Youths, some 30,000 foreign workers – sucked into a huge construction project

along the old Polish-German border, *Unternehmen Bartold* – Operation Bartold. Named by Karl Hanke for Vogt Bartold, the mythical 13th Century coloniser of Silesia, the massive undertaking aimed to create an impregnable barrier, an *Ostwall* – eastern wall – in a semi-circle from Trachenberg, thirty miles north of Breslau, past the rural towns of Militsch, Neumittelwalde, Gross Wartenberg and Namslau. An anti-tank ditch twenty feet wide and thirteen feet deep would be dug, and behind it a network of trenches and machine-gun nests.

Makeshift camps, such as the one in which Peter Bannert found himself, sprang up across Silesia to accommodate the influx of diggers. Workers found themselves living in tents, in empty factories, barns, in outhouses, in school buildings. Facilities were rudimentary. Pits were dug on the edge to serve as 'toilets' and thunderboxes provided, but the smell was so overpowering, many did not have the stomach for using them. Food came courtesy of field kitchens, invariably soup or some form of broth, which was often so weak that the diggers poured it back into the vat in disgust. Life was rather better for the Party leaders overseeing *Bartold*. They enjoyed better accommodation, better food, a *very* generous allocation of alcohol – many turned up on duty drunk – and various other privileges. They exploited their special position, swaggering around the ditches in their brown uniforms. Above all, they drove their workforce ruthlessly and relentlessly.

Hugo Hartung, chief dramatist at the city's opera house and now a reluctant soldier, was woken daily at 3.30am for roll-call at 4am, before marching off to his place of work near Trachenberg. Sometimes the men sang *Graue Kolonnen marschieren in der Sonnen* – Grey Columns March Towards the Sun – as they headed out of camp. Before sunrise, they were digging the fertile Silesian soil. As the sun climbed higher in the sky, so the number of workers collapsing grew. These were middle-aged or elderly musicians, men more accustomed to the violin or flute than the spade, who struggled to dig the wet clayey soil. Ballet dancers, dressed in colourful swimsuits which conjured up images of summer at the beach, fainted.

The *Hitlerjugend* toiled with spades, shovels and pickaxes for six hours in the torrid August heat, then underwent two hours of *Wehrertüchtigung* – preparatory military training – practising marching and parade ground exercises with spades. One day, their instructors told them, they would swap spades for rifles and defend the very trenches they were digging.

Older men in uniform enjoyed free afternoons. Hugo Hartung explored a part of Silesia he did not know. He picked blackberries, bathed in the Bartsch, a river which once formed the border between Poland and Germany, and lay on the ground staring into the sky. Sometimes he would hear the faint hum of Allied bomber columns streaking their faint vapour trails across the heavens.

Evenings were almost idyllic. Hartung and his comrades sat around camp fires and sang childhood songs or folk tunes, or debated how the war might end. Peter Bannert and his fellow Hitler Youths would regularly march into Neumittelwalde, singing as they went – *Marianka, come, let me kiss you*, or *Master, have no mercy*. The town's only cinema offered standard fare: the musical *Der weiße Traum*, the ever popular musical drama *Wunschkonzert* or Veit Harlan's colour melodrama *Immensee*. Once the projector bulb burned out; the boys sang as they waited for someone to drive to the next town to get a replacement.

And in the morning, the diggers returned to the trenches and anti-tank ditches – and found them half-collapsed where the soil had given way overnight.

The propaganda machine painted *Bartold* as an unqualified success, of course. "Thanks to a tremendous effort, the populace of Germany's eastern *Gau* have created a protective position many hundred kilometres long and given assurance to German troops fighting before the borders of the Reich that the homeland is giving them strong support with this energetic action." Peter Bannert believed the propaganda. "The Russians will bleed to death at our positions," he wrote home with pride, "and victory will be ours." The voices of dissenters were far more numerous, however. Youngsters joked that the Russians would need only thirty-two minutes to break through the *Ostwall*: they'd spend thirty minutes laughing and just two minutes to overcome the fortifications. "This will not stop one Soviet tank," Hugo Hartung overheard one Army officer complain. "If one really falls into this network of ditches, the next one will already be driving across it." How could ditches and walls of earth hold back the enemy, people asked, where the concrete and steel of the Atlantic Wall had failed, while one senior officer inspecting the works told diggers: "It's wonderful that you're working, but it's all for nothing." [49]

Beyond the huge eastern wall its citizens were digging along the old Polish frontier, Breslau possessed a handful of weak concrete and earthen fortifications dating back to the Great War. Napoleon had razed the city's ancient walls and bastions, so a century later a series of infantry positions – or *I Werke* – numbered forty-one through forty-three had been hurriedly thrown up to protect Breslau from the north, and a fourth built in Gräbschen cemetery, three miles south-west of the city centre.

Trenches and anti-tank ditches dug by hand, a few light field fortifications, such were the domain of *Generalmajor* Johannes Krause when he arrived in the Silesian capital on September 25. Breslau had been earmarked as a *Festung* – fortress – and the fifty-one-year-old general its commandant. Krause was an artilleryman with relatively little front-line experience – he had spent most of the war in Greece. But he knew what the designation 'fortress' meant. If war came to Breslau, then the city would be defended to the last round.

Johannes Krause found Breslau not merely lacking in fortifications, he found it lacking in men. His staff were aged officers and ranks fit for only light duties. His garrison troops were two battalions of reservists and militia, almost all old or sick men. His artillery comprised captured French, Russian, Yugoslav and Polish guns, but some lacked the optic equipment and firing tables their inadequate crews, once again elderly soldiers unfit for the battlefield, would need to fire them. As for the working batteries, they had too few shells so it was almost impossible to train. [50]

Johannes Krause's rank and experience counted for naught in the face of the Party. He had no say in *Bartold*, how the ditches were dug, how the trenches were laid out, how the bunkers were built. When his men tried to install machine-guns, they found the weapons would not fit. They spent weeks chipping more than an inch off the concrete pedestals the guns were to sit upon. Few if any of the beds the garrisons of the *Ostwall* would need had arrived. Farmers refused to surrender their vehicles to move material from railway stations to the entrenchments because they were collecting the turnip harvest. Not that much material arrived by train in the first place anyway – there was insufficient fuel in Breslau to move items from depots to the stations, and there were too few wagons on the railways to carry them into the countryside.[51]

The shortcomings of the *Reichsbahn* did not merely bedevil the enormous fortification programme, however. The railways were central to plans to evacuate Breslau's civilians should the city be directly endangered. And on paper, these plans were first-rate: 100 trains a day would carry Breslau's citizens westwards. Johannes Krause thought it was beyond the capacity of the *Reichsbahn* and urged Hanke to evacuate 200,000 Breslauers – the elderly, the sick, children and young mothers – now. The *Gauleiter* dismissed the general's suggestion. "The Führer would have me shot if it went to him with such matters now, in the deepest peace!"[52] That deepest peace was about to be shattered.

It had been dark for a little over an hour on Saturday 7 October as Hugo Hartung made his way through the city centre towards the shores of the Oder. He had been relieved from his duties at Schöngarten airfield and permitted to lay on a concert by singers and musicians from his opera house at a makeshift hospital in a converted government building. As he arrived at the hospital, the sirens began to howl. The theatre director was unperturbed. For three months, first digging the *Ostwall*, then back at the airfield, he had watched "silver flashes beneath a blue sky flying in formation, as if on exercise", his heart skipping a beat as the American bombers approached Breslau. They had always avoided the city, continuing on to the synthetic oil plant at Heydebreck, eighty miles to the south-east. Tonight, however, the dreaded 'Christmas trees' – coloured marker flares to aid the bomb aimers – appeared over the Silesian capital. The flak thundered. The bombs fell – one fell barely 300 feet from the hospital, shattering windows. Hartung watched as gravely-wounded patients were brought on stretchers from the upper storeys into the cellar. A soldier whose legs were lacerated was brought into the temporary operating theatre in the cellar, where staff worked by candlelight. It was an hour and a quarter before the all-clear sounded. There was no thought of giving the concert now. Hugo Hartung stepped outside and surveyed the damage. Under the bright moonlight, he could see widespread fires on both sides of the Oder. The Rhenania-Ossag oil depot was on fire. The trams no longer ran. It was the first significant raid Breslau suffered: sixty-nine people were killed, among them thirty-seven women and thirteen children. The city's status as 'air raid shelter' was over.[53]

A fortnight later, the Reich's desperate position was reinforced. On Friday 20 October, Karl Hanke climbed a small white podium in the centre of Schlossplatz, surrounded by a handful of standard bearers and rather more Party and Wehrmacht leaders. The few huge swastika banners on the edge of the square hung limply in the still autumn air. Hanke looked out across a sea of people; he estimated perhaps 100,000 Breslauers had gathered on the parade ground, while those who could not hear his words in person listened on the city's public address system. Two days before posters had appeared on billboards, on lampposts, on advertising columns across the Silesian capital:

> After five years of the most bitter fighting, the enemy stands close to or on the German border on several fronts thanks to the failure of all our European allies. They are gathering their forces to smash our Reich, to destroy the German people and its social order. Their ultimate aim is the eradication of the German people.

The needs of the hour, the decree continued, demanded "a second great effort" by the German people, namely calling to arms every man capable of bearing them "to wage a merciless struggle wherever the enemy sets foot on German soil". Thus was born the *Volkssturm* – literally 'people's storm' – a national militia of men aged sixteen to sixty. In Breslau it was Karl Hanke's personal army. It was his to form, it was his to command.[54]

Over the coming three weeks, the men of Breslau were expected to register for the new force. Any man who could carry and use a weapon as well as carry out a short march was regarded as fit to fight. Every city block was expected to provide a *Gruppe* – squad – every *Zelle* of eight blocks a platoon, every *Ortsgruppe* a company and every *Kreis* a battalion. The Sunday closest to the anniversary of the Munich putsch in 1923 was chosen for the solemn act of swearing-in the *Volkssturm* ranks. And so on Sunday November 12, men dressed in civilian clothes, in the uniforms of railway workers, boys in the brown of the *Hitlerjugend*, men fresh from work in Breslau's factories took the oath:

> I swear this holy oath by God that I will be unconditionally loyal and obedient to the Führer of the Greater German Reich, Adolf Hitler. I vow to fight heroically for my homeland and would rather die than give up the freedom – and with it the future – of my people.[55]

Afterwards, these new warriors marched through the Silesian capital. "The march pasts created an image of very large reserves of men still capable of fighting," one Propaganda Ministry report observed. "This fact not only had an effect on the populace and soldiers, for whom it is an added incentive in battle, but has also shown dubious foreigners that the German nation is still strong."[56] The reality was rather different. Photographs show mostly aged Breslauers, some portly, some thin, all wearing caps and hats, some smiling, some looking pensive, some looking doleful. The *Volkssturm* man had every reason to feel doleful, for the force he had just been sworn into was a desperate last throw of the dice. Far from emanating strength, calling up old men and boys showed that the Reich was morally bankrupt. The Soviets showered Silesia with leaflets lampooning the *Volkssturm*, not the "mightiest wonder weapon of the Reich", rather an army of "grandfathers driving tanks and young lads with pistols". It continued:

Hitler wails, Himmler threatens

As if they'll still get a response.
Himmler's levy cannot
Save Hitler's Reich any longer.[57]

It could not. For Hitler's Reich could not even equip this 'storm' it had summoned. Each man had to provide his own clothes: either dyed Party uniforms or a weatherproof suit, plus shoes, a coat, rucksack, blanket, flask and canteen. He received a black-red arm band with the inscription '*Deutscher Volkssturm: Wehrmacht*'. Training was equally rudimentary. Instructors were ordered to dispense with lengthy lectures and move straight to the practical demonstrations. "No long-winded explanations but exercises with the weapons! No tedious talk, rather training of the mind and body."[58] They should "arouse the love of shooting which exists in every German man. You can only learn to shoot by shooting, and learn to shoot well by shooting a lot. It doesn't matter how you shoot, rather that you hit." Where there were insufficient weapons or ammunition, the men were to resort to practising "digging trenches, establishing an all-round defence with barriers, camouflage, understanding the terrain".[59] *Volkssturm* commanders – almost all Party leaders – were expected to follow their Führer's example. "Strive to live, to fight, to believe like Adolf Hitler." They were expected to listen to the older men in their charge "who have already experienced so much in life", to praise rather than chastise. "Appeal to the men's hearts so that they will go through fire for you. One word of encouragement and you will see for yourself that each man will do his utmost to improve his efforts." The commander must use every opportunity to "promote love for our people and for our Fatherland" as well as "the most fervent hatred of the enemy".[60]

Within a month, there were more than forty *Volkssturm* battalions across Lower and Upper Silesia. Each one should have been equipped with nearly 650 rifles – a carbine per man, two dozen grenade rifles and three-dozen light and heavy machine-guns, but the experiences of *Breslau-Land 3 Battalion* were typical. For 600 men, most dressed in civilian clothes, there were around 100 captured Russian, Italian and French rifles with just fifteen rounds apiece.[61] The one weapon which they possessed in abundance, however, was the *Panzerfaust* – armoured fist – a small hand-held anti-tank weapon. It was cheap, easy to use standing up, kneeling or lying down, and effective, capable of penetrating up to eight inches of armour. Its use demanded nerves of steel – the target could be no more than 300ft away – but instructors told their men not to be afraid of the steel colossi from the East:

The T34 takes 13,000 hours to build, weighs 20,000 kilogrammes, 15,000 kilogrammes of high-grade steel, and costs 182,000 Reichsmarks.
    It can be destroyed by a *Panzerfaust* which takes fifty-three minutes to build, weighs six kilogrammes, 4.9 kilogrammes of steel and costs eight Reichsmarks.
    What else does it need? An iron heart, a well-aimed shot. Do you still believe in the superiority of size?[62]

The men were shown training films. There were booklets, the *Volkssturm*'s own newspaper *Der Dienstappell* – Call of Duty – filled with instructional material, there were posters and pamphlets such as *Panzerknacker* – tank cracker – packed with cartoons, sketches, slogans: 'work together like a football team'; 'if you're well camouflaged, you're half-way there'; 'better sweat than blood'. And there were short rhymes to learn:

Der schwerste Panzer geht in Brand
Nimmt Du die Panzerfaust zur Hand!

The heaviest tank goes up in flames
When you grab the *Panzerfaust*!

Slogans began to appear on the façades of Breslau's buildings – 'Never capitulate in the face of anything!' 'Germany will and must be victorious!' 'There can only be peace if we are victorious!' 'It is better to die heroically than be a traitor of the Fatherland!' 'We will give the enemy hell for every metre of German soil, and fighting in the ruins we will win a new life!'[63] – while the *Schlesische Tageszeitung* published the *Song of the Lower Silesian Volkssturm*:

Comrades, do you hear the fanfares,
With their old familiar battle cry
Always in times of crisis and danger
Called us to arms and were heralds of victory.
Once again the storm signals howl.
Once again the bells sound in the tower,
Once again the flags billow like blazing torches.
People go to battle.
Comrades, grab your rifles
Panzerfaust and hand-grenades at the ready.
The enemy wants to lay waste to our land and *Volk*
We want to deny him defiantly.[64]

As the year drew to a close, the city's propaganda leader, Dr Schulz, tried to assure his masters in Berlin that Breslauers felt "greater confidence and hope in a favourable outcome to the war."[65] Schulz's assurances flew in the face of all the evidence on Joseph Goebbels' desk. Some people, even in the Party, were beginning to lose their heads, he acknowledged. They no longer believed his propaganda machine. They no longer believed claims that the Russians would slaughter civilians. They did believe that Budapest would soon fall, that the situation at the front was "very threatening". By the end of 1944, the propaganda minister realized, large sections of the German public, "wanted peace at any price".[66] The people of Breslau clung to the wildest of hopes, almost all involving Silesia's patron saint, Hedwig, buried in Trebnitz, fifteen miles north of the city. People who hadn't been to church in years, who criticised the 'reactionary' clergy, suddenly began praying at Hedwig's grave for salvation – and she had appeared to them. Just like the Mongols in 1241, the apparition said, the Red Army would suffer a decisive defeat on Silesian soil and Germany would be saved. Others claimed they had seen the saint in the skies above Breslau, stretching her arms over the city. That was why, they said, it had not been bombed. Such rumours spread rapidly through the city – and throughout Silesia – because, Ulrich Frodien observed, "apart from this, they heard nothing but catastrophic report after catastrophic report."[67]

Frodien was right. There was little to cheer Breslauers as 1944 drew to a close. The air raid sirens now sounded on average once a week – instead of once every two months – although no more bombs fell. Besides sending thousands of Breslauers to dig, Karl Hanke had ordered those left behind to work ten-hour days – and had cancelled leave. All but a handful of newspapers and journals had been culled, and those which survived – the Party's own *Schlesische Tageszeitung* was among them, naturally – invariably ran to no more than four pages. Since September 1, all theatres, variety clubs, cabarets, orchestras, circuses had been closed, their artists and employees sent to the *Ostwall*, to factories, to armament works. Touring the workshops of the Rheinmetall-Borsig plant in Hundsfeld one day, works director Herbert Rühlemann found a sixty-year-old actor pushing a carriage around on the production line. The man smiled at Rühlemann and told him – convincingly – that he loved his new job. "We should not forget he was an actor," the engineer observed, "and a good one."[68]

The city still possessed some of the attractions of a metropolis. After summer and autumn in the small provincial town of Neumittelwalde, Peter Bannert revelled in life in a big city. There were bouts at the Jahrhunderthalle, there were trams, cinemas, and, above all, beer. On Sundays, the Hitler Youth and his comrades would head into the city for a feast – meat salad, broth, sausage, beers, all for four marks apiece.[69] Lower Silesia's farmers would take a break from looking after their herds and head into the city for a holiday of a day or two. Surplus animals and poultry should have been surrendered to the state. But a vibrant black market thrived in the city – geese, sausages, chickens, pig fat, all were readily available for the right price, or with a little haggling. One farmer 'paid' for his stay at the small Dresner Hof hotel near the central station with a dozen geese. It was not unusual. The owner's daughter recalled that her mother "hardly bothered" with ration books. "By 1944, barter had reached the height of perfection."[70]

As 1944 turned to 1945, Hugo Hartung found himself back on duty at Schöngarten airfield, half a dozen miles west of the city centre. The forty-two-year-old had been granted leave to enjoy the festive period with his young family. Like many Breslauers that Christmas, the Hartungs sought reassurance from the church. The focal point for Protestants was the twin-towered cathedral where "more Christmas candles burned than ever", while Catholics headed for the imposing Dorotheenkirche with its steep roof, or the Matthiaskirche in the heart of the university quarter, kneeling before the altars in ever greater numbers. Heavy snow fell – so heavy that the trams no longer ran and the electric wires around the Ring arced, bathing the Rathaus in an eerie green light for an instant. Hartung's children were entranced by the magical sight and by the mangers in the churches, but not the theatre director or his wife. They were seized by a feeling of anxiety walking through the narrow alleyways of the old town which "strangled our throats such that we were barely able to speak". Returning to Schöngarten had done nothing to lessen that anxiety. The tension "was by now becoming unbearable". Hartung and his comrades were all too aware of the Soviets' "mighty concentration of troops and material". Their offensive "had to be unleashed any day".[71]

Notes

1. Bannert, pp.54-57.
2. Hitler's speech and New Year in the Goebbels household based on TB Oven, 31/12/44; TB Goebbels, 31/12/44 and 1/1/45; *Schlesische Tageszeitung*, 2/1/45.
3. *Führer durch das Deutsches Turn- und Sportfest Breslau 1938*, p.9.
4. Davies and Moorhouse, *Microcosm*, p.263.
5. Cited in *Microcosm*, p.327.
6. Hupka, *Meine Heimat Schlesien: Errinerungen*, p.63.
7. Thum, p.351.
8. Frodien, p.142.
9. Ibid., pp.192-3.
10. *Schlesische Tageszeitung*, 12/3/33.
11. TB Goebbels, 1/8/37.
12. *Völkischer Beobachter*, 28/9/36.
13. TB Cohn, 27/9/36.
14. Frodien, p.133.
15. *Kristallnacht* based on Ascher, p.170; Tausk, pp.182, 192; TB Cohn, 10/11/38; *Schlesische Tageszeitung*, 11/11/38; and Frodien, pp.132-4.
16. Höntsch, p.304.
17. Konrad, pp.7-8.
18. Hupka, *Meine Heimat Schlesien: Errinerungen*, p.146.
19. TB Cohn, 28/8/39 and 31/8/39 and Tausk, pp.227-8.
20. TB Felber, 1/9/39 in BA-MA RH20-8/1.
21. Frodien, pp.95-6.
22. Hartmann, *Wehrmacht im Ostkrieg: Front und militärisches Hinterland 1941/42*, p.131.
23. Bannert, p.28.
24. Henkel, pp.77-8.
25. Frodien, p.165.
26. TB Cohn, 13/8/40.
27. Ibid., 14/11/38.
28. *Microcosm*, p.393.
29. SD Meldung, 20/9/43, 16/12/43.
30. *Microcosm*, p.389 and IMT, xv, p.202 and *Völkischer Beobachter*, 29/8/44.
31. SD Meldungen 29/4/43 and 2/9/43.
32. Frodien, pp.98-9.
33. SD Meldung, 6/1/44.
34. Ibid., 13/12/43.
35. *Schlesische Zeitung*, 31/7/44 and *Schlesische Tageszeitung*, 31/7/44.
36. Herbert Rühlemann, 'Father Tells Daughter' in IWM 02/23/1; *Microcosm*, pp.387-8, 400-1; *Less Than Slaves*, p.151.
37. NMT, ix, pp.964-6.

34   HITLER'S FINAL FORTRESS

38. NMT, ix, p.1422 and Manchester, pp.574-81.
39. SD Meldung, 21/2/44.
40. After the speech Goebbels noted smugly in his diary: "Despite the seriousness of the hour, I believe that my stock among the broad masses remains as high as it ever did." The account is based on *Völkischer Beobachter*, 9/7/44, TB Goebbels, 8-9/7/44, TB von Oven, 9/7/44. By contrast, Hitler's final visit to Breslau in November 1943 – in the same hall – was a secret affair, only reported to the public several days after the event. The Führer spoke to several thousand officer candidates, an address he typically gave in Berlin's Sportpalast, but moved to the Jahrhunderthalle because of Allied air attacks on the capital.
41. *Schlesische Tageszeitung*, 12/5/44.
42. Based on *Schlesische Zeitung*, 31/7/44; *Schlesische Tageszeitung*, 12/5/44 and Terp, p.72.
43. *Schlesische Zeitung*, 31/7/44.
44. *Schlesische Tageszeitung*, 31/7/44.
45. NA FO898/187, p.600.
46. SD Meldung, 7/8/44.
47. *Schlesische Tageszeitung*, 30/7/44.
48. Ahlfen, p.71.
49. *Bartold* is based on Bannert, pp.46-52, Hartung, pp.13-15; SD Meldungen 28/10/44 and 12/11/44; *Lausitzer Rundschau*, 8/1/05; *Gross Wartenberger Heimatblatt*, Nr.1, 1995; Noble, pp.108-09, 118-19; Becker, p.97; Grieger, p.4. Breslau's civil servants, public employees and factory workers were not exempted from this massive undertaking. Every Tuesday and Friday they left their places of work, caught trains from the central station before 5am and were dropped off 'near' the digging sites – the reality was usually a two-hour trek on foot through the Silesian countryside before they could actually start work. It was after 10pm by the time they returned to the city. Their reward for their toil: stamps for bread, stamps for fifty grammes of meat and fifty grammes of fat, plus two or three cigarettes. See Becker, p.97.
50. Based on Ahlfen and Niehoff, *So Kämpfte Breslau*, pp.13-14 – hereafter cited as *So Kämpfte Breslau* – and Becker, p.97.
51. Gleiss, ix, pp.11-12.
52. *So Kämpfte Breslau*, p.18.
53. Hartung, pp.20, 26.
54. The rally in Breslau was mirrored across the Reich. Upper Silesian *Gauleiter* Fritz Bracht addressed "tens of thousands of people" in front of his headquarters in Kattowitz. "Now is it too late for our enemies," Bracht assured his audience. "Now it has truly become a total, a holy war, one we have been forced to wage. It will end one day, suddenly perhaps. And the bells which will then announce peace to the world, will be the bells of German victory." *Oberschlesische Zeitung*, 22/10/44.
55. Seidler, p.126.
56. Ibid., pp.130-2.
57. Siebel-Achenbach, p.28.
58. Mammach, p.61.
59. Ibid., p.63.
60. Seidler, pp.187-8.
61. Mammach, p.68.
62. Messerschmidt, p.466.
63. Seidler, pp.287-8.
64. *Schlesische Zeitung*, 10/11/44.
65. Noble, p.180.
66. TB Goebbels, 9/11/44.
67. For the rumours circulating at the end of 1944 see Frodien, p.116; Fritz Neugebauer, 'Tatsachenbericht unserer Erlebnisse während der letzten Kriegszeit, 1945', p.7 in IWM 95/4/1; and Hartung, p.31.
68. Rühlemann, 'Father Tells Daughter', p.428 in IWM 02/23/1.
69. Bannert, p.55.
70. Dittman, Ursel, 'Memoirs', p.2 in IWM 07/15/1.
71. Hartung, pp.38-9.

CHAPTER 2

The Bridgehead

Just one more leap is needed for final victory
Marshal Ivan Konev

The mortars rained down continuously on *Oberleutnant* Hans Jürgen Hartmann's bunker. Here, more than 200 miles east of Breslau, was the "easternmost balcony of the German front" – a network of trenches stretching for more than seventy miles through central Poland to hem in the Red Army's bridgehead over the Vistula. For more than three months, Hartmann and his comrades in Infantry Regiment 514 had manned positions at the north-eastern end of the salient. Germans called it the Baranow bridgehead, the Russians named it after the town of Sandomierz. It was a demoralising existence for the defenders. By the end of 1944, Hans Jürgen Hartmann's nerves were shot. The sight of the shadowy ruins and empty trenches near the village of Łukawa, half a dozen miles north of Sandomierz, filled him with horror every time he carried out a night-time patrol. The turret of a Russian T34 tank slowly rusted away in one abandoned trench, now covered by a white blanket after the first light snowfall. To the *Oberleutnant*, war in the Baranow bridgehead seemed to be hibernating. There was rarely any shooting, let alone any fighting. "But appearances are deceptive," the twenty-three-year-old wrote in his diary. "We cannot be frivolous for even one minute." The moment one of Hartmann's men stood up in the trench, his head visible above the parapet, a Soviet sniper would shoot. The officer had toyed with doing just that. That way, he admitted, "I would finally have peace."

Christmas in the regiment's bunkers had been "shitty". All manner of gifts had been supplied: cigarettes, wine and schnapps. But the men did not feel like celebrating. In the half-light of bunkers lit by candles, the food turned cold. The wine stayed in the bottle. "Christmas songs, wrapping paper, Christmas this, Christmas that, the things scrimped and saved for at home – what does all that matter in our lonely, grey world of the trenches?" Hartmann wrote. The men talked long into the night, gathered around a small Christmas tree. They talked about their families, about the bombing of German cities, about the sporadic post – the bespectacled Hartmann had sent his family in Dresden his latest portrait; he had received no mail in return – about Christmases past, in peace and in war. "As far as was possible, we didn't discuss the future," wrote Hartmann. "What would I have been able to say to them?"

The mood at New Year was better. Yet nothing had changed. Still no post. No alcohol for eight days. "We're now waiting, morning after morning, for that distant loud noise which could take place any day and signal for us the end of this unnatural calm," Hartmann noted in his diary. "Yes, we expect the major Russian offensive to begin any day."[1]

Half a dozen miles away in Sandomierz, Lieutenant Vassily Ivanovich Malinin could hear a handful of aircraft overhead in the night sky. It was rarely quiet in the historic small town which straddles the Vistula. For several weeks, the correspondent with the Soviet Sixth Army's front-line newspaper, *Down With The Enemy*, had watched the build-up of forces: trucks and armour continuously crossed the bridges Red Army engineers had thrown across the river the previous summer and autumn. As they approached Sandomierz they passed posters pinned to trees or road signs, or erected by the roadside, proclaiming, *We will reach Berlin!* German artillery had tried to disrupt the build-up. Shells fell sporadically in Sandomierz's centre. Russian gunners responded with heavier salvoes aimed at German lines half a dozen miles to the north. The infantry trained. They practised neutralising enemy bunkers and the art of street fighting. That would, one battalion commander told the journalist, "definitely come in handy". Occasionally Vassily Malinin visited the front, staring across the eighty or so metres of wasteland between the Russian trenches and the foremost German lines. Bunkers, trenches, connecting trenches, all were easily identifiable. By day there was random fire from enemy mortars and machine-guns. By night, the Vistula landscape was bathed in artificial light by flares which the Germans launched almost without interruption from dusk until dawn. It was, Malinin observed, "a sign that they are afraid." Tonight the light show had an aural accompaniment. Several German aircraft circled above Sandomierz, dropping bombs on the town. Many did not explode. "Hitler's machine," Malinin noted in his diary, "is beginning to stutter."[2]

It was five months since the Red Army had first crossed Poland's great artery with the very last gasp of its great summer offensive which drove the Germans out of Byelorussia, out of Galicia, out of eastern Poland. It threw its forces across the Vistula at Magnuszew, three dozen miles south of Warsaw, at Puławy, seventy-five miles south of the Polish capital and at Baranow, another sixty-five miles upstream. For a month, the German Army had tried to crush the bridgeheads and drive the Soviets back over the river. The best they could achieve was to limit the Red Army's foothold on the left bank of the Vistula – but that foothold was still enormous. When the front settled in September 1944, the bridgehead at Baranow was forty miles deep and followed the river for fifty miles; the smaller foothold at Puławy was a mere eight miles deep. Russian and German alike knew that these bridgeheads would be the springboards for the Red Army's next push west, whenever it came.

Almost every day during the autumn, sound-ranging equipment and troops watching for muzzle flashes reported the arrival of fresh batteries at Puławy. The numbers, *Oberst* Paul Arnhold noted with concern, "rose to utterly overwhelming proportions". But how, the senior engineer with LVI Panzer Corps wondered. Any attempts to throw a bridge across the Vistula here – anywhere between 200 and 300 yards wide – had been thwarted either by German artillery or by dive-bomber attacks. There were no ferries, no boats. Low-level aerial reconnaissance provided the answer: 'underwater bridges'. Arnhold had first encountered them before Moscow – bridges whose roadway ran about six inches *beneath* the surface of the river. Every effort had been made to disguise the bridges – the wooden boards which served as the road were camouflaged. Such caution did not extend to the approaches, however; the build-up of traffic on either side of the river gave the locations away. Destroying these structures proved rather more challenging. Artillery found it difficult to hit the bridges. When they did, the damage was quickly repaired. The solution was mines, floated down the Vistula. The Navy was reluctant to give Arnhold the weapons, unconvinced that army pioneers could use them. Their reluctance seemed justified initially. The current carried the mines downstream initially, but then drove them towards the bank; they exploded long before they reached the Russian bridges.

Arnhold now focused on the islands in the middle of the Vistula as launchpads for his mine attacks. The islets were already occupied, not by the Red Army, but by geese. The officer likened them to the geese of the Roman Capitol which had alerted the garrison when the Gauls tried to storm it: neither side had succeeded in occupying the islands because of the deafening cackle of the geese, which immediately prompted a hail of artillery fire. One island, 400 yards long, was finally cleared of the birds, but that barely made the task of Arnhold's pioneers any easier. To reach it they had to wade for more than 100 yards through the Vistula with the water up to their chests. In the river, the salt plugs on the mines dissolved and the metal detonating arms were freed, sticking out like antennae. The weapons were now live – and would explode with the slightest of shocks. Two nights running, four men volunteered to take the mines out to the island. And two nights running, the mines drifted towards the bank and detonated prematurely. But on the third night, the mines struck the nearest bridge and destroyed it. "Utterly exhausted, but with a beaming smile, the men came back to our island," Paul Arnhold recalled. "They had probably been swimming against the current for fifteen to twenty minutes." Night after night these 'kamikaze swimmers', as they became known, struck out into the Vistula and released their mines. Some hit the bridges, some did not. Arnhold recommended four of his men for the Iron Cross, but LVI Panzer Corps' commander *General der Infanterie* Johannes Block dismissed the request. "Tossing a couple of mines into the water," he told the *Oberst*, was "not an heroic act." Arnhold suggested his general watch this 'tossing' in person. A brave man, Block did just that, wading into the Vistula then cowering under artillery fire on the island. He watched the swimmers set off with the mines. "If the men do not handle them as carefully as raw eggs, then they'll explode – and they'll go up with them," Arnhold pointed out. Twenty minutes later four explosions shook the Vistula valley as the closest underwater bridge was destroyed. That same evening, Johannes Block returned and pinned Iron Crosses on these kamikaze swimmers.

The days of these mine attacks were numbered, however. First the Russians subjected the island to such a pounding from their artillery there could be no thought of launching mines. Then they stretched wires across the Vistula upstream of the bridges, causing the mines to detonate prematurely. The build-up in the Puławy bridgehead continued unimpeded.[3]

Fifty miles upstream, so too did the massing of Soviet forces at Baranow. On clear days, Hans Jürgen Hartmann could look down the Vistula valley and see a road lined with trees stretching to the horizon. Day and night Russian guns, tanks and endless supply columns rolled along it. The direction was always the same: to the west. "No one disturbs them, no artillery, no aircraft," Hartmann fumed. "The sight of these masses, even for brief glimpses, is depressing enough." The junior officer contrasted Russian preparations with his own company's. His men raided the ruins of nearby homes for anything they could get to shore up their positions: boards, joists, nails, spades and axes, plus a little extra to decorate their foxholes. At night the men dug fresh trenches, but to what end Hans Jürgen Hartmann did not know. "It must be an intoxicating pleasure marking this tangle of scrawled lines on large charts in beautiful colour," he observed in his diary. "Red in front of the main defensive line, green for the second line, brown for the third, purple for the fourth, on top of that the hundreds of cleverly-placed communication trenches, the ditches to it, the dummy positions, the switch positions, this completely idiotic network where only rats and mice cower, which not one German soldier will ever occupy – because there aren't any."[4]

The reason there weren't any German soldiers was simple: 1944 had broken the back of the German Army on the Eastern Front. At the dawn of the year it held the Ukraine and the shores of the Crimea, it was camped outside Leningrad. A relentless series of offensives drove the Wehrmacht from the 'cradle of the revolution', from 'Russia's breadbasket'. The bloodletting reached its climax in Byelorussia, in Galicia, in eastern Poland, in Romania over three summer months. Between July and September, the German Army lost nearly 6,000 dead *every day* on the Eastern Front, more than half a million men in all. By the time the front on the Vistula stabilised, the Fourth Panzer Army was holding the front at Baranow with just three or four men every 300 feet. It was short of a dozen battalion commanders, 121 company and 140 platoon leaders. The typical infantry division had begun the war 17,000 men strong, supported by four dozen artillery pieces, more than 600 vehicles, 900 carts (and nearly 5,000 horses to pull them). By 1944, the average division was reduced to 12,000 men, thirty-nine guns, 1,300 carts yet only 3,200 horses.[5] Rear services, the Luftwaffe and the Kriegsmarine were combed out for men, as was the rest of the Reich – the railways, the postal service, the civil service, schools and universities, public utilities – under 'total war' measures introduced in the summer of 1944. The Nazi apparatus had no scruples about calling up the 1928 year group – boys aged sixteen, as *Reichsführer* SS Heinrich Himmler told senior officers: "A nation has to be willing and we must be willing, if necessary, to send fifteen-year-olds to the front to save the nation. I know that it caused many to shake their heads. These gentlemen didn't think logically. It is better for the young to die and the nation to be saved than the young to be spared and an entire nation of eighty or ninety million go under."[6] Boys, men, former sailors, airmen, it was still not enough. As 1944 drew to a close, the German Army was short of at least 600,000 men. In the East, the Red Army outnumbered it almost three to one.[7]

Inferiority in men was compounded by inferiority in material. That year the Wehrmacht lost just short of four million rifles and more than a quarter of a million machine-guns. The battles of 1944 had cost it some 6,000 Panzer IVs and Vs (Panthers) – by far the most numerous models – as well as more than 850 of the pre-eminent German tank, the Tiger. Despite the efforts of the Reich's armament industry, which had produced 18,000 panzers and *Sturmgeschütze* – self-propelled guns – in 1944, the armies in the East could muster a little over 1,600 panzers as 1945 opened, and a good third of these were out of action. Beyond the shortage of armour there was a shortage of fuel: the loss of the Romanian oil fields, the sustained Allied bombing campaign against synthetic oil plants and the Reich's rail network severely restricted the movement of the panzers. As 1944 faded, it was not the panzer, not the Panther, not the Tiger, which was the German Army's weapon of choice, but the *Panzerfaust*. This small, simple anti-tank weapon had become, one SS general believed, "the principal weapon of our entire conduct of the war".[8] This from an army which had given the world Blitzkrieg.

If the German Army had abandoned Blitzkrieg – by necessity rather than desire – the Red Army had embraced and adapted it. In the summer of 1944, Russian tanks had demonstrated that they too could slice through defences, lunge far into the enemy's rear and trap hundreds of thousands of soldiers. The methods of the summer of 1944 would be refined for the winter offensive: a lightning artillery barrage, a foray by reconnaissance parties to probe the German defences, then a bombardment of unparalleled intensity, followed by the painstaking clearance of mines by the pioneers and engineers. Only then could the armour be unleashed – more than 3,500 tanks and self-propelled artillery were poised to strike at Baranow alone. Once let off the leash, they were not to stop until they had crossed the Oder.

Like the Wehrmacht, the Red Army was never the mechanised, armoured behemoth the propaganda image might project. There were, to be sure, some 100 tank brigades as 1945 began. But there were nearly *500* infantry – or rifle – divisions, and 100 artillery divisions. Outside the armoured brigades, the horse was as common a method of transport as the truck. Infantry marched into battle, or rode on tanks. The Mosin, a sturdy if unspectacular rifle, was their trusted weapon, the DP their standard-issue light machine-gun with its trademark 'pan' magazines which were exhausted after just forty-seven rounds. The men lived on a diet of porridge for breakfast, cabbage soup or broth, a bit of bread, tinned meat or tinned fish for their main meal. They received 100 grammes of vodka every day and a double ration on holidays such as May 1 or November 7. But in such a vast, disparate nation, there never was an archetypal 'Ivan' or *frontovik* – front-line warrior. There were educated men, and there were men whose vocabulary stretched to barely 2,000 words. There were idealistic warriors – one in four Red Army soldiers was a member of the Communist Party – and there were men who clung to their religious beliefs, however much the Party tried to eliminate God. There were men from the industrial heartlands who generally fought better than peasants, but then peasants from northern Russia were more fearsome warriors than those from the south of the country. The Red Army, like the nation for which it fought, was a melting pot of peoples. Nazi propaganda talked repeatedly of the 'Mongol storm' or 'Asiatic hordes', but Slavs – Russians, Byelorussians, Ukrainians – were by far the most numerous of the Soviet Union's many nationalities represented in the ranks. There were, of course, Mongols. There were Siberians. There were Georgians. There were Kalmycks. There were Uzbeks and Tajiks (they didn't like the cold). Uzbeks did not get on with Ukrainians and Russians, while Ukrainians were frequently treated with suspicion.

As 1944 ended, they stood more than six million strong – despite the terrible toll four years of war had taken. The past twelve months alone had demanded more than six million casualties, a quarter of them dead. Two in every five tanks or self-propelled guns – nearly 24,000 in all – had been lost, plus more than 43,000 artillery pieces and mortars. Yet Soviet industry had made good all these losses, while the ranks of the Red Army stood 500,000 men stronger at the end of the year than it had at the beginning.[9]

Human losses had in fact proved more difficult to replace than equipment. Three out of four tank men never returned from the war – not entirely surprising as the T34, the outstanding Soviet tank of the war, "quickly went up in flames – very badly", one surgeon recalled.[10] Other arms fared no better: after three months' fighting one mortar company commander observed that all of his men had either been killed or wounded,[11] while one pioneer leader told his troops: "A pioneer platoon commander only lasts two months."[12] By 1945, instead of their requisite 9,000 to 11,000 men, many infantry divisions were barely half that strength. A rifle company commander recalled that the ranks of his division, 213th Rifle, were never more than sixty per cent filled, while he never led more than thirty-seven men in his company; the paper strength was seventy-six.

Not even the enlistment of some 800,000 women could plug the gaps in the Red Army's ranks. They served in every arm of the Soviet armed forces. They served at the front. As pilots. As tank crew. As infantry. As snipers. As anti-aircraft gunners. As machine gunners. As medics. They served behind the lines. As cooks. As laundrywomen. The men struggled to adjust to the sudden appearance of women in a male-dominated world. After rifle training, driver Tamara Davidovich picked violets, then wrapped them around her bayonet. Back at camp her instructor called her forward. "A soldier has to be a soldier, not a flower picker," he berated Davidovich, sentencing her to extra duties.[13] A group of female snipers pitched up at the front only to be told they were being kept in the rear. "No, we're snipers," they protested. "Send us where we belong." They were despatched to a regiment where a colonel explained to them they were soldiers first, women second. "Pay attention, girls, you've come here to fight, so fight and don't do anything else. Here there are boisterous men and no women. Damn it, how can I explain it to you? It's war, girls . . ."[14] Others, such as nurse Maria Boshok, did not find it hard to banish all feminine thoughts from her mind. "I told myself that that I didn't want to hear any words of affection in this hell," she recalled. "How can you think about pleasure there? About luck? I did not want to associate love with it." At school Boshok had enjoyed herself. In war she never smiled. "When I saw a young women doing her eyelashes or putting on lipstick, I was angry. I was firmly against it."[15]

If womanly thoughts could be suppressed, feelings of compassion and horror could not. Tamara Davidovich and her comrades were ordered to collect the dead from the battlefield – "all very young chaps, barely adults". But it was only when they saw the corpse of a girl that they fell silent. "We were silent all the way to the mass grave."[16] Maria Boshok went to war as a nineteen-year-old nurse. After six months, friends thought she had aged a decade. It was, she observed, understandable, having spent "every day in fear, in terror", surrounded by "people dying constantly. Dying every day, every hour. In fact, apparently, every minute. There were not enough sheets to cover them up." The dying always stared upwards, never to the side, never at the nurses, always upwards "as if they were looking to heaven."[17]

It wasn't only the foe who dealt these *frontoviki* death. More than 150,000 Red Army men were shot for desertion, for cowardice, for self-wounding. Behind the front, *zagraditelnye otriady* – blocking detachments – were set up with orders to shoot any man who panicked or retreated without orders. Lesser infractions might result in a spell of hard labour in the gulag, or worse still, the *shtraf* battalions. The ranks of these *shtraf* – penalty – units were filled with men who had shown cowardice in the face of the enemy, or indiscipline. Joining them were "criminals, bandits, thieves, demoted officers, soldiers who had failed to fulfil orders".[18] They were given the most dangerous missions in battle – attacking the unassailable, clearing minefields, storming over open ground – where they would "atone for their crimes with their blood".

Despite their notoriety, the penal units were relatively few and sparingly used. On a day-to-day basis, the arbitrary nature of their officers was of far greater concern to the ordinary Red Army soldier. Some could be "sincere, intelligent and just", infantryman Nikolai Litvin recalled. And some could be petty tyrants.[19] Such a man was mortar company commander Vladimir Gelfand's senior. "There's not a single soldier, not a single NCO or officer who's not been scolded in the most obscene language at least once by the captain," Gelfand wrote. The captain progressed from verbal to physical abuse: deprivation of sleep, beatings, a fist to the face. On several occasions he pulled out his pistol and shot it in the direction of the men who had incurred his wrath.[20] Ukrainians suffered the most – especially those from territory liberated during the push west in 1944. "They had no combat experience and had been exposed to a lot of Fascist influence during the occupation," one divisional commander observed. "We could not compare them with Leningraders who had withstood the blockade and had been steeled in numerous battles."[21] After one heavy barrage, a Soviet commander complained: "All the West Ukrainians throw themselves into the rearward trenches. We cannot win any war with them!"[22] The Soviets did little to endear themselves to the Ukrainians however. Before every battle, one officer told Ukrainian soldiers under his command he regarded them as Fascists who would have to atone for their crimes in blood. "At any time a man's name could be called out and an order read out saying he was condemned to death as a Fascist agitator and enemy of the Soviet Union. The commander shot the men dead on the spot," Ukrainian deserters told their German interrogators. "Every Ukrainian soldier wants to leave the Red Army as quickly as possible and desert to the Germans."[23]

One Ukrainian scrambled over no-man's land towards Infantry Regiment 514's lines, "a very young chap, a soldier for just a month, evidently rounded up in the newly-conquered lands". The deserter promised Hans Jürgen Hartmann that more would follow. He was right. A second, "just a kid, leapt over the trench, visibly relieved". At dawn the next day, two more figures in earth-brown uniforms scampered into the German trenches near Zawichost, "one of them even with a '*Geil Gitlarr'*!"[24]

Otherwise, life on the easternmost extremity of the Baranow bridgehead was relentlessly monotonous. Every day Hartmann saw to his duties: bunker construction, cleanliness of the latrine, construction of posts, the gathering of ammunition cartridges, drainage of water in the trenches, visibility, observation of the enemy, contact with neighbouring units, the cleaning and care of weapons, and a hundred other trifles. And every day his men received lectures or instruction on five different subjects: the gathering of cartridges, the wearing of earmuffs, gas and air-raid drills, a reminder not to wear felt boots when it was wet, a reminder to use boot polish and toilet paper sparingly, about observation of the enemy or keeping their unit's postal address secret, about behaviour in captivity – and on the toilet. And the war? The war, Hartmann observed, "seems to have been forgotten". There were occasional raids on German lines by the Russians, more to keep the minds of the *frontoviki* active and "alleviate a little of the boredom". But all day and all night, a couple of Red Army snipers observed the 514th's lines, "shooting accurately if someone holds his head too long and too carelessly above the trench, or carelessly walks through the trench standing upright."[25]

The men in Hans Jürgen Hartmann's company wore a *feldgrau* – field grey, although the colour was more a dirty green – tunic, perhaps covered by a padded dirty white winter jacket. On their head was the felt field cap or *Stahlhelm* – steel helmet. In their hands, the MP44 machine-pistol was replacing the Mauser 98K rifle as the standard-issue weapon. It was a first-rate weapon, effective up to 400 yards, but it devoured ammunition at an alarming rate. So too did the standard-issue German machine-gun, the MG42, known as the *Hitlersäge, Singende Säge* or *Knochensäge* – Hitler saw, singing saw or bone saw – thanks to the noise it made as it dispensed up to 1,500 rounds a minute. The field kitchen provided the men with a breakfast of bread and jam, or perhaps *Schmalz* (pork or goose fat), a lunch normally consisting of stew and an evening meal of bread, meat and possibly a little cheese, all washed down with *Ersatz* – substitute – coffee. The ordinary German soldier, the *Soldat* or, more commonly, the *Landser*, enjoyed a few days' rest behind the front at the *Soldatenheim* – soldiers' home. Some units, such as 6th Infantry Division, formed cabaret troupes, while members of the *Deutsches Frauenwerk* – German Women's Organisation – distributed charitable donations and food. What the *Landser* wanted most was the *Feldpost* – field post – letters from home, from family, from friends, from loved ones. But by late 1944 the *Feldpost* service was faltering. Lack of mail was a common complaint; the combing out of the postal service for soldiers and, above all, the wrecked rail system in the Reich meant it was not getting through.[26]

What *Feldpost* did leave or arrive in the trenches was scrutinized by the German Army's censors. And in the autumn of 1944, despite the crushing defeat he had suffered, despite the fact that his homeland was subjected to bombing by day and night, the *Landser* still believed in Adolf Hitler. Sifting letters and postcards from the front, the staff of Fourth Panzer Army – driven 150 miles westwards from the Bug to the Vistula during the summer battles – learned that their men abhorred the attempt to kill their Führer at his East Prussian headquarters on 20 July. From 291st Infantry Division: "Every soldier on the Eastern Front rejects the *putsch* outright." From the panzer army's own staff: "Our faith in the Führer is much stronger now, our belief in victory much more confident and certain." From 72nd Infantry Division: "Adolf Hitler will never capitulate, he will never give in, never lose his nerves, in short, he means more to us *Landsers* than you can understand." Many ordinary soldiers hoped that, "there'll be a purge of our nation so that we're finally rid of the parasites".[27]

They were not to be disappointed. In the wake of the 20 July plot, the German Army truly became Hitler's Army. The military salute was replaced by the *deutsche Gruss*, the straight-armed Nazi salute. Hitler's trusted lieutenant and head of the SS, Heinrich Himmler, was put in charge of training and providing replacement soldiers for the front line. 'Courts of honour' were established to expel from the Armed Forces officers connected or suspected of connection with the 20 July putsch. By the autumn of 1944, the 'Nazification' of the Wehrmacht was complete, as one senior SS officer gloated. "There's not one branch of the Wehrmacht, one inspection, General Staff officer course, or *Kriegsakademie* which manages to avoid having a number of SS leaders on its speaker programme."[28]

In reality, the German Army was Adolf Hitler's Army long before the July putsch. For years the German soldier had been subjected to National Socialist indoctrination through newspapers, leaflets, speeches, talks. "Faith in the Führer and his ideology is the bedrock for the life of all German people," he was told. Or: "A fanatical will to fight and the persistence of belief in victory is rooted in National Socialist ideology." The soldier of Adolf Hitler placed "blind faith in the Führer" and drew his strength "from his total faith in victory and belief in our Führer, Adolf Hitler."[29] On leave he was ordered to ignore the damage inflicted by Allied bombers and put rumourmongers and pessimists in their place. If anyone at home asked: "How much longer will the war last?" he was to respond immediately: "Until we have won."[30] Nazi indoctrination reached its apotheosis with the *Nationalsozialistische Führungsoffizier* – National Socialist Leadership Officer – the German equivalent of the Red Army *politruk*, who was charged with imbuing the German soldier with Nazi ardour, of creating a single fighting community of officers and men. "Wars of this proportion are decided neither by numerical nor material superiority," their instructions stated. "The only decisive factors are the high values possessed by a nation: bravery, iron discipline, honour and the nation's consciousness of being the standard bearers and the protagonists of a lofty idea."[31] The methods of the National Socialist Leadership Officers mirrored those of the *politruks*: an apt passage from *Mein Kampf* was posted on daily orders as a 'thought for the day', there were lectures, films, community evenings for the men with folk music, a few of the Führer's inspirational words, a rousing speech and fighting songs to finish things off. The walls of houses near the front were daubed with slogans: "Victory or Siberia!" or "We fight for the lives of our women and children!" Youngsters handed out leaflets urging the German soldier not to leave his post but to halt the Soviet onslaught. The men were encouraged to stop singing songs from the Reeperbahn or the *Der blaue Engel* in favour of those of the Nazi movement, such as the *Horst Wessel Lied*. The word *Katastrophe* – catastrophe – was stricken from the soldiers' vocabulary and replaced with *Notstand* – crisis.[32] Subtle methods did not always work, however. One *Leutnant* tried to encourage his men to fight to the bitter end by using the fable of the two frogs which fell into a jug of milk. "The first gives up the struggle and drowns, while the other thrashes about as long as he can and puts up a fight until the milk has turned to cheese and he has saved his life," the officer explained. His men simply fell about laughing.[33] Other efforts to rally the men were more blunt, more successful. The National Socialist Leadership Officers would foster hopes of new weapons, of revenge for the bombing of the Reich's cities and, above all, they would stoke the flames of hatred for the foe from the East. 'Asiatic subhumans', 'red mob', 'hordes from the steppe', 'red beasts' – no pejorative was overlooked when it came to demonizing the Red Army. "Asia has never triumphed over Europe," one officer assured his men. "This time too we will stem the Asiatic floodtide."[34] Pamphlets like *Wofür kämpfen wir?* – What are we fighting for? – were handed out, featuring articles with titles such as 'What fate do the Bolsheviks have in store for your parents, your sisters, your wives, your children?'[35] Bolshevism, the booklet explained, presented "a dangerous threat to all of Western Civilisation. Many a European, *ja* many an Anglo-Saxon would be shaken to his core if he could see the true face of Bolshevism." It was down to the German soldier to defend "all of cultured civilization from Asiatic subjugation! What matters now is which ideology wins: the Jewish-Bolshevist demon of materialism or the creative ideology of German idealism, National Socialism."[36] Such propaganda fell on fertile ground. "Such a people may not and cannot triumph over the culture of the West," one *Unteroffizier* wrote home. "There's probably no point wasting any words on the subject as it will never happen."[37]

It was more than belief in National Socialism, in Adolf Hitler, in the struggle to protect Germany from the 'hordes from the steppe' which kept the German soldier fighting in the winter of 1944. Fear played a significant role too. Like the Red Army, the Wehrmacht had long since used the *Strafkompanie* – punishment company – to discipline men for lesser infractions, forcing them to clear mines or bury the dead in no-man's land. For singing this ditty,

Es geht alles vorüber
Es geht alles vorbei
Erst geht der Führer
Und dann die Partei!

It will all be over
It will all be done with
First the Führer
Then the Party!

one *Gefreiter* was sentenced to two years in prison. Passing sentence, the judge observed: "There can be no doubt about the corrosive effect of the lyrics of this song."[38] More serious offenders were sent to the *Bewährungsbataillon* – probationary battalion – to prove themselves by "exceptional bravery" on particularly dangerous missions. As the Reich's plight grew worse, such legal 'niceties' were invariably dispensed with. An officer had the power – "it was not only his right but his duty" – to shoot men on the spot for disobedience; there was no point delaying matters by beginning court-martial proceedings.[39] Officers who slandered or insulted their Führer, who "undermined the German people's power to resist" with reckless or insulting remarks, faced execution.[40] Cowardice had to be punished with "the most ruthless severity";[41] defeatists, shirkers and deserters faced execution. Behind the front lines the feared *Kettenhunde* – chain dogs, so called because of the distinctive dog tags around their necks – the military police, were "more dangerous than any Red Army soldier".[42] Any soldier found away from his unit without the authorised papers faced immediate execution. They were hung from trees or from lamp posts, with signs hung around their necks: "That's how we deal with cowards"; "I'm hanging here because I was too cowardly to defend my Fatherland"; "I made a pact with the Bolsheviks".[43] Perhaps as many as 20,000 German soldiers were executed, most in the final year of the war. Their families were sent a blunt notification:

> While the entire German nation is involved in the most bitter defensive struggle, your son neglected his duty as a German and as a soldier in the basest way and defied laws which preserve the fighting strength and life of the German nation. In view of the severity of his crime and the demands of the fifth year of war, only the most severe punishment could be imposed.
>
> I can assure you that your son died like a man. His final words were for his parents.
>
> I must point out that obituary notices and obituaries are not permitted in newspapers, journals and the like.[44]

By late 1944, there was a final method of Nazi tyranny to keep the German soldier in his place: the *Sippenhaft*. Not only were the deserters themselves sentenced to death, but their families faced arrest and would be deprived of any pension or pay. "Every deserter will find his just punishment," Heinrich Himmler warned. "His ignominious behaviour will entail the most severe consequences for his family."[45] It was soon extended to cases of men taken prisoner "without being wounded or fighting to the bitter end".[46] The threat of death and the *Sippenhaft* or not, 6,000 *Landsers* were deserting from the front every month.

Outnumbered, outgunned, facing draconian punishment, with the danger of his family being arrested, with little news from home, the German soldier doggedly held the line in the East. There were still many *Landsers* who believed the words of their leaders, who believed in the 'wonder weapons', who believed in Germany's star. "As long as we have our Führer, there is no reason to doubt victory," one *Leutnant* assured his wife in Breslau. "There will soon be a turning point in the fortunes of war, soon we will strike once more." An 'old *Ostkämpfer*' (eastern warrior) from Striegau, thirty miles west of Breslau, told his wife not to worry. "Even if the roar of battle has come a little closer to our border, there's no reason to drop your head," he wrote home. "Fight even more fanatically, be even more ready for action, work and above all be confident." The wife of a soldier from Görlitz in south-west Silesia admired her husband's confidence. "I really couldn't think any other way," he wrote back. "Every day I see new units, replacements for us, and all manner of weapons arriving. We have brought the Russians to a halt here. Their attacks are beaten off under very heavy losses on his side, his armour losses are considerable." Victory, he predicted, "will be ours. The very good fighting spirit of the men and now the homeland which is prepared to make every effort are our guarantors of victory."[47] Others, like gunner Werner Adamczyk holding the perimeter of the Baranow bridgehead, believed it would be "just a matter of time" before the Wehrmacht was rolling west again. "We simply were outnumbered in everything – in men, artillery and tanks," he recalled. "I never saw a smile on any face any more. Joking around had stopped. We just lived in mental misery until our survival responses were triggered by Ivan's next major attack."[48] Dominating all thoughts, wrote one *Gefreiter* defending the front on the Vistula, was "that great longing for peace". But what sort of peace, he wondered. "When it finally comes, how much misfortune, murder, misery and destruction will it have inflict on our homeland, *ja*, over all mankind."[49] An *Unteroffizier* in the Fourth Panzer Army readily admitted that his comrades talked openly of peace. "No one believes in victory any longer," he wrote. "Everyone hopes that it will soon come to an end. It doesn't matter on what terms, just get the war over with. This is not some wish, the hopes of one person, that's how we all talk, think, wish."[50] *Oberleutnant* Walter Blöhs, an adjutant in Panzer Grenadier Regiment 90 weighed up his men's combat experience against Russian numbers. "What use is it against an enemy who's four, five times as strong?" he asked himself. "Courage and experience are no use." The Russians enjoyed such superiority, possessed so many men, so much material, "while we have to save every litre of fuel, every shell", Blöhs fumed. "We only have the skin on our backs to defend ourselves." Conversation in the bunkers and dugouts revolved around a single question: what happens now? "The many defeats we suffered last year, the heavy losses in men and material, the vast area which we have given up – all this has a negative impact on the morale of the men when it comes to approaching the battle with a great deal of confidence," Walter Blöhs observed. Yet he also noticed something else. Privately, they may have felt it, but among comrades not a single man said: "If only this was finally over!"[51] Hans Jürgen Hartmann continued to lead his men into the trenches to dig and to practise attacks. It would have been better, he mused, to teach his men how to retreat, or how to receive a wound which would take them home to the Reich for treatment. "This year we've not been successful anywhere – on no front, on no sea, and certainly not in the skies of the homeland," he lamented. "Yet despite it all, we still believe in final victory, we want to cling to this hope with every sinew."[52] And so the *Oberleutnant* fought on. His comrades fought on. They fought not for a great idea, not for Western Civilisation, but for each other, and above all for their families. "If we imagine what will happen if we're defeated," a doctor in a panzer division recorded in his diary. "Our wives surrendered to the despotism of these Asians, our children abducted, and we ourselves will be in forced labour somewhere! Better to be dead than a slave!"[53] The men, one Silesian officer recalled a quarter of a century later, "thought only about our women and children and what would happen to all of them if the enemy continued advancing. That was what still held us together." Did the men want to die for Adolf Hitler? an interviewer asked. "*Nein*," the officer said forcefully. "Who was Hitler anyway?"[54]

Adolf Hitler expected the men at Baranow and Puławy to die, of course. He expected them to die – but not just yet. All through October, November and December 1944 the evidence of the Soviet build-up on the Vistula was placed before him. He ignored it and frittered away what reserves in men and, above all, material the Reich still possessed in the Ardennes. He ignored it again on Christmas Eve when it was clear that the offensive in the West had failed. "Who's responsible for producing all this rubbish?" he flashed at Heinz Guderian, as the Chief of the General Staff presented the latest ominous intelligence assessment of Red Army forces massing in Poland. "It's the greatest bluff since Ghengis Khan."[55] The real bluff came from Hitler and his acolytes with their talk of wonder weapons, of new tanks, of jet aircraft turning the tide of war. The Führer was dreaming of the summer. Fifty new divisions, manned by soldiers born in 1928 – sixteen- and seventeen-year-olds – would "decide the war". German industry would work at full tilt to equip these new formations. "The war will reach its climax in the summer of 1945," he predicted, "and the summer will also bring its decision."[56] His generals in the East spread the word. "Never had so many tanks and aircraft been built, in none of the years of war had so much ammunition been produced, so many new guns sent to the front, as in this fifth year of war," Fourth Panzer Army's commander General Fritz-Hubert Gräser assured Hans Jürgen Hartmann and his comrades on a visit to the front. The Russians "could pump what they liked into the Baranow bridgehead". They would find anti-tank guns, panzers and reserve divisions waiting for them "like never before". The men of Infantry Regiment 514 were filled with fresh hope. "It was truly intoxicating listening to him," Hartmann wrote. "The production figures alone were so incredible that now the turning point had actually been reached."[57]

The figures *were* incredible. Or rather they were fantasy. For each mile of Gräser's 116-mile front there were in reality just 176 men, five artillery barrels, just two combat-worthy panzers, a couple of working *Sturmgeschütze*, and three anti-tank guns. The predicament of Gräser's superior, *Generaloberst* Josef Harpe, was equally dire. The previous July, Army Group A's front had stretched for 378 miles, held by 123,000 front-line infantrymen. By the beginning of 1945, the front was fifty miles longer but defended by 30,000 fewer *Landsers*.[58] Harpe's talented chief-of-staff, *Generalleutnant* Wolfdietrich von Xylander, had devised an imaginative solution. Xylander proposed evacuating German lines a couple of days before the Russian attack, falling back to a line of fortifications several miles to the west. It would spare the troops the brunt of the Soviet barrage and shorten their lines by a good sixty miles. Maybe there, perhaps on a second prepared line which followed the River Nida, twenty miles west of the Baranow bridgehead, but certainly along the border of Silesia, Xylander reasoned, the Russian offensive would be brought to a standstill. Above all this grand plan, named *Schlittenfahrt* – sleigh ride – would "keep the enemy away from German soil".[59] During a four-day tour of the Eastern Front, Harpe convinced Heinz Guderian of the wisdom of 'sleigh ride'. He promised to put it to Hitler at their next encounter.

At his headquarters in the Sandomierz bridgehead, a telephone call was put through to Ivan Konev. Eclipsed by Georgi Zhukov as the Soviet Union's most famous general, the shaven-headed marshal was at least his equal on the battlefield and surpassed him for ruthlessness. Like Zhukov, the forty-seven-year-old general had served in the Tsar's army. Unlike Zhukov, however, he had served as a political commissar in the Red Army in the 1920s. But Ivan Konev was no Party crony who had earned his position through political connections. He had trained at the famous Frunze Military Academy, served in the Far East during the skirmishes with the Japanese in the late 1930s, and been recalled to the western USSR in the spring of 1941 when war threatened the Motherland. The men knew him as 'the general who never retreated' – an inaccurate sobriquet, for Konev had not merely been defeated, he had very nearly been executed after his armies were crushed at Vyazma in October 1941 in one of the greatest battles of encirclement in history. He survived, and led new armies with aplomb that winter as the German advance was first halted then turned back before Moscow. It was in the Ukraine, commanding the front – the Russian equivalent to an army group – which bore the region's name, that he made his mark, in bitter, bloody fighting. Victory at Korsun earned Konev the marshal's baton, but he was rarely interested in the trappings of rank, covering his uniform with a cloak when he visited the front line so the men did not feel shy or embarrassed in his presence. Wherever he went, so did his library: Livy, Pushkin, Tolstoy. It was the only luxury Ivan Konev afforded himself. His quarters were usually a small cottage or hut. He rarely drank – and castigated members of his staff who did, one sign of his fearsome temper. Above all, Konev was exacting, of his staff, of his men, of himself. He never underestimated his enemy, demanding his men study their foe, know their positions, their methods, their minds. He was a master of deceit, using all manner of tricks to fool the enemy about his intentions. And when the attack came, Ivan Konev accompanied it with a tremendous artillery barrage to crush the enemy's means of communications, to wipe out his staffs, to stun his troops.

For the past three or four months, the marshal had been orchestrating plans for the latest lunge westwards by his 1st Ukrainian Front, striking out of the Sandomierz bridgehead, through Kielce, Radomsko, past the famous religious shrine of Częstochowa, finally coming to a halt on the Oder somewhere near Breslau. A second, lesser thrust would liberate Krakow then continue towards the industrial heartland of Upper Silesia. Joseph Stalin used a single word to impress its importance on his marshal: gold. Konev heeded the message. His build-up for the thrust from the Vistula to the Oder was on a staggering scale. He massed more than 3,500 tanks and self-propelled guns at Sandomierz (plus 400 dummy ones for good measure). There were 17,000 artillery pieces and mortars, more than 900 miles of trenches were dug and 1,100 command and observation posts erected. Some 10,000 bunkers and dugouts were built for the men and 11,000 emplacements were built for guns and mortars. Engineers threw thirty bridges across the Vistula, and more than 1,200 miles of roads were built or improved. With eleven days to go until the beginning of the offensive – 20 January – Ivan Konev was well satisfied with his work. "The main part of the preparation was finished," he wrote. "As is always the case before major events, a good deal was still to be done."

Now he received a telephone call. On the other end of the line was the acting Chief of the General Staff, Alexei Antonov. Stalin wanted the offensive brought forward. It would begin not in eleven days' time, but just three, on Friday, 12 January. The 1st Ukrainian Front, the marshal assured Antonov, would be ready in time.[60]

As Ivan Konev was telling Moscow he could bring his attack forward, Heinz Guderian was closeted once more with Adolf Hitler at his headquarters near Frankfurt. The files of Guderian's intelligence staff, *Fremde Heere Ost* – Foreign Armies East – were bulging with evidence of an impending Soviet offensive. That very Tuesday, 9 January, a Russian deserter had described how the attack would begin "in three days" and reach German soil "in a single bound".[61] Aerial reconnaissance revealed thousands of Soviet aircraft lined up on the airfields of Poland, poised to strike at the Vistula and East Prussia. "The Soviets no longer have so many planes," Luftwaffe chief Hermann Göring interjected. "They're simply decoys."[62] Adolf Hitler concurred. He flew into a rage at the latest predictions of impending doom compiled by Foreign Armies East. Its head ought to be committed to a lunatic asylum, he yelled at Guderian, before finally regaining his composure. He had chided the general long enough. Now he praised him: "The Eastern Front has never possessed such a strong reserve as now. That is your doing. I thank you for it." Guderian snapped back: "The Eastern Front is like a house of cards." If it was penetrated at any point, it would collapse. It needed tanks. It needed guns. It needed men. The Führer brushed the general's protestations aside. "The Eastern Front must help itself and make do with what it's got."[63]

Josef Harpe's open-topped staff car raced along the road from Kielce to Krakow. The *Generaloberst* pulled up his fur collar to protect his face from the icy wind blowing across the plains of southern Poland. Filled with unease, the general had paid another visit to Fourth Panzer Army's lines around the Baranow bridgehead. It was the small hours of 10 January by the time Harpe's car finally pulled up in front of the school where the general and his staff were accommodated. As Harpe entered the building, *Generalleutnant* von Xylander approached him. The tall, thin chief of staff looked at his general with a serious expression. "The Führer refused everything," he told Harpe.

"The front stays where it is. And the situation stays as it is. The Führer does not believe there will be a Russian attack."[64]

In a large hospital tent in a forest outside Staszów towards the southern edge of the bridgehead, there was lively talk among the officers of Third Guards Tank Army: regimental, brigade, divisional, and corps commanders. The sides of the tent were covered with maps and sketches, marked with red and blue lines and arrows. In the centre, there was a huge sandpit with the terrain of the Vistula landscape carefully duplicated. An officer shouted: "Attention!", and Marshal Ivan Konev, accompanied by several generals, entered the tent. Third Guards Tank Army's chief of staff Bachmetjev took the floor, outlining the plan of attack, moving his pointing stick over the sandpit. Konev studied the sandpit closely, then turned to the officers standing around the tent. "Our 1st Ukrainian Front possesses a mighty punch and firepower," the shaven-headed marshal told the assembled commanders. "We're almost on the border of Fascist Germany. Just one more leap is needed for final victory. We have the great honour of being among the first to cross the frontier." The watchword of the coming offensive was speed, Blitzkrieg Soviet-style. "Don't get drawn into small fire-fights," he impressed upon the men of Third Guards Tank Army, "the steel arrow" of his front. "Detour around resistance. Don't hang around in towns. Thrust into the heartland. Don't worry about your flanks. Penetrate deep into the heart of Germany." But Ivan Konev added a word of caution. "Nothing does more harm than underestimating the enemy's strength," he warned. "A bitter struggle awaits us." He pointed to the lines of German fortifications which surrounded the bridgehead. "The German soldier is still strong and doesn't retreat without orders, and the units committed against us are commanded by experienced generals." And on native soil, the German soldier would fight with even greater fanaticism. But then Ivan Konev smiled. "What Soviet soldier doesn't dream of storming the lair of the Fascist beast?"[65]

That had become the Red Army's battle cry by 1945. No longer "Liberate the Soviet Motherland from the Fascist German occupiers." Now it was "Deal with the Fascist beast in his lair!", "Raise the banner of victory over the Fascist lair!" or "Forward, we are liberating our brothers and sisters from Fascist slavery!" The letters of the *frontoviki* are filled with contempt and hatred for their foe – *Nemtsy* (Germans), *fashisty* (Fascists), *gitlerovtsy* (Hitlerites) and, especially, Fritzes. German soldiers were, one Russian major observed, "the only fighters in Europe who deserved our respect,"[66] but that didn't stop the men branding their enemy 'beasts' or 'barbarians' – the same invectives used by the German propaganda machine to describe Soviet soldiers. They felt imbued with a holy mission to wreak vengeance "for the misery they inflicted on Leningrad and Byelorussia". No distinction was made between 'Nazi' and 'German', between SS and Wehrmacht. "The entire German Armed Forces – from commanders to soldiers – took part in plunder," senior Party leader Mikhail Kalinin declared. "Every German, from Hitler to the common man, was an accomplice in the tortures and murders."[67] In every division, even battalion, every company, *politruks* – political agitators – sought to "educate personnel along the lines of love of the Motherland, loyalty to their oath and burning hatred of the enemy", especially when an offensive was imminent.[68] During the autumn of 1944, more than forty visits by officers and political leaders in one of Konev's tank armies were arranged to the death camp at Majdanek near Lublin, liberated that summer. They returned to their troops and encouraged "the soldiers to hate the enemy using material from the Lublin camp", while newspaper articles urged: *Pomni Majdanek, voin Krasnoj Armii!* – Remember Majdanek, Red Army warriors![69] By far the most virulent – and popular– anti-German propaganda came from the pen of journalist Ilya Ehrenburg. His exhortation "If you kill one German, kill another – there is nothing more amusing for us than a heap of German corpses" had been widely disseminated among the troops in 1942. Two more years of war did nothing to mollify the propagandist. "It is not only divisions and armies marching on Berlin," Ehrenburg wrote after Majdanek had been liberated. "The grief of all the innocents from mass graves, ditches and gorges are marching on Berlin. The cabbage patches of Majdanek and the trees of Vitebsk where the Germans hanged their unfortunate victims, the boots and shoes of those men and women and children shot and gassed at Majdanek: they are all marching on Berlin." To Ehrenburg, it was imperative there should never be another Majdanek: "We do not want our children to have to fight again. Finish it properly! Finish it in such a way that they will not start again! Make them forget how to fight. Pull out the sting, break off their claws," he urged. "It is time to finish off the Germans." [70]

There were selfish motives for fighting, not least a plethora of medals: for the defence of Leningrad, Moscow, the Caucasus, Stalingrad, and the highest distinction of all, Hero of the Soviet Union; more than 11,000 were awarded. Of far greater use to the ordinary Ivan, however, was money. The destruction of a panzer earned an anti-tank gun crew 2,000 roubles – three times the monthly wage of a private, two weeks' pay for a sergeant. But the simplest – and strongest – incentive was to end the war as quickly as possible and return home. "The quicker we get to Berlin, the quicker we get home, the quicker we see our beloved families and friends again," a company commander wrote to his wife in Minsk. "What I would not give to experience that day!"[71] By 1945, the *frontovik* was "tired of fighting and looked anxiously towards the war's end," one officer recalled,[72] while a former metal worker, now a senior sergeant in a signals company, wrote home to Kiev:

> Your love has protected me from enemy bullets and shells up to now. We will only feel joy and happiness when we are united once more. For four years, we have overcome one difficulty after the next in the hope that we would be happy once more, that Fate would unite us once more, that we are never separated again until the end of our lives. But all these are hopes, all this still lies before us.[73]

There were still a few Soviet soldiers willing to desert, to risk crawling over the minefields to stumble into German lines. A Ukrainian deserter ignored the political commissar who threatened him and his fifty-nine compatriots and crossed Infantry Regiment 514's front near Łukawa. He reached the second line of trenches – given grandiose names such as *Panther*, *Tiger I*, *Tiger II*, *Neger* (Negro) *I* – before he ran into a German soldier, so weakly occupied were they.

It was the last flurry of excitement for the men of the 514th. Otherwise life went on as normal. At first and last light the men gathered corn for the company's horses. Before, afterwards and in between, the *Landsers* were on guard, on watch, perhaps for fifteen or sixteen hours a day. "We're simply waiting for the great offensive which must come any day," Hans Jürgen Hartmann observed. The Russians were "pumping their bridgehead full to bursting, always more, always fuller, week after week" until one day, Hartmann predicted, it would "burst with a roar."[74]

Notes

1. Hartmann, *Zwischen Nichts und Niemandsland*, pp.591-4.
2. *Wrocławska epopeja*, pp.143, 145, and Gleiss, i, p.123C.
3. Arnhold, pp.7-14.
4. Hartmann, *Zwischen Nichts und Niemandsland*, pp.581-2.
5. Kunz, p.200.
6. Ibid., p.167.
7. Kunz, pp.151-4 and Magenheimer, pp.45-9.
8. Kunz, p.232.
9. Glantz and House, *When Titans Clashed*, pp.292 and 306.
10. Alexijewitsch, p.322.
11. Gelfand, p.77.
12. Alexijewitsch, p.228.
13. Ibid., p.77.
14. Ibid., p.208.
15. Ibid., pp.257-8.
16. Ibid., p.77.
17. Ibid., p.257.
18. Art of War Symposium, p.70.
19. Litvin, p.13.
20. Gelfand, pp.57-8.
21. Zeidler, p.132.
22. Magenheimer, pp.92-3.
23. BA-MA RH2/2468.
24. Hartmann, *Zwischen Nichts und Niemandsland*, p.552.
25. Ibid., pp.547, 554, 567, 569, 581.
26. Adamcyzk, p.348.
27. BA-MA RH13/48.
28. Kunz, p.116.
29. Messerschmidt, pp.324, 344, 374, 377.
30. NA WO204/985.
31. NA WO204/987.
32. Messerschmidt, pp.430-1, 466.
33. Kunz, pp.243, 246, 247-8.
34. Messerschmidt, p.466.
35. Zoepf, p.117.
36. Cited in *Das Russlandbild in Dritten Reich*, p.161.

37. Müller, Sven Oliver, *Deutsche Soldaten und ihre Feinde*, p.189.
38. Messerschmidt, *Was damals Recht war*, p.63.
39. Seidler, *Die Militärgerichtsbarkeit der Deutschen Wehrmacht*, p.188.
40. Messerschmidt, p.375.
41. Seidler, *Die Militärgerichtsbarkeit der Deutschen Wehrmacht*, p.173.
42. Frodien, p.120.
43. Wette, *Der Krieg des Kleinen Mannes*, pp.282-3.
44. Seidler, *Die Militärgerichtsbarkeit der Deutschen Wehrmacht*, p.227.
45. Shulman, p.278.
46. Messerschmidt, p.368.
47. See BA-MA RH13/48 and RH13/49.
48. Adamczyk, pp.346-8.
49. Schleicher, Karl-Theodor and Walle, Heinrich (eds), *Aus Feldpostbriefen junger Christen 1939-1945*, p.326.
50. BA-MA RH13/49.
51. Asmus, ix, pp.39-40.
52. Hartmann, *Zwischen Nichts und Niemandsland*, pp.581-2.
53. Fritze, Eugen, *Unter dem Zeichen des Aeskulap*, p.269.
54. Gunter, *Letzter Lorbeer*, pp.19-20.
55. Guderian, pp.382-3.
56. TB Goebbels, 4/1/45.
57. Hartmann, *Zwischen Nichts und Niemandsland*, p.588.
58. BA-MA RH19 VI/33.
59. Thorwald, pp.30-1 and Ahlfen, p.39.
60. Konev, pp.5-14; Werth, p.706.
61. Hastings, *Armageddon*, p.277.
62. Freytag von Loringhoven, p.126. In fact, some 10,500 Soviet aircraft were lined up to support the winter offensive. *Luftflotte* 6 – Air Fleet 6 – which provided aerial support for the central sector of the Eastern Front had barely 300 fighters to confront them. Things had actually improved for the *Luftflotte*. Six months before it had been outnumbered forty to one. In January 1945, the enemy 'only' possessed a thirty-five-fold superiority. See DDRZW, 10/1, p.497.
63. Guderian, pp.386-8.
64. Thorwald, p.31.
65. Based on Jakubowski, pp.590-1, Polewoi, p.100 and Dragunski, pp.209-12.
66. Hastings, *Armageddon*, p.133.
67. DDRZW, 10/1, p.705.
68. Ibid., p.702.
69. DDRZW, 10/1, p.702 and Zeidler, p.121.
70. Zeidler, pp.120, 121.
71. Scherstjanoi, p.32.
72. Art of War Symposium, p.72.
73. Scherstjanoi, pp.29-30.
74. Hartmann, *Zwischen Nichts und Niemandsland*, pp.581, 598, 600.

CHAPTER 3

God Has Washed His Hands of This World

An entire city with more than one million
inhabitants was beginning to die.
Gefreiter Ulrich Frodien

It was pitch black in the camp which served as the headquarters of 55th Guards Tank Brigade. After the feverish preparations of the preceding day, it was quiet now. Still the brigade's commander, Colonel David Dragunsky, could not sleep. He spent the night fretting about the impending battle, about the fate of the men in his charge, before he finally fell asleep.

His adjutant shook him awake. "The time has come." Bugle calls brought the brigade's field headquarters to life. Infantry, tank crews and artillerymen scrambled out of their dugouts, buttoning up their uniforms as they rushed to their vehicles and guns. Tarpaulin and camouflage nets fell to the ground, engines clattered and exhaust fumes mixed with the clear winter air.[1]

Gefreiter Ernst Dippel was half way through his night-time guard duty in woods near Szczucin on the southern extremity of the Baranow bridgehead. Dippel and his fellow tank destroyers in *Jagdpanzer* Company 1168 had spent the previous month building pens for their vehicles. Despite their toil, the protective pens, built from felled trees, were still not finished. Worse, the company was recovering from a dose of food poisoning after celebrating the end of the old year with a special meal: potato salad washed down with half a bottle of red wine each, and a 'dessert' of a bar of chocolate. The 'seasoning' for the salad had actually been rat poison.

The first hour of Dippel's duty had passed without incident. But as the second began, a little after 5am on Friday, 12 January, the sky in the east turned red, followed a few seconds later by a terrible thunder.[2]

Pravda correspondent Boris Polevoy peered through the slit windows of fine stables perched on high ground overlooking the Sandomierz bridgehead. Once the property of a Polish aristocrat, paintings of racehorses hung on the walls. Until recently, it had still been used – the odour of horse manure lingered. Polevoy ignored the smell and enjoyed the view of the Polish landscape which the stables offered. At 5am precisely flares bathed the terrain in a reddish light and artillery salvoes began to crash.[3]

Hans Jürgen Hartmann was writing reports in his bunker following a night patrol near Łukawa, half a dozen miles north of Sandomierz. It was still dark when he heard "a mighty thrashing" in the distance. He rushed up the bunker steps and watched transfixed as clouds to the west and south-west were "lit by countless incessant flashing lights beyond the horizon". Hartmann dispatched runners to alert his platoons. "For weeks we'd awaited this moment," he wrote. "Now it had been bubbling and simmering over there for half an hour already without the slightest pause." Half an hour became an hour. Then two. The first streaks of dawn tried to break through the winter sky. Yet the Russians in the trenches opposite were still strangely subdued.

The barrage was short but stunning. As the Soviet guns fell silent, the first reconnaissance patrols moved forward and occupied the foremost German trenches after a brief fight. With the first light of dawn – a monotonously grey January morning – Boris Polevoy followed them. He had seen nothing like it. Not at Stalingrad, nor at Korsun in the Ukraine twelve months before. "A huge plough seemed to have smashed through everything," he wrote. Paths through minefields were marked by signs. *Frontoviki* followed them, bunched together.[4] The defenders were so shaken by the bombardment and the foray by reconnaissance parties that they were convinced this was the main assault. It was merely the prelude. In the sectors earmarked for a breakthrough at Baranow there were 350 guns for every mile of front – "real punch" as the *frontoviki* called it. At 10am they opened fire. There was, Soviet captain Naim Chafisov observed, "an almighty howling, the distinct howl of artillery, thousands of guns went off ceaselessly – artillery, mortars."[5] Fourth Tank Army commander General Dmitry Lelyushenko watched "plumes of smoke, fire and dust compounded with snow" rise up. "The ground quivered and the very earth of the battlefield was blackened."[6] The timbers of Ernst Dippel's bunker came loose. The windows shattered. In the middle of the hurricane, the order was given: "Men to the *Jagdpanzer*!" Dippel and his comrades ran across a mile of open ground under direct shellfire. Most were veterans of the Eastern Front. They knew when to throw themselves to the ground and when to run. Finally they reached the copse where their *Hetzer* – rabble rouser – tank destroyer, a 75mm anti-tank gun mounted on a panzer chassis, was waiting. As he closed the hatch, Dippel realized he had left his crew's headphones and microphones behind. There was no question about not returning for them. He rushed back, grabbed them, then ran once more to his tank destroyer. He reached it safely. "I must have had a guardian angel," he concluded.[7]

David Dragunsky gathered his brigade in a forest. There were veterans of Bialystok, Leningrad, Odessa and Moscow in the ranks. A Hero of the Soviet Union held aloft the red banner of the Guards – a title bestowed upon units which had distinguished themselves in battle. The brigade's commissar, Dragunsky and his chief of staff knelt down. A couple of men swore an oath to their Motherland and to the flag, while a few men fixed the colours to Dragunsky's tank. There was a thunderous "Hurrah!" from the tank crews, then their colonel gave the order, "Mount up!"[8]

At Łukawa, the barrage persisted. Three hours. Four. Five. Six. Seven. Still no attack. But disquieting reports began to reach Infantry Regiment 514: deep penetrations by Soviet forces. "It happened just as we had secretly feared," Hans Jürgen Hartmann conceded. "One step and already the fragile wooden fence of the German front was in tatters . . ."

It was 2pm when Ernst Dippel's company finally received orders to counter-attack. At first it was as if they were on manoeuvres, with mounted infantry sitting on the *Hetzer*'s hull, rolling over heavily frozen ground covered with a light sprinkling of snow. The tank destroyers came to a halt on a line of hills, watching Russian infantry swarming down the wooded hillside opposite. They directed their machine-guns and high-explosive shells at the Soviet troops. The enemy attack stopped.

Dippel's company stood firm. Its neighbours did not. To the left and right, 304th Infantry Division's front caved in, its artillery positions overrun by Russian tanks. In danger of being encircled, the *Hetzers* fell back with the onset of darkness.[9]

Karl Hanke was writing at his desk in the Palais Hatzfeldt, the seat of government in Breslau for more than half a century. The palace was the city's largest – and finest – but the *Gauleiter*'s office was rather small and dominated by the imposing, light wooden writing desk. The plush brown carpet muffled his secretary's footsteps as she paced the room. "We expect the Wehrmacht communiqué shortly," the radio announcer declared. Tense minutes passed. And then the dispassionate voice of the announcer once more: "The long-expected Bolshevik winter offensive has begun on the Vistula front. After extraordinarily strong artillery preparation, the enemy advanced on the western front of the Baranow bridgehead initially with numerous rifle divisions and armoured formations. Bitter fighting flared up. Diversionary attacks south of the Vistula and in the northern part of the bridgehead were repulsed . . ."

Eva Arlt watched Hanke nod quietly to himself. The twenty-three-year-old walked up to the *Gauleiter* and smiled. "Amazing really that they're risking everything, in their situation."

Hanke stared at her. "Who?"

"The Russians, of course, who else?"

"But where's the risk?"

"But Karl, they're at the end of their strength. They only have a couple of American tanks which have got through our blockade up there in Murmansk."

"Dear child, that's the wisdom of the propaganda office. Do not rely on it too much."

"You're a defeatist, Karl. According to my oath of office, I must report you to the *Gau* leadership." Eva Arlt put her hand on Hanke's shoulder. "Are you really worried?"

"*Ja*," he answered, "It's very serious. I wish we had at least a quarter of what the Russians have today. The Americans have literally fed them with tanks, ammunition and especially aircraft . . ."

"Aren't they at the bottom of the Arctic Ocean?" The secretary's question tailed off. Karl Hanke changed the subject. "Since yesterday I've had a book on my bedside table, a book about the Mongol invasion of Silesia, a book about the Battle of Liegnitz, in which Duke Heinrich with a handful of determined men brought the Asian flood to a halt," he told his secretary. The *Gauleiter* walked to the window, moved the net curtain back and looked down on to Albrechtstrasse. A few Breslauers hurried through the snow. "*Ja*, it's coming to us – we must prepare ourselves well."[10]

In Berlin, Joseph Goebbels was struggling to make sense of patchy reports. Some suggested the Russians had advanced two, perhaps four miles, others that they had punched through the German front to a depth of eight miles. "At present we can't say whether it's a success or a failure," he noted impatiently. There was only one certainty that Friday evening. "There's nerve-splitting tension," the propaganda minister observed. "It will probably continue for several days."[11]

Night came to Łukawa with still no attack. Hans Jürgen Hartmann and his men were relieved, marching back to their quarters in the village of Chrapranów, six miles away. At the opposite end of the Baranow bridgehead, David Dragunsky's armour had reached the right bank of the Nida in driving sleet. His tanks had advanced more than a dozen miles. The Red Army was now within 200 miles of Breslau.[12]

It was nearing daybreak on 13 January by the time Hans Jürgen Hartmann and his men reached their quarters in woods at Chrapranów. Their beds beckoned, but first the *Landsers* checked their weapons, ammunition, food supplies, then tossed their kit on to baggage trucks just in case they had to move out suddenly. They did not. The men slept until midday, but when they woke Chrapranów was buzzing with rumours: some said Kielce, fifty miles to the west, was in danger, others that it had fallen. "Things here," wrote Hartmann, "look completely black and gloomy."[13]

David Dragunsky's T34s forded the River Nida after artillery and mortars had smashed the dam and lowered the water level. The tanks rumbled past destroyed earthen bunkers and other fortifications, overrunning village stations and German airfields, whose garrisons were convinced the armour was their own. The Russian armour bore down on the town of Jedrzejow, two dozen miles south-west of Kielce, which sat astride the roads to Kraków and Silesia. After a brief skirmish on the edge of Jedrzejow, German troops fell back on the town. Dragunsky's tank simply drove straight after them. Jedrzejow fell into Soviet hands – and with it several thousand prisoners, their stores, and a train waiting at the station carrying Russian forced labourers. Breslau was now just 160 miles to the west.[14]

Long after nightfall this Saturday, orders were suddenly handed to Hans Jürgen Hartmann: fall back to the regimental command post in a manor house in Grochocice, just half a dozen miles away. It was midnight by the time his company was ready to move out. By then, the area was under heavy Soviet artillery fire. "In the darkness, there were only the milky stars in the moonless sky and the weak glow of light from distant muzzle flashes and shells landing."[15]

Hartmann had no idea of the scale of the catastrophe which had befallen his army. Fourth Panzer Army was disintegrating by the hour, its armoured reserves, 16th and 17th Panzer Divisions, simply bypassed, the only substantial natural barrier, the Nida, crossed. There was a hole forty miles wide and twenty-five deep in the army's front. It would never be closed. Before the night was out, the Russians would complete the German Army's destruction on the Vistula.

The ground near Zwolen, a dozen miles west of the Puławy bridgehead, rumbled and trembled "like an earthquake" under the weight of thousands upon thousands of shells. A "continuous roar" surrounded *Oberst* Paul Arnhold in the small hours of 14 January. It was impossible to make out the muzzle flashes of the Russian guns because "a single red glow of fire marked the course of the curved front". The east wind whipped up an impenetrable wall of dust and smoke, blinding German artillery observers. Their guns fired back blindly. Paul Arnhold had been at Verdun. He had been on the Somme and in Flanders. Nothing compared with the barrage he was experiencing now. Every telephone line was wrecked. Heavy losses were reported. The bombardment paused briefly, then resumed, leaping into the depths of the battlefield to pummel any reserves LVI Panzer Corps was trying to bring up. Now was the moment for the waves of Red infantry to swarm forward. "But they did not come – at least not towards us in the Puławy bridgehead."[16]

Hans Jürgen Hartmann was struggling to orient himself on a hilltop west of Chrapranów as he tried to locate his regimental command post. "Nothing at all in every direction except lightly rolling empty fields as far as the eye could see," he fumed, save for a village spread out before them which was under Russian artillery fire. Hartmann summoned his platoon leaders. They would have to go through the village – "back into hell" – to reach their command post. Sporadic shellfire was already landing on the men's position, unsettling the horses hauling the company's carts. Hartmann led his men from the front but barely had he set off than the entire hillside was subjected to a ferocious enemy barrage. He heard a cry, saw fire, was thrown around and then slammed into the ground. As he regained his senses he was surrounded by blackness, the smell of powder, moaning, whimpering, screaming. He stood up slowly. Then man next to him had half his skull missing. A second was covered in blood and groaning "My stomach, my stomach." Three *Landsers* were just charred corpses. Slowly Hartmann began to feel a sharp pain in his upper left thigh – and something damp, blood.[17]

Beyond Zwolen, Paul Arnhold watched the landscape swarm with Soviet tanks. Zwolen was the key to thwarting any Soviet breakout at Puławy: five roads met in the town, the most important of them leading west to the city of Radom. Arnhold's pioneers had laid 20,000 mines around the town. *Sturmgeschütze* self-propelled guns were dug in on the approaches to the town. Anti-tank guns were fixed in concrete at road junctions. And two dozen miles to the rear, on call when the battle came, there should have been Tiger and King Tiger tanks. There was no fuel for such large-scale reserves. They were scattered around the front piecemeal. Even then, they were crippled by a shortage of fuel. "They formed the steel skeleton of the Vistula front," Arnhold recalled, "but only a stationary one. If they had fired all their ammunition, if their turrets would not move, then their crews could only blow them up in the worst case." For now, the *Sturmgeschütze* were picking off the enemy tanks "one after another" – the German gunners knew the terrain and the distances precisely – but "for every shot-up T34, two new ones appeared".[18]

In Breslau, 14 January was *Opfersonntag* – the Sunday of sacrifice. The city's 600,000-plus inhabitants were expected to surrender whatever clothes they could spare: uniforms, shoes, boots, but also textiles, underwear, anything which might aid the *Landser*. It was only the beginning of the sacrifices which this Sunday would demand.

That afternoon, Party functionaries began knocking on doors across the city – an action repeated in towns and cities in every eastern *Gau* of the Reich: the first wave of the *Volkssturm* was being called up. Fourteen-year-old Hans became the latest member of the Illmer family to be called up. There were no uniforms for boys, only men. "The trousers had to be turned up three times," his nine-year-old brother Jürgen recalled. "His tunic could have served as a coat and his coat reached the heels of his boots. His cap – that was his headgear – stretched from the bridge of his nose to behind his collar." Under any other circumstances, the Illmers would have laughed. Jürgen felt envious initially, his mother cried constantly. Teenager Christian Lüdke felt proud to be wearing a uniform. "Now I'm a soldier," he boasted to his parents. His mother cut him short. "Oh God, now they're taking the children as well."[19]

It wasn't merely the *Volkssturm* stirring in Breslau. So too were the garrison troops and labour service. The time had come – too late, of course – to resume work on Karl Hanke's fanciful barrier of ditches, trenches and hastily-erected pillboxes which would shield the Silesian capital. Except that now work was taking place not along the old German-Polish border but on the edge of Breslau: in Weide, just four miles from the city centre, or Lohbrück, a mere three miles from the Ring. Senior lawyer Max Warzecha was ordered to build fortifications along a small tributary of the Oder, the Lohe. The temperature never rose above fifteen degrees below zero. Most of the men fell sick, including Warzecha who was struck down with a heavy cold. As for the work, it was fruitless. "The ground was frozen solid," the lawyer recalled. "Pickaxes broke."[20]

Other steps to prepare Breslau for the impending onslaught were more practical – and successful. The city's hospitals began to transfer their patients west. Attractive young sisters from the *Nationalsozialistische Volkswohlfahrt* – the Nazi welfare organisation – dressed in their smart brown uniforms with white aprons and bonnets sat "for hours on end" drinking coffee in the carriages of hospital trains, while volunteers from the German Red Cross toiled in temperatures of twenty degrees below zero. This was how Red Cross sister Lena Aschner spent her fiftieth birthday: lifting stretchers carrying groaning people from morning until almost midnight. "My hands are blue with cold and torn to shreds," she wrote, her work done. "My arms ache, my eyes are barely open." The hospitals had been emptied.[21]

The strongpoint at Zwolen held out for a good twenty-four hours. It was not lack of numbers, not lack of fuel, not lack of shells which brought about its downfall, but orders from above – and not orders to retreat. No, a handful of self-propelled guns were ordered to leave the safety of the position and hold open a line of retreat for German troops falling back from the perimeter of the Puławy bridgehead; Arnhold's pioneers would close the barrier through the minefield when the last German armour passed. In the confusion of night and fug of smoke and haze lying over the battlefield, ten Soviet tanks slipped through the gap, followed by mounted infantry who held the barrier open. "The result," Paul Arnhold recalled, "was indescribable chaos. In the darkness, friend and foe could no longer recognise each other."[22]

The fall of the strongpoint was repeated across LVI Panzer Corps' front, which simply melted way. Entire units were at best regarded as scattered across the Polish landscape, at worst simply written off. "Displaced troops wandered around the terrain, looking to link up with others or heading for the rear in the hope of finding a unit again," Arnhold remembered. The *Oberst* was given fresh orders: head for Radom to rally the men. He did, gathering nearly 600 troops and half a dozen *Sturmgeschütze*, resolving to block the road to Tomaszow with this makeshift formation.[23]

Perhaps the official communiqué from Hitler's headquarters had Arnhold's unit in mind when it referred to "strong German combat formations" offering the enemy "bitter resistance". The missive played up Soviet losses – 245 tanks destroyed in a single day – and skirted around the subject of German casualties. It was, the communiqué insisted, still a "defensive battle", just one which had "shifted" from the Baranow bridgehead to the Vistula, Nida and the southern foothills of the Holy Cross Mountains near Łysa Góra.[24]

It was mention of Łysa Góra, 200 miles east of Breslau, which electrified Ulrich Frodien's father. Herr Frodien, a former army doctor, had taken his son into the Lower Silesian countryside, convinced fresh air and hunting in the Silesian countryside were the best convalescence for the eighteen-year-old; Ulrich's thigh had been smashed, his head and chest peppered with shrapnel following an artillery strike on the Eastern Front the previous autumn. Until now that front "had always seemed a world away" to the inhabitants of Germanengrund, two dozen miles north of Breslau, but not now. Young Ulrich watched as everyday life in the village broke down:

> Fear and helplessness spread through the village. Every office, every authority, every arm of the Party – if they were still contactable by telephone – remained silent or was as good as useless. Every man aged fifteen to sixty-five was called up by the Wehrmacht or *Volkssturm*, the women were completely left to their own devices. They had to face every decision alone.[25]

Twenty-five miles away, the housewives of Oels were celebrating the pig slaughter festival as they did every year. "It's a little oasis in the desert-like austerity of the war," enthused Erna Seiler. Boiled belly pork, sauerkraut and wellwurst – boiled pork sausage, a Silesian delicacy – were particularly tasty. "But the shadow of the Russians, growing closer by the day, weighs heavily upon us," the thirty-eight-year-old confided to her diary. The owner of the sub-post office burst into the festival. The Party leadership was holding an urgent meeting on the situation. "They'll probably talk about the evacuation of specific villages," Seiler noted excitedly. They did not. "There's no talk whatsoever of leaving," Erna Seiler wrote. "On the contrary, we're told it's the anxious types who talk about packing. They should be ashamed of themselves for spreading disquiet among the populace. The Eastern Front holds and will continue to hold!" The *Frauenschaft*, the Nazi Party's organisation for women, was more interested in debating how to celebrate Shrove Tuesday on 13 February. Long before then, Oels would be in Russian hands.[26]

Despite the assertions of Nazi Party functionaries, the Eastern Front was *not* holding. There no longer was an Eastern Front, not a continuous German line at any rate, just pockets of German units scattered across some 7,000 square miles of central Poland. Konev lunged along the Vistula towards Kraków and Upper Vistula with his left flank, towards Breslau and the Oder with his right, while his right-hand neighbour – and bitter rival – Georgy Zhukov pushed his 1st Byelorussian Front towards Łódź, Poznań and the lower Oder. Some *Landsers* struggled westwards in the wake of the Soviet armour, others were simply overrun. Command was paralysed. Near Radom, 19th Panzer and 6th *Volksgrenadier* Divisions had lost all communications with the outside world. They were in danger of being overwhelmed – but their commanders would issue no orders to retreat for fear of "getting it in the neck".[27] Other leaders were prepared to make independent decisions. The remnants of 17th Panzer Division were surrounded in a forest outside Kielce, led by their thirty-seven-year-old commander, Albert Brux. The Silesian was a brave man – he held the *Ritterkreuz* with Oak Leaves – but not a foolish one. He summoned his staff and gathered his men around him, then ordered them to lay down their arms. After interrogation, his captors showed him around the battlefield. "What remained of the division was a cemetery of men and vehicles," he lamented. "Piles of metal skeletons scattered on the roads – this was all which was left of my panzers and armoured cars."[28] *Generalmajor* Max Sachsenheimer – at thirty-five the second youngest general in the German Army – and his 17th Infantry Division suffered no such fate. Sachsenheimer was struck by the morale of his men as they fought their way back from Puławy, still singing the national anthem as they went into battle. "Each man fought doggedly, for himself and for his comrades, to beat a path back to Germany," Sachsenheimer recalled. He watched as the heaviest Russian tanks, Josef Stalins, were destroyed by *Panzerfaust* right in front of him. But it could not go on like this. Ammunition and, above all, food was running out. Hunger sapped the men's strength while Sachsenheimer's artillerymen blew up gun after gun "after the last shell was fired" as the Soviet ring tightened. Some of the 17th Infantry broke out – "a forest,"

Sachsenheimer wryly observed, "proved to be very useful". But as a coherent fighting unit, 17th Infantry Division ceased to exist. "From this moment on, every man was on his own."[29] Signaller *Oberfeldwebel* Helmut Reiche found himself somewhere near Kielce with thirty men and no contact with the rest of Panzer Grenadier Regiment 90 – or any other German unit. "In our situation, there are two choices," he decided. "Captivity or smashing our way through. There's no question of the former." Reiche and his comrades moved by night, stealing food from the homes of Poles. Each morning there were fewer and fewer men at roll call. They found the Polish landscape teeming with individual *Landsers* or small clusters of German soldiers trying to make their way west. They also found signs of battle: dead German and Russian soldiers, an abandoned German field ambulance, its patients dead.[30] Walther Nehring somehow managed to keep his XXIV Panzer Corps intact, pushing it westwards, seeking the path of least resistance. Like a rolling snowball, Nehring's 'wandering pocket' accumulated dispersed German units as it barrelled across Poland. "Only if we all stayed together could we reach our goal, while breaking up into individual groups meant death or captivity," the general wrote. Among the units gathered by Nehring were elements of 20th Panzer Grenadier Division. "The strange thing was," wrote its commanding officer, *Generalleutnant* Georg Jauer, "that despite all our worries and concerns, we never felt that we would die in the pocket. Each man trusted the next man, and everyone gave his all."[31] It took ten days for Nehring's corps to batter its way back to German lines after a 150-mile odyssey. And sometimes it was bluff rather than blood which aided escape. One senior NCO hollered "like a general" at a *Major* directing traffic at a bottleneck to let his vehicle through. The bluster succeeded. Elsewhere, several grenadiers wore Polish clothes over their uniform. A Russian field kitchen asked them for help. While the cooks yelled, the signallers pushed. They were even rewarded with a little food for their exertions. After that, the Germans vanished into the night.[32]

Paul Arnhold and a handful of men crept through the fields of the Pilica valley trying to avoid the Russian columns – with headlights on full beam, so secure did they feel – pushing west. The *Oberst* had been unable to hold the road to Tomaszów Mazowiecki with his scratch force and fled in a staff car, until it was shot up by Soviet armour which overhauled the retreating Germans. Arnhold had no map – he used the stars to guide him as he trudged "hungry and half frozen" through deep snow, through thicket, through clearings, somewhere south of Tomaszów, occasionally crossing a road in darkness in the gaps between the Soviet convoys. But roads were a trifling obstacle compared with the icy Pilica, anywhere between 120 and 200ft wide here. Most of the river was frozen, save for a central channel, but Arnhold sought a stretch where there were islands; the ice there was thicker.

He found none, but on the edge of Tomaszów he found a farm surrounded by a wooden lattice fence. That, the *Oberst* determined, would serve as a makeshift bridge. He and his pioneers began dismantling it, then slid it over the ice. Several figures came out of the farmhouse and called out in Russian. The pioneers did not respond. The Russians opened fire. The Germans dropped the fence and simply ran over the ice – until the ice ran out and they plunged into the Pilica. It wasn't far to the opposite bank, no more than a couple of strokes, but Arnhold's thick coat "became as heavy as lead" in the river; the ice was too thin to support the officer's weight. So began, says Arnhold, "a desperate fight, a struggle with my last ounce of strength against the end, either at the hands of a bullet from a machine pistol of a dozen shooters or by drowning in the icy waters of the Pilica." Finally he found ground beneath his feet and climb out of the river as erratic tracer fire struck the far bank. He was joined by four comrades, one who had left his boots behind in the thick Pilica mud. The soldier cut his soaked coat into strips and wrapped them around his bleeding feet so he could continue on his way. The pioneers were cold, wet, barely able to focus because they had not eaten in days, but there was no thought of stopping because they would freeze to death.

With every step their boots squelched, the water in their sodden coats froze – so stiffly that when Paul Arnhold tripped in the dark, a piece simply snapped off. The men's teeth chattered constantly from the cold – a snow storm now added to their misery – and tension. "The cold went right through us – to our feet, legs, our entire bodies," the *Oberst* remembered. "The damp began to freeze. Death by freezing accompanied our every step. There was no point arguing with it. That uncompromising certainty never loosened its grip on us. It spurred us on, allowed us no break."

Finally they stumbled across a cottage whose elderly inhabitant allowed them in and even fed them. The pioneers dried their clothes by the open fire, but food and warmth made them drowsy. They fell asleep. "I suddenly woke up because my feet felt as if they were on fire," Arnhold recalled. "When I drew them back, it was already too late: the soles had been too close to the embers and had caught fire. In that short space of time, they warped so badly that I felt as if I was standing on a pipe."

They rested for a couple of hours until the first signs of dawn, then it was time to leave. Their clothes and boots were still wet. For the first few steps shivering and goose pimples went through the pioneers' bodies. But what, thought Paul Arnhold, were goose pimples compared with the "threatening spectre of the Bolsheviks breathing down our necks?" He hobbled through the deep snow in his burned shoes, every step painful. Just one thought possessed him and his comrades: reach the Oder. But the Oder lay 150 miles away. [33]

The blame for this catastrophe was not Adolf Hitler's. Or at least the blame for this catastrophe was not Adolf Hitler's *in Adolf Hitler's eyes*. As ever, he blamed others for his own arrogance and ignorance. He blamed the low morale of the troops at the front – especially the officers. He blamed his generals for failing to warn him about the Soviets' strength. Above all, he blamed Army Group A's commander Josef Harpe, who was promptly sacked. In his place, Ferdinand Schörner, Hitler's favourite, a general whose ability was invariably overshadowed by his ruthlessness and fanaticism. "I think Schörner can do it," Joseph Goebbels wrote. "He will put right the desolate state of affairs caused by Harpe. We will leave no stone unturned in making the necessary forces available to him."[34]

Already dispatched to halt the Red Army advance were the tank destroyers of *Oberst*

Hans-Ulrich Rudel specialist ground-attack unit, *Schlachtgeschwader* 2, transferred from Hungary to Silesia. Germany's most decorated warrior, Stuka pilot, tank destroyer *par excellence* and sole recipient of the *Ritterkreuz* with Golden Oak Leaves, Swords and Diamonds, found the situation at Udetfeld* outside Katowice confused – and confusing. Ground crew told Rudel Russian tanks were just two dozen miles from Częstochowa – or perhaps they were panzers trying to break through to the west. Within twenty minutes, Rudel's wing was airborne and flying low over Częstochowa. A tank was moving along the main road, a second, then a third. They looked like T34s, but Rudel was convinced they had to belong to 16th or 17th Panzer Divisions. He circled the city. No mistake. They were T34s with infantry mounted who now began to take pot shots at the German aircraft.

Tram cables and tall houses made it difficult for Rudel to manoeuvre for an attack but he nevertheless left three tanks ablaze courtesy of his Stuka's cannon. *Schlachtgeschwader* 2 continued east following a railway line and main road. It wasn't long before they came across more Soviet armour rolling west, closely followed by a column of lorries carrying infantry and supplies, plus several anti-aircraft guns. The terrain here was far better suited to tank destroying – no obstructions to hinder the Stukas' movements. At last light Rudel's unit set down on the runway at Udetfeld, out of ammunition. They left behind eight shot-up Russian tanks.

Until now Rudel and his comrades had almost regarded the destruction of enemy tanks "as a kind of sport". But no longer. "I am seized with an uncontrolled fury at the thought that this horde from the steppes is driving into the very heart of Europe."[35]

Despite Hans-Ulrich Rudel's intervention, Częstochowa could not be saved, as wounded soldier Wolfdietrich Schnurre discovered. The holy city had largely been evacuated as the twenty-four-year-old *Landser* was taken to the military hospital, with Częstochowa already under enemy fire. Only a few surgeons and medics remained – and most of those had drowned their sorrows with alcohol. For the first time in weeks, Schnurre was treated to a shower, then a proper bed. The soldier slept soundly and dreamed vividly of "roaring claps of thunder and raging lightning." He awoke. It was no dream. With tank shells exploding all around, two orderlies carried the soldier to the station and put him on a train. It was the last one to leave Częstochowa.[36] The Red Army was now just 100 miles from Breslau.

One by one the towns and cities of Poland were falling to the Red Army: Kielce, 15 January. Częstochowa and Radom, 16 January. Warsaw, 17 January. *Pravda* proclaimed 400 towns and villages liberated in the first three days of Konev's offensive. "Glory to the outstanding men of the Red Army!" the official Communist Party organ trumpeted. "Forward under the victorious banner of Lenin and Stalin, to the West!"[37]

The Nazi empire in the East crumbled as quickly as the Red Army advanced. Four days into the offensive, the first orders were issued to evacuate the great city of Łódź –

---

* Today the site of Katowice International Airport

renamed Litzmannstadt by the Nazis in honour of the Great War general who captured it. As the wheels of the civic apparatus began to turn, there was a sound rarely heard in Łódź: the air-raid siren. For an hour, Soviet bombers pounded the city, paralysing the tram network, overwhelming fire-fighters and the German administration. No evacuees left Łódź that night. The first train only departed the following lunchtime.[38]

Bombs also began to fall on the ancient seat of the Polish kings. That aside, life in Kraków was still remarkably normal. The trams ran. The black market thrived. Cinemas and restaurants were still open. But outside the city, all was not normal. Police and soldiers stood guard on the roads leading from Kraków to ensure no one left without permission.

The Army had already abandoned Kraków; the sacked Josef Harpe had fled with his staff, but the city's Nazi overlord conducted business as usual – for one day at least. In the magnificent coronation hall – 'the hall of columns' – of Wawel Castle, Hans Frank held a farewell dinner for three dozen members of his staff. Five years before, Frank had been 'crowned' ruler of the rump of Poland as its Governor General in a suitably tasteless Nazi ceremony. Hans Frank was not a king. He was a god. "There is no authority here which is higher in rank, influence and authority than the Governor General," he proclaimed. He was as good as his word. He had ruled his domain as brutally as any tyrant in history. And now as his rule crumbled, he was overcome by self-pity. "I stood alone in the great coronation and congregation hall with its panoramic view over the wonderful old city and thought about the path which had brought us to this point."[39]

In the face of this inexorable advance, as many as five million German civilians fled. They fled because civilians always flee in the face of an invader. They fled because memories of Russian actions in the German East a generation before were long. But above all they fled because they feared the 'Mongol onslaught' coming from the East. The German soldier called his foe 'Russki' or 'Ivan' out of grudging respect. The best the Nazi propaganda apparatus could manage was 'Bolsheviks'. More typically the newspapers and newsreels branded the Soviets an 'Asiatic horde', 'Mongols', 'beasts'. It had proof they were 'beasts', too: in November 1944, the Red Army had seized, then been driven out of, the East Prussian village of Nemmersdorf. The returning Germans found numerous dead civilians – the actual figure is disputed – "almost every one of the murdered in a bestial fashion," a *Volkssturm* soldier recalled.[40] War reporters, photographers, foreign correspondents, newsreel cameramen all descended on Nemmersdorf, while Germany's newspapers were told to warn their readers that if the Red Army overran the Reich "the systematic and terrible murder of every single German would take place and Germany would be turned into one big cemetery".[41] The newspapers obliged – and struck terror into the heart of every inhabitant of the German East.

The cities of the occupied East emptied first – Łódź, Kraków, Kalisz, Poznań and their satellite towns and villages – then the border settlements of Silesia. They called it *die grosse Flucht* or *der grosse Treck* – the great flight or great trek – an exodus of millions in temperatures of twenty degrees below. Farmers limbered their carts and wagons, but most people moved on foot, pulling hand carts, carrying suitcases, rucksacks strapped to their bodies, mothers cradling babies as they tried to hold on to the hands of older children. There was little order, almost no organisation. Party officials who had insisted such a never day would never come, often fled hastily, leaving the people to their fate. Sixteen-year-old soldier Hubertus Kindler and his comrades watched as a column of Nazi dignitaries, their wives dressed in fur coats, their vehicles filled with every imaginable item, passed a line of refugees. The Party leaders stopped only to force the poor refugees to move their carts out of the way.[42] It was left to fellow Silesians to offer these people aid. Breslauer Hanne Hübler was staying with her family in a village inn in Friedrichslager, Upper Silesia, when the first refugees appeared on the lane outside the hostelry:

> Weeping and crying came from the carts, some horses fell down, and in front
> of our window, two cars collided, overturning one, a grandmother fell so badly
> that she was carried into the restaurant with a battered face.

The refugees rushed inside and huddled around the oven while the innkeeper and his wife did their best to provide coffee, soup and milk. "Our hearts trembled seeing so much misery, illness and loneliness all in one place, for this trek of refugees was the first shock to seize our hearts," wrote Hübler. One tearful woman pleaded for help warming her two children. The youngsters were carried to the oven, while their mother kissed and stroked them. They did not move. "Your children are frozen," a *Volkssturm* doctor curtly pronounced. Wailing, the woman threw herself on top of the corpses. Finally she was wrenched from them. Her face racked by agony, she had to watch as they were laid to rest by the roadside – the macabre ceremony made worse by the time it took to dig the frozen earth. Hers were not the only victims of this trek; two babies had frozen in their nappies as they lay in the carts. "We had the greatest sympathy for the poor unfortunate creatures," Hanne Hübler recalled, "but we didn't in the slightest think that the same fate would overtake us as well."[43]

The treks moved at two, three, perhaps four miles an hour. They were frequently passed by Soviet armour bound for the Oder. Journalist Boris Polevoy was moved by the sight of "a column of women, elderly people and children, pulling their possessions in hand carts and prams, or pushing bicycles with bundles hanging from them." Younger children clung to their mother's backs or were cradled in their arms, older ones held on to their hands. It reminded the thirty-six-year-old of the autumn of 1941 when his wife had fled the city of Kalinin with the couple's seven-month-old son in almost identical circumstances. "Now it was the Germans' turn," the *Pravda* correspondent observed. "Such a sight did not provoke gloating among the soldiers. They looked upon this sad column with sympathy."[44] Frequently, however, the Red Army showed the refugees no mercy. "Russian aircraft dived at our trek repeatedly," wrote one Upper Silesian. "The horses ran away, there were many dead and a child was lost in the confusion."[45] Hubertus Kindler came across the remnants of a trek mauled by Soviet tanks. What was still warm gave off steam in the cold, while the survivors stood by the side of the road crying, unable to comprehend what had happened. "It was terrible to look at," he recalled. "People, animals, beds, household effects, hay, straw, oats. They had simply shot at everything, even the horses, at everything which moved."[46]

The first of these wretched columns began to file through Breslau on 17 January. Red Cross volunteer Lena Aschner watched as the refugees crossed Passbrücke, near the Jahrhunderthalle.

> The overloaded small hand carts and sleds wobble between the carts and horses. A small, heavy-laden sled overturns. Amid the chaos, its owner tries to right it. The column cannot stop. Onwards, only onwards. She struggles in vain to put her legs between the overturned sledge runners, she cannot stay up, falls down crying for help and grabs on to another cart. Everyone tumbles over, screaming in confusion.

Frau Aschner and her friends helped the woman up. Her entire calf was torn, her leg broken, blood running down it in torrents. Yet she didn't want to go to the nearby clinic for treatment – she would lose her place in the trek. Aschner handed her some bandages. With a tired, tear-stained, smeared face she thanked her then returned to her place in the column and continued on her way. Another woman passed, her heavily-laden cart falling apart under the weight. She kept slipping and falling over. It was too much. She grabbed the heavy sack of bedding on the cart and threw it into the road, screaming "Let the shit lie there, I don't give a damn anyway." The bundle joined sacks, packages, suitcases, broken carts and sledges lining Uferstrasse. A few Breslauers handed out coffee, but the refugees took no more than a couple of gulps before rushing back to their carts to resume their journey. "Nobody stops if they're injured on the way – they're bandaged up," wrote Aschner. "Everyone hurries on their way. Their strides are tired, weary, their faces wealthy, grey, tear-stained. They can hardly still move their feet forward. But onwards."[47]

Office worker Max Hamsch was returning home when he was drawn to strange noises: slurping, trampling, crying. The sight presented to him was one he had never seen – and would never see again: a herd of cows filling the entire road, stretching out of sight, escorted by a few soldiers, elderly farmers and prisoners of war. "Blood's already flowing from the udders of some of the poor creatures because they cannot be milked," Hamsch observed.[48] Schoolgirl Ursula Scholz also remembered the cries of pain from the unmilked cows. The sixteen-year-old had been ordered to help at the nearby Freiburger Bahnhof, reuniting children and mothers, hauling luggage, distributing food. As she headed there, the streets were already filled with a "ghostly column" of refugees. Aside from the bellowing cattle, the only sounds were "the shuffle of footsteps of utterly exhausted people who totter next to their carts, the occasional crying of a child, the clattering and snorting of horses". Abandoned dogs accompanied the trek, howling and barking. "How much longer," wondered the schoolgirl, "can we still lie in our warm beds before the fate of life on the country lanes with temperatures twenty or twenty-three degrees below overtakes us?"[49]

The wounded Hans Jürgen Hartmann pondered the same question. The junior officer had been taken first to his regimental command post, then to Kalisz, and finally to an overcrowded hospital in Poznań, surrounded by "lacerated, groaning, stinking bodies". He spent two days there, watching surgeons and nurses overwhelmed by the number of casualties, orderlies constantly carrying "heavy stretchers back and forth with the dreadful wrecks of men", before the hospital was evacuated. There was no luxury of a hospital train for the wounded officer, but an unheated passenger train which hurried through the night. "An icy wind sweeps over the light snow on the fields and penetrates into our compartments through cracks in the windows," Hartmann recalled, unable to sleep. The faces of his comrades haunted him: "Steinberg, Iglhaut, Schmidt, Kober, Treder, Jonny, Greiner and Teige – Iglhaut especially, groaning covered in blood and Steinberg, his skull horribly smashed in half." He stared out of the window at the endlessly flat terrain. "Unless there's a miracle, soon Russian tanks will roll over these tracks too," Hartmann reasoned, "and this land too will go down in a sea of blood and futile tears."[50]

By the early afternoon of 17 January, the Red Army vanguard was less than five miles from Kraków. The city possessed some of the most comprehensive defences of any of the Reich's bulwarks in the East – far more robust than those shielding Breslau. There was nothing to hold them, or Kraków itself: 3,000 soldiers, police officers and Party functionaries, most unfit, with no heavy weapons and only a handful of *Panzerfaust*. The garrison commander, *Generalmajor* Hermann Kruse, had no intention of defending the city – and told Hans Frank he should evacuate Kraków. The Governor General wasted no time in following the general's advice. Shortly after 1pm, a column of vehicles and trucks packed with documents and looted *objets d'art*, left Wawel Castle "in the most wonderful winter weather and brilliant sunshine", led by Frank in his Mercedes.[51]

It was growing dark as battalion commander *Hauptmann* Georg Christian Kreuter arrived in Łódź. There was little of his battalion left, to say nothing of his division, 25th Panzer. During the night much of its armour had been blown up after running out of fuel, while Kreuter had been wounded in the arm during fighting in the Pilica valley. He asked his commander, *Generalmajor* Oskar Audörsch, not to take him to a hospital – "it seemed too risky" – but to the central station. There Kreuter found "all hell let loose", especially when the air raid sirens sounded for the second night running. One woman wailed hysterically, unnerving everyone around her. And yet trains were still running to Poznań and Breslau, and a commuter train was waiting in the sidings. The officer decided to leave Łódź immediately, forcing his way with difficulty into an overcrowded carriage. Around 9pm, it pulled out of the city.[52]

Georg Kreuter had made the correct decision. As his train lumbered through Łódź's suburbs, the first Russian tanks were already in Zgierz and Aleksandrów Łódzki, little more than half a dozen miles from the city centre. Their appearance provoked panic among the remaining German populace. Too late, the authorities tried to evacuate Łódź. But the telephones no longer worked. Most officials had fled. The garrison had fled.

Many Germans never received the order to leave. They left on their own initiative. On foot. By night. Through the snow. With Red Army tanks breathing down their necks. "The scenes of flight remained burned into the memory of everyone who witnessed them," recalled mayor Hans Trautwein.[53]

The Wehrmacht communiqué still talked of the battle in the "great Vistula bend", of "bitter resistance" from German units striking in the rear of the Soviet armoured spearheads, but really, as *Leutnant* Wilfried Nordmann realized, "it was a simple race with the Russians". The thirty-five-year-old lived on no more than three hours' sleep every night and a couple of slices of bread daily during the retreat. "So you see how much eating as well as sleeping are more habits than necessities," he observed drily. Each time Nordmann and the remnants of his *Werfer* rocket battery believed they had escaped the Soviets and grabbed a couple of hours' sleep, the cry 'Tanks' would wake them – and the retreat continued. Nowhere did a German unit make a stand. "We actually waited for someone to say, 'As far as here and no further'", Nordmann recalled bitterly. "But wherever we went, the senior staff had already cleared off so that the poor *Landsers* were left entirely to their own devices."[54]

What attempts there were to halt the Soviet advance were at best piecemeal, at worst simply steamrollered. Two first-rate divisions, the *Hermann Göring* and the *Brandenburg*, were hastily transferred from East Prussia to central Poland. Committed before they were ready, they were caught up in the tide of German troops fleeing west. At least their ranks were filled with trained soldiers. Not so the *Volkssturm*. Joseph Goebbels received pleas for men from across the Reich's eastern provinces. All he could offer them were militia. "Once again the hour has come when we must scrape together our forces from all four corners of the Reich and hurl them at the threatened places."[55]

Poznań's *Volkssturm* was one such formation hurled at a threatened place. The place was Ostrów Wielkopolski, eighty miles north-east of Breslau. As the men stepped off the troop train, Russian rifles were thrust into their hands and they were ordered to safeguard the roads in and out of the town. At least half of them had never served before. They certainly had no idea how to use the handful of *Panzerfaust* they'd just been issued with; instruction was hurriedly provided during a brief pause in marching. When they finally took up their positions outside Ostrów, nothing happened apart from heavy artillery fire from both sides. After a night in the open, the *Volkssturm* men were ordered back to town to embark on a train once more. As they crossed the tracks, they were caught by heavy machine-gun fire; one company and a platoon were all but wiped out. Another platoon approached the station building in front of which was a tank; its leader was certain the tank was German – certainty reinforced by the crew's gestures. When the *Volkssturm* troops were just 100 yards away, the tank opened fire. The platoon was wiped out. Another *Volkssturm* company was still holding the road into Ostrów when tanks appeared in its rear. The men assumed they were German. They were not. At point-blank range, machine-guns and anti-tank guns opened fire. Only two men survived the bloodbath: one who pretended to be dead, another who was badly wounded.

What was left of the battalion rallied in woods outside the town. The men were despondent. Of 350 troops originally sent to Ostrów, only 200 were left. "The Bolsheviks chased us around like rabbits on a hunt," seethed Otto Albrecht, formerly Poznań's superintendent. He filed a complaint to his political masters:

> It was a crime to send us so untrained and so unskilled in war against our worst enemy, the Bolsheviks. The battalion went into combat completely untrained. There was just a handful of men who knew how to use Russian rifles, no one knew how to use the machine-gun at all, to say nothing of the *Panzerfaust*. No one knew how to use the *Panzerfaust* before it was explained to us shortly before we went into action. And this is the only weapon which a simple soldier can use successfully against a tank.[56]

Thirty miles to the south, soldiers were beginning to occupy the fortifications of the Bartold line, built with so much sweat by Silesians the previous autumn. The codeword *Walküre* – Valkyrie – flashed around the scattered units of *Wehrkreis* VIII, and training units, militia, garrison troops, and reservists were alerted. The school for non-commissioned officers in Frankenstein was emptied, Luftwaffe cadets at Schöngarten airfield abandoned their training and formed companies of soldiers. Anti-aircraft gunners protecting the Berthawerk were ordered to prepare their 88mm flak guns for ground combat. Soldiers were posted at railway stations and road junctions to round up any retreating troops, irrespective of their rank, and form them into a makeshift battalion for Breslau's defence. And on the Bartold line, *Volkssturm* men with aged rifles and just eight rounds apiece stood guard next to an anti-tank ditch thirty feet wide and five feet deep. Despite all the toil of 1944, the fortifications were still incomplete. To strengthen Karl Hanke's great barrier, they began unrolling barbed wire.[57]

One hundred miles south-east of Breslau, military chaplain Joseph Ozanna was riding a tram in Beuthen, one of the cities in the sprawling Upper Silesian industrial conurbation. Two women climbed on and began talking excitedly. They had just succeeded in fleeing from Częstochowa, fewer than forty miles away. "A Party member in uniform screamed at the women and threatened to arrest them for spreading false news," the priest wrote. The women, not the Party official, were right. Joseph Ozanna returned home immediately, determined to move his family to safety.

At first he walked, then ran down the country lane leading to Golassowitz, three dozen miles south of Beuthen. "You must get away with the children," he told his wife Christa breathlessly. "I will go to my mother," Frau Ozanna decided in a flash. Her mother lived in Breslau.[58]

Ulrich Frodien and his father were also making for the Silesian capital. They drove as quickly as the roads, covered by a thick blanket of snow, would allow. They passed goods trains, crammed with German refugees from central Poland – the Warthegau district, colonised after the 1939 invasion – "naked fear and deep despair etched on their faces," the young soldier recalled. "These first German refugees made a deep impression on me. What was the point of sacrifices and toil at the front if our own people now had to flee?"

It was late on 17 January by the time their car entered the Silesian capital, its streets pitch black "apart from a blanket of snow which glistened wonderfully thanks to our car's headlights". Barely had they returned to their apartment than the telephone was ringing – constantly. "Are you still there?" Friends, family, patients asked. "Are you staying in Breslau or leaving?" "What should we do, what should we take with us? "What's the best way to get out of the city?" "Is the front holding, what have you heard?" "The Müllers have already fled."[59]

From the window of his office in the Rheinmetall-Borsig works in Hundsfeld, Herbert Rühlemann watched "an endless stream of horse and wagon, hand-drawn carriages, bicycles and people" moving westwards. They moved slowly, but never stopped. It was sufficient to unnerve the armament plant's director. He climbed into a works car with a colleague and drove south along the Oder. They stopped after about ten miles of negotiating lanes buried by snow, but oddly devoid of traffic, when they reached a bridge spanning the river. *Volkssturm* men stood guard, with orders to blow the crossing if it was threatened. Rühlemann and his colleague drew the same conclusion: "working would come to a stop in less than a week". They resolved to send their families west.[60]

Already rolling west were the workers and heavy plant of Breslau's sprawling FAMO works. Just a fortnight earlier, some 8,000 people had been employed here, but now engineers were dismantling its machinery and operating equipment, loading them on hundreds of freight cars, and sending them to Schönebeck on the Elbe, ten miles south-east of Magdeburg.[61]

At Krupp's Berthawerk in Markstädt, managers had fled, but not the workforce, as Hugo Hartung discovered. Hartung and a few fellow artists were relieved of duties protecting Schöngarten airfield and ordered to organise an evening of classical music and recitals for staff and directors of the Berthawerk. Except that "none of the leading figures for whom our evening had been arranged was present," the former theatre director observed. "There was a chilly, uncomfortable feeling in the half-filled hall." It was half-filled with good reason: that afternoon a telegram had been handed to the Berthawerk's directors outlining the Red Army's rapid advance.[62]

The torrent of refugees from the East soon swamped the Silesian capital. Scenes at the Hauptbahnhof were chaotic – and harrowing. Soldiers struggled to control the crowds. A few helped to load the carriages, luggage first, the people on top. It was not unusual for owners and suitcases to become separated – or for children to travel on one train, mothers on another, but not necessarily to the same destination. Women with small children besieged the hut on the platform run by the Nazis' welfare organisation. Soup had run out; the volunteers handed out hot water instead. "People press, bump, look for someone, climb over the piles, call out inaudible names across the crowd," wrote Red Cross volunteer Lena Aschner, trying to offer help to the exodus. "Everyone fights for a place close to the track so that they can find a place when the next train comes." She noticed a fair-haired woman slumped on one of the piles of luggage, staring at the feet of passers-by. "Suddenly she leaps up and looks around like a madwoman, runs to a pram, hauls the child out, not giving a thought for its frightened, screaming mother, presses it to her chest and runs off," wrote Aschner. "Someone succeeds in taking the wailing child from her and returning him to his mother." Frau Aschner took the woman to one side, gave her a cup of strong coffee and sat down with her. The woman had come on foot from Oels, just eighteen miles away, pushing a pram. When she reached the Hauptbahnhof, she had tried to change her baby's nappy – only to discover it had frozen to death.[63] A shiver went down the spine of veteran policeman Otto Rogalla as he watched an "endless train of human misery" pass through the station, people "with rucksacks on their backs, children on their arms and horror etched on their faces". Some had lost their children in the chaos of evacuation, others carried dead babies who had frozen to death during the journey, while lost youngsters screamed for their mothers. Rogalla and his fellow officers directed this torrent of refugees, as best they could, to temporary quarters, and reunited mothers and children. But deep down, the policemen felt stiff, "as if paralysed," Rogalla recalled. "We had never thought something like that was possible to us." It slowly began to dawn on the officers that soon they too would suffer the same fate.[64]

It was even worse for those on foot. "Columns without end" passed through the city "by day and night", Catholic priest Paul Peikert noted. "The sight of these haggard, withered people who had to leave the land of their fathers with what little possessions they had was terrible." Peikert's housekeeper passed the corpses of eight children and an old man in a ditch, while there was talk of trucks filled with the dead heading for the city's cemeteries. "Silesia," wrote Peikert, "hasn't experienced such hardships since the Thirty Years War, and given its scale that hardship must be called minor."[65]

Normal life in Breslau ground to a halt. From a tram nine-year-old Jürgen Illmer watched staff at the Luftwaffe headquarters burn huge piles of documents in full view. In the distance there was the dull crash of explosions as the frozen earth was blown up to create anti-tank ditches.[66] "You could see things breaking down almost by the hour," Ulrich Frodien recalled. Snow was not cleared from the streets. Rubbish was not collected. Trams became less and less frequent. Traffic lights stopped working. Nazi Party officials disappeared from the streets. Cinemas and restaurants closed. "In just a few days, the routine changed completely," the *Gefreiter* noticed. "A feverish unease had seized Breslau. I smelled it, it already stank like a front-line city, it stank of fires and death."

After more than five years of war and rationing, shopkeepers were issuing double, even triple rations. "You might as well take it before Ivan gets his hands on it!" they told customers. Frodien was sent by his mother to pick up her fur coat from a store in Gartenstrasse, close to the central station. It was already closed, its shutters and bars lowered. The young soldier clambered over rubbish bins and entered the back of the shop. Inside, receipts and order forms were scattered over the floor, order books were piled up, there was even some money left in the till. And there were coats, jackets, capes, cloaks by the hundred. Sable, mink, wolf, sheep, fox and others. "For a poor soldier, who had frozen often enough on cold nights, it was a staggering sight," Frodien recalled.

He tried on an officer's fur-lined coat. It fitted perfectly. "But then I hung it back up in the cupboard resignedly," he lamented. Plundering was punishable by death.[67]

It was dark on Thursday, 18 January by the time Christa Ozanna reached Breslau's Hauptbahnhof after a couple of changes of trains and a delay of several hours. "Somewhere in the East and West there was war," she thought. "In Breslau you forgot about it." Just before 7pm, she walked through the door of her mother's home in Kronprinzenstrasse. Suddenly the air-raid siren howled. The family hurried into the cellar of the apartment block. "No reason to be alarmed," the concierge assured everyone. "Nothing is happening." But then bombs fell. The cellar walls shook, the building shook. Plaster fell from the ceiling. Dust and sand was whirled around, stinging eyes and choking throats. It went on like this for ninety minutes until the all-clear sounded. The Ozannas returned to their apartment, collected their thoughts, and prayed before going to sleep.[68] Jürgen Illmer's family rushed to his uncle's house – he had built a concrete bunker in his garden with heavy iron blast doors. Before they got there, the sky was lit by 'Christmas trees', the bombers' marker flares. The shelter itself was shaken repeatedly by loud explosions, not Russian bombs but German 88mm flak batteries in nearby Birkenwäldchen. It lasted only half an hour. As the all-clear sounded, the Illmers stepped out of the bunker and saw "the bright glow of fire over our city". The oil tanks by the Oder were aflame, a handful of homes had been hit by bombs, but otherwise there was little damage and no one killed.[69]

Barely had the sirens abated than the loudspeaker columns spread around the city crackled and a tinny voice announced coldly:

> The civilian populace must evacuate every district of Breslau east of the Oder immediately. The Oder bridges in the city are being prepared for demolition by engineers. Every inhabitant in the eastern part of town must leave his house immediately and proceed on foot to the western side of the city where every step has been taken to prepare for their arrival.[70]

Every step had *not* been taken, and Breslau's Party leaders knew it. The head of Silesia's propaganda office nervously walked around his office in Charlottenstrasse. Barely a fortnight earlier, Dr Schulz had reported that the Führer's New Year speech had been a fillip to morale in the city. Now he questioned the decision of his masters. "What are we going to do with the people?" he asked his deputy, Carl Wichmann, adding: "How many are there actually?"

"A good two hundred thousand," Wichmann answered.

"*Ja*, Carl, and what are going to do with them?"

Wichmann shrugged his shoulder. "We can't do anything more. At such times, the fate of individuals does not matter," he added coldly.

That was something Schulz, a former officer in a panzer regiment, could not tolerate.

"But we can't let these people freeze outside, let those 200,000 go wild, half-starved when it's twenty below again."

"One thing you cannot be, not now, not ever, is weak," his deputy warned. Carl Wichmann still believed his own propaganda. The handful of Russian tanks in Oels were scouts, at least sixty miles ahead of the bulk of the Soviet forces. It would be weeks before the Red Army stood at the gates of Breslau. "By then," he smiled at Schulz, "by then our wonder weapons will have come into play."[71]

To Ulrich Frodien, the radio announcement had been both horrifying – and electrifying. "It suddenly dawned on me: here an entire city with more than one million inhabitants was beginning to die," Ulrich Frodien recalled. "A world was going under – my world, my home, and I was an eyewitness. I told myself that what was happening here now I would never be able to witness again in my entire life, that it would be in the history books and that I was there, a direct participant, if I survived." There was only one thing to do, the teenage soldier decided: *get out and see what is happening.*

In the small hours of 19 January he crossed the Oder and headed in the direction of the Jahrhunderthalle. At the Passbrücke, over the arm of the old river, he ran into a "long column of refugees" trying to reach the city centre. "In the bone-chilling cold children screamed for their families, old people collapsed," Frodien observed. "Hand carts and sledges became stuck in the snow. Many people were too exhausted and too distraught to cry out loud and – this was very eerie – the constantly-falling snow and the thick blanket of snow smothered all loud noises like a powerful muffler."[72]

In Rosenthal, just a couple of miles north of the city centre, former union official Otto Rothkugel helped his family pack, calmly but purposefully. His daughter and wife each had a bicycle and trailer. The latter were filled with whatever bedding, warm clothes and food they could hold – including two freshly-slaughtered turkeys.

Otto would not be accompanying his family. The forty-seven-year-old had been called up by the *Volkssturm*. He buried the supplies he would need to sustain him in a neighbour's cellar under a pile of sand. Next came tubs filled with clothes and underwear, valuable household items, plus the radio. It too was hidden, then more sand poured in until it filled the cellar. Rothkugel then bricked up the entrance. Just to make sure, he stuck several old barrels on top. "No stranger would be able to tell there was a cellar there," he declared proudly.[73]

Barely a mile away in the 'garden city' suburb of Karlowitz, thirteen-year-old Hans Eberhard Henkel's mother grabbed the family silverware, photographs, clothes and documents. "Children, we're going for a couple of days to the other side of the Oder," she assured her offspring. "Once things have cleared up, we'll come back." A few minutes later the Henkels and five other families stood in front of their block with suitcases and rucksacks. The women cried at the top of their voices.

The Henkels loaded their trunks on to a pram and began pushing it down Wichelhausallee, then across Hindenburgbrücke and into the heart of Breslau. "A torrent of people moved over the bridge, heavily laden, fleeing into the city," recalled Hans.

His friend Manfred, barely fifteen, parted company with the refugees. As a member of the *Hitlerjugend* he had to stay behind to defend Breslau.

The Henkel family was quartered in the huge, but spartanly furnished apartment of an *Ortsgruppenleiter*. They lay on mattresses in otherwise empty rooms. It would be their penultimate night in the city.[74]

Karl Hanke tried to appeal for calm. "A few Soviet tanks" had clashed with *Volkssturm* units on the Silesian border – and been repulsed. To be sure, some districts on the right bank of the Oder had been evacuated. "If the same steps are required in Breslau, the appropriate orders will be issued in good time," the *Gauleiter* assured the city's inhabitants. "Comrades! Maintain your calm and do not let careless chatterboxes and scurrilous gossipmongers make you nervous! Steps have been taken to ensure the safe return of Breslau's women and children, if evacuation becomes necessary."[75]

Saturday, 20 January barely dawned. An almost black layer of cloud hung over the city as heavy snow fell. The wind whistled through the streets of Breslau, driving the snow into huge piles in front of corner houses. It was, wrote police officer Otto Rogalla, "one of those days which gives the impression that God has washed his hands of this world."[76]

School had been cancelled for Horst Gleiss so he and his *Hitlerjugend* comrades could collect clothes for the *Volksopfer* collection. Instead, the fourteen-year-old went with his mother into the city centre to buy a winter coat. The Gleisses found the streets of Breslau filled with unending columns of farmers from the Silesian hinterland. Breslauers stared with disbelieving eyes at these refugees from Hünern – six miles from the city centre. From Ransern, also six miles from the centre. From Oswitz, just four miles away. The farmers drove their cattle, their sheep, their horses and other animals to the west. Panzers, anti-tank guns, armoured vehicles and infantry tried to make headway against them, moving eastwards.

Whatever the time of day, the schoolboy observed large crowds gathered in front of loudspeakers, hanging on every word of news which they sputtered out infrequently. Some time that afternoon, the announcer spoke once more. "Attention! Attention! Citizens of Breslau! . . . Women and children leave the city on foot in the direction of Opperau and Kanth . . ." Opperau lay five miles south-west of the city centre, Kanth ten miles beyond it. It was snowing. The temperature fluctuated between fifteen and twenty degrees below zero. For thousands, the order to evacuate Breslau would become a death sentence.[77]

Horst Gleiss stared through the windows of the family apartment in Benderplatz at the crowd of people in their thick winter coats, fur hats, earmuffs and sheepskin mittens, ignoring snow two feet deep and temperatures of twenty below, and huddling around the loudspeaker column. When the speaker urged them to flee towards Kanth, the group quickly dispersed. The fourteen-year-old was torn between feelings of pride and abject fear: pride at living through a historic moment in his country's history and fear that his fate was beyond his control. Above all, he realized that the war he had experienced – in the newspapers and newsreels – "was actually no experience of war at all." Now things would turn "deadly serious. There will be merciless murder here."[78]

Jürgen Illmer's mother telephoned the barracks to ask permission for fourteen-year-old Hans to leave the city with them. "Leave in this situation is impossible," the voice on the other end of the line coldly informed her, adding that fleeing the city would be regarded as desertion, punishable by death. Frau Illmer put the receiver down and turned to Hans. "Please, take off your uniform immediately. You're still a child and you're coming with us." He did. It was stuffed with some bed sheets in a large red canvas bag and left in the cellar.

As the Illmers packed, the doorbell rang. A neighbour wanted some razor blades so she could kill herself. For half an hour Frau Illmer pleaded with the woman to change her mind. In the end she walked away.

Young Jürgen crept into the dining room and grabbed the last packet of his favourite chocolate drink – "a reminder of better times and was brought out for birthdays and special rewards". There was still space for it in his small rucksack next to the various pairs of shoes shoved inside.

His brother Hans filled a leather suitcase with the family silver, plus bread, sausages, butter and a jar full of salt, while their mother put more food and cutlery in a large leather shopping bag.

After an hour's packing, the Illmers were ready to leave. With tears in their eyes, the family stepped out into the street in the dark. There were twenty inches of snow on the ground, it was twenty degrees below zero, and there was a solemn procession of people wandering down the road, their hoods pulled up, hauling hand carts and sledges.

The Illmers stopped briefly at a relative's house to bid farewell. "We're only leaving Breslau temporarily," Jürgen's mother comforted them. "In fourteen days the situation will have calmed down, then we'll see each other again." No one believed her.

They headed out into the streets once more, not for Kanth, but for Hartlieb on the southern edge of the city. Frau Illmer knew the stationmaster, but that proved of little use. Bells announced the approach of trains. Each time they rang, Jürgen and Hans got off the floor and stepped to the front of the platform where they jostled with the crowd, including three Lithuanians smoking Soviet-made Pappirossi cigarettes. "They were filled with a fear of the Russians," Jürgen recalled. "They said they'd rather lay their heads on the tracks than fall into Russian hands." No train stopped. They continued on their way to the Sudeten Mountains. So overcrowded were they that people squatted on the running boards of the freight wagons.[79]

After assisting refugees at the Freiburger Bahnhof, schoolgirl Ursula Scholz now faced the prospect of joining this exodus. She and her sister Margot filled home-made rucksacks with documents, clothes, a towel, a few small pots and a plate to eat from. They pulled the rest of their possessions – clothes and blankets crammed into a trunk – behind them on a sled. Having witnessed the scenes at the station, the Scholzes resolved to walk.[80]

Having waited unsuccessfully for a train, Hans Eberhard Henkel's mother decided the only solution was to make for Schweidnitz, thirty miles south of Breslau, on foot. "You will freeze," one woman admonished her. "Tanks will drive over you." Frau Henkel pressed on undeterred. "Come, children, we have a lucky star!"[81]

Luck came to the aid of Dr Theofil Peters. Peters had spent days at the Hauptbahnhof in vain. Now desperate, he headed to Party headquarters in the slender hope of obtaining a travel permit for his car. He was in luck. He bumped into a former patient from the Upper Silesian village of Pitschen, now a career Party man. "We Pitschen folk must stick together," he told Peters and handed him fuel and travel permits to allow the family to escape to Berlin.[82]

It was approaching midnight at Hartlieb station and still the Illmers were waiting. They were about to return home when the bells rang again. The family automatically rushed out on to the platform. But this time the train stopped. Four passenger carriages had been laid on for the people of Hartlieb. There was space for all those waiting – just. As the train got under way, recalled Jürgen, "we realized for the first time all that we had left behind". Only now did the tears truly flow. Jürgen sobbed over his electric train set, Hans over his fishing tackle. "Children, don't be sad," their mother told them. "Think about everything that I have left behind." The train eventually reached its destination, Schweidnitz. It too was overcrowded, but the stationmaster refused to open the first-class waiting room, convinced its fine furnishings would be ruined by the crowds.[83]

As the third week of January 1945 began, there were as many as 600,000 Germans struggling west through Silesia. There were ethnic Germans from Romania, the Ukraine, the Baltic, Bessarabia, who had come 'home to the Reich' in 1939 and resettled in Poland – at the expense of the native population, of course. There were the rural and urban populations of Silesia. There were wealthy farmers with their well-fed horses and fine wagons, loaded with beds, household goods, hay, straw. There were less affluent farmers with small gaunt horses pulling canvas-covered carts. Their families lay inside and shivered, despite the bedding and blankets. The farmers ran alongside the carts, their eyebrows and beards frozen, their horses covered with hoarfrost as thick as a finger. There were the ill and wounded from Breslau's hospitals, frogmarched down country roads, clinging to carts and supported by fellow patients. There were lengthy columns of Russian prisoners of war accompanied by armed escorts. In their ill-fitting, faded blue-grey prisoner suits, they shuffled along, hands in their pockets, some hauling sledges carrying the sick. There were *Landsers* hoping to slip away with the trek, hiding under the tarpaulin of a farmer's cart having discarded their weapons and uniforms. "*Ja*, there's one with us," refugees would admit when questioned by the military police checking refugee columns on the roads leading out of the city. The fate of the deserters was unequivocal – and brutal. Near the Hundsfelder Brücke the bodies of hanged soldiers swung in the cold wind with a cardboard sign around their necks: 'For cowardice in the face of the enemy.'[84] The *Bonzen* – Party big shots – also sought to hide among the refugees. On the Kanth road, Otto Rogalla stopped a senior Party figure dressed in civilian clothes and carrying two pigskin suitcases stuffed with winter clothing, jewellery and bundles of Reichsmarks. He shouted at the policeman, told him he had orders to go to Berlin – but could not produce them. "Then he tried the soft touch," Rogalla recalled, "offering me money and jewels." The bribe did not work. Otto Rogalla handed the *Bonze* over to the criminal police to take back to the city. "I had done my duty but I did not feel good about it," he admitted.[85]

The policeman stopped military vehicles and pleaded with their occupants to take women and children with them. Mothers beseeched soldiers: "Carry this for me, guide my child for me." Children screamed, farmer's wives begged anyone they met to give their horses and children shelter for a night. The exhausted, frozen beasts stumbled along, dragging heavily-loaded carts. Babies whimpered. A girl asked her mother: "*Mutti*, do we still have far to go?" Anyone who fell in the road was simply crushed by the crowd, by people trampling, by the wheels of carts. Mothers were frequently separated from their offspring in the throng. Women pushed prams and were delighted when their children finally fell silent, unaware that they had frozen to death, despite the pillows and blankets protecting them. Fritz Neugebauer peered into a pram pushed by a young mother from Trebnitz. "Dear madam, your child has lips which are completely blue. He could freeze to death," he warned her. "*Ach*, Jesus, I couldn't do anything," she sighed. Neugebauer touched the child. It did not move.[86]

Barely a day into the evacuation, there were more than fifty graves of children in the city's Südpark. There were many more on the country lanes outside Breslau. The ditches along the road to Liegnitz filled with frozen babies as well as suitcases, bedding, and clothes, while the corpses of forty small children were laid to rest on straw in the market square of Neumarkt. For the most part, the dead were simply left by the wayside. There was no time, nor means to bury them. Their fathers at the front had no idea that the snow was their only blanket. "None of them closed their eyes," secondary school teacher Lucia Kusche remembered. Occasionally, a corpse was covered by a piece of paper but that, thought Kusche, "was even more tragic because it was so squalid." Search parties were sent out to recover the dead. Sixteen-year-old *Bund Deutscher Mädel* girl Vera Eckle was collected by a *Volkssturm* man in an open truck filled with blankets. It headed down the road to Kanth, finally coming to a halt when the mass of people prevented any further progress. From the cab, Eckle stared at children stumbling along, weighed down by the layers of clothes keeping them warm; an elderly woman puffed and wheezed, an old man on crutches constantly slipped on the ice. "Get out, come on, get out girls, take the blankets with you and pick up the dolls!" the *Volkssturm* man yelled at the schoolgirl. She did. But which dolls? And then she stumbled over a bundle on the ground. Eckle picked it up – then dropped it immediately. "For God's sake, they're children, the corpses of children," she screamed and burst into tears. The *Volkssturm* soldier showed no compassion. "*Jawohl*, they're children which German women have tossed away to save their own skin," he snarled. "We can't allow our leader to see this so gather them up as quickly as possible." The burial parties were simply overwhelmed by the task facing them. There were too many corpses for the trucks to carry; 400 dead children and adults were found along a single short stretch of road.[87]

Breslauers gave this exodus a chilling name: the Kanth death march. Of the 60,000 people who responded to the instructions to leave the city, perhaps 18,000 died. It is not figures which have the power to convey the horrors of this trek, but the plight of the individual. Housewife Frau Hanisch had dutifully left her home city with four-month-old daughter Gabi. Now she lay in the hall of a makeshift hospital somewhere south-west of Breslau, writing the bitterest letter of her life, trying to explain to her mother how her daughter had died.

She had wrapped Gabi in two blankets, before slinging the most vital items, including powdered milk and a bottle, in a rucksack, then struck out into the night. In the suburbs, the women grouped together while Party officials drove up and down the streets in loudspeaker vans urging people to flee the city. Occasionally, cars stopped and took a handful of people with them. Most were not so fortunate. The refugees skidded and slipped on the ice. Those with prams often abandoned them because they would not move. Soon they began to toss their luggage into the roadside ditches, unable to carry it any more as the snow fell heavily.

And then the first dead children appeared, some in the ditches, some laid out in the market squares of Silesian hamlets. Women sat in front of the houses, trying to rest. Frau Hanisch banged on the doors of several homes, hoping to warm up some milk. No answer. She gave up and sat down in the snow, watching this endless column of women trudge past for half an hour. And then on to the next village. "I counted the trees along the avenue, hauling myself from tree to tree," she wrote.

> Possessions thrown away simply lay in the middle of the road. Women sat on their sledges, wanting to rest. The cold always drove them on, however, until they simply stayed sitting on them and perhaps froze to death with their children. I saw many who sat there with their back resting on a tree. Sometimes larger children stood next to them crying. Motherly love is surely the greatest love. However strong any love might be, we are but weak creatures in the end.

It was beginning to grow light as Frau Hanisch approached Kanth. After two hours of crying, her daughter had finally fallen silent. Her mother began to bang on the doors in the hope once more of warming some milk. Other mothers hurled snowballs at windows. No doors opened. "They will get their just dessert for their hard-heartedness," Frau Hanisch wrote bitterly. The milk in her baby's bottle had frozen. She resorted to breast feeding, but her daughter was not interested. Despite the continuous icy wind, she continued towards Kanth, down a road lined with the corpses of children.

Finally she found a house still occupied and rushed inside. She unwrapped Gabi from her blankets. The baby was silent. A woman standing next to her said simply: "She's dead." Hanisch wrote:

> I do not know what I can still say, dear mother, but now everything is so different

from what it was like before – even with this tragedy. I could not cry over Gabi any longer. But nor did I want to leave her behind. I continued with her.

She carried her dead daughter until her frostbitten arm could stand it no longer, then wrapped the corpse in blankets and buried her deep in the snow somewhere beyond Kanth. "Gabi was not alone there," she wrote to her mother. Eventually soldiers in a car took pity Frau Hanisch and took her to a temporary hospital. There she was surrounded by fellow Breslauers, many struck down with pneumonia. There were mothers suffering from ulcers and frozen chests having tried to breastfeed their babies on the way, a handful hallucinated about Breslau, about their husbands, about their children. One of Frau Hanisch's neighbours lay in the middle of the road; all three of her children had died on the march.[88]

The scenes in Breslau's stations – the Hauptbahnhof and Freiburger Bahnhof especially – were no less distressing. People abandoned their last possessions in the hope of saving their skins. Beds, prams, carts, suitcases packed with belongings were piled up in mountains. Mothers weighed down by luggage often lost their children in the crowd. Station staff would try to call out the names of the missing above the hubbub. Sometimes they reunited mother and child, more often than not they failed. Pregnant women gave birth prematurely because of the fear and anxiety of flight. In the rush to get on trains at the Hauptbahnhof, sixty to seventy children were crushed to death or trampled. Lena Aschner noticed a woman curled up in a corner of the central station. Two children stood in front of her, crying, stroking her hand and face. The youngsters were shaking with cold after four days on the road, did not know where they were, and now their mother was sick. She foamed at her bloodless blue lips, her head slumped against the wall. Aschner carried her to a neighbour's house until she warmed up, while the children received a little food. The next day, with the mother recovered, the family were taken to the Freiburger Bahnhof and put on a train. To where, no one knew. "I'm just glad to get away from this hell!" the mother cried from the window as the train pulled away. Ursel Dittman found a "real hotchpotch of humanity" on the platform of a goods station. The twenty-nine-year-old had packed two suitcases, one with food including the geese the family had been given as payment at their hotel, one with papers and documents, plus a little bedding and underwear. Her mother put on a black Persian lamb coat, Ursel a coat of canine fur dyed to look like brown mink. Underneath were jackets and sweaters to keep the cold at bay. At the station were mothers with babies, some newborn, others a few weeks old, plus hospital patients hobbling around on crutches, a few with broken limbs, some almost delirious. A hospital train pulled in and the Dittmans grabbed the first seats they could find, next to two middle-aged ladies, a younger woman and an elderly lady who looked as if she'd already lost her mind. For several hours, the train sat in the station before finally setting off – the position of the sun assured the anxious passengers it was moving west. At times it travelled so slowly that people stepped off in the dark, convinced it had stopped, among them the distraught elderly woman.[89]

This, of course, was not what the rest of the Reich learned of the mass flight from Silesia's capital. "If you believe that there's mood of disaster or panic in Breslau, then take another look around now," the *Völkischer Beobachter* reassured its readers. "In three days, Breslau evacuated many thousands of people – only women and children – an achievement of which the Party, authorities, as well as the *Reichsbahn* and the deputy for local traffic at the *Oberpräsidenten* can be proud." State radio, meanwhile, described how "women and children marched in columns towards safety." It was too much for one Breslauer, who immediately penned a letter to the *Reichsrundfunk* – anonymously. "Just now we have listened to reports from Silesia and Breslau," he complained. "It's a long time since we heard such a god-damned pack of lies."[90]

Faced with death on the snow-covered country lanes of Silesia, many Breslauers resolved to stay in their native city. Having packed to flee, Ursula Scholz was stopped by her mother, who was convinced she did not have the strength to withstand the trek. Some Breslauers feared their homes would be raided if they left. Others openly welcomed the prospect of the Soviet invasion, convinced the Russians would treat them fairly "because they are good Communists."[91] Others still chose another way out of their predicament. Climbing the stairs to the family's third-floor apartment, Ulrich Frodien noticed the door to the flat below, owned by a popular doctor, was ajar. Frodien nervously pressed the doorbell. No one stirred. He went inside and called out. No answer. As he walked into the surgery, the eighteen-year-old was confronted by the sight of the elderly doctor's contorted body lying on top of a desk. On the patients' couch, her eyes rigid and wide open, her face distorted, lay the doctor's aged housekeeper. "They must have been dead for some time already because the smell in the room, heated by the still-warm oven, was so foul that I turned around on my heels and closed all the doors behind me," Frodien recalled. "I had seen and experienced enough at the front, but these corpses right next door, in my home, upset me."[92]

The teenage soldier rushed upstairs, fearing his father might have done the same. Instead, Herr Frodien stood in his bedroom, trying on the staff surgeon's uniform he had not worn since the campaign in Poland. He sat down on the edge of the bed with his son and outlined their plan of escape: he would march into the office of the hospital and demand orders to take recovering soldiers, like his son, to another hospital – outside the city. Only with such an order could they leave Breslau. "It was an extremely daring plan," his son remembered, "but it was also a game of *va banque*." His father possessed no papers, no service record, no pay book, not even a dog tag. It was a plan based entirely on bluff. "My father fastened his belt and put his medals on his chest – he served as a front-line soldier in World War I from the age of fifteen to nineteen," his son wrote. "I was very impressed." Hopefully so too would be the *Feldwebel* in the hospital office.

And so Herr Frodien made for the hospital; his son headed into the city seeking a way out of Breslau:

> We did not know whether we would meet again in three hours time as planned.
> It was one of those unreal situations when you would like to speak to express

our affection, gratitude and hope to each other, things which as men we could simply not express given the way we were brought up then, and when a gesture tries to replace words. My father thrust his pistol into my hand and said: 'Take it for the worst case.'[93]

It took two days and nights for Ursel Dittmann to reach Dresden – normally a 150-mile journey of only four hours. The train continued west, but not the Dittmans. They stepped off at Dresden's high-vaulted central station where they found "a milling crowd of nationalities" and a Red Cross soup kitchen handing out broth, bread, coffee and milk.[94]

The Frodiens had decided to leave the city by the Hauptbahnhof. Father and son packed two rucksacks and an old sailor's bag with a few personal belongings. Everything else was left behind. For Ulrich that was no hardship, but his father's face turned to stone. He had settled in Breslau in 1921 "without a pfennig to his name" and spent the next quarter of a century building a new life as a successful doctor. It had all been in vain.

For the last time, the Frodiens passed through their large apartment, through the surgery with its still gleaming medical instruments, then down the stairs where there was a lingering smell of decomposition and out into the Strasse der SA. "Start forgetting right now that I'm your father!" Herr Frodien admonished his son. "From now on you will address me as '*Herr Stabsarzt*', and don't forget to stand to attention when you do." If the Frodiens were discovered as father and son "we'd both be hung from the nearest tree." But at that moment, all Ulrich could do was laugh. "*Jawohl, Herr Stabsarzt!*"

Hans Eberhard Henkel and his family spent three nights on the road: the first on an estate with numerous farming families, the second in a village kindergarten, well stocked with toys, the third with a friend of young Hans in Rogau-Rosenau in the shadow of the Zobten mountain.

War had yet to touch this village. The Henkels breakfasted on fresh bread, butter and warm milk, then caught a scheduled train to Schweidnitz. There, Hans observed, "people didn't seem to appreciate the impending chaos". Shops opened as normal, smart soldiers from the garrison marched through the streets. "It seemed that Breslau was located in a different world," he recalled. "Perhaps it was also the famous lull before the great storm."[95]

By now, the first refugees were beginning to pass through the city of Görlitz, on the western extremity of Silesia. Whatever Nazi propaganda assured or promised, *Hauptmann* Arthur Mrongovius realized an unimaginable catastrophe had befallen his beloved land. "So now places which I have come to love and cherish during my lengthy spell in Silesia are already under threat," he observed. "For almost 150 years no enemy has set foot on this soil. The enemy inherits a rich heritage." Now, he concluded, was "not the time to be faint-hearted!"[96]

Eleven wounded soldiers, including Ulrich Frodien, hobbled and staggered to the Hauptbahnhof. The evacuation of the city was now in its fifth day, but still there was a vast crowd seeking salvation. On the forecourt mountains of luggage were piled up, prams, hand carts, bags, baskets, sledges, household goods tied together with string and rope. The strong pushed the weak aside. Police, soldiers and railway officials tried to maintain order, but Breslauers were no longer prepared to follow instructions. Some fought or struggled, most ignored the announcements which the loudspeakers occasionally spluttered out. Not that anyone heard them, for above everything was an awful cacophony.

> It was like a loud groan, made up the moaning and whimpering of completely overburdened and desperate people, the screaming of children, the crying of babies, the shouts of distraught mothers who had lost their children in the chaos and whose cries became ever louder the less chance there was of finding their children again.

Half a century later, Ulrich Frodien still heard this terrible din in his nightmares.

When a hospital train pulled into the station, his father stood in front of his 'men', then with a slight smile ordered: "Fall in, pick up your luggage, single file, by the right, march." Eleven *Landsers* hobbled and limped behind 'their' *Stabsarzt*, who showed the travel permit to the military police. The men were allowed to pass, then they quickly disappeared inside the train. Frodien's father was still in character: "*Gefreiter*, kindly take notice – your rucksack is not properly tied up." But then the doctor whispered: "Now just keep your mouth shut. Everything's worked wonderfully. None of those swine asked me for identification. Long live Prussian military efficiency." The doctor headed to the first-class compartment. The men found themselves in a carriage filled with sick men, beds stacked one on top of the next. The train was well heated but, Frodien remembered, "the stench of pus, shit, blood, urine took your breath away." Otherwise, the wounded were provided for admirably. There was a laundry, a galley with a seemingly endless supply of pea and bacon soup, a dedicated water supply, a carriage which served as a makeshift operating theatre, a pharmacy, medics and nurses. Badly injured soldiers groaned loudly, but death to most came quietly. Barely had a man expired than the nurses carried away the corpse and changed the bed linen ready for the next patient. The train made its way laboriously through Silesia. As it passed through stations, Frodien noted their names: Kamenz, forty-eight miles from Breslau; Glatz, fifty-five miles; Mittenwalde, seventy-five miles away. The destination was Regensburg in Bavaria. "What," he wondered, "will the future bring?"[97]

Notes

1. Dragunski, p.214.
2. Dippel, p.14.
3. Polewoi, p.105.
4. Ibid., pp.105-6.
5. Kempowski, *Das Echolot*, i, p.10.
6. Duffy, p.68.
7. Dippel, pp.14-15.
8. Dragunski, pp.215-17.
9. Dippel, p.15.
10. Schimmel-Falkenau, pp.120-1 and OKW Communiqué, 12/1/45.
11. TB Goebbels, 13/1/45.
12. Hartmann, *Zwischen Nichts und Niemandsland*, pp.601-2 and Dragunski, p.217.
13. Hartmann, *Zwischen Nichts und Niemandsland*, pp.601-2.
14. Dragunski, pp.220-1.
15. Hartmann, *Zwischen Nichts und Niemandsland*, pp.603-4.
16. Arnhold, pp.15-16.
17. Hartmann, *Zwischen Nichts und Niemandsland*, pp.604-5.
18. Arnhold, pp.17-19.
19. Based on Echolot, i, p.150 and *Die Grosse Flucht*, ZDF documentary, 2001, Episode 3, 'Festung Breslau'.
20. Documenty Nr.4 and Gleiss, i, p.100D.
21. Echolot, i, pp.236-7.
22. Arnhold, pp.17-19, 26-31.
23. Ibid., pp.17-19, 26-32.
24. OKW Communiqué, 14/1/45.
25. Frodien, pp.97-8.
26. Echolot, i, p.242.
27. Hinze, *19 Infanterie und Panzer Division*, pp.793-4.
28. Gleiss, vii, p.582.
29. Ahlfen, p.52.
30. Asmus, ix, p.41-2.
31. Paul, *Endkampf*, pp.56-7.
32. Asmus, ix, pp.41-2.
33. Arnhold, pp.59-70.
34. TB Goebbels, 15 and 17/1/45.
35. Rudel, pp.160-2.
36. Echolot, i, pp.574-5.
37. *Pravda*, 17/1/45.
38. Rogall, pp.47-8.
39. TB Goebbels, 20/1/45, Schenk, p.359 and Hargreaves, *Blitzkrieg Unleashed*, pp.271, 274.
40. Dollinger, p.288.
41. Scherstjanoi, p.296.
42. Knopp, *Grosse Flucht*, p.163.
43. Gleiss, i, pp.362-3.
44. Polewoi, pp.150-2.
45. Schwarz, p.36.
46. Knopp, *Grosse Flucht*, p.163.
47. Echolot, i, pp.468-70.
48. Gleiss, ix, p.56.
49. Waage, pp.11-12.
50 Hartmann, *Zwischen Nichts und Niemandsland*, pp.610-11.

51. TB Goebbels, 20/1/45 and Schenk, p.360.
52. Echolot, i, pp.463-4.
53. Rogall, pp.48-9.
54. Echolot, i, pp.667-70.
55. TB Goebbels, 15/1/45.
56. Rogall, pp.208, 210-11, 213.
57. Based on *So Kämpfte Breslau*, p.19, Gleiss, vii, pp.83, 102 and Becker, p.86.
58. Ozanna, pp.166-8.
59. Frodien, pp.114-16.
60. Ruhlemann, pp.436-7.
61. *So Kämpfte Breslau*, p.90.
62. Hartung, p.52.
63. Echolot, ii, pp.569-71.
64. Van Aaken, p.159.
65. Peikert, pp.25-7.
66. Echolot, i, p.799.
67. Frodien, pp.116-17, 122-3.
68. Ozanna, pp.166-8.
69. Echolot, i, pp.657-8.
70. Frodien, p.118.
71. Schimmel-Falkenau, p.163.
72. Frodien, pp.118-19.
73. Gleiss, i, p.208.
74. Henkel, pp.11-12.
75. *Schlesische Tageszeitung*, 20/1/45.
76. Van Aaken, p.189.
77. Gleiss, i, pp.204, 215.
78. Gleiss, i, p.218.
79. Echolot, i, pp.799-802.
80. Waage, p.12.
81. Henkel, p.13.
82. Echolot, i, p.805.
83. Ibid., i, pp.799-802.
84. Neugebauer, pp.9-11.
85. Van Aaken, pp.189-91.
86. Based on Neugebauer, pp.9-10 and Echolot, ii, pp.103-4.
87. Based on Grieger, pp.7-8, Becker, p.106, Knopp, *Grosse Flucht*, pp.161-2 and Peikert, p.31.
88. Becker, pp.107-10.
89. Based on Becker, pp.104-05, Peikert, p.30, Echolot, i, pp.798-9 and Dittman, pp.5-7.
90. Based on *Völkischer Beobachter*, Munich edition, 29/1/45, NA FO898/187, p.226 and Haack, pp.23-4.
91. Becker, p.105.
92. Frodien, pp.128-9.
93. Frodien, pp.129-31, 132, 138.
94. Dittman,pp.5-7.
95. Henkel, pp.13-14.
96. Echolot, ii, pp.82-3.
97. Frodien, pp.140-54.

CHAPTER 4

The Reckoning Has Begun

So much inhumanity everywhere, senseless inhumanity
Captain Grigori Klimov

S ome time on Sunday, 21 January bill posters began to appear on advertising
columns across Breslau. Their message would soon be repeated in its newspaper
and over the wire radio.

Men of Breslau

Our *Gau* capital has been declared a fortress. The evacuation of women and
children from the city is under way and will soon be completed. Everything
possible will be done to care for women and children!

Our task as men is to do everything which is necessary to support the troops
fighting. I call upon the men of Breslau to join the defence of our fortress. The
fortress will be defended to the last.

Who cannot bear arms must use all his strength to help with public services,
with supplies, with maintaining order.

Men of the Lower Silesian *Volkssturm* who successfully fought against
Bolshevik tanks on the edge of our *Gau* have shown that they are prepared to
defend our home to the last. We will be no less ready.

Hanke[1]

Henceforth the city would never be simply Breslau, always *Festung* Breslau. One by
one, the towns and cities on the Eastern Front were also declared fortresses –
Königsberg, Poznań, Schneidemühl, Danzig, Küstrin, Frankfurt. They would fulfil
the role of fortresses of old: surrounded, they would tie down enemy forces, hindering
the Russian thrust westwards. They would hold out until relieved. Except that no
Festung had ever been relieved. All had fallen. Karl Hanke had signed Breslau's death
warrant.

Breslau in January 1945 was a fortress in name only. It had not been a bulwark for more
than a century, since Napoleon tore down the city walls. "Breslau is no fortress," Red
Cross volunteer Lena Aschner commented. "It is lost. Everyone knows it. The people,

86

the Wehrmacht and the SS." A Party diehard disagreed. "We must sell our lives as dearly as possible," he admonished Aschner.[2]

And so in the third week of January 1945, Karl Hanke and his fortress commander began summoning what forces they could. The *Gauleiter* drafted every male Breslauer aged sixteen to sixty into the *Volkssturm*. Johannes Krause went even further, demanding *every* inhabitant of the city aged ten and above help "the final preparations for the battle for your home city". Those final preparations meant gnawing at the very vitals of Breslau. Trees were felled, bushes pulled up, rubble, monuments, wrecked vehicles, overturned trams piled up, barbed wire laid across streets to form makeshift barriers. "Even the dead have no peace in their graves," electrician Hermann Nowack noted as gravestones were uprooted to feed the barricade moloch. "It's one of those tragicomedies – these barricades actually hinder our movements more than they put a stop to the Soviets," wrote schoolboy Horst Gleiss. On the right bank of the Oder trams went no further than the Scheitniger Stern. Beyond there, Breslauers needed special passes – and a good deal of agility – to negotiate the forest of fallen trees blocking the streets. Tarmac and paving slabs were ripped up so foxholes five feet deep could be dug for soldiers and *Volkssturm* to combat Russian tanks with *Panzerfaust*. "Russian tank crews will need just fifteen minutes to get past such a barrier," one *Landser* sneered. "Fourteen minutes to stop their belly laughs, one minute to push the junk away." All sixty-four bridges over the Oder and its tributary, the Weide, were prepared for demolition, their approaches mined. Slogans were daubed on the walls at every street corner: 'Every house a fortress', 'If you retreat, death will march towards your home', 'Today the front is everywhere – fight against the cursed spirit in the rear'. [3]

Across Breslau, across Lower Silesia, forces began to muster to defend the *Gau* capital. *Unteroffizier* Hans Gottwald and his Grenadier Regiment 51 comrades were enjoying an evening at the cinema in Liegnitz, forty miles west of Breslau, when the film was interrupted and the men were ordered to return to barracks. By morning, the regiment was rolling towards Breslau against a tide of refugees, the sound of weeping children the only noise coming from the columns. The army trucks bumped down dirt tracks, finally coming to a stop in the suburb of Opperau, five miles from the heart of Breslau. Here there was more noise – from carts being packed, from stables being emptied, from yet more weeping children. The soldiers tried to offer the inhabitants reassurance. "You'll be back home again in a couple of weeks!" they called out. Stony, disbelieving faces stared back at them. Hitler Youth Manfred Preussner and his comrades were dropped off at a school in an open truck where they received Wehrmacht uniforms and weapons. Preussner was delighted. "Finally what we'd dreamed about since childhood had come true," he wrote happily. "We were proper soldiers at the age of sixteen."[4]

Every day new *Volkssturm* were sworn in – and almost every day Karl Hanke addressed them, sometimes in a square, sometimes in a courtyard, sometimes on Schlossplatz, sometimes as many as 2,000 at a time. His watchword? "Harm the enemy wherever possible!" The enemy was on foreign soil, men in the *Volkssturm* knew "every

nook and cranny" of Breslau and its suburbs. "Use each night to creep up on the enemy
and harm him!" the *Gauleiter* urged, invoking the memory of Erwin Rommel by
repeating the late field marshal's battle cry. "*Meine Herren*, there is no shame in dying
for Greater Germany. Attack!" The freshly sworn-in soldiers would shout a few '*Sieg
Heils*' for their Führer, sing the national anthem, then march off to the front.[5] Among
them was Otto Rothkugel. Having seen his family leave the city, the retired union official
reported to his *Volkssturm* company. An aged Italian rifle was thrust into his hands, plus
ten rounds of ammunition. There was no instruction, no order. The company, Rothkugel
observed, was "a shapeless mass. Everything looked so disorganised. And on the
opposite bank of the Oder were the Russians."[6]

Except that by now, the Russians were also on the left bank of the river. They had tried
to force it on 21 January near the small village of Gross Döbern, forty miles upstream
of the Silesian capital. Schoolboy Josef Wszyk watched Soviet troops trying to build a
pontoon bridge across the Oder outside the village of Gross Döbern. It was almost
complete when German planes appeared and bombed it. Fresh bridging equipment was
brought up. The Luftwaffe attacked again. "This was repeated until the Oder turned red
with blood and carried thousands of dead Russians in the direction of Breslau," Wszyk
remembered.[7]

The Red Army proved more successful downstream. On the night of 22 January, VI
Guards Mechanized Corps crossed the Oder at Steinau, forty miles from Breslau. The
crossing caught the Germans unaware. A steamer chugged down the river from Breslau
ferrying supplies. As it approached Steinau, Russian tanks opened fire. The steamer
sank within three minutes. Still the Germans were none the wiser. A couple of hours
later another vessel appeared. It suffered the same fate.[8]

There was no continuous front around Breslau this third week of January – Russian
or German. Soviet spearheads may have reached, even crossed, the Oder, but the bulk
of the 1st Ukrainian Front was still spread across huge tracts of Upper and Lower
Silesia. Ivan Konev's thrust towards the regional capital was inexorable. On 21
January his troops stormed historic Kreuzberg, sixty miles east of Breslau. As two
intelligence officers rifled through the home of the *Kreisleiter*, searching for important
Party documents, the telephone rang. "Is that you, Franz?" a gruff voice asked.
"Where the hell have you been? I've been calling you since early morning. You should
have at least left someone manning the phone." One of the Russian officers answered
in German. "Are you drunk, Franz?" said the voice. "Or have you lost your mind?
The Ivans are attacking and are already approaching your town. And you're bumbling
around God knows where." The voice was that of Karl Hanke.[9] That same afternoon,
Russian artillery began shelling Namslau, thirty-five miles from Breslau. The next
day, Luftwaffe ground crew blew up more than a hundred unserviceable aircraft in
Oels, a mere eighteen miles from the Silesian capital.[10] The town itself was "eerily
quiet" *Major* Günther Tenschert noticed. "There were a few fires flickering, but the
black night hung like a black ribbon over everything." Tenschert, commanding a
scratch unit of convalescing Eastern Front veterans, fell back through Oels just in

time. Twenty-four hours later, 269th Infantry Division also had to pass through Oels – but they had to fight their way through; the Russians had encircled the town. The men found the airfield ablaze. They grabbed anything white they could find – curtains, sheets, even a chemist's overalls – and threw it over their *feldgrau* jackets to camouflage themselves. "The glow of fire and flares light up the narrow gap which we're breaking through individually or in small groups," wrote the 269th's Kurt Awe. Tiger tanks held the gap open while furious anti-tank and machine-gun fire from both sides dissected the field. A couple of officers sat on a wall, pointing the way to safety for their men. At least one panzer was hit and towed off the battlefield. As for the men, those who reached a plain beyond the airfield were loaded on to trucks and driven away under shell fire.[11]

It was almost midnight on 24 January by the time Oels was in the hands of the *frontoviki* of Fifty-Second Army. Soviet accounts say the small town was "liberated". German accounts speak only of the suffering of Oels' inhabitants. Entire streets were razed. The town hall, the fourteenth-century Propstkirche, the Catholic church, the meeting hall, the high school, all were burned.[12] The people of Oels fared no better than their bricks and mortar. Thirteen men, women and children were found murdered in the house of a leading local Nazi, while one elderly inhabitant found the corpse of his wife in the cellar. "She'd been raped with her clothes tied together over her head."[13]

The rape, plunder, murder and arson were repeated across Silesia. Oels was the rule, not the exception. Looters rampaged through the village of Albrechtsau, ancestral home of one of Prussia's great military dynasties, the Blüchers. They smashed any statues of the family, forced their way into the field marshal's tomb and scattered his remains around the village; his head was never recovered. Another vault next to the Blüchers' tomb was also raided and a mummified woman dragged out. The shroud was removed and the naked figure was left standing in full view.[14] The historic heart of Kreuzberg was burned down: the Ring, the railway station, the pharmacy, its chemicals exploding, the homes of Party officials.[15] German stragglers passing through the village of Freyhan in the wake of the Russian advance came across the bodies of an elderly couple in front of one of the many smashed, looted houses. "The man had been shot four times in the head," an officer wrote. "He had clearly wanted to stop his wife being raped. Both perhaps hoped that things would not be so bad and so had not fled. Now they lay there with heartbroken eyes which captured the horror of the final moments of their lives."[16] A dozen miles from Breslau, the villagers of Jungfernsee endured "days and nights only imaginable in hell," their Catholic priest recalled. His church was ransacked, his clothes scattered around the vestry, trampled on and covered in dirt. As for the rest of the village, "the doors had been kicked in and hung off their hinges, each room was in such a chaotic state that it brought tears to your eyes. Everything turned upside down, smashed, crushed, ripped to shreds. There are no words to describe the devastation". The priest found two women hiding in a stable and vowed to take them under his wing. The house of God offered no protection; one night four drunken Russians burst into his vicarage, and thrashed the priest and two women he was sheltering.[17] In Gerlanden, a small village south-east of the Silesian capital, soldiers

searching for quarters found a young woman dead in a farmhouse, lying naked on
mattresses. Her breasts had been sliced off. Knitting needles were sticking out of her
windpipe.[18] Kanth, to where 60,000 Breslauers had fled only days before, also
succumbed to the relentless Red Army advance. When it fell, the Russians "acted like
out-and-out beasts," one forty-year-old housewife later testified. "We suffered as if we
were in hell." That first night she was raped a dozen times. "I kept wanting to hang
myself but I did not have the chance because Russians constantly came in and out of
the house." The priest was killed trying to protect seven elderly nuns. A factory owner
was shot dead, a post office employee locked in a cellar and left to starve. Some of
Kanth's women were eventually transferred to a Soviet field hospital where they were
assaulted "by one bandit after the next". One young girl was raped and beaten until
her innards were hanging out "in front and behind". She died. The housewife took ten
sleeping pills to end her misery, only to wake up three days later.[19]

    None of this should have happened. The *frontovik* marched on to German soil with
unequivocal orders not to rape, not to plunder, not to burn or loot. But as he did so, he
passed signs by the roadside: 'Red Army Soldier: you are now on German soil: the hour
of revenge has struck'; 'Here is damned Germany'; 'Soldier: you are in Germany. Take
revenge on the Hitlerites.'[20] He read the words of Ilya Ehrenburg. *Nastala rasplata* –
the reckoning has begun – he proclaimed in *Red Star*:

> We forget nothing. We march through Pomerania but before our eyes is
> destroyed, bleeding White Russia. Now we want to bring that pungent smell of
> burning, which seeped into our soldier's coats at Smolensk and Orel, to Berlin.
> In front of Königsberg, Breslau and Schneidemühl we think about the ruins of
> Voronezh and Stalingrad. Soldiers of the Red Army who are now attacking
> Germany's cities will not forget how mothers in Leningrad carried their dead
> children away on small sledges. Berlin has still not paid for the torture of
> Leningrad.[21]

The *frontovik* had seen his motherland despoiled, he had seen the towns and villages
of the Ukraine and White Russia razed. "We had seen so much destruction, so many
corpses," recalled Semyon Sipernyak, advancing on Breslau. "And so we were angry
with the Germans. Some were filled with hate, others less so. Some had lost their father
or their mother, others only distant relatives. Some had more reason to hate, others
less."[22] And so to many Red Army soldiers, what happened to the people of Silesia was
not revenge, it was justice. "You cannot imagine the deep satisfaction which our
soldiers and officers feel, regardless of their rank or education," veteran soldier Sergei
Grebenik assured his family in the Ukraine. "The Germans will now suffer all the same
misery which they inflicted upon us in 1941."[23] The fascist hordes, one infantryman
gleefully wrote home, "will turn to ash and we will carve the names of those whose
blood was spilled for the good of mankind on the remains of Hitler's lair."[24] Another
frontovik told his family enthusiastically: "We warriors of the Red Army, sons of the
Soviet Union, are now telling German hangmen that they have sung their little song to

the end and the day when the Red Army raises the victory banner over Berlin is not far off."[25]

And this *was* a just cause. This was a war of liberation. "Everywhere we run into Poles and Russians returning from slavery," one Red Army war correspondent wrote to a friend. "They tell terrible stories."[26] A torrent of people and nations streamed east. Public buildings were opened as makeshift quarters. Guards and traffic police tried to persuade these refugees – Russians, Ukrainians, Danes, Czechs, Slovaks, Serbs – to wait a few days. "Attempts were made in every tongue," *Pravda* correspondent Boris Polevoy wrote. "Railway traffic would resume in a few days and they would be carried home." But no. They headed home on foot. "Their desire to put places connected with so many terrible memories behind them was stronger than reason," the journalist noted. "With rucksacks on their backs they moved along their road, meeting troops on the way, waving cheerfully at them and sometimes even singing."[27] Many liberated Russians, one of Konev's staff reported, "expressed the wish to join the ranks of the Red Army so they could take revenge for their ill-treatment at the hands of the Germans."[28] Some were even afforded the opportunity to do so – courtesy of Karl Hanke. Around 6,000 Russian prisoners of war had been moved out of the camps supporting the Krupp works at Markstädt, bound for Strehlen, two dozen miles south of Breslau. They never got there. Hanke ordered the prisoners turned around and marched back to Markstädt. They never got there either. They were liberated by their Red Army comrades. Fed and re-armed, they joined the battle for Breslau.[29] The 3,000 inmates of the camps serving the chemical weapons laboratories at Dyhernfurth on the Oder were less fortunate. In driving snow they were force-marched towards Gross Rosen concentration camp west of Breslau. Their fate remains uncertain. Some say they were liberated by Soviet troops, others claim that two out of three were either shot or died on the journey. Those left behind in Dyhernfurth were shot, while any fair-minded Germans who tried to offer the prisoners food or medicine were either turned away or, in the case of two people, butchered by local Nazis.[30] Perhaps as many 2,000 prisoners died on the march from Dyhernfurth – a terrible toll, albeit one dwarfed by Auschwitz. From 18 January the roads of Silesia began to fill with columns of prisoners as the camp complex was emptied. Healthy – or rather *healthier* – inmates marched west, the young, the elderly, the infirm were left behind, their guards with instructions to kill them. In all, perhaps 60,000 prisoners were sent west, their destination Gross Rosen. As many as one in four died on the way. SS *Obersturmbannführer* Rudolf HTss was sent to Auschwitz to oversee the death camp's evacuation. HTss struggled eastwards through Silesia against a torrent of refugees. He never got to Auschwitz. He never got to the right bank of the Oder. He did, however, find the tortured souls of the death camp, "stumbling columns of corpses" on the Silesian roads and country lanes. No provision had been made for the inmates on this death march. There was no food, no shelter – the public buildings were filled with civilian refugees fleeing the Red Army. Instead, the corpses of shot prisoners – executed by their SS guards when they could march no further – littered the roads every few hundred yards. When his staff car stopped next to one cadaver, he heard a pistol shot. "I ran towards the sound, and saw a soldier in the act of stopping his motor cycle and shooting a prisoner leaning against a tree," he wrote. "I shouted at him, asking him what he though he was doing, and what harm the prisoner had done him. He laughed impertinently in my face, and asked me what I proposed to do about it. I drew my pistol and shot him." It wasn't the death of the prisoner which haunted Rudolf Höss – some one million people, almost all of them Jews, had been exterminated at Auschwitz under the SS officer's command. It was the disintegration of order, the loss of slave labour which might prop up the tottering Third Reich economy for a few more weeks.

Gross Rosen was "crammed to overflowing". Höss sent any prisoners who arrived by train westwards. A few scraps of food were tossed their way. "Dead SS men lay peacefully in the open cars between dead prisoners," the *Obersturmbannführer* recalled. "Those still alive sat on top of them, chewing their piece of bread. Terrible scenes, best not described." It was time, Rudolf Höss decided, to put a stop to the evacuations. He headed for Breslau and the regional SS commander, Ernst-Heinrich Schmauser. Schmauser merely handed Höss a message from Heinrich Himmler: not a single healthy prisoner should remain in any concentration camp in Silesia.[31]

Himmler's orders were not carried out to the letter. When Konev's troops liberated the Auschwitz complex on January 27, they found nearly 350,000 men's suits and more than 800,000 items of women's clothing. They also found almost 8,000 men, women and children alive. Boris Polevoy made his way through a group of about 200 men "all wearing the same canvas jackets, striped trousers, peakless caps and wooden-soled plimsolls". They were, the journalist observed, "wretched, a pale green, yet with a bashful, disbelieving smile etched on their emaciated faces". One of them broke ranks and dashed into a field, grabbed a handful of snow and put it in his mouth. Several others followed his example. Others slid down a narrow, icy gutter. When the first one slid and fell over, those following rolled over him. Liberation had brought out the child in these grown men, Polevoy realized. "Everyone laughed, happy like schoolboys on their way home." Most prisoners surrounded their liberators, hugged them in tears. But Vassily Petrenko, commander of 107th Rifle Division, also remembered a large group of apathetic people simply standing around, neither laughing nor crying. The youthful general toured the camp, still littered with the detritus of life and death: clothes, suitcases, spectacles, toothbrushes, seven tonnes of women's hair. "What sort of people commit such unimaginable crimes?" Petrenko asked himself. His men demanded retribution. "We will not take one more German prisoner," they told their commander. "We must destroy them like rabid dogs for the crimes they have committed." Polevoy branded the camp "a factory of death", its fields "soaked in human blood and fertilized with human ash", its survivors martyrs. "The Red Army saved them – and dragged them out of hell." Auschwitz's liberators "had a feeling that we had done something good," Lieutenant Ivan Martynushkin recalled. "A very good deed, that we had somehow fulfilled our duty." But four years of war had rather inured the *frontovik* to such sights. "I had seen the destruction of villages," Martynushkin continued. "I had seen the suffering of our own people. I had seen small children maimed. There was not one village which had not experienced this horror, this tragedy, these sufferings."[32]

Martynushkin's reaction was typical of men and women brutalized by the war in the East. Normal feelings of empathy, of compassion, of basic humanity had been numbed, suppressed. When an elderly German woman whined tearfully at Russian field surgeon Nina Sakova: "I have lost two sons in Russia," the doctor snapped. "And who is to blame? How many have *we* lost?" The Frau began to speak. "Hitler . . ." Sakova interrupted her. "It wasn't Hitler alone. It was your children, your men as well." The old woman fell silent. Sakova felt no sympathy. "My mother starved during the war," she then said. "My brother lay in hospital, badly wounded. In our family, only the women are left." Mikhail Koriakov watched a junior officer walk up to a herd of cows being driven along the lanes of Silesia. He unsheathed his knife and stabbed one of the beasts in the base of the skull. Its legs gave way, the animal fell down and the rest of the herd stampeded, bellowing madly. The officer wiped the blade on his boots and rejoined his comrades. "My father wrote me that the Germans had taken a cow from us," he told his fellow officers. "Now we are even." Captain Grigori Klimov passed the corpse of a young woman lying in a ditch, the lower half of her body naked, a beer bottle between her legs. Hundreds of his fellow Russian soldiers passed the body. Not one thought to move it to one side or bury it. He shook his head. "Where did just retribution end and crimes begin?" Klimov asked himself. "So much inhumanity everywhere, senseless inhumanity . . ." In years to come, the officer felt the wrath of the German people, but he could not apologise. The Germans, he said, "can ask God for a reckoning."[33]

This blunting of emotions perhaps explains, but does not excuse, what happened to the populace of Silesia at the hands of the Red Army. So too, perhaps, does sexual frustration. "We were young, strong," one *frontovik* admitted forty years later. He'd been without a woman for four years, so too had many of his comrades. There were simply not enough *Fräuleins*, he lamented. And so ten men raped one German girl. They seized twelve-year-olds. "If they cried," the soldier recalled, "we'd hit them, stuff something in their mouths." Decades later he could not understand – or justify – his crimes, but in 1945 all he feared was whether Russian girls learned what happened in Germany. "We felt ashamed in front of them." The men of the Red Army had been starved of sex for years, one Russian major admitted. "So sex-starved," he continued, "that they often raped old women of sixty, or seventy, or even eighty – much to these grandmothers' surprise, if not downright delight."[34] But there are few expressions of delight to be found in the testimonies of the countless victims . . .

But above all it was alcohol which fuelled the rape and murder, the senseless destruction. And there was plenty to drink in Silesia. "There's schnapps and spirits," one 1st Ukrainian Front soldier from Krivoj Rog wrote, "we drink every day, each man as much as he needs and as much as his heart desires . . ." Many *frontoviki* drank to forget. As one soldier wrote home, "it's impossible *not* to drink here. It's hard to describe all that we experience here. If we've had a drink, it's easier."[35] But alcohol also made it easier to kill, to loot, to rape, to ignore orders. Discipline, particularly behind the front line, broke down. One drunken Russian tank commander killed two gun crews by firing into his own ranks. Soldiers rode around on stolen bicycles. Some replaced their caps or helmets with bowler or top hats. Horse-drawn carts headed east packed with all manner of household furnishings. "The men in the first wave barely had enough time to collect the watches and jewellery," wrote Captain Mikhail Koriakov. "The second wave, supporting the advance, was less in a hurry – the men had time to go in for girls. The men in the third wave never found any jewellery or untouched girls, but they combed the town and packed suitcases." Ivan Konev attempted to curb the excesses. "This has nothing to do with fighting," he raged. "All it does is destroy precious items." The marshal promised severe punishment for acts of arson or senseless destruction. Looting had to cease immediately. Guilty soldiers faced being sent to penal units. Commanders who failed to halt indiscipline would be "called to account." *Red Star*, the official newspaper of the Russian Army, joined in the condemnation of the atrocities. Having stoked the anger of the *frontoviki* just days before, it was now urging restraint. "If the Fascist two-legged beasts had the nerve to rape our women in full public view and to plunder, then it does not mean that we must do the same. Our revenge is not blind, our anger not unreasonable."[36]

To many Silesians, the Russians' revenge *was* blind, their anger unreasonable. "What fate do the Bolsheviks have in store for our people and you, my love?" one junior officer defending Silesia asked himself. "Women and mothers would be raped, disgraced, deported to Siberia – that's if they don't just let them starve or exterminate them." If anything happened to him, Breslau *Volkssturm* man Hermann Krätzig told his wife Margarete, "then pray that I have not fallen into enemy hands. Protect yourselves, my beloved, from this dreadful fate. The enemy knows no humanity." The atrocities played into the hands of the Nazi propaganda machine. It had warned the German people an Asiatic storm threatened them in the East. Now the prophecy was being fulfilled. The Russians, Joseph Goebbels noted, "act like barbarians in the conquered region. Stalin has probably modelled his method of torture on Genghis Khan's column." There could be no more talk of mercy, the propaganda minister decided. "The German people must defend their lives – and any method of doing so is just."[37]

Any method *was* used. But they were not just. In one Silesian village, Russian soldiers were found sitting at tables in German kitchens dead after gorging themselves on poisoned schnapps, cucumbers, bacon. There were numerous instances of captured Russian soldiers being executed on the spot by their German foe. "You cannot still call on us to take prisoners!" one *Landser* told his commander after seeing the corpses of raped women. Female Soviet soldiers were often shot. "Each one of us always had a bullet left for ourselves – better to die than to go into captivity," one battlefield nurse recalled. One of her friends was taken prisoner. "When we re-took the village two days later we found her: her eyes were gouged out, her chest cut open. She was impaled on a stake." In the frost, her body had been entirely frozen, her hair turned grey. Signaller Vladimir Archipov came across the bodies of twenty comrades who had been taken prisoner by German troops. They had been quartered, their eyes gouged out. "So when our lads had taken prisoners, they gave them a good thrashing," he wrote home to his family. "Today some SS troops were captured. They were beaten by our lads because of their SS uniforms. They were made to feel our hatred." They were not the only ones. Ambulance driver Pavel Chochlov found the villages of Silesia littered with the corpses of German officers and men; in one perhaps fifty *Landsers* who had surrendered then shot to a man "on the orders of a Russian officer". After one particularly bitter struggle for a village involving Chochlov's regiment, enemy troops filed out of the houses. "Don't shoot them yet," the Siberian's commander told his men. "They'll all be rounded up, then we'll shoot them." He was as good as his word. As the final German soldiers were driven out of the last house in the village, they were lined up and shot. One female Red Army soldier admitted that any captured Germans "were not shot dead – that would have been too easy for them. We stabbed them like pigs with spears, chopped them to pieces." This was not hearsay. It happened. "I saw it with my own eyes," she recounted forty years later. "I waited for the moment when their eyes bulged with pain." They bulged, and she felt no mercy. "They burned my mother and my young sister at the stake in the middle of the village."[38]

This was *Pravda*'s celebrated "flame of war" raging across Silesia in January 1945. "Silesia is the forge of Hitler's Germany," the Communist Party organ told its readers. "Without metal, machines, fuel, grain no one can fight. Soviet troops have halted all industrial activity in Silesia and seized an important part of the land. Germany's eastern lands have turned into a battlefield."[39]

Russian killed German. German killed Russian. And now in Breslau, German killed German.

In the fading light of Sunday, 28 January, a large crowd began to gather outside the Nazi Party headquarters in Albrechtstrasse. They watched as the city's finance director, Dr Wolfgang Spielhagen, was led out under armed guard. An educated, civilized man, Spielhagen knew that Breslau's fate was sealed and sent his wife, Eva, and their daughters, Gisela and Sonny, to the safety of Berlin. He too sought work in the capital, but there was none at the Ministry of the Interior. Browbeaten, he returned to Breslau to resume his duties. Instead, he was arrested on the *Gauleiter*'s orders and charged with cowardice. Punishment was swift – and barbaric. The finance director was tied to a recording truck which then drove around the Ring. It stopped in front of a statue of Frederick Wilhelm III. Spielhagen tried to speak but a volley from a dozen *Volkssturm* men felled him. Still the official was not dead. A Party stalwart strode up to the dying man and fired several pistol shots into Spielhagen's head. The corpse was wrapped in a few blankets and tossed in the back of the truck. Karl Hanke quickly issued a proclamation to the people of Breslau:

> The deputy mayor of the city of Breslau, *Ministerialrat* Dr. Spielhagen, informed the mayor of the capital of the *Gau*, *Gauamtsleiter* Leichtenstern, that he was moving to Berlin to look for a new post.
> On my orders *Ministerialrat* Dr. Spielhagen was shot dead by a *Volkssturm* squad in front of Breslau Rathaus.
> He who fears an honourable death dies in disgrace!

The news was subsequently relayed by state radio in Berlin. It was the first Frau

Spielhagen heard of her husband's demise. She never received official notification of his death.[40]

The murder – for that is what it was – of Wolfgang Spielhagen had nothing to do with honour or disgrace. It had everything to do with Karl Hanke flexing his authority – and eliminating any potential foes.

"He left his Lower Silesian homeland as a miller's assistant and returned as *Gauleiter.*" So eulogised the flagship journal of the Third Reich, *Das Reich*, about the man charged with leading the defence of Breslau. Like most of the Nazi hierarchy, Karl August Hanke was a nobody who became a somebody courtesy of fate and favouritism. Born the son of an engine driver in the small western Silesian town of Lauban in August 1903, he left his native land before he turned seventeen to serve in the rump of the German Army left after the Great War. He lasted no more than a year in the ranks before enlisting at a millers' school in Saxony to learn a trade. The young Hanke then mastered the miller's art, working in Bavaria, the Tirol and his homeland, before moving to Berlin to teach the subject at a technical school. It was in the German capital that Hanke joined the Nazi Party. He rose rapidly through its ranks: within three years he was the senior Party official in west Berlin, a position which made his job at the technical school untenable. It was in Berlin that he forged his two most important relationships, one with architect Albert Speer who found Hanke "uncomplicated but intelligent and highly energetic," the other with Joseph Goebbels – which would have fateful consequences. The *Gauleiter* of Berlin and future propaganda minister selected Hanke as his adjutant. In time he would rise through the ministry to become its under-secretary. He soon became appalled by his master's philandering – and the slight to Goebbels' wife, Magda. Hanke was a couple of years younger than Frau Goebbels, tall, with a goatee beard to disguise his youth, and thinning swept-back black hair sitting on a high forehead. He oozed energy, yet was quiet, almost shy, possessed a dry sense of humour and deep-set eyes "filled with life". By the summer of 1938, the simmering relationship between the minister's wife and his deputy was threatening to boil over. Hanke was besotted and talked of marriage, listing Goebbels' indiscretions – as many as forty – and rounding up scorned actresses to testify against his master. Frau Goebbels took her grievance to Hitler, who forbade any divorce, ordering the Goebbels couple to reconcile their differences. Karl Hanke pursued Magda for another twelve months – in vain. Distance finally brought the affair to an end. In August 1939 as a reservist *Leutnant*, Hanke joined an armoured training unit which accompanied 3rd Panzer Division into Poland as a reservist *Leutnant*. He remained in the army throughout the winter, now assigned to another panzer division, the 7th, as adjutant to its commander, one Erwin Rommel. Hanke presented Rommel with the *Ritterkreuz* for his exploits in France in the spring of 1940. Erwin Rommel was set to repeat the favour. He recommended Hanke for the same decoration; the *Leutnant* had routed a French counterattack single-handedly when it threatened 7th Panzer's advance near Avesnes. (He had also saved his commander's life by machine-gunning French bicycle troops when Rommel blundered into them.) But the future Desert Fox promptly withdrew the citation when Hanke crassly pointed out he was senior to his general thanks to his Party status. That Party status would now elevate Karl Hanke to the post of *Gauleiter* of Lower Silesia when the unwieldy province was split in January 1941 and the out-of-favour existing leader, Josef Wagner, sidelined.

Karl Hanke's hagiography claimed he arrived in Breslau with "a raft of original plans", a new broom to sweep away bureaucracy. He certainly carried out Nazi policies energetically, none more so than the eradication of Breslau's Jewish population. It was his intention, he declared, to "make Breslau free of Jews" and he immediately set about clearing the 1,800 apartments in the city still occupied by Jews. Hanke was as good as his word. By the summer of 1943, the Jews of Breslau were no more. The *Gauleiter* of Lower Silesia was left in no doubt of the consequences of this 'Jewish resettlement action'. 'Resettlement' meant 'extermination' – the head of the SS, Heinrich Himmler, told him so at a conference of Party leaders in Poznań in October 1943. But Karl Hanke also witnessed the business of extermination, visiting Auschwitz. According to his friend Albert Speer, the visit left the *Gauleiter* shaken. He urged Speer never to go there – "never under any circumstances". It was a rare crack in Hanke's ruthless edifice. For the most part, however, he showed no sympathy, no mercy. At least 1,000 people were executed during his unforgiving reign. Not without good reason did the city's inhabitants refer to their leader as *der Henker von Breslau* – the hangman of Breslau.

It was hardly surprising that Breslauers never warmed to Karl Hanke. He was at best an awkward public speaker, at worst plain awful. He was overbearing and often abused his ever-growing powers. "Hanke had an exaggerated sense of his own worth," schoolboy Horst Gleiss recalled. "In person, he was overbearing, his appearance was brutal, he was tight-lipped and non-committal." Above all, Breslauers viewed their *Gauleiter* as a "carbon-copy Hitler" who "enjoyed playing the role of dictator". Except that in the winter of 1945, Karl Hanke wasn't simply playing.[41]

Hanke's clearing of the decks did not end with the execution of Wolfgang Spielhagen. The *Ortsgruppenleiter* and mayor of Klettendorf, the mayor of Brockau, a senior civil servant, all left their posts, ostensibly without orders. All were sentenced to death. Ordinary Breslauers were not spared. Looting and theft were now punishable by death. "Whoever misappropriates the property of evacuated comrades when there is no crisis forfeits their lives," Hanke decreed. Widow Maria Bramer and the divorcée Walli Langer took food, luxury items and curtains from an abandoned apartment. They had acted "solely out of greed and hedonism". They were shot. The same fate befell four foreign workers, also found in abandoned apartments. Two soldiers who threw away their uniforms, donned civilian clothes and returned to their homes were caught by a Wehrmacht patrol. Before the day was out they had been condemned to death by a flying court-martial and shot. Another *Landser* who plundered an abandoned house, stealing women's clothes, wine and champagne, was shot dead. Defeatism also meant the death penalty. Party member and *Zellenleiter* Gerhard Malek "had a special duty to be loyal to his Führer and nation". Instead, he distributed Soviet leaflets among fellow armaments workers. He was shot dead on Hanke's orders. No one was safe, not even the fortress's staff. Intelligence officer, *Major* Hans Meyer, was charged with undermining fighting spirit by making "demoralizing remarks" in front of a large group of soldiers, *Volkssturm* troops and civilians. Krause spoke up on Meyer's behalf. A standing court martial ignored him. Meyer was shot dead. "I resolved to cast off all inhibitions in dealing with the utmost severity against those who paralyse or harm the overall will to stick it out as a result of their thoughtless or irresponsible actions," Hanke told Breslauers unapologetically. He described a selfless *Volkssturm* man, a sixty-year-old government inspector, he had encountered who suffered frostbite after spending a week in a foxhole. "How can I look such men in the face if I deal leniently with weaklings?" [42]

And still Karl Hanke was not done. Next he turned his attention to Breslau's universities, which had decamped to Dresden, 150 miles to the west. The *Gauleiter* expected a repeat of 1813, when the city's university had been the fount of the national uprising against Napoleon. Instead of rushing to the flag to defend their Fatherland, he chided Heinrich Blecken, director of the technical high school, they had scurried to safety. Blecken could not agree. In six years of war, the city's universities had given their all. At least 500 students had been slain on the battlefields of Europe. There were no longer any able-bodied students at his technical high school. The only men on its books were 250 war-wounded amputees and foreigners. The figures were similar at the university. "One more combing out of the students now in Dresden to find some men still capable of bearing arms is utterly pointless," Blecken protested. "You cannot wage war with one-armed or badly wounded students." The *Gauleiter* brushed the chancellor's objections aside. One-armed students could still man barricades. He despatched a special courier to Dresden bearing an appeal:

> Lecturers and students of Breslau's universities!
> Why do you not defend your universities with us on the Oder? Do you think you can save the Fatherland by your current actions? We know that scientific work is vital even in wartime. But in times of the gravest danger academic youths and their lecturers must defend the sites of their scientific work with weapons in their hands.
> We will defend Breslau and the Oder with bitter determination. We are waiting for you, because we do not want to believe in the self-abandonment – and with it the moral death – of our Breslau universities! [43]

Breslau's students did not return, but others did. Just days after fleeing the city, refugees began to make their way back to recover their possessions – against the instructions of Karl Hanke. [44] At the Freiburger Bahnhof, Lena Aschner saw a woman trying to head back to her apartment to retrieve her papers and money. Brownshirts blocked her way. She tried to slip past them. One of the SA men struck her in the neck, grabbed her dress and threw her against the wall. The woman staggered, straightened herself up and screamed: "You damned dogs! You'll die like dogs, our Lord will see to it!" [45]

Her job as a doctor did allow Annemarie Hegenscheidt to return to the city. She borrowed a baggage cart from the Hotel Savoy, now derelict, its red curtains fluttering in the wind which whistled through the broken windows. She hauled it to Fürstenstrasse in the north-east of the city, where every house, every apartment block lay empty. Her flat was just as she left it. She packed her books, climbed through the open cellar window of a neighbour's house to retrieve her microscope. By the time she had gathered everything, it was dark – too late to leave. She lay down on her bed – "it seems to have been waiting for me in a ghostly manner" – and tried to sleep as shells crashed all around.[46]

By the end of January, artillery fire and bombing were Breslau's nightly soundtrack. The Red Army stood outside Hundsfeld, barely five miles from the city centre. Its howitzers were lined up on the Trebnitzer Heights fifteen miles north of the Silesian capital. It had forced the Oder at Märzdorf, a dozen miles upstream of Breslau, then at Peiskerwitz, ten miles downstream. "You can easily hear the thunder," post office employee Wilhelm Bodenstedt wrote to his wife. "It doesn't upset people." Perhaps the fifty-year-old was trying to be reassuring, because the bombardment *was* upsetting Breslauers – and beginning to change the face of their city. The roads were peppered with bomb craters. Front doors had been blown in by the pressure of explosions and window panes shattered. Kaiser Wilhelm Strasse was scarred by artillery strikes, so too Tauentzienplatz.[47] Fritz Neugebauer visited his Aunt Gertrud to celebrate her birthday. She and her husband Horst sat calmly in their fourth-storey apartment, refusing to leave the city. "*Ach*, it doesn't matter where we die," she told Fritz. After sharing memories and eating cake, Fritz parted company with his aunt with the words: "We'll see each other again in a mass grave." It was 11pm by the time he left, yet the trams were still running. The No.6, its lights dimmed, scraped over shattered glass strewn across Feldstrasse. Suddenly the sirens droned, two bombs landed nearby. The tram ground to a halt. Neugebauer and the driver dashed into the alcove of a house and waited for the raid to end. The tram did not resume its journey. Neugebauer returned home on foot "through empty, sinister streets, making detours because of the barricades". For Fritz Neugebauer this was the signal to leave Breslau. The next day he headed to the Ring and the savings bank, withdrew 800 Reichsmarks, then took his family to the village of Leuthen, a dozen miles away.[48]

Lena Aschner stayed. Every day she selflessly helped refugees at the Hauptbahnhof. As she crossed Tauentzienplatz returning home late one evening, she was caught in an air raid. Bombs landed barely 600 feet away, throwing Aschner against the wall of a house.

I can't hear or see. I stagger on and begin to run filled with a mad fear, I stumble over a piece of wall, fall, get up and run, run for my life until I reach my staircase out of breath, sink into a corner and am unable to go down to the cellar.

A soldier came to her aid and helped her down. "I suddenly realize that my head hurts. Blood streams down my face." The people in the shelter washed and bandaged her, then handed the housewife a glass of cognac. "It burns my throat and stomach, but I soon get better."[49] *Volkssturm* soldier Alfred Hardlitschke took shelter in the cellar of the Menzel fur store on the Ring to escape one Soviet raid. "The civilian populace is filled with a thousand fears and we sit in our cellar like a mouse in a trap, and wait for Death. This is terrible," he wrote to his wife. A bomb interrupted his letter. The neighbouring building had been hit. The cellar filled with dust, the windows in the passageway shattered, walls fell down. "If only it was over soon." His letter is unclear as to whether he meant the bombing or his life.[50] During one ten-hour bombardment, fifteen shells landed close to Paul Peikert's St Mauritiuskirche. The Lobe theatre, the Lazarus hospital, the friary, plus numerous homes were all damaged. "It was barely possible to sleep for one hour," Peikert wrote. His parishioners were "extremely depressed and despondent" – several families even gassed themselves. Across the city there were at least half a dozen suicides daily.[51]

And yet life in Breslau went on. The trams ran – at least those in the inner city and lines to the southern suburbs did. They no longer ran as frequently, but they were free to ride now. There was still a postal service – and 1,800 people working in the central post office to deal with the several hundred sacks of mail daily. Nazi Party officials still stamped ration cards on Mondays as they had done throughout the war. Food was one thing Silesia's capital did not lack. Thanks to its status as Germany's 'air raid shelter', the warehouses on the Oder, on the Sandinsel and in half a dozen other locations across the city were filled with flour. And in the freezer warehouse there were 32,000 sides of pork, 150,000 rabbits, 150 barrels of fat and five million eggs. "The food's very good and there's plenty of it," one *Volkssturm* soldier wrote. "In the evening there was sausage and fatty sausage for the grease – 100 grammes of each. At mid-day there's always a large bowl of roast meat and potatoes." But otherwise normal life in Breslau broke down. Rationing and shortages meant there was little, if any fuel. The electricity supply was erratic. The average daytime temperature in early February was seven degrees Centigrade – outdoors *and* indoors. Snow piled up in roads – no one shovelled it to one side. Indeed, hardly anyone could be found in the streets, no people scurrying to work, no children playing, just soldiers. By night, dogs scampered from door to door, howling, in search of their master who had fled. The Gestapo and most of the SS, including its intelligence service which kept an eye on the city's morale, abandoned Breslau for the safety of Saxony – taking a truckload of files with them. More important papers were also shipped west: some of the oldest manuscripts in the city library, the papers of the sixteenth-century humanist Thomas Rhediger, the writings of fifteenth-century chronicler Jean Froissart, parchments from before the millennium and the signature of Martin Luther. But far more of Breslau's treasures were left behind. Refugees, the sick, machinery from the city's factories, forced labourers, troops, all took precedence on trains heading west, ahead of cultural heritage. The technical high school's Professor Günther Grundmann had urged Karl Hanke to evacuate Silesia's treasures the previous autumn. The *Gauleiter* refused. Now the desperate Grundmann tried to persuade the local head of the *Reichsbahn* to spare him a few carriages. The response was curt: "Too late, professor!"[52]

Breslauers could still listen to the radio, but the city's transmitter which had broadcast to the world for fifteen years, stopped broadcasting early on the evening of 26 January. The airwaves were not silent for long. Within a week, the Russians were broadcasting on the same frequency. The *Schlesische Tageszeitung* continued to appear daily, no longer published in Breslau, rather *Festung* Breslau. It was, however, reduced to a single sheet – perhaps two at weekends. The Propaganda Ministry in Berlin suggested ideas for articles to its editor Herbert Zeissig. There was a myriad of birthdays to celebrate: the centenary of a Potsdam publishing house, the eightieth birthday of geographer and polar scientist Erich von Drygalski, the sixtieth birthday of theatre director Franz Ulbrich, the death of the Nazi poet Sepp Keller on the Italian front – and on and on. Zeissig was not, however, to make any mention of history professor Alexander Graf Schenk von Stauffenberg – brother of the man who tried to kill Hitler the previous July. The editor of the *Schlesische Tageszeitung* preferred to offer more practical advice – what to do in an air raid, where to find a dentist, how to trace relatives evacuated from the city – and tried to raise the morale of the 200,000 or so people still in the city. The newspaper encouraged the troops defending Breslau to strike up a tune. "The odds are stacked against soldiers who no longer sing." It talked of the "struggle at Breslau's gates", of "defence to the bitter end", of the "Soviets' countless losses", of "huge craters" left by the impact of V2 rockets in London, of *Volkssturm* men who destroyed two dozen Russian tanks with *Panzerfaust*. And on 30 January – the twelfth anniversary of the Nazi assumption of power – it carried a clarion call by Karl Hanke: "Even during these days we look full of faith to the Führer. He can count on all of us. The German people will not let him down now." A Luftwaffe unit defending Breslau held a collection in Hitler's honour, donating more than 60,000 Reichsmarks – a lowly soldier earned just fourteen a month – for the reconstruction of Silesia's homes after the war. At midday, the city's streets resounded to songs from the heyday of the Nazi movement as the *Hitlerjugend* paraded. It was all a prelude to the main event: a speech by the Führer, just as he had given every 30 January. The overture on the state radio – an hour of excerpts from Wagner's operas – was longer, more dramatic and more stirring than Adolf Hitler's limp speech. At twenty minutes long, it was his shortest public pronouncement – and the last time the people of Breslau would hear their Führer. His address was almost a carbon copy of his speech four weeks before, except that now he acknowledged that "tens and hundreds of thousands" of Germans in the east had suffered a "terrible fate". But, he continued, "whatever suffering our enemies might inflict on German towns, the German countryside and above all our people, it pales compared with the irredeemable misery and misfortune which would befall us if the plutocratic-Bolshevik conspiracy was victorious." There was only one course of action, Adolf Hitler told his people, to "make our hearts stronger than ever and steel ourselves with our holy determination to bear arms wherever and whatever the circumstances until in the end victory crowns our efforts." To Joseph Goebbels, the speech was "firm, virile and full of character". He thought it would leave a deep impression on the German people. He was wrong. There was, one Breslauer wrote, "nothing comforting" in the Führer's words, "only a list of the Nazi Party's achievements and we've all had our fill of those."[53]

The word of God proved far more potent than the words of Adolf Hitler. At nightfall on Sunday, 28 January, Breslauers filed into St Barbarakirche on the western edge of the old town. The church was overcrowded, understandably, as worshippers from every parish in the city and every denomination had been invited to a united service. The priests told the huge congregation they would stand shoulder-to-shoulder with them in their hour of need. "We do not wish to be hindered by any false fear," they declared at the end of the service. "We seek help and advice in common prayer and concentration on the word of God, in whose hands all fates are safe."[54]

The Church was a clear threat to Nazi authority. Relations between the Church and the Party had always been uneasy. Now they began to disintegrate. Nazi thugs repeatedly attacked one priest for refusing to leave the city. Joachim Konrad protested. That night he was woken by the thud of rifle butts against his door. "A group of suspicious-looking characters forced their way in, threatened me, swore in the most vulgar manner and stole my telephone." After that, he spent the nights elsewhere. At the end of January, every priest was ordered to leave the city – ostensibly for their own safety, in reality to eliminate any challenge to Party rule. The priests revolted. They refused to leave. Now, more than ever, they were needed: the wounded needed comforting, the dead burying, the people moral and spiritual support. A deal was struck. Thirty-five Catholic and nine Protestant ministers were allowed to remain.[55] They would serve as the city's soul and conscience throughout the siege.

To Paul Arnhold, Breslau still offered salvation. The pioneer officer's party of stragglers from LVI Panzer Corps was reduced to just three men, moving by night through the forests and woods of Poland, through undergrowth, over streams, grabbing rest and food from isolated cottages. They stumbled across one dwelling in a copse, "wonderfully warm although it also smelled of old people who had lived with cats for many years". The soldiers didn't care about the smell, only about warmth and food. The elderly Polish occupants brought out a foul-smelling potato stew. The men refused to eat it. "Experience told us that even in the poorest cottage there were better things kept hidden somewhere for the winter," the pioneer officer wrote. The soldiers threatened the couple, who opened up a hole in the ground and pulled out two loaves and some salted meat. "We could not contain ourselves and attacked it like wild animals," Arnhold recalled. "We paid the price for doing so; a short time later we brought it all back up again. Our weak stomachs could not cope with something like that any more."

The soldiers grabbed some sleep and tried to clean themselves after a fortnight on the run. "We carefully removed our boots and shoes," Paul Arnhold wrote.

What was left of our socks and foot-cloths had gone hard from dried blood and pus. My soles were just pus-filled flesh, but the worst pain came from inside. As I'd been running for three weeks on soles which were burned and warped, my metatarsal was horribly inflamed. When I stood up, the pain coming from it was unbearable. In addition, my ankles had swollen badly where the top edge of my boots rubbed with every step. Our feet were a pathetic sight. In normal times, no one would have believed it possible that we could run even one more step.

As darkness came, the three soldiers set out for the Oder, perhaps still sixty miles away. "As we left, the two elderly people signed the cross behind us. Their eyes were filled with sympathy and a little sadness; they probably gave us only a very slight chance of surviving." The *Oberst* had now been on the move for three weeks:

> Three weeks by day and night in snow and ice, hungry and hunted like wild animals. None of us had washed or shaved for three weeks. We had not changed our clothes for three weeks. We had worn our uniforms for three weeks. During the 'bathe' in the Pilica they had been soaked. Then they had frozen solid in the icy storm, and then we'd been hunted and harried in our wet gear. We huffed and puffed for three long weeks through undergrowth covered in snow and over vast expanses of snow. The uniforms were torn a thousand times by the brittle frozen branches and thorns. Ten days after our swim in the Pilica, our clothes were still damp.
>
> My beard, with its many silvery-grey streaks, had grown so thick that my hands could reach into it. We'd not been able to wipe our arses for three weeks. But what's the use of telling this to someone who hasn't experienced it? That little scrap of *Pravda* was more important for our [Russian] Machorka cigarettes than a civilisation which wouldn't have suited us anyway. For three weeks we'd been living like creatures in the jungle, ready to kill anyone who stood in the way of our progress, and ready to kill anyone who refused to give us food. Our mindset had become so primitive that we could no longer think of anything other than food and getting to the Oder. There were only three of us left now.
>
> Never did we want to raise our hands in the air! Never! If we'd fired the last round and thrown the last hand-grenade, then we would have smashed the enemy's face in with our bare rifles![56]

Feldwebel Karl-Heinz Wolter also sought the left bank of the Oder. Rather than slip through, the signaller and his comrades in the Hermann Göring Division – one of two first-rate units transferred from East Prussia and caught up in the maelstrom of retreat in Silesia – intended to punch their way across the river. The nearer the Oder, the more awful the sights. "Dead Russians lie around in heaps, between them women wearing shawls," Wolter wrote. "Death caught up with them at their guns and anti-tank guns. The hard frost and white snow meant the dead had not changed at all – it was as if they were still alive. It is terrible."

The signaller's vehicle had to swerve around a motorcycle and sidecar, blocking a junction. Wolter wanted to scream at the two riders. He just about contained himself. "When we pass near to them, I see from their almost white, waxen faces, that they are dead, killed. Their stance on the motorcycle did not recognise death. The cold has only slightly changed them."

Pioneers had thrown a bridge over the Oder near Steinau. Its approaches were strewn with the cadavers of horses, their stomachs bloated, shot-up vehicles and other abandoned equipment. On the bridge, the engineers valiantly stood in the pontoon boats to ensure the makeshift bridge, its sleepers and boards bound by rope, could take the strain.

The left bank of the river offered little comfort to Wolter and his comrades. Soviet artillery filled the air with iron. Its harvest was rich. "Dead soldiers, dead horses and smashed guns line our route of advance," the *Feldwebel* wrote. He continued:

> I see a dead artilleryman. His horse stands in front of him, its head lowered. Both soldier and horse are still bound to each other by the reins held by the stiffened hand. The animal stands on three legs, a foreleg was half shot away.
>
> Only very occasionally have I been moved as I have been by this image of the dead gunner and his wounded horse.[57]

Thirty miles upstream at Peiskerwitz, trainee Waffen SS non-commissioned officers grappled with the Red Army. The SS men had arrived in Silesia just six weeks earlier, but the training at Deutsch Lissa, eight miles west of Breslau, abruptly stopped when the Red Army reached the Oder. Now, in the darkness of 28 January, the SS troops marched towards Peiskerwitz to eradicate the Russian bridgehead. It was a daunting prospect, for the sky over the village, *Untersturmführer* Hendrik Verton recalled, was "blood red", flashes lighting up the horizon constantly with each shell fired by the Soviet barrage, while wounded or distraught German troops ran away. The Dutchman and his comrades pushed through copses under heavy mortar fire, finally reaching a forest beyond Peiskerwitz, just short of the Oder dam. "The flash of fire of exploding shells cast the snow-covered forest in an eerie light," wrote Verton. "Dead Russian sharpshooters hung in the trees – we were never entirely sure whether they were not simply playing dead." The screams of the wounded reverberated around the trees, while the SS troops could hear the Russians on the opposite side of the dam cursing and moving their mortars into position. Verton's company commander gave the order to attack. With a loud hurrah, the company rushed up the steps in the side of the dam and stared down at the Russians, who had wrapped white sheets around their earth-brown uniforms as camouflage. There was a brief – and wild – exchange of fire before the SS fell back "silently or screaming", leaving their dead on top of the dam, dragging some of the wounded, leaving the others to crawl to safety. Peiskerwitz was ablaze. "Shadows jumped past the flames – we weren't sure whether they were friend or foe," the Dutch volunteer recalled. The decimated company sought shelter in farmhouses, sheds and cellars and enjoyed their first cigarette of the battle. The baggage column brought up food; its place on the wagons was taken by the dead, hauled away into the night.

Hendrik Verton spent ten days at Peiskerwitz. "The young unshaven faces of my chums were thin now and angular, our uniforms gave us no warmth. Outside was grey, only grey," he wrote. In the grey of dusk, it was impossible to tell where the heavens ended and the firmament began. "It matched our fighting spirit." Verton's unit had lost a hundred men in the fighting for the village. No more than two dozen SS troops marched out of Peiskerwitz.[58]

As they did, a thaw was setting in. The virgin white snow of January was turning to a dirty grey blanket in February. As the snow receded, the ghosts of the past fortnight appeared: the half-frozen corpses of Verton's comrades. There were far worse sights in the ditches, fields and roadsides of Silesia. The thaw revealed as many as 80,000 corpses, victims of the flight from the Russian advance. Special burial parties were sent throughout the *Gau* to find and bury them.[59]

The fighting had yet to reach the heart of Breslau, or even its suburbs, but it was consuming the villages which ringed it on the left bank of the Oder. The airfield at Schöngarten, just seven miles west of the city centre, was becoming untenable as a base for aircraft: ground-attack planes on the standings were pounced upon by Soviet fighters, which scattered ten bombs across the field and caused more damage to the barracks than the aircraft, leaving rolls of paper, pencils, pens and other stationery strewn across the field. Schöngarten's commanders heeded the warning and evacuated the base. Two days later, the last aircraft were flown away in a snowstorm, the Junkers transport aircraft kicking up huge clouds of fine snow as they started up. Just Hugo Hartung and his company of reluctant soldiers were left at the airfield. They had one final duty: to offload a transport of wounded being flown in that night. "We stand for hours freezing at the edge of the runway and wait for an aircraft landing," the theatre director wrote. "We can hear it circling in the snow clouds above us." The men fired flares but to no avail; the pilot could not find Schöngarten in the storm. After a while a ball of flames lit up the night: the aircraft had crashed with all its crew and its passengers.

There was no longer a need for Schöngarten, but there was for its men. After priming the five-ton bombs left behind so the airfield could be blown up, the stragglers received orders to join the Breslau garrison and defend the city. It did not go down well with the men, who decided to plunder Schöngarten's stores before leaving. "It is like the land of milk and honey," Hartung wrote. There were vast supplies of food and cigarettes. The cattle and pigs were slaughtered. "We find so much meat in our soup or in our stew that's often too much for us." The men felt guilty. "We do not like it either when we hear that refugees are starving in the streets."

Hartung's company received its baptism of fire a few days later in the village of Kriptau on the south-western edge of the airfield. As they moved down the road, the men passed the first corpse, a Luftwaffe man, his eyes wide open. They collected his weapons, removed his dog tags, but did not bury him. As for Kriptau, it was devoid of any Russians until late in the day when the rattle of tank tracks sparked panic. An inexperienced non-commissioned officer simply ran away, back to the airfield. A Hitler Youth, serving as a bicycle messenger, was killed by a shell splinter, a popular Berliner was killed by heavy machine-gun fire. "The confusion reaches its climax during the night," Hartung wrote. He was sent with another reluctant soldier, the former chief producer at the opera, to observe the Russians from the edge of a forest. Flares continually rose into the sky. The two men could hear the Russians talking, their shrill whistles piercing the night. No one came to relieve the two observers. "So we lie, almost frozen stiff by the cold, for six long hours on the edge of this eerie forest." In the small hours, another tank scare. Russian armour fired at the centre of Kriptau. One of the NCOs fell into a cesspit out of fear. With Soviet tanks on three sides, the men had orders to fall back to the airfield. They had achieved nothing.[60]

The skirmishes at Peiskerwitz and Kriptau were repeated in Breslau's outlying villages. And always the defenders fell back towards the city. *Leutnant* Wolfgang Chutsch was sent with a makeshift company to re-take the village of Gerlanden, a dozen miles southeast of Breslau. Chutsch was an artilleryman recovering from wounds suffered in the Carpathians the previous autumn. He was ordered to Breslau not as an artilleryman but an infantryman. He was put in charge of a company of *Volksdeutsche*, ethnic Germans from the Black Sea, 120 of them in all. "They only spoke broken German – slowly."

Gerlanden had witnessed ferocious fighting. Several houses were wrecked and in the centre of the village the body of a *Leutnant* hung over a fountain with his head down, just touching the water. There were more dead nearby: numerous *Landsers* sprawled on a dung heap. A few of Gerlanden's elderly residents dared to emerge from their hiding places. Cattle and pigs, terrified and in many cases wounded by the recent fighting, scurried around. "We gave some of them the *coup de grâce* and enjoyed some meat as a result." Chutsch's company spent a couple of days clashing sporadically with Russian troops in the next village, Zottwitz, and living on a diet of cigarettes and meat – the latter courtesy of the animals slaughtered in Gerlanden. Of the sixty-six men the artilleryman had led into battle, three quarters were casualties thanks to Russian machine-gun and sniper fire. Wolfgang Chutsch was one of them, wounded by shrapnel from a Russian shell which missed his heart by two inches.[61]

Schütze Karl Friedrich Oertel was not wounded, but he was exhausted. The twenty-year-old philosophy student had been sworn in on 20 January and sent into action two days later. He had looked forward to battle. "This new year will bring a great decision, one whose effects will echo far into the future," he had written at the end of 1944. "It will bring an end to the most terrible of wars – the time is ripe." The reality was less enticing: "long, terribly cold hours in my foxhole". Many of his comrades fell victim to frostbite, but not Oertel. "I am overtired," he admitted in a letter home, "yet after ten hours in a quiet spot I cannot sleep properly. These days have been very hard for me but I probably need them to grow up." He assured his family: "I am full of confidence."[62] *Volkssturm* man Hermann Krätzig also tried to reassure his wife Margarete, eighty miles away in Greiffenberg. "Things will not turn out so badly because we expect the counter-effects to make visible progress soon. I have trusted my future to Fate. Don't let your head drop! Against fate!"[63]

Hermann Krätzig was one of 25,000 men defending Silesia's capital – soldiers, militia, scratch units, garrison troops, 850 Waffen SS non-commissioned officers from a training school, 5,000 Luftwaffe personnel, 1,700 police officers and nearly 9,000 *Volkssturm*. They possessed 1,200 machine-guns, a dozen howitzers, nearly fifty field guns, 120 flak guns and 11,000 *Panzerfaust*, but barely any ammunition.[64]

This mixed bag of troops was led by a mixed bag of seventy officers, many of whom "had never been in combat and did not know what to expect or how to prepare for it," Siegfried Knappe observed. "The place was a military mess." The twenty-eight-year-old officer had been flown into the city to help the *Festung*'s staff. As the new operations officer, Knappe's tasks were many: designating defensive lines, overseeing the digging of trenches, ensuring the evacuation of the wounded, making provision for refugees still passing through the city, maintaining order, keeping vital public utilities running – "all in addition to normal staff functions". He never slept more than two hours without interruption, or for more than five hours in any twenty-four-hour period. "Slowly, with time," wrote Knappe, "everything began to function better."[65]

Everything except the fortress commander. Johannes Krause was sick. He spent the opening days of February 1945 confined to bed with pneumonia. The telephone at his bedside rang. The new army group commander, Ferdinand Schörner, was in Breslau – and demanding to see Krause. Krause refused. The telephone rang again. An aide took the call. As he replaced the receiver, he turned to the fortress commander. "*Herr General*, you must come. Schörner is stomping around like a madman and threatening to shoot you. He has brought his firing squad with him." Krause refused. A few minutes later, another staff officer appeared at the fortress commander's bedside. Schörner was now "foaming at the mouth" and had ordered his firing squad to "lock and load".

Now Johannes Krause rose from his bed, dressed and headed to the *Wehrkreis* headquarters. There he found Ferdinand Schörner, not foaming at the mouth but rather conciliatory. The army group commander rose, then shook Krause's hands. "I am sorry that you are so ill," he apologized. "You must be able to see that under these circumstances I have to relieve you. A sick commanding officer cannot lead the struggle as it demands. The Russians are close. Now get yourself to bed and get well very quickly."

In his place, Schörner chose an experienced pioneer officer, *Generalmajor* Hans von Ahlfen. He took charge of *Festung* Breslau on the morning of 3 February "with orders not merely to hold out," he proclaimed to the city's inhabitants, "but to beat back."[66]

And so, proclaimed the city's newspaper, "*Festung* Breslau stands armed". It left its readers in no doubt about what was expected of them – and what fate awaited Silesia's ancient capital.

If such an undamaged, such a wealthy, and such a beautiful city has to turn to rubble house by house, and we hold on in its ruins, then it will be an even more precious treasure than when it possessed all its former beauty.

The general stands beside the president of the *Reichsbahn*, the Hitler Youth leader crippled by the war stands next to the leader of a large organisation. For each and every one of them, there is a single, clear mission: the city must be held. And whoever does not know how to use the *Panzerfaust* is starting to learn about it. This people will not go under.[67]

Notes

1. *Schlesische Tageszeitung*, 22/1/45.
2. Echolot, iii, pp.478-9.
3. Based on Frodien, p.124, Becker, p.125; Gleiss, *Pennäler, Pimpf und Volkssturmmann*, p.2, Gleiss, i, pp.282, 517 and Gleiss, vii, p.872.
4. Gleiss, viii, pp.21, 29, Ibid., vii, p.549.
5. See *Schlesische Tageszeitung*, 28/1/45, 31/1/45 and 3/2/45.
6. Gleiss, i, pp.247, 279.
7. *Als die Deutschen weg waren*, pp.30, 32-3.
8. Magenheimer, p.99, Duffy, pp.94-5.
9. Polewoi, p.150.
10. Gleiss, vii, p.422.
11. Based on BA-MA RL7/531, Ahlfen, pp.89-90 and Römhild, Helmut, *Geschichte der 269. Infanterie-Division*, p.270.
12. Gleiss, vii, pp.424-5.
13. Becker, p.30.
14. Kaps, *Tragödie Schlesiens*, p.362.
15. *Vertreibung und Vertreibungsverbrechen 1945-1948: Bericht des Bundesarchivs vom 28 Mai 1974*, p.265 and Schwarz, pp.50-1.
16. Arnhold, p.188.
17. Kaps, pp.386-9.
18. Gleiss, vii, p.803.
19. Vertreibung, i, pp.452-3.
20. Werth, p.846, Alexijewitsch, p.323 and Naimark, p.74.
21. Ilya Ehrenburg, 'Nastala rasplate' in *Krasnaya Zvezda*, 30/1/45.
22. Knopp Documentaries.
23. Echolot, iv, p.685.
24. Ibid., ii, p.370.
25. Ibid., iii, pp.162-3.
26. Ibid., iv, p.634.
27. Polewoi, pp.181-2.
28. Scherstjanoi, pp.56-7.
29. Ahlfen, p.74.
30. Gleiss, vii, p.357.
31. Höss, pp.190-2.
32. The liberation of Auschwitz is based on Polewoi, pp.140-1, Knopp, *Der Verdammte Krieg*, iii, p.146, *Pravda*, 2/2/45, and Rees, Auschwitz, pp.264-5.
33. Alexijewitsch, p.323, Koriakov, p.67, and Knopp, *Der Verdammte Krieg*, iii, p.163.
34. Alexijewitsch, p.25 and Werth, p.863.
35. BA-MA RH 2/2683 and Zeidler, p.151.
36. See Koriakov, p.68, BA-MA RH 2/2470 and 'Nase mscenie' in *Krasnaya Zvezda*, 9/2/45.
37. Echolot, iv, p.683, Gleiss, vii, p.493, TB Goebbels, 25/1/45.
38. For details of atrocities on both sides see Scherstjanoi, pp.56-7, Ahlfen, p.169, Alexijewitsch, pp.24, 143, Echolot, ii, p.830 and BA-MA RH2/2681.
39. *Pravda*, 31/1/45.
40. Gleiss, i, pp.577, 578B-C and *Schlesische Tageszeitung*, 29/1/45.
41. This brief biography of Hanke is based on material kindly provided by Michael Miller, plus Rudolf Sparing, 'Karl Hanke' in *Das Reich*, 11/3/45, TB Oven, 9/7/44, Schimmel-Falkenau, p.118, Speer, *Inside the Third Reich*, p.52, NA WO309/140 and Gleiss, ix, p.478. His affair with Magda Goebbels can be found in Goebbels' diaries of 1938-39 as well as David Irving's biography of Joseph Goebbels, Anja Klabunde's biography of Magda Goebbels, and Speer, *Inside the Third Reich*, pp.214-15, 218. Details of his relations with Rommel and service in France are based on *The Rommel Papers*, pp.39, 42; Irving,

Trail of the Fox, pp.43, 44, 52-3 and Manteuffel, p.67. Hanke's role in the Holocaust can be found in *A Community Under Siege*, p.214, Microcosm, pp.392-3 and Speer, *Inside the Third Reich*, pp.506-07.
42. Details of Hanke's ruthless acts can be found in *Schlesische Tageszeitung*, 1/2/45, 3/2/45, 5/2/45, 6/2/45, Documenty, No.32, and Gleiss, vii, pp.759-60.
43. Gleiss, vii, pp.817-18 and *Schleschiche Tageszeitung*, 5/2/45.
44. NA FO898/187, p.187.
45. Echolot, iii, pp.478-9.
46. Ibid., iii, pp.573-4.
47. Kain, pp.319-20.
48. Neugebauer, pp.18-19.
49. Echolot, iii, p.693.
50. Ibid., iii, pp.800-02.
51. Peikert, pp.37, 42.
52. Life in Breslau based on Becker, p.132, Majewski, p.68, Haack, p.29, Gleiss, i, p.240, Gleiss, vii, pp.208, 872, and Hornig, pp.116-18.
53. Propaganda in Breslau based on Gleiss, i, p.475 and Geiss, vii, p.707, Echolot, ii, p.141, and *Schlesische Tageszeitung*, 30/1/45, 31/1/45, 4/2/45. Hitler's speech of 30/1/45 in *Schlesische Tageszeitung*, 31/1/45. Rundfunkprogramm, 30/1/45 in Kempowski, iii, p.153 and Gleiss, vii, p.678.
54. Hornig, pp.27-8.
55. Konrad, pp.11-12 and *So Kämpfte Breslau*, p.18.
56. Arnhold, pp.147-50, 157-8.
57. Echolot, iii, pp.162, 353-4.
58. Fighting for Peiskerwitz is based on *So Kämpfte Breslau*, p.20, Gleiss, vii, pp.616-18, 651-3, 677, 950-1 and Verton, pp.139-40.
59. Peikert, p.272.
60. Hartung, pp.45-8, 54-5.
61. Gleiss, vii, p.803, 861.
62. Bähr, pp.438-40.
63. Gleiss, vii, p.924.
64. Ibid., vii, p.547.
65. Knappe, *Soldat*, pp.303-5.
66. Gleiss, ii, pp.66-7. Krause left Breslau three days later for treatment at a specialist lung hospital in the Sudeten Mountains. *So Kämpfte Breslau*, p.21.
67. *Schlesische Tageszeitung*, 25/1/45.

CHAPTER 5

In Defiance of Death
and the Devil

Every house of Fortress Breslau, which has been entrusted to us
by the Führer, will cost the enemy rivers of blood
Generalleutnant Hans von Ahlfen

For ten days there had been an uneasy lull along the Oder. Scratch German forces had finally given up the struggle for Steinau, allowing the Red Army to expand its bridgehead unfettered. There was fierce fighting in Breslau's satellite villages. But otherwise the war had stalled. Each evening, history-professor-turned-reluctant-soldier Heinrich Appelt lay in a foxhole on the left bank of the Oder, observing the Russians on the other side of the river. It was relentlessly tedious. Nothing happened apart from ice floes drifting down the thawing Oder. "Very occasionally – and probably without any good reason – there was the sound of a gunshot, but apart from that this sector of the front was utterly quiet," Appelt recalled.[1]

One reason for the quiet was the ice floating past Heinrich Appelt. The thaw which had uncovered so much horror on the Silesian country lanes also seriously hindered the Red Army's thrust westwards. A thick sheet of ice moved inexorably down the Oder, carrying pontoon bridges and ferries away and crushing them. The approaches to the river became a morass. "The splashing in the gutters is like angelic music to our ears," Goebbels' secretary Wilfred von Oven noted with relief. "*Ja*, you can say without exaggeration that the Soviet offensive has largely ground to a halt for the time being."[2] Ferdinand Schörner agreed. The Soviet onslaught had "stalled at the Oder". The climax, the army group commander assured his men, "has undoubtedly passed".[3] It had passed, at least in part, thanks to Schörner's uncompromising leadership. The fifty-two-year-old Bavarian was an able commander, but his abilities were surpassed by his ruthlessness. His methods were draconian – he hanged stragglers on trees with placards around their necks: "I am a deserter and have refused to protect German women and children" – and his beliefs were pure National Socialism. "In this Asiatic war we need revolutionary officers who can carry men with them," he told his commanders. "I demand clear and obvious fanaticism, nothing less." He banned words such as 'withdrawal' or 'breaking off', lambasted staff officers for their "obsession with retreating" and "overestimating the Bolsheviks", and demanded commanders prefix every mention of Soviet units in their reports with the word *sogenannt* – so-called. "We shall not do Stalin the favour of confusing his deliberately deceptive designations with our factual terms."[3] But in February 1945, 'so-called' was a far more apt description for many of Ferdinand Schörner's formations. "No longer was one division the same as the next, one regiment identical to another," wrote Hans von Ahlfen. There were still elite units, the armoured units, the Hermann Göring panzer division or the Brandenburg panzer grenadiers, which received the pick of men and material but which were "rushed around to and fro like the fire brigade". There were *Kampfgruppen*, the remnants of divisions smashed in the retreat from the Vistula. There were makeshift formations recruited from training schools, cadet academies, police units. And there were divisions comprising soldiers previously considered unfit for battle – men with stomach complaints who needed, but rarely received, a special diet, or troops with eye or ear problems. "Company commanders were forced to carefully plan how they used their personnel so that those with eye and ear conditions were on double guard duty at the same time," von Ahlfen wrote. "The man with eye problems acted as the ears, the man with ear troubles acted as the eyes." Had Germany's plight not been so grave, it would have been farcical.[4] The German soldier now defending Silesia fell into one of two categories, Soviet intelligence observed: men who had abandoned all hope, who cared only that the war would end, and men – "a large number" – who were convinced some new weapon would turn the tide of the war. "Retreating into a belief in miracles has become even stronger as a result of the successes of the Russian offensive. Soldiers do not want to – and cannot – bring themselves to contemplate an unfavourable outcome of the war."[5] Veteran artilleryman Klaus-Andreas Moering had already abandoned all hope. "Villages and towns smell and are falling apart," Moering wrote home. "In homes there are radios where you can pick up voices and sounds from all over the whole world yet we don't know how things are twenty kilometres away." The former teacher was growing increasingly fatalistic. "I almost doubt that we will see each other again because probably no one will get out of this." Klaus-Andreas Moering was right. He would be killed in the offensive Ivan Konev was about to unleash.[6]

The shaven-headed Soviet marshal was well pleased with the accomplishments of his 1st Ukrainian Front. In four weeks of fighting it had advanced nearly 400 miles, smashed more than sixty German formations, killed perhaps 150,000 enemy soldiers, and seized a good 40,000 prisoners, 5,000 guns and mortars, plus 300 panzers. Land, prisoners and booty were all well and good, but the real prize was Berlin, and Ivan Konev was a long way from the Reich's capital. Silesia – and above all Breslau – blocked his way. His solution? Another lunge across the province to the River Neisse, 100 miles to the west, would provide his troops with the springboard for the drive on Berlin. Two pincers, one advancing out of the bridgeheads at Steinau and a little upstream near Dyhernfurth, a second south of Breslau striking out of the Brieg bridgehead, would seal off the Silesian capital. The city would either fall to the Red Army – or be left to wither and die in the rear as Soviet troops continued towards the Neisse. Ivan Konev could commit eight armies in his onslaught – history has rather blandly branded it 'the Lower Silesian operation'. He outnumbered his foe two to one and enjoyed a fivefold superiority in guns and armour. Yet compared with the assault launched four weeks earlier, this was a pauper's offensive. "Oh, how far we now are from the Vistula," war correspondent Vasily Malinin lamented – rightly. The 1st Ukrainian Front's railheads still stood behind the Vistula. The troops were at the end of a 300-mile supply line. Fuel and ammunition were at a premium – there was only enough ammunition for a brief initial barrage. It would be more than sufficient.[7]

Before dawn on Thursday, 8 February, aircraft of 4th Bomber Corps attacked German troop concentrations, artillery positions and command posts ringed in a semi-circle south of Breslau. Ten minutes later, Konev's guns opened fire with a thirty-five-minute barrage while pioneers cleared a path through minefields. In drizzle mixed with snow, Soviet engineers stood up to their hips in the icy waters of the Oder to prevent the wall of ice drifting down the river from devouring four ferries.[8]

Hauptmann Heinze was woken by the Soviet barrage plastering his battalion's positions a dozen or so miles north-east of Liegnitz. The reservist officer had broken off his convalescence to lead a makeshift force of Silesians rounded up on leave and formed into a battalion. They were well equipped – winter clothing, assault rifles, carbines, Czech machine-guns – and determined to defend their native soil, but they lacked leaders: most of their NCOs "had never smelled gunsmoke". After just three days of skirmishing in woods around the Dyhernfurth bridgehead, Heinze's battalion was exhausted. It would never recover. As darkness gave way to a sullen grey this Thursday, the reservist could make out a battalion of Russian troops supported by two tanks advancing sluggishly towards his lines – the boggy ground impeded their movement. When the tanks paused near a farm, Heinze seized the opportunity. He grabbed a *Panzerfaust*. "Then a bang, sparks flew up. Gotcha!" Three mounted infantry slid off the Soviet tank which burned, but was not knocked out. A comrade tackled the second tank with a *Panzerschreck* – the German counterpart of a bazooka. Again the tank was hit, but not destroyed. The two wounded beasts withdrew to the relative safety of a copse and began to shell the farm. "A cow was bloodily torn to pieces," the *Hauptmann* recalled. He was struck in his left foot by a splinter, his adjutant was gravely wounded. After defending their ground heroically, Heinze now saw his men falling back – and fresh Soviet armour bearing out of the woods. "Continued resistance here was pointless," he decided, and ordered a withdrawal.[9]

The thin German veneer holding the Oder shattered. By the end of the second day of Konev's offensive, his men were fighting in Liegnitz, forty miles west of Breslau, where empty or partially-filled trains pulled out of the station because inhabitants "preferred to remain rather than make a journey into the unknown". Many felt betrayed by their mayors, by their local Party leaders, by National Socialism. Despite stories of Russian atrocities, some even openly welcomed the Red Army with the greeting 'Heil Moscow.' *Pravda* correspondent Boris Polevoy found the roads to Liegnitz strewn with abandoned cars and trucks filled to the roof, bicycles, motorcycles, helmets, rifles, coats, uniforms. Roadside ditches were littered with trunks, rucksacks, gasmasks, rifles, photograph, even a "vase which belonged in a museum". And there were corpses, "heaps of German soldiers" and the cadavers of horses. The fighting for Liegnitz was brief, but ferocious – and offered a foretaste of the impending battle for Breslau: German and Soviet troops clashed in the streets, in houses, in rooms, on rooftops, even in the cellars and underground passages of Liegnitz. By the morning of 10 February the town was in Russian hands, its fall celebrated with a twenty-gun salute in Moscow. That same day, Red armour seized Bunzlau, seventy miles west of Breslau, in a heavy snow flurry. More alarming for Breslauers, on this same Saturday Russian tanks were seen rolling along the Autobahn from Liegnitz towards their city. Breslau was about to be encircled.[10]

The renewed thunder of cannon was the cue for the final exodus before the Soviet jaws shut. The new offensive caught Breslauers off guard. They expected the enemy to come – just not from the south. Now those who had postponed the decision to leave the city three weeks earlier delayed no longer. Post official Josef Dittman waited for night to shroud Silesia before grabbing his bicycle and pedalling to Schweidnitz. Some of his employees tossed their belongings into the final mail train to pull out of the city. "Refugees begged us to take them along," Wilhelm Beier recalled. "We did what we could. When the train departed our mail carriage was crammed with women and children." Annelies Matuszczky and her family hauled two small handcarts towards the Freiburger Bahnhof, the only station still open. It was 1am on the ninth before the Matuszczkys reached the concourse. As they did, the air raid sirens wailed. The station shelter was full. Hundreds of Breslauers stood on the forecourt with their carts and simply waited for the all-clear. When it came, ninety minutes later, the throng shuffled inside and found a half-empty train pulling out of the station. The next scheduled train, eight hours later, was cancelled. Finally, in driving rain, a train was provided – "no seats of course and terribly dirty, but empty at least," Annelies wrote. For four hours it sat outside Freiburger Bahnhof before beginning a tortuous journey to Schweidnitz, just thirty miles to the south-west. It took more than eighteen hours to get there. It was the last train from Breslau: just an hour after it pulled into Schweidnitz, Russians captured the line. No more trains left the Silesian capital.[11]

Other facets of everyday life in Breslau were also disappearing. Party functionaries began to burn documents, stripping off their brown uniforms, donning *feldgrau* in their place. For the final time, the band of the local army unit, *Standort Bataillon Breslau*, performed in the courtyard of the cuirassier barracks. The men had barely finished their third march when Russian aircraft circled over the base. The musicians and their audience scattered – although no bombs fell. Never again did the men perform together during the siege. They swapped their instruments for rifles, machine-guns and *Panzerfaust*.[12] By day and night there was a new sound: the crash of entire blocks in the south of the city being demolished to provide rubble for the barricades. Field guns were moved into position in Scheitniger Park. Once popular with Sunday strollers, the park now also served as a makeshift cemetery. Shocking though this was, what happened on the opposite side of Horst Wessel Strasse turned Breslauers' hearts to stone. They had grown up with their beloved zoo, which could trace its history back eight decades. By the winter of 1944-5 it was one of the few zoos in Germany still open – most in the rest of the Reich had long since put down many of their animals as a result of the Allied bombing campaign. Now the same fate awaited the beasts of Breslau: fortress commander Hans von Ahlfen feared they might escape and attack the populace. He ordered the animals shot. First to face the executioners were the wolves. "They looked at us mistrustfully, shrewdly," recalled Dr Herbert Kraeker, the only native Breslauer in a group of pioneers given the bitter task of killing the creatures. "They stood there motionless, wonderful to look at, and died without a sound." The sound of the carbines unsettled the monkeys in a neighbouring pen, but it was the bears in their open enclosure who were shot next.

> Probably believing they would get some food and delighted to see people again, they faithfully came to the ditches begging, but the first bullet was already hurtling into their fur. It barely grazed the thick fur and a small stream of blood ran red. The second bullet struck it in the middle of the head. A spurt of blood as thick as an arm shot from its nose and mouth, it swayed, fell down, one last twitch and it was all over. The other brown bears stood there upright but retreated back to their caves when they saw and heard this sad occurrence. Only by using sticks, and a great deal of cunning and guile could they be enticed out again. Another tranquiliser bullet, a shot to the head, sometimes one more as a *coup de grâce* and the awful groaning and howling ended.

The execution squad moved on to the polar bears. The zoo's director could no longer watch. He turned his deathly-pale face away, tears streaming down it, as his life's work was systematically destroyed. Kraeker continued:

> The moaning cries of the mortally-wounded animals shattered the silence. All the white bears rolled slowly into the ditches with last spasms. Now the rest of the Asian black bears stood in front of us, begging us, pleading with us. It didn't work. We went to the lions, leopards, tigers and hyenas. The same sad drama. They were slain up close and personal. They tried to defend themselves against the carbines by beating their large paws. These regal animals lay dead in front of us. There was no other solution available to us.

Perhaps the Russians knew what was afoot, for as the killing party moved through the zoo, the district was bombed heavily. The exhibition hall in the grounds of the Jahrhunderthalle, opposite the zoological gardens, burned. And in the zoo itself, gaps were torn in the aviary fence. Its exotic occupants fled, seeking sanctuary in Scheitniger Park. For days afterwards, the otherwise bleak and lifeless park was coloured by these bright birds, whose songs at night brought a touch of spring to life in the fortress.[13]

On the opposite side of the city, boys from two *Hitlerjugend* battalions, 55 and 56, mustered excitedly in the hall of Dietrich Eckart School. Today there was a 'comradeship evening' – a feast of cake and cocoa. Their leader Herbert Hirsch insisted they use '*Du*' rather than the more formal '*Sie*', whatever the rank. And tonight the highest rank of all was present, the head of the Hitler Youth, Artur Axmann. The *Reichsjugendführer* had struggled against a torrent of refugees heading west on Silesia's roads, but finally his staff car arrived at the former girls' school, now a makeshift headquarters for Hirsch's teenage soldiers. Axmann was impressed. "They created an outstanding impression, mentally and physically," he wrote, and Hirsch assured him that his boys had "received good training". That 'good training' comprised intense physical instruction in a nearby park and instruction in the use of first the rifle, then the *Panzerfaust*. The youngsters gathered on a railway embankment and watched as several anti-tank weapons were fired. At least one *Panzerfaust* exploded prematurely, killing one boy and wounding several others. Artur Axmann learned none of this – but he was left in no doubt that Breslau was a city under siege. Throughout the two hours he spent with the boys, Soviet Po2 biplanes dropped bombs constantly. "Although we all agreed not to let anything disturb us, whenever the monotonous droning stopped – replaced by a hissing-buzzing noise – we ducked automatically," sixteen-year-old Manfred Preussner recalled. The festivities over, Axmann left Breslau that evening to continue his visit to *Hitlerjugend* units defending Silesia. He narrowly escaped capture by Soviet tanks on the Autobahn outside Breslau.[14]

Just a few miles to the north, Soviet forces were now bearing down on Hendrik Verton's SS unit in Deutsch Lissa. The town was deserted – not just every civilian, but every soldier had pulled out, save for Verton and his comrades. They had one final duty to perform before they too abandoned Deutsch Lissa: to cover the last bridge spanning the Weistritz, the sole natural barrier opposing the Red Army west of Breslau. At midnight, the SS troops crawled into the cellars of houses along the river to take shelter as pioneers destroyed the crossing. "There was a deathly silence," wrote Verton. "The eerie calm was just like New Year's Eve, a few minutes before midnight." Then there was a deafening explosion which shattered the calm. In the cellar "we heard stones and bricks raining down in the streets for several seconds". When the troops emerged from the cellar the bridge had gone and "the roofs of houses looked like a hurricane had passed. Doors and window frames lay scattered in the streets and gardens between pieces of glass."

It was another day before the Russians attacked Deutsch Lissa. For more than twenty-four hours, the SS troops stood guard along the right bank of the Weistritz, bailing their foxholes out with their mess tins. At first light on the fifteenth, the Red artillery opened fire, first with individual shells, then growing into a barrage as the day became brighter and brighter. "We awaited the end, shaking in our foxholes," wrote Verton. "The pungent smoke from the explosions forced its way up our noses. Howling shells flew over our foxholes and splinters whistled in every direction. The earth shook, lumps of sand and stones drummed on our steel helmets." No one was wounded – only direct hits on the foxhole could do that.

We never got a single second to orientate ourselves [Verton continued]. But in this hurricane of fire the Russians could not attack either.

You couldn't defend yourself, you only wanted to crawl even deeper below ground. You forgot about the cold and sleeping. We felt the air pressure of the shells roaring low over our foxholes. The enemy barrage lasted an eternity and I believed the world was going under.

I didn't know what was happening to my comrades. It seemed unlikely that my neighbours on my left or right were still alive. When there was a sudden pause in the barrage, I dared to peer cautiously over the edge of my foxhole and noticed that the terrain had become ghostly. Acrid swathes of grey smoke hung over the cratered landscape. My right-hand neighbour was torn apart next to his foxhole. I called the man on my left and a steel helmet cautiously lifted out of the ground. Thank God he was alive and unharmed.

As the guns fell silent, the coarse cry of 'Urrah' carried through the haze as Russian infantry swept across the Weistritz plain – and over a bridge their pioneers had thrown across the river. "Dark figures appeared everywhere in front of us on the white, snow-covered landscape," Verton recalled. "Wide-eyed we watched the approach of the superior enemy." The SS unit's left flank caved in, leaving Verton's platoon cut off. "There was no other choice left to us than to sell our lives as dearly as possible," he wrote. Verton's machine-pistol glowed as he fired round after round. The Soviet infantry were slowed, but not stopped. "There were only a very few comrades left, standing or sitting – unprotected – on the edge of their foxholes, firing their last rounds. Death was so near now. I no longer had any hope. Life unwound at a furious pace." Suddenly, the platoon leader pointed excitedly at a stream which meandered through open ground to a nearby copse. The men left their foxholes and plunged into the icy water, holding their weapons above their heads. Machine-gun fire whistled over their heads, but every man who left his foxhole along the Weistritz made it safely to the wood and from there to the village of Saara. The exhausted soldiers sought food in the farmhouses on the edge of the hamlet. They found an elderly woman sitting in her kitchen wrapped in blankets, a black cat on her lap. "We wanted to take this old farmer's wife with us, but she refused to leave."[15]

In a flurry of snow, the Soviet pincers – Sixth Army from the west, Fifth Guards Army from the south-east – locked around 10am on Shrove Tuesday, 13 February, in the village of Domslau, eight miles south of Breslau. The pincers did not lock tightly, however. In places, the encircling ring was barely two miles thick initially – as the remnants of 269th Infantry Division discovered that evening. The 269th had done its job. It had parried the Soviet advance when Breslau's defences were weakest. Now it was needed elsewhere. Its artillery and support vehicles had already been sent south before the gap closed. The fighting troops, however, had to bludgeon their way out on the cusp of February 13-14. Ten *Sturmgeschütze* supported their bid for freedom. The bulk of the infantry made it, but not the armour. It found its path blocked in Gallen, ten miles outside

Breslau. "The village," recalled assault gun commander *Leutnant* Leo Hartmann, "was riddled with anti-tank guns and mortars". At dawn on the fourteenth, the six remaining *Sturmgeschütze* fell back past burned-out vehicles. The guns were ordered to support the defence of the city. The spare crews were ordered to slip through the ring of encirclement on foot. "I don't know how many succeeded," Hartmann wrote. "I did not." He swam through the icy waters of the Lohe then spent a day lying motionless "soaked to the skin" in no man's land between German and Russian lines just four miles from the city centre. He was found by the *Volkssturm* and carried to a field hospital before rejoining his unit, the grandly-titled *Panzerjäger Abteilung Breslau* – Breslau tank destroyer detachment.[16] A dozen or so miles away, what was left of 408th Infantry Division began to fall back towards the city. The troops passed through the village of Leuthen, empty save for one elderly woman who refused to leave the place of her birth. She not merely remained in Leuthen, she reported the Red Army's progress to *Generalmajor* Max Sachsenheimer and his scratch force. The reports were alarming. Sachsenheimer's men were cut off. Breslau was encircled. Germany's second-youngest general received orders to surrender all his field guns, all his vehicles, all his flak to the city's garrison, then break out. Fourteen hundred men set out on foot in three groups that night. Some clashed with Red Army troops on the Autobahn bridge at Kostenblut, others on a country estate. Some 800 men escaped. The rest were either dead or abandoned the attempt and joined the defenders of Breslau.[17]

There were no more concerted efforts to break out of the Breslau *Kessel* – cauldron – but there was one determined attempt to break *in*. Paul Arnhold had now been on the move for four weeks – but at least he was on native soil. He had passed through the village of Freyhan, forty miles north of Breslau, in the first week of February. From there the officer and his two companions had wandered west to the forests east of Trachenberg, then east to the farmland outside Trebnitz, and finally west once more to the banks of the Oder near Auras.

The approaches to the river were still covered in snow. The three men used white bed sheets as camouflage but they could not silence their footsteps – crunch, crunch, crunch. A handful of Russian troops stood guard on the Oder, but preferred singing to shooting – "they'd probably been at the schnapps again," Arnhold observed. Occasionally flares arced over the river, there were sporadic bursts of machine-gun fire, but otherwise the *frontoviki* were paying little attention to the Oder. As Monday, 12 February turned to Tuesday, Paul Arnhold and two *Landsers*, Rosseck and Feiner, struck out across the river in a raft.

> Full of desperation, we thrust our paddles into the water as if we were at a rowing regatta – we didn't worry about splashing or anything else for that matter. All that mattered was our poor, naked lives.
> In fact, we were naked aside from the shrouds wrapped around us. We had to do it – we just had to. Thanks to our manic efforts, our eyes were popping out of heads and our veins on our forehead were as thick as fingers. But the raft was

too heavy to be propelled through the swirling current into open water using our
little paddles. It almost looked as if we were driven back again despite our insane
efforts.

As the trio reached the main flow of the Oder, the noise of the paddles thrashing around
in the water finally triggered the Russian response. One flare, then another. Both fell
into the river, hissing. Three more flares, then five, six, seven. "It became as bright as
day – in fact brighter than day – along the entire river," Arnhold recalled. "There was
nothing we could do other than play 'dead rabbits'. Someone saw us and fired his
machine-pistol in our direction. Then three, four, six machine-pistols fired and a
machine-gun joined in."

Rosseck went into the water, then Feiner and finally Arnhold. "When I went into
the cold water between two ice floes, I was certain that now everything was over," he
wrote. "All too often these past few days I had imagined what would happen if we were
forced to swim in the icy water again. I had dismissed such thoughts as nightmares. And
now we were in the water again!"

The Russians aimed most of their fire at the raft, which quickly sank, while the three
men negotiated the ice floes in a desperate struggle to reach the left bank. Rosseck was
hit, but Arnhold hauled him to a sandbank. As the two men set foot on it, Russian
artillery began shooting. "The fire never relaxed," Arnhold wrote. "The Russians seemed
to be enjoying the change and fired everything they had." The pair crawled and swam
through thirty feet of river and bushes before a mound finally offered some shelter.

I fell down here with the wounded Rosseck and – just like him – could not get
my breath back at all. More dead then alive, we lay here in our underpants and
shirts, wet, with every limb shaking from the cold and excitement. We would
perhaps have stayed there, croaking miserably, because we could not find the
strength to stand up. Our spark of life was so close to being extinguished.

Mortar shells started to land. Reunited with Feiner, Arnhold and Rosseck crawled across
100 or so feet of ground before yelling: "Hallo! Hallo! Haaaallooo! There are three
German soldiers here – where are you?" No response. "Hallooooo! Hallooooo!
Hallooooo! There's a German *Oberst* here with two men. Where are you? Help us!
We're freezing to death. Tell us where you are!" Still no answer. "We've seen you
shooting. Tells us for God's sake where you are! One of us is wounded. We're all
freezing to death! Haalloooooo!" Finally, an answer through the night: "*Hier*!"

The three remnants of LVI Panzer Corps had run into a *Volkssturm* battalion holding
the Oder's left bank. They were led to the battalion headquarters where they were given
civilian clothes, warm soup and a hot bath. "It was no pleasure," Arnhold recalled. "The
pain when thawing out was so unimaginable that we passed out on a few occasions. We
could have screamed. But we had to get rid of five weeks of dirt, blood from our wounds,
pus from our frostbitten feet before we could eat something. It was like Christmas – in
hell!"

Sufficiently cleaned, Paul Arnhold was taken into Breslau, where he reported to von Ahlfen. His comrades volunteered to join 269th Infantry's breakout that night. "Much as I wanted to, I could not go with them," he wrote. "It was only now that the full extent of my exhaustion became clear. I could barely go on as I hobbled to the hospital located in a large bunker in the city centre." Medics immediately decided the *Oberst* should be flown out of the city.[18]

Siegfried Knappe also had orders to fly out of Breslau and rejoin Ferdinand Schörner's staff. After two gruelling weeks in the fortress, Knappe was exhausted; he fell into a deep sleep on a bed in the barracks at Gandau – despite the constant crashing of shells outside and the sound of infantry fighting to the west of the airfield. Finally, a little after 7pm on the fifteenth, two Junkers 52 touched down. Russian shellfire was erratic, but the crates of ammunition the aircraft brought in were unloaded hurriedly anyway. The staff officers climbed into the empty transporters with their kit. In a matter of minutes, the aircraft rolled down the field. As it lifted off the ground, the pilots banked sharply, trying to gain altitude circling over Breslau. That gave passengers "a spectacular view of a large city surrounded by a pearl-like string of burning villages". The muzzle flashes of artillery marked the Soviet front line. Knappe could also see flashes of heavy flak followed a few seconds later by the bursts of red shells close to the Junkers. After barely thirty minutes, the aircraft set down at Schweidnitz. "The tension, which I had hardly been aware of during the excitement of the flight, began to drain from me," he remembered. "I also felt an enormous sense of relief at being out of a city under siege."[19] Hugo Hartung was experiencing the full effects of that siege. All through 15 February the airfield at Schöngarten was subjected to a Soviet barrage. Hartung took shelter in the fire station; his less fortunate comrades were pinned down in their concrete foxholes on the airfield perimeter, unable to move thanks to the presence of Russian snipers. Only at nightfall were the airfield's defenders able to fall back to the officers' mess, left in a desolate state – "dirt and rubbish, leftovers from meals, puddles of wine and liquor". The company tried to settle down for the night when a messenger rushed in: "Alarm! The Russians are at the airfield fence!" Rushing outside, they found wild shooting and tracer hissing across the runway. Hartung continued:

> Everywhere the villages are on fire. We hear the terrible bellowing of cows in the burning stables, and also the shrill cries of people. Fires have broken out in the middle of the airfield. The cinema is aflame. Running and ducking, we look for cover in the officers' houses. Dead lie in the road everywhere.
>
> In the midst of the hellish noise of the barrage, the voice of a Soviet loudspeaker booms – it seems like it's coming from very close by: 'Come to us! Come to us!' After that, distorted by the volume, there's the *Internationale*, *Lili-Marleen* and the *Viennese Waltz*. Once we hear the 'Urrah!' of attacking Russians, partially to our rear. Palls of black smoke drift across the red sky and form strange figures.

The men took cover in the cellar of an officer's house on the edge of the field – but not for long. A shell crashed through the water main, plunging water into the cellar. As the men dashed outside, they ran straight into direct Russian fire. In the small hours of the sixteenth, a messenger somehow reached them: Schöngarten was being abandoned. Its defenders were to pull out.[20]

That same morning Breslauers awoke to the realization their city was surrounded. The day's edition of the *Schlesische Tageszeitung* carried an appeal by the fortress commander:

> *Festung* Breslau is encircled.
> That comes as no surprise to us, for a fortress must always expect to be encircled and to fight while encircled. All that matters is that every person remains steadfast in the fortress despite – and precisely because of – this encirclement.
> Everyone! Whether you are a man or a woman, old or young, soldier or *Volkssturm* man!
> We must now prepare ourselves for artillery fire, fire from other heavy weapons and bombs smashing into the fortress. All this is completely normal in the defence of a fortress.
> It would therefore be unworthy of every Breslauer to lose courage under this fire. Think of the many fortresses which have been encircled and successfully defended in our great history.
> We want to show the same courage, bravery and steadfastness as our forefathers did defending their fortresses.
> – Von Ahlfen, Generalmajor
Festungskommandant[21]

Encirclement also prompted calls for the city's surrender – but not from the Red Army directly. No, the call to capitulate came from a German, former Party member and regimental commander Luitpold Steidle, who had joined the anti-Nazi *National Komitee Freies Deutschland* – National Committee for a Free Germany – in captivity. Leaflets bearing Steidle's appeal began to drift down across Breslau. "Any further resistance is utterly pointless and senseless," he implored. "The only outcome will be the total sacrifice of your men for Hitler's long-since-lost war and the ultimate destruction of our homeland." The German response was printed in the city's daily newspaper. "We refuse to deal with the Red Army, which brings terror and destruction to our beautiful Silesian home," the *Schlesische Tageszeitung* declared. The article, which bears all Hanke's hallmarks, continued:

> What counts for us is the Führer's order to defend *Festung* Breslau to the last. We will carry out the mission of this German bulwark of culture on the Oder, which brave German warriors have defended and held for centuries with their blood and their willingness to make sacrifices . . .

> Warriors of *Festung* Breslau! This affects everything! It affects our people and our beautiful German home! We want to defend both to our dying breath. So to battle in defiance of Death and the Devil! We will meet the Red invader wherever we can. Their skulls will run with blood in the ruins of our beloved city. We are fighting for a just cause. We believe in our victory and God will stand by our strong hearts.[22]

Few believed the rhetoric. "Breslau will be quickly overrun," a reservist wrote to his wife. "The end of the war might soon be upon us and we want to hope that we will see each other again safely." *Sturmgeschütz* commander Leo Hartmann remembered "the most incredible rumours were circulating. Everyone believed we'd be relieved. But no one believed that the city could hold out more than three weeks." Others sought refuge in revelry. The first night of encirclement, one officer found two city centre bars "almost filled to overflowing", food was in more plentiful supply "than before the war" and the wine cellars were raided. It was not just officers enjoying a final night of debauchery. Accompanying many of them were finely dressed women, "most of whom looked like courtesans".[23]

There were at least 150,000 people now trapped in Breslau – and only one in four was a warrior. Nazi Party documents suggest there were 80,000 civilians still in the city when it was surrounded: 6,500 men capable of bearing arms, 30,000 men and women capable of working, 5,000 mothers, nearly 9,000 children, 24,000 elderly, sick or infirm, and more than 4,000 foreign workers. The true figure is probably nearer 115,000, but no one knows with certainty.[24]

The 37,000 or so warriors in the fortress consisted of one division – the 609th under Great War veteran and artilleryman Siegfried Ruff – which had not existed just one month earlier, and five equally hastily formed regiments, each named after its commander. They were deployed around the forty-five-mile perimeter of the ring, more accurately an oval, on a north-west to south-east axis. Luftwaffe ground units meshed together under *Oberst* Wolf Wehl defended the southern perimeter of the cauldron. In the west, *Major* Karl Hermann Hanf commanded men from a former non-commissioned officers' school, holding the line alongside the youthful *Obersturmbannführer* Georg Besslein and his regiment of Waffen SS replacement and training units. On their right, troops from the city's barracks at Karlowitz and Rosenthal safeguarded the northern front under *Oberst* Hermann Sauer, while thirty-four-year-old *Oberstleutnant* Walter-Peter Mohr defended the north-eastern line with a newly formed replacement and training unit. The three regiments of the 609th – Kersten, Reinkober and Schulz, comprising reconnaissance units, trainee NCOs, anti-tank gunners, officer cadets and men of 269th Infantry Division unable to escape encirclement – completed the ring of defenders in the east and south-east of Breslau. To each regiment was assigned at least one *Volkssturm* battalion under the overall command of the city's SA chief, Otto Herzog. Herzog was no fair-weather Nazi; a reserve officer, he had fought – and been wounded – in the campaign in France in 1940. He energetically set about organising the city's 38

Volkssturm units into 'combat' and 'work' battalions depending on the men's experiences, plus two battalions comprised solely of Hitler Youths.

Against them were ranged an entire Soviet Army, the Sixth, led by the energetic – and young – Vladimir Gluzdovski. The forty-one-year old Georgian had served in the Red Army since the age of sixteen, fighting in the Civil War, defending the Soviet capital in 1941, and leading three armies westwards when the tide of war changed. With wiry jet-black hair, a wry smile often etched across his face, a cigarette invariably in his right hand, and with political commissar Vassily Klokov almost always at his side, Gluzdovski had commanded Sixth Army for barely two months. He was even-handed, sometimes stubborn, and regarded as one of the brighter young brains in the Red Army. He committed six rifle divisions to the siege of Breslau – 181st, 218th, 273rd, 294th, 309th and 359th – some 50,000 men armed with more than 1,000 field guns and howitzers, but only a few dozen armoured vehicles. In the small hours of 17 February Gluzdovski would unleash his forces to crush Silesia's capital.[25]

For most Breslauers, there was little if any distinction between the different stages of the struggle for their city. It had been under siege for a good three weeks now. No longer did the air raid sirens sound. There was no need. Somewhere in Breslau was always under bombardment by day or night, be it from Soviet aircraft or Soviet artillery. "Smoke from fires constantly hangs over the city," a bomber crewman in 82nd Guards Bomber Regiment wrote to his mother as he sat "next to an oven, formerly owned by a German, on a chair, formerly owned by a German". Daily he watched "bombs exploding, setting houses on fire and destroying them." He felt no pity. "Just imagine the Germans finding their graves under the ruins of their houses. Now these Fritzes are all learning what destroyed cities are and what war means."[26] With the impact of each bomb or shell, doors shook and shutters clattered, but it was windowpanes which suffered most. City streets were strewn with fields of broken glass. Breslauers patched their shattered windows up with boards, wrapping paper, cardboard – less as protection against the bombs and shells than to keep out the cold, made worse by the now intermittent gas and electricity supplies.[27] Other damage was beyond repair. A shell smashed through the medieval wall of St Barbarakirche on the western edge of Breslau's old town as *Pfarrer* Ernst Hornig led morning prayers. It lodged in the bars on the windows in the north vault. It failed to explode, but it did send clouds of dust billowing through the church. Hornig led his worshippers into the cellar of the adjacent parsonage. At least two more artillery strikes followed, smashing the harmonium, peppering the heavy vestry door "with holes like a sieve". Despite the devastation, Ernst Hornig felt the protective hand of the Lord. "Had the first shell exploded, there would have been dead and wounded," he wrote. "We know that we have been saved, as if by a miracle." But never again did the bells of St Barbara toll to summon the devout to worship – the congregation were convinced the church had been targeted because of the ringing.[28] "Everyone wonders whether Breslau will share the fate of the other major cities of the Reich. Breslau is a beautiful city with marvellous icons of its historic Christian culture, it has architectural structures seldom found in a city," wrote Paul Peikert. "Dominsel, the town hall, the wonderful old churches – is all this to go down in ruins because military insanity wants to turn every house, every church, every cellar into a fortress? What will we achieve if Breslau holds out a couple more days as a result, if what is left is an endless field of ruins? It's as if the world has been gripped by a mania for destruction. The moloch of war devours everything."[29] The answer would come on Tuesday, 20 February.

Shortly before dusk on 16 February, more than fifty dots appeared in the sky above Breslau. As the sun began to dip in the west, the aircraft broke formation. "Huge puffed-out red mushrooms suddenly appear in the sky, falling slowly to earth," wrote battalion adjutant Erich Schönfelder.

> Dark shapes dangle on the ropes beneath these mushrooms, causing a great deal of consternation. The occasional person points to the sky at first with an expression of the surprise, then one of horror. Now hundreds are looking up to sky – *Landsers* and civilians. They stop walking, look up in disbelief at this strange sight, until from somewhere there's the shrill cry of terror: "Paratroopers, red paratroopers! The Russians are using airborne troops to take hold of the airfield."

Hugo Hartung and his comrades grabbed their carbines and began wildly shooting at the aircraft and the parachutes. "Cease fire," their flak commander screamed. "You're shooting at our planes!" Breslauers, too, quickly realized that the parachutes brought supplies, not death. "As quickly as the horror took hold, it's vanished again," Erich Schönfelder noticed. The canisters were scattered: some landed at Gandau, some drifted into the Oder a few yards away, and some landed near the Soviet lines – so close that German troops gathering them came under mortar fire. Breslauers cared little for the ammunition and weapons the canisters contained, but a rumour quickly flashed through the city: the post had been dropped and would soon be distributed. For most inhabitants, it was the first news from the outside world, from loved ones evacuated, in four weeks.[30]

The air supply of Breslau began encouragingly. For the loss of just seven aircraft and sixteen men in the first six nights of operations, 315 tonnes of supplies were delivered. The aircraft did not leave the fortress empty. They carried more than 1,600 people out of the encircled city, including Paul Arnhold. The pioneer officer had been joined at Gandau by his two comrades from their bitter trek from the Vistula to the Oder – neither man had been able to break through the Soviet ring around Breslau. Medics determined they should be flown out at the first opportunity. But they would not share the same aircraft as Paul Arnhold, there was no room. They accompanied the *Oberst* to the door of the Junkers 52 under heavy artillery fire. The pioneer officer was tempted to climb out as Rosseck and Feiner waved forlornly. When a salvo landed not fifty yards away, the pilot throttled the engine up and the transporter raced down the runway. "For all three of us, it was a sad departure," Arnhold wrote. "I was not ashamed to wipe away a couple of tears." The Junkers headed west for an hour. The sky suddenly turned blood-red – Dresden was still aflame, four days after the city had suffered one of the heaviest air raids of the war. The Junkers "flew over thousands of fires" before touching down west of the city. From there, the officer was put on a hospital train and sent to the spa town of Bad Elster. His convalescence would last just four weeks. Before the end of March, Paul Arnhold was back on duty.[31]

On the western edge of Breslau's defensive perimeter, Hendrik Verton and his *Regiment Besslein* comrades watched Soviet engineers with admiration as they tried to build a temporary crossing over the Weistritz in Deutsch Lissa. The SS troops emptied their machine-guns at the opposite bank. Tracer fire created an eerie impression as the shells hissed into the river. The Russians responded with heavy fire, enveloping the Germans in clouds of smoke and brick dust. Under this protective umbrella, the pioneers finished their bridge. By morning, a handful of assault troops gingerly crossed and formed a small bridgehead. They would soon be cut off.

Hans von Ahlfen had monitored the Soviet engineers on the Weistritz. He had allowed them to throw a bridge across the river. Now he committed his secret weapon. He sent pioneer *Leutnant* Hans Kohne with three remote-controlled miniature tanks – Goliaths – each packed with a 165lb explosive charge. With German artillery and mortar shells crashing down on the left bank of the river to drown out the noise the small tanks made, Kohne manoeuvred his Goliaths on to the bridge. When they reached the main span, the officer detonated them. Three flashes, then the makeshift crossing was enveloped in clouds of thick black smoke. It took an eternity for it to clear, but when it did Kohne could see that two stretches of the bridge had been destroyed and one of its pillars had crashed into the Weistritz.

The Soviet attack disrupted, Verton and his comrades booby-trapped the cellars of abandoned homes in Deutsch Lissa, on the right bank of the Weistritz, fixing hand-grenades to door handles "so that the Russians at least faced a little resistance". *Regiment Besslein* fell back through the night – "the clattering of our gasmasks was the monotonous and ever-present rhythm of our march" – first through the deserted village of Stabelwitz, seven miles north-west of the city centre, bound for Schmiedefeld on the western edge of Breslau. After three weeks in the front line, the city offered sanctuary to the worn-out soldiers, a chance to wash and sleep properly for the first time in weeks. "To us," wrote Hendrik Verton, "Breslau seemed a peaceful oasis in the middle of a hell of fire and death." His company would quickly discover it was not.[32]

Werner Zillich and his *Regiment Schulz* comrades were enjoying a break after their labours on the edge of Brockau, five miles south-east of the city centre. The men were satisfied with their work. They had finished digging foxholes and the village was well fortified for the coming assault – the front door of every apartment or house in Brockau, and many of the internal doors, had been booby-trapped with mines. "If somebody opened the door, they would be blown into the air," eighteen-year-old Zillich recalled. Now it was time for breakfast – and Brockau was richly stocked; its inhabitants had left behind copious supplies of preserved fruit and meat. One of the men fetched a pail filled with jam. And then 'Stalin's Organs', the multiple rocket projectors, opened fire. "We could tell," wrote Zillich, "that they were aiming for us." The troops dashed for their foxholes. SS *Sturmmann* Zillich was too slow. The holes were full. He threw himself to the ground and waited for the onslaught to end. Eventually, it did. The men climbed out of their foxholes. One looked across at Zillich and called for a medic. The SS soldier stood up, bemused. "This lad still doesn't notice anything," his comrades laughed. A shell had smashed the pail of jam and splattered his coat. "They thought it was blood, that I was wounded," Zillich recalled. "Terror and joy at the same time." Shortly afterwards the men heard the crash of explosions coming from Brockau: Red Army troops were searching the houses – and paying a fearful price. "We do not know how many were killed," Zillich said, "but all hell was let loose because there was no attack in the coming days."[33]

Vladimir Gluzdovski's attack faltered at Brockau, but elsewhere the first day of 'Operation Breslau' saw five outlying villages fall to his Sixth Army, among them Krietern, not three miles from the city centre. "Houses burn, a pungent mist hampers breathing and hinders vision. Eyes water," wrote war correspondent Vassily Malinin, who took part in the village's capture. "This merciless, bloody struggle for every house, for every floor continues. It's not uncommon for the walls of houses which fall down to bury soldiers of both sides in the ruins." After the lightning thrust from the Vistula to the Oder, Malinin realized that fighting in a city was an entirely different proposition. He found the roads blocked by stone barricades, houses blown up by the defenders to leave streets impassable. Each night at 8pm precisely, the apartment blocks and villas of affluent Breslau society were dynamited. Sometimes they were still occupied, but the inhabitants were given no time to gather their possessions. Furniture, clothes, family heirlooms, all added to the mountains of rubble. The Red Army responded in kind, blowing up walls and hauling guns through the breaches, then directing their fire at the German positions. In narrower streets it was almost impossible to determine from which window machine-gun or sniper fire came. An advance of two hundred yards was something to be celebrated. "Two hundred yards in the city, in street fighting – that's a lot. That's two, sometimes even three houses," the war correspondent noted. For it seemed every house, every floor of every house, every room of every house, had to be contested. "If our soldiers don't comb out the entire house – from attic to cellar – then we're not certain the house is free." There were veterans of the struggle for Stalingrad in Sixth Army's ranks, but for most of Gluzdovski's soldiers the initial fighting in Breslau's suburbs was a new experience. They were men, battalion commander Captain Nikolai Nemakin remembered, who had mainly grown up in villages and fought in the open. "The labyrinth of streets and squares of a sprawling, burning city, full of acrid smoke and clingy soot which hung in the air everywhere seemed like out-and-out hell, something they had never experienced," he wrote.[34]

The defenders of Breslau were also adjusting to their first exposure to street fighting. Lessons were brutal and bloody. After sporadically firing on Russian positions near the sprawling Südpark, Max Baselt's *Hitlerjugend* platoon was subjected to a ferocious barrage. The mortars took a direct hit, so too the men bringing up crates of ammunition. When he returned from fetching ammunition, fifteen-year-old Baselt found his comrades either dead or wounded, their faces grey and covered with dirt. It was their own fault, the teenager reasoned. "Our stupidity! The best protection against being discovered is changing position quickly." They had failed to do so – and paid the ultimate price. The gravely wounded were pushed to a field hospital in a wheelbarrow, the lightly wounded walked on foot. "Everyone is still stunned, hardly anyone speaks," Baselt wrote. That evening, Baselt's section leader held roll-call in the shadow of the imposing red-brick water tower which dominated the southern Breslau skyline. The *Unterscharführer* had started the day with eighteen men. Now he had nine.[35]

Otto Rothkugel and his companions in *Volkssturm Bataillon Peschke* were ordered to build machine-gun emplacements near the FAMO works on the western edge of the city. The Russians quickly observed their activity and began to plaster the goods station which served the factory. "As the house where we were billeted was close to it, our cellar shook and it felt like we were in a boat which was rocking," Rothkugel wrote. "We were constantly afraid that the house would collapse and we would be buried under the ruins." Sometimes there were lengthy pauses in the barrage. "Some of us thought about the end and called upon God to help even if at other times we wanted nothing to do with God."[36]

In nearby Schmiedefeld, Hendrik Verton's company took shelter in cellars as Russian artillery and mortars began to pummel the village.

> We sat or stood in the dark cellar in silence. Shells crashed outside in quick succession. Now and then wounded *Landsers* staggered down the cellar steps and reported with horror that hell was raging in the street. In the end, soldiers from every branch of the armed forces were crammed in the cellar. Between the explosions, the wounded cried.

Russian infantry did not attack Schmiedefeld, but the barrage had left the village in ruins: houses were wrecked, the main street "had been ploughed up by numerous hits". Once again the Waffen SS troops pulled out, this time halting in the grounds of the now abandoned and overgrown Linke-Hofmann works. "We now realized that we had to defend a city, because from time to time civilians cautiously entered the surrounding houses to save their most important items," Verton recalled. "They would carefully lock their empty, but still intact, apartments as if that would save them."[37]

A few hundred yards away, Hugo Hartung dug in on the railway embankment. His company received no instructions on entrenching. He and a comrade, an Upper Silesian farmer, dragged building material from nearby gardens to create a makeshift foxhole. A professor hauled a mattress to make his hole more comfortable. When the company's battle-hardened *Unteroffizier* returned, he berated the reluctant soldiers. The positions were pathetic, while the red mattress was the perfect target for Russian aircraft. A mile away, the church in Neukirch "burned like a torch and the fires in the south-west of the city grew." The gardeners' huts where the day before Hartung's company had found shelter were now ablaze. "The warm flow of embers blew pleasantly towards us on this bitterly cold night," he wrote, while transport aircraft rumbled overhead, bound for Gandau airfield, a couple of miles to the east.

The following morning the Luftwaffe troops were pulled out of the line. They spent the day resting with a couple of civilians and several women in an inn "whose owner was still serving beer". For the first time, the soldiers learned that the city was encircled and Dresden had suffered "a terrible air raid". After twenty-four hours' rest, the company returned to the embankment before first light on 19 February. From his foxhole, Hugo Hartung stared at a small mound of sand. He named it the Wendelstein after a crooked-peaked mountain in Bavaria. "I very much enjoy the sun rising up on my little Alpine peak," he wrote. "Gleaming, it stands out against the dark-blue February sky." He continued:

> These wistful memories do not last long, however, because as the sun rises, the Russian artillery wakes up and shoots at our positions. One shell lands not fifty metres from us and causes a hail of splinters to fall on our foxhole. Rifle shots strike the tracks and the rain of gravel from the embankment which drums against our steel helmets after each impact is particularly unpleasant. A lark, the first this spring, provides the treble in this hellish concert. Unruffled, its chirps grow louder.

At midday the Luftwaffe troops were relieved. They had walked barely one hundred yards from the embankment when the Soviet artillery opened fire. The first shells landed in the foxholes the men had just left.[38]

After just three days, Gluzdovski's troops had smashed Hans von Ahlfen's southern ring and pushed to within two miles of the city centre, crossing the main railway line which ran through the suburbs along a sweeping semi-circular embankment. A battalion of Hitler Youths was ordered to drive the Soviets out of a copse in Südpark and beyond the embankment at the foot of the park. Fifteen-year-old Peter Bannert described the attack:

> Then the sound, a whistle! We jumped up and ran to Südpark. We fired into the dark while we roared at the top of our voices. As I leapt up, various men who had been lying next to me did not move. "Hey, we're off!" I screamed at them. When I touched one of them I realized that it was a dead Russian. I quickly ran after my comrades.
>
> Our attack surprised the Russians and they fled back through an underpass behind the railway embankment. Südpark was captured! As I ran past, I saw a number of abandoned anti-tank guns, which were half dug into the ground between the trees. We'd been shot at with them. A dead Russian soldier hung in front of the entrance to a bunker. He looked as if he was still alive and wanted to alert his men inside.

The attack began to stutter just beyond the underpass as Russian machine-guns opened fire. Bannert took cover behind a tree trunk. From there he could just make out dark figures leaping from foxholes on the railway embankment. Bannert fired his rifle at them wildly while his comrades crept or rushed back to his left and right. It was time, he reasoned, to fall back too. He fired his *Panzerfaust* then began to run to the rear, only to be struck in his right thigh by shrapnel. He used his rifle as support to reach German lines, then was sent to a first-aid post. A week later, lying in a hospital bed with the wounded badge pinned to his uniform, he wrote proudly to his parents. "We turfed the Russians out of Südpark with our counter-attack. A number of dead Russians and six captured guns! Perhaps you have already read about the *Kampfgruppe Hitlerjugend*."[39]

Perhaps they had. For the Party mouthpiece, *Völkischer Beobachter,* trumpeted the bravery of the boys defending Breslau. It championed the "fanatical doggedness and determined fighting spirit" they displayed 'routing' a Soviet regiment. One hundred and twenty boys had left 170 Ivans dead on the battlefield, seized several prisoners and captured a "rich booty – anti-tank guns, mortars, machine-guns, handguns and ammunition." In doing so, the newspaper declared, they had "set a glorious example. They struck the hated enemy where they found him. They stood firm and attacked." In short, opined the Nazi organ, they had lived up to the old adage: "The flag means more to us than death." Other Nazi accounts of the battle for Breslau were no more accurate. Sudeten Germans in Kaaden – today Kadaň in the Czech Republic – were assured their compatriots were not suffering. "The trams are running again. The newspaper is published every day." There was fighting, of course – "sometimes it's more lively than others" – but the defenders of Breslau were "filled with self-confidence". Inside the fortress, there was a whispering campaign to raise the troops' morale. Propaganda officers spread rumours that "new weapons" were being used *en masse*, that a new counter-offensive along a sixty-mile front had been unleashed in Silesia aimed at Breslau and was making excellent progress. In an address to the nation, propaganda minister Joseph Goebbels repeated the lies. Germany would deliver her enemies "blow upon blow" courtesy of new U-boats and a renewed V-weapon campaign, and her conquered territories in the East would be liberated.

> Just as our forefathers did so often in our history, so we too will smash the Mongol storm against the heartland. Like them, we will defend ourselves with fanatical fury and dogged hatred, so that one day the legend – that after days of fierce fighting the dead continued to fight on in the heavens in the ominous darkness of night – can be recounted about us too.
>
> And even if in the end we have to cling to our soil, even if we have to sacrifice our last remaining possessions, even if no end to the suffering and terror can be predicted, we will not give up the lawful right of our nation to life, freedom and a future. We prefer to die rather than surrender!

Priest Paul Peikert was not fooled. "These are the same old propaganda lies which have been used repeatedly for the past two years, from Stalingrad to the present day." He was right.[40]

Tuesday, 20 February 20 had been a cold but sunny winter's day. The night which followed it was moonlit. An hour after dark, Russian bombers approached from the east. Flares quickly outshone the moon, turning night to day. For the next three and a half hours it "rained bombs" on both sides of the Oder as the heart of Breslau was pummelled. "The foundations of houses shook, an indescribable noise filled the air," Peikert wrote. "People in cellars prayed and begged for this terrible curse to pass. Because the houses shook awfully, everyone feared that the houses would collapse on top of them and bury them. The bombs seemed so close that everyone believed the entire neighbourhood would collapse in ruins." Peikert led the occupants of his air raid shelter in prayer. With the cross in his hand, the Catholic priest blessed parishioners with the words: *Ecce crucem Domini; fugite partes adversae! Vicit Leo de tribu Juda*! Behold the cross of the Lord; flee, ye enemy armies – the lion of the tribe of Juda is victorious.

When the bombing ended, the priest tentatively stepped outside. He expected to see his church, St Mauritius, in ruins. It was not, nor was his rectory. Another house of God was not so fortunate. St Augustinus, a fine neo-Romanesque church in the south of the city, had been levelled. In ruined houses next to the Holteihöhe gardens by the Oder, the corpse of a soldier was found; his uniform had been ripped from his body by the force of a bomb blast. Kaiserbrücke was barely passable. Lessingbrücke no longer was; a second of its arches had collapsed into the river. "The city leaves a rarely-seen impression of neglect," Peikert wrote. "Most windowpanes are smashed, the streets are full of rubbish and littered with shards of glass from the windows." Post official Conrad Bischof agreed. "Breslau is turning more and more into a field of ruins," he recorded in his diary, resignedly accepting the destruction of his home town. "It's a pity for beautiful Breslau but it must sacrifice itself for Germany – that's obvious." Paul Peikert could not agree:

This air raid has left people utterly depressed. Everyone awaits the nights to come with a great deal of concern – the air raids are bound to get heavier. Everyone asks why, what for? *Ja*, the war which we waged has become madness, absurd. We cannot change its outcome. Criminally caused by our regime, it is the worst crime not only against our people, but the entire world. Every day the senseless continuation of this war devours countless human lives, destroys our cities and villages, makes an entire nation homeless and poor. How terribly has God's judgment been unleashed against our nation, whose leadership has committed outrages against everything which God stands for these past dozen years.[41]

Early on the morning of 22 February, the paratroopers of 25th and 26th *Fallschirmjäger* Regiments hung around on the edge of Jüterbog airfield, fifty miles south of Berlin. Just twenty-four hours before they had been blown kisses by the young women of Schwedt on the lower Oder, perhaps convinced they would defend the city. Now, ninety miles away, all manner of rumours passed from company to company as Junkers 52 idled on the tarmac. The men's commanders asked them to gather round: the garrison of Breslau needed reinforcements. "Our faces became hard and serious, for we knew what it meant to fight in a fortress," *Oberjäger* Rudi Christoph wrote. "But we wanted our men to hold their own because now we had to defend our regional capital. You see our battalion consisted mainly of Silesians and Sudetenlanders – and they would rather fight in Silesia than Pomerania."[42]

Late that day, the men were divided into groups of sixteen for the flight to Breslau, 200 miles away. Shortly before midnight the *Fallschirmjäger* boarded their aircraft. At five-minute intervals, Junkers rolled down the Jüterbog runway. The paratroopers sat calmly on the linen benches. Some slept. Company commander *Oberleutnant* Albrecht Schulze van Loon put his steel helmet on his lap and let his dachshund settle in it. For nearly two hours, the transporter droned towards Breslau until the eastern horizon began to glow red.

We see the fires and the flashes of gun barrels [Schulze van Loon wrote]. Anti-aircraft searchlights nervously sweep the sky. We get closer with our engines throttled down. The Russians have heard us. Because only one aircraft can land, the Russian air defences concentrate on every single aircraft. The searchlights thrash about wildly. For a few seconds it's as bright as day in the aircraft. We are above the city. The searchlight has seen us. It swings back and has us in its beam. Like a pack of wolves, the others join it and will not release us from their bright beam. The beams are fixed firmly on us, a signal for the light and heavy anti-aircraft guns. Light anti-aircraft shells shoot up to our left and right – as if someone in the sky above was pulling up a shining pearl necklace. The salvoes from the anti-aircraft batteries explode in front of us, behind us and next to us. It's like running a gauntlet in the sky. Suddenly we're hit. Fuel sprays in our faces, all the windows have shattered. The machine drops 2,000 metres. The air is full of iron. I move my dachshund and put on my steel helmet. The searchlights will not release us from their grasp. The pilot is able to regain control of the aircraft fifty metres above the rooftops. Only the middle engine is still turning. The propellers on the left and right are not moving. The aileron is shot to pieces and fuel is still spurting into the cabin, but it does not set on fire.

We cannot land at Gandau. Each shot-up aircraft must look after number one. Otherwise it would block the runway to subsequent aircraft. We try to escape in the direction of Schweidnitz. Once again we cross the front line. The searchlights capture the aircraft behind us. But the burning city provides us enough light anyway and so the Russian infantry creeping slowly across roofs and through the streets see us and fire rifles and machine-guns at us for all they're worth.

The front lies behind us. In front of us towers the Zobten, a peak which rises several hundreds metres above the plain. We stick our heads out of the windows. Treetops sway beneath the left wing. There's the aromatic smell of resin.

We land in Schweidnitz on literally the last drop of fuel. We leap out and take a deep breath first of all. A hole one metre across yawns on the tank in the right wing. The aircraft is riddled with shrapnel and bullet holes. Each man feels his body. No one is wounded, but an *Obergefreiter* has a shiner. A piece of metal struck him in the eye.[43]

Twenty Junkers 52s touched down at Gandau that night, delivering 295 paratroopers. Minutes later, eighteen aircraft lifted off again carrying nearly 350 wounded men and civilians.

Like the plane carrying Albrecht Schulze van Loon, Rudi Christoph's Ju52 was diverted. The radio on his aircraft failed, the wings started to ice up. It turned around and set down on an airfield near Dresden. Two nights later, he tried again. As the *Fallschirmjäger* climbed into their Junkers – its doors left open to speed loading and unloading – they were warned that Gandau would be under fire when they landed. The eastern horizon glowed red as the transporter approached Breslau. On final approach a red flare was fired to warn the Junkers off. For the next twenty minutes the aircraft circled Breslau. The first strains of dawn were glimmering in the east as Christoph's aircraft landed under heavy artillery fire. Three other Junkers were destroyed as they approached Gandau; one flew into a factory's chimney.

Rudi Christoph and his comrades were put on a bus once used by the *Gau* orchestra and driven through the city to their billets at the new labour exchange, the *Fallschirmjäger* regiment's headquarters. Each man received several hand grenades, then was driven to the front line in a truck constantly attacked by Soviet fighter-bombers. The wagon halted next to a railway embankment in the western suburb of Mochbern, where the paratroopers filed into the cellars of abandoned houses "and waited for things to happen". Nothing did. After the strains of the night, the day passed "waiting and sleeping. We occasionally saw a comrade whom we'd already given up on, and learned from him that so-and-so was no longer alive," Christoph wrote. "It was clear to us that this time it was serious."[44]

Hans von Ahlfen had committed Rudi Christoph and his fellow paratroopers into battle immediately – and reluctantly. *Fallschirmjäger* had a fearsome reputation, justifiably. But the *Fallschirmjäger* of Breslau were not the *Fallschirmjäger* of Crete, Monte Cassino, Normandy. Many were pilots without aircraft who had re-trained as infantry. They had seen little fighting. They had plenty of *Panzerfaust*, but no mortars, no machine-guns. "In a nutshell, it was a good – but still young – unit, not yet suited to conditions in Breslau," he said – and told Ferdinand Schörner as much. "The *Fallschirmjäger* battalion is good," the army group commander snapped. "I expect the utmost energy from you now."

The paratroopers were foisted on Hans von Ahlfen. The fortress commander did not want them – but Karl Hanke did. He used his Party connections to ensure the *Fallschirmjäger* were flown in. Until now, Ahlfen had been given a free hand to direct the battle for Breslau. But with the fighting now devouring the city's suburbs, the

Gauleiter was a constant presence at the general's daily conferences in his new headquarters in the cellars of the Liebichshöhe, an ornate folly built on a hill overlooking the city's historic moat.

Ahlfen did not impress Hanke. The general was defeatist: in private he conceded that the war was lost. His defeatism had clearly infected the men, for in barely a week's fighting, the Russians had advanced to within two miles of the city centre. He had opposed the use of paratroopers. But his greatest sin was to challenge the *Gauleiter* over the location of a new airfield for the fortress. The Russians were already closing in on Gandau, and its loss meant the fall of *Festung* Breslau. Work had begun on a replacement in the east of the city on the site of the 1938 *Sportfest*. The fortress's Luftwaffe liaison officer, Wilhelm von Friedeburg, and a civic engineer scoured the city. They came up with one alternative location: along the Kaiserstrasse and across the Scheitniger Stern. The street was lined with apartment blocks and lampposts, trees ran down the central boulevard and tram wires overhead, the imposing gothic Lutherkirche with the tallest steeple in the city dominated the landscape. All would have to be flattened by tons of explosives and thousands of people. It would create "a swathe of destruction" – and one usable only in favourable wind conditions. Ahlfen rejected all thoughts of blasting a runway down Kaiserstrasse, but not Karl Hanke. The *Gauleiter* prevailed.[45]

Hans von Ahlfen may have disagreed with Breslau's *Gauleiter* on many issues, but he quickly adopted Karl Hanke's motto – who fears an honourable death will die in disgrace. A platoon leader who left his men and looted a flat, stealing a bizarre haul – two swords, a travelling manicure set, hair lotion, an officer's belt, perfume and tins of powdered milk – was condemned to death. The standing court martial went even further: it also condemned him to lose his *Wehrwürdigkeit* – worthiness to serve – and the loss of civil rights for life, which was now not especially long. A drunken reservist officer who was half an hour late carrying out an order was treated more leniently. Stripped of his rank, he was committed to the front line as an ordinary soldier. And any man who abandoned his post and fell back without orders, Ahlfen ruled, would be executed. *Pionier* Franz Polak did just that. He was shot. So too *Gefreiter* Richard Misof. *Feldwebel* Richard Brener loitered in an abandoned apartment rather than rejoin his men. He too was shot. The sharp tongue of fifty-five-year-old *Volkssturm* man Martin Mayer earned him the death penalty for "subversive remarks". *Obergefreiter* Alfred Lieske, *Gefreiter* Paul Piontek, and *Kanonier* Josef Smolka and Anton Drong decided to desert *en masse*, downed weapons, tore up their pay books and tried to cross to Russian lines. Courage deserted them when Soviet troops opened fire. The following morning a reconnaissance party found them hiding in a stable. All four men were shot on Ahlfen's orders.

> These death sentences should serve as a warning to every soldier and at the same time give decent soldiers – and the entire fortress as well – the satisfaction that cowardly traitors face a merciless, shameful end. The summary execution of

cowards and shirkers not only eradicates them, it also brings down shame upon their families by wiping out their honour and condemns them to poverty, depriving them of all benefits.[46]

The fortress commander could praise as well as chastise his men. He singled out Walter-Peter Mohr's regiment for inflicting casualties "at least fifteen times higher than our own death toll" on the Red Army in fighting in the south of the city. "Comrades," he urged, "keep fighting like this." The general continued:

> Every house of Fortress Breslau, which has been entrusted to us by the Führer, will cost the enemy rivers of blood. Always remember how the Bolshevik foe has raped our wives, murdered our children and brothers or led them into forced labour.[47]

It would be one of the final orders Hans von Ahlfen issued.

Hermann Niehoff was returning to his command post near the Upper Silesian town of Ratibor, looking forward to the cup of coffee prepared for him by a staff officer. Niehoff was pleased with his work this first day of March: his 371st Infantry Division, a *Feld, Wald und Wiesen* – bog-standard – division, had cleared up a Soviet penetration and thrown the Russians back to their starting positions. The *Generalleutnant* had twice led these men, mostly Westphalians and Rhinelanders, firstly in the Ukraine when he had brought them out of encirclement, then through the winter of 1944-5 and the retreat from the Vistula to Upper Silesia. As he approached his makeshift headquarters, he noticed the staff car of the army group commander parked outside. Perhaps, he mused, Ferdinand Schörner had come to congratulate him on correcting the front line. He had not. "Your division is an undisciplined mass and that is solely and only down to the failure of your supervision," the general scolded Niehoff. The divisional commander was taken aback. Schörner's tirade continued. One by one, officers were called in and arrested or dismissed. Niehoff spoke out. "Schörner, who up to now had ranted and raved, now began to roar," he recalled. "*Generalleutnant* Niehoff, you are hereby relieved of command. Go immediately to Mährisch-Ostrau and await my further orders!" he bellowed. Schörner turned on his heels and walked out.

Niehoff's batman grabbed his general's possessions, put them into a staff car and drove his master the twenty miles to the industrial city. The general hardly spoke a word on the journey. Barely had he arrived in Mährisch-Ostrau than a teletype was thrust into his hand. "A new mission in a most difficult location is planned for the general at the suggestion of *Generaloberst* Schörner." At that moment the telephone rang. It was Schörner. "Niehoff, I have big plans for you," he said. "The Führer himself has ordered that you should fly to Breslau immediately. Take over command from *Generalmajor* von Ahflen. Niehoff, you must hold the fortress to the last man and to the last round." Schörner paused, then added chillingly: "If you fail in your task not only will you face the death sentence, but your family too will also bear responsibility." The army group commander gave Niehoff a few minutes to collect his thoughts. He used them to write a brief note to his family:

> My Dear!
>   In this hour of the hardest decision I send you and our children my most heartfelt wishes.
>   God give me the strength to survive.
>   I know what is expected of me. Live well!
>
> Your father[48]

Before leaving for Breslau, Niehoff was invited to dine with Seventeenth Army commander Friedrich Schulz – "a final meal before execution" – he wryly observed. "Schörner has also asked me to pass the following on to you," Schulz imparted. "If you succeed in holding Breslau for three or four days, then he will reach you by road and extend his hand to you." Schulz leaned forward. "Between us," he whispered, "the first attempts to form such an assault group have been made. But in three to four days, that's an illusion. If you perform your miracle and, shall we say, hold on for fourteen days, then this thrust might come to something."[49]

After dark on 3 March Hermann Niehoff arrived at an airfield – "little more than a crudely flattened field with old barracks on the edge" – just outside Schweidnitz. The flight into the fortress was brief – Breslau lay a mere thirty miles to the north-east, but more than half of the territory his Junkers would cross was occupied by the enemy. His pilot warned him the flight would be "ticklish". To Niehoff, the Junkers seemed too large, too cumbersome, too slow for the job. He asked for a parachute. "There's only one for me and my radioman," the pilot told him. "But if my crate is caught by the batteries of searchlights I won't be able to get out and will go down with it in a spin." The general took his place in the cabin and placed his trusted Mauser pistol on his knee. And then the cabin was bathed in light. Outside there was "a huge circle of flames, an inferno of bright fire." Anti-aircraft guns flashed and the fingers of searchlights groped. The sound of exploding shells was drowned out by the droning of the Junkers' three engines. Suddenly the pilot turned to Niehoff. "We've got to go back. My engines are hit." The transporter returned to Schweidnitz. Another was sent at 3am. It was not far from the city when it too turned back: icing made control impossible.[50]

It was late on the fifth before Niehoff made another attempt to enter the fortress. The flight this time was uneventful, but not the landing. As the Junkers 52 rolled to a halt on the runway at Gandau, rifle bullets ricocheted off the fuselage. Niehoff, a veteran infantryman, jumped out of the aircraft and threw himself on to the ground. Rifle and machine-gun bullets struck all around. "Wonderful reception," the general muttered. Dashing from one pile of rubble to the next, a staff officer guided Niehoff to safety. "Travelling on foot is not advisable, *Herr General*," the officer told Niehoff, pointing to a motorcycle and sidecar. The two men lifted the vehicle over the cadaver of a horse, then set off for the command post, carefully skirting around the craters in the streets. "The accompanying soundtrack," Niehoff recalled, "consisted of exploding artillery shells and bombs. The gaps between them were filled by the rat-a-tat-tat of machine-guns."

The new fortress commander was led into his headquarters on the Liebichshöhe. He walked through an old beer cellar, now empty, then down two flights of stairs to the offices from where the battle for the city was directed. The damp concrete walls were covered with situation charts and street maps. Niehoff's own room was equally spartan: small with a single table, a couple of chairs and a wire bed. He was introduced to his staff: his deputy *Oberst* Kurt 'Papa' Tiesler, a former headteacher from nearby Oels and holder of the *Ritterkreuz* – "a typical, dependable front-line soldier"; the operations officer, the one-armed *Major* Albrecht Otto – "an exceedingly sympathetic officer, whose first glances radiate confidence and calm"; his adjutant Martin Boeck, the supply officer *Major* Fuchs, and the other members of a staff which Niehoff immediately realized was too small for the task. And finally there was the crestfallen von Ahlfen. As he sipped a cup of tea and shared a few slices of bread with his predecessor, Hermann Niehoff told his old friend from infantry school in Munich that he had orders to send him out of the city on the next aircraft. Von Ahlfen nodded silently. But far from curtly dismissing von Ahlfen, Niehoff would allow him to command for several more days while he got a feel for the struggle for the Silesian capital. It was a wise move. For the first time, Hermann Niehoff learned of the megalomania of the *Gauleiter*. "Despite little combat experience and having only spent a short time in the field, Hanke believes he's the supreme commander in the fortress," Ahlfen warned, adding dolefully. "The judgment of the *Gauleiter* counts more than the judgment of the military commander."

As the two men conferred in their bunker, Soviet loudspeakers blared their propaganda from Russian to German lines: *Hoff nie auf Niehoff, bevor der Hanke hängt* – Don't put your hopes in Niehoff before Hanke hangs him.[51]

Notes

1. Gleiss, vii, p.728.
2. TB Oven 1/2/45, 3/2/45.
3. Schörner's leadership is based on BA-MA RL7/531, TB Goebbels, 9/3/45, Kaltenegger, *Schörner*, p.278, and Kunz, p.220.
4. Ahlfen, pp.54-6.
5. Echolot, iii, pp.803-4.
6. Echolot, iv, p.684.
7. Konev, p.46, Gleiss, ii, p.267.
8. Gleiss, vii, p.945; Konev, pp.52-3; Majewski, p.26.
9. Ahlfen, pp.110-13.
10. Based on BA-MA RH2/2129, BA-MA RH2/2683, *Pravda*, 12/2/45, Gleiss, ii, p.267 and Dragunski, pp.236-8, 241.
11. See Gleiss, ii, pp.226, 251, 263 and Gleiss, vii, pp.980-1.
12. Gleiss, ii, p.264A.

13. Ibid., ii, p.264B.
14. Based on Gleiss, ii, p.252D, Gleiss, vii, pp. 549, 983-4 and Axmann, pp.407-8.
15. Gleiss, vii, pp.1078-9 and pp.1226-8.
16. *So Kämpfte Breslau*, pp.31, 35-6; see also Gleiss, vii, pp.1107-08, 1261.
17. Ahlfen, pp.124-5.
18. Arnhold, pp.188-9, 230-54, 259-60.
19. Knappe, pp.311-12.
20. Hartung, pp.56-7.
21. *Schlesische Tageszeitung*, 16/2/45.
22. Gleiss, vii, pp.1272-3, *Schlesische Tageszeitung*, 18/2/45.
23. Gleiss, ii, p.508C and Gleiss, vii, pp. 1111 and 1261. Similar bacchanalian scenes would be repeated in Berlin two months later.
24. Based on Gleiss, ii, p.328C and HGr Mitte papers in the author's collection.
25. Majewski, pp.32-4.
26. Scherstjanoi, pp.52-3.
27. Gleiss, vii, p.1152.
28. Hornig, p.65.
29. Peikert, p.69.
30. Based on Gleiss, vii, p.1279, Hartung, p.58 and Arnhold, pp.260-1.
31. BA-MA RL7/535 and Arnhold, pp.260-2.
32. Verton's account of fighting on the Weistritz is based on his memoirs in Gleiss, vii, pp.1302, 1315, 1345, 1397-9 and Verton, pp.149-50. The Goliath attack can be found in *So Kämpfte Breslau*, pp.46-7; Verton, pp.149-50.
33. Gleiss, vii, pp.1311-12.
34. Based on Malinin's diary in Gleiss, ii, pp.553, 667, 710, Peikert, pp.73-7 and Majewski, pp.51-2, 54.
35. Gleiss, ii, pp.568A-B.
36. Ibid., ii, pp.588-9.
37. Gleiss, vii, pp.1397-9.
38. Hartung, pp.59-60.
39. Bannert, pp.75-7, 80.
40. Propaganda accounts based on *Völkischer Beobachter*, 28/2/45, *Kaadner Zeitung*, 24-25/2/45, Wette, Bremer and Vogel, *Das letzte halbe Jahr: Stimmungsberichte der Wehrmachtpropaganda*, p.382, *Schlesische Tageszeitung*, 1/3/45 and Peikert, p.82.
41. Based on Peikert, pp.73-7 and Gleiss, vii, p.1421.
42. Based on Gleiss, vii, pp.1433, 1480.
43. Gleiss, vii, pp.1716-17.
44. Christoph's experiences are based on Gleiss, vii, pp.1433, 1480, 1616, 1620-1 and Ramm, pp.192-3.
45. *So Kämpfte Breslau*, pp.49-51, 52-3.
46. Punishments based on Documenty No.35, No.49, and *Schlesische Tageszeitung*, 21/2/45.
47. Documenty Nr.65.
48. Gleiss, iii, pp.56, 65, 66 and *So Kämpfte Breslau*, pp.60-1.
49. Gleiss, iii, p.117.
50. Ibid., iii, p.118-19, 121.
51. Ibid., iii, pp.183, 190-1, Van Aaken, pp.202-04, *So Kämpfte Breslau*, pp.55-6.

'As if a wave of fanaticism and belief breaks in front of the tribune...' Participants in the *Deutsche Turn und Sportfest* extend their hands to Hitler in Breslau's Schlossplatz, 31 July 1938

'The flower of Europe...' (*Above*) Looking east from the tower of the Elisabethkirche across the Ring towards the twin steeples of the St Maria Magdalena. (*Left*) The city's university and (*Below*) The Kreuzkirche and twin-steepled Cathedral seen from one of the Oder promenades

'The howl of machines...' Breslau, the 20th Century metropolis. (*Above*) Trams and cars compete for space outside the Hauptbahnhof. (*Right*) The Liebichshöhe pleasure gardens; in its cellars Breslau's fortress commander would direct the city's defence. (*Below*) The Jahrhunderthalle, a cathedral of concrete and steel

Breslau. Jahrhunderthalle

DER FÜHRER

KOMMT

Deutsches Turn-u. Sportfest 1938

'A wonderful future is in store for all of us, together...' (*Above*) A large swastika banner hangs from a building in the Ring. In the foreground the impressive Rathaus, beyond it the modern Sparkasse bank built between the wars. (*Left*) 'The Führer's coming...' A poster heralds Hitler's arrival at the *Deutsche Turn und Sportfest* in July 1938 and (*Below*) A May Day rally in Schlossplatz in 1933 urges 'Chains must be broken'

Ketten müssen gebrochen werden

'The roads of Adolf Hitler...' The German dictator opens the 100th kilometre of Autobahn in Breslau in September 1936. (*Inset*) 'A carbon-copy Hitler...' A formal portrait of *Gauleiter* Karl Hanke (picture courtesy of Michael Miller)

'People go to battle, Comrades, grab your rifle...' (*Left*) *Volkssturm* men raise their rifles and cheer during a mass rally in Breslau at the end of October 1944. (*Below left*) A propaganda poster depicts old and young standing shoulder-to-shoulder 'for freedom and life'. (*Below*) Karl Hanke addresses *Volkssturm* at a swearing-in ceremony in Schlossplatz in February 1945. '*Meine Herren*, there is no shame in dying for Greater Germany. Attack!'

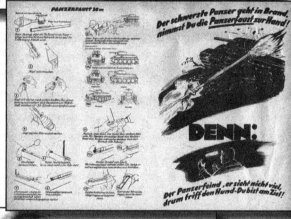

'No long-winded explanations but exercises with weapons...' (*Above*) Police and (*Below*) *Volkssturm* conduct machine gun training during the winter of 1944-45 and (*Right*) A leaflet explains how to use the *Panzerfaust*

'Just one more leap is needed for final victory...'
(*Above*) Soviet artillery push a field gun across
the Oder. (*Left*) The uncompromising Marshal
Ivan Konev. (*Below*) 'An almighty howling...'
Red Army rocket launchers open fire on 12
January 1945

'The flame of war...' (*Above*) Soviet horse-drawn troops race through a burning Silesian village. (*Right*) The *Schlesische Tageszeitung* warns of the 'fateful struggle for our home' on 22 January 1945. (*Below*) Soviet troops of 293rd Rifle Division assault the village of Brockau, just five miles southeast of the centre of Breslau, in late January 1945

welcher am 10. April 1945 in
Breslau im 46. Lebensjahr den
Heldentod starb.
Er wurde in Breslau begraben.

Christliches Andenken
an unseren lieben, unvergeßlichen
Gatten, Vater, Sohn, Bruder,
Schwager und Onkel
Unteroffizier
Franz Berger
Pointler in Straß Nr. 17

Gebet.
Allmächtiger, ewiger Gott! Du lenkst
die Geschicke der Menschen u. Völker;
erbarme dich unseres für die Heimat
gefallenen Sohnes und Bruders.
Dein unerforschlicher Ratschluß hat ihn
aus dem Lärm der Waffen in die
Heimat des Friedens gerufen; laß ihn
bei die Barmherzigkeit finden und
lohne seine Treue bis in den Tod
mit dem unverwelklichen Kranz des
ewigen Lebens, durch Christus, unseren
Herrn. Amen.   29

Bestellt durch Großpointner St. Georgen
Druck von A. Heidenbörfer, Böcklabruck

Zum Andenken im Gebete
an
unseren lieben, unvergeßlichen Sohn
Stabsgefreiter in einem Flakartillerie-Rgt.
Karl Thaler
Hausbesitzerssohn von Laufenbach
Pfarre Taufkirchen a. d. Pr.
Inhaber des Eisernen Kreuzes 2. Klasse,
der Ostmedaille und des Flak-Kampfabz.
welcher am 6. März 1945 in der
Festung Breslau im 29. Lebens-
jahre den Heldentod fand.

Th. Ebner, Taufkirchen a. d. Pram

✝
In Christus
Jesus erwartet
seine Auferstehung
unser lieber Sohn
und Bruder

Hermann Holzer
Angestellter der Bundesbahn v. Leiten
Nr. 10, Pfarre Marchtrenk
der am 26. April 1945 in Breslau
gefallen ist, 19 Jahre alt.

Wer ihn kannte, hatte ihn lieb.

Du hast ihn uns geliehen o Herr,
und er war unser Glück. Du hast
ihn von uns zurückgefordert und
wir geben Dir ihn ohne Murren,
aber das Herz voller Wehmut.
(Hl. Hieronymus)

Vater Dein Wille geschehe!

DRUCK: H. ZAUNER LAMBACH

'Death cards' commemorate those killed
defending Fortress Breslau. (*Clockwise from left*)
Nineteen-year-old Hermann Holzer ('Anyone
who knew him, loved him'); 'Our dear,
unforgettable husband, father, son, brother,
brother-in-law and uncle' *Unteroffizier* Franz
Berger, killed on 10 April; and twenty-eight-
year-old flak gunner Karl Thaler who 'found a
hero's death on 6 March'

(*Below*) 'Furious machine gun fire...' Soviet
troops rake a street

(*Above*) A T34 and self-propelled gun move across Hindenburgplatz while (*Right*) Artillerymen push an infantry gun into position. (*Below*) A Russian artillery observer makes use of one of Breslau's many church towers

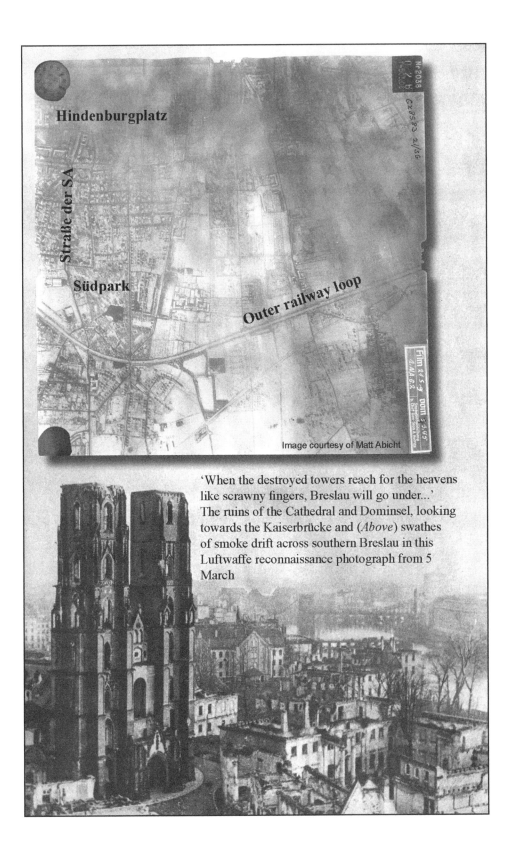

Hindenburgplatz

Straße der SA

Südpark

Outer railway loop

Nr. 2038

Image courtesy of Matt Abicht

'When the destroyed towers reach for the heavens like scrawny fingers, Breslau will go under...' The ruins of the Cathedral and Dominsel, looking towards the Kaiserbrücke and (*Above*) swathes of smoke drift across southern Breslau in this Luftwaffe reconnaissance photograph from 5 March

'Danger threatens with every step...' Soviet infantry assaults a Breslau street and (*Inset*) A rare moment of tranquillity – Dmitri Baltermants' iconic *Tchaikovsky, Germany 1945*

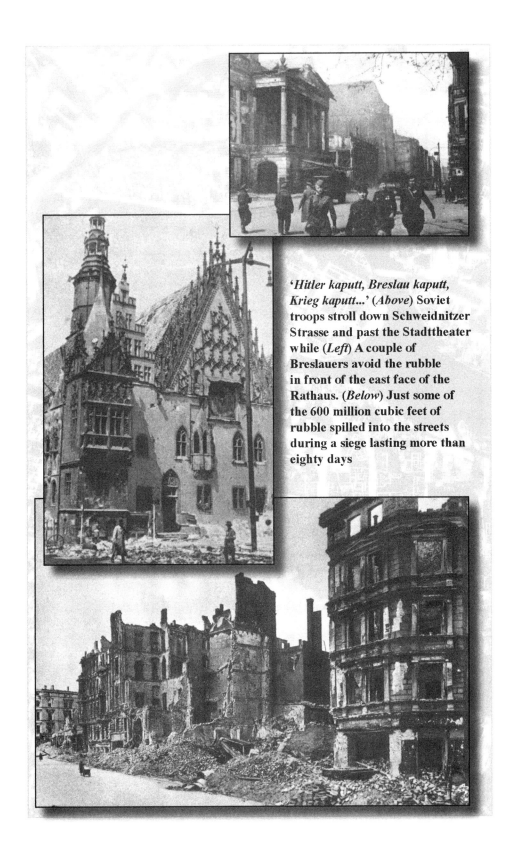

'*Hitler kaputt, Breslau kaputt, Krieg kaputt...*' (*Above*) Soviet troops stroll down Schweidnitzer Strasse and past the Stadttheater while (*Left*) A couple of Breslauers avoid the rubble in front of the east face of the Rathaus. (*Below*) Just some of the 600 million cubic feet of rubble spilled into the streets during a siege lasting more than eighty days

Kreuzkirche

Sandkirche

Cathedral

(*Above*) An aerial photograph of the
Sandinsel and Dominsel gives an indication
of the devastation in the city. (*Right*) The
last defender of Fortress Breslau, Hermann
Niehoff. (*Below*) The ruins of Schlossplatz,
Hotel Monopol and the Dorotheenkirche,
stripped of most of the slates on its steep roof

'We people from the Vistula came to these ruins to build a new Polish Wrocław...' (*Above*) Looking northeast across the ruined gabled houses of the Ring towards the Sandinsel and Dominsel in 1945 and (*Below*) The same view in the early 1960s

St Michaelkirche   Sandkirche   Kreuzkirche   Cathedral

CHAPTER 6

The Breslau Method

Oh, you beautiful Breslau, how you have changed,
how you have turned into a field
of ruins and all because you are no fortress,
you were merely turned into one with words
Conrad Bischof

The first day of March 1945 was bright, mild, wonderful. The sun was strong enough now to melt the snow by day. The first spring bulbs were poking through the surface of the earth, the first green shoots timidly and slowly appearing. This augury of spring was the only hope. Life in Breslau, librarian Friedrich Grieger observed, "has gradually become like that of a besieged medieval fortress". By day the streets were empty, except for military vehicles and fire engines. At first and last light, civilians rushed to and from their places of work, or dashed with pails to water fountains. Shops remained open. Butchers, bakers, grocers – all preferred to close, but were ordered not to by the Party. They received little custom, for as electrician Hermann Nowack wrote, "a shell can come through the window or door at any moment". The traditional greeting of 'Heil Hitler' had long since been replaced by another: *Bleib übrig* – stay alive. In many parts of the city the mains had failed, flooding the churned-up streets. By night there was a macabre firework display as Russian searchlights, flak and tracer sought transport aircraft bound to and from Gandau airfield, while their loudspeakers proclaimed the latest Allied successes and repeatedly broadcast demands for Breslau's surrender.[1]

Karl Hanke delivered his response on the evening of Saturday, 3 March. His speech was carried by the wire radio network across the city and, beyond Breslau, by state radio. It was mercifully short; the *Gauleiter* was neither a great writer nor passionate orator. Tonight his words were aimed less at the defenders of his city than what was left of Hitler's ever-contracting empire. "When the history of the struggle for *Festung* Breslau is written one day, then it will have to remember all the men and women who today simply do their duty, unaware that they are setting an historic example." At first light each morning, "tens of thousands of dutiful men and women" cleared rubble, rubbish and dust from the city's streets "so that messengers, ambulances and trucks can make their way". The people of Breslau had demonstrated to the entire world "that determined resistance halts even our Bolshevik foe". He singled out the *Volkssturm* – "sixty-year-olds have often acted like young soldiers" – and the Hitler Youths. "Anyone who has seen these youths with their own eyes knows the truth of the words: with us comes the new age." That new age would see the Silesian capital built anew, Hanke continued:

> We do not know what Fate has decided for us and *Festung* Breslau; but one thing we do know when we look into the eyes of our youngest and most faithful of our fanatical youths: whatever happens after we're gone, they will rebuild, yes here in Breslau, yes here in Lower Silesia, and for those who come after us it will be easy – just like the colonists of 1241 – to rebuild this city greater and more beautiful than it once was.

He called on the rest of the Germany to summon "the Reich's final forces" to help the beleaguered city. Until that day of relief arrived, Breslauers would fight. "We in *Festung* Breslau vow to stand unshakeably with our faith in the Reich and the Führer, never to falter even though even more bitter days may come, to fight as long as there is an ounce of strength within us!"[2]

Waiting at an airfield outside Schweidnitz for his flight into Breslau, Hermann Niehoff had listened to Karl Hanke's speech. Now, three nights later, he would meet Breslau's political master face-to-face for the first time. It was nearing midnight on 6 March as a group of junior SS officers led the general along a long corridor in Breslau's *Oberpräsidium* and down numerous flights of stairs. The bowels of the Party headquarters, Niehoff realized, were "utterly bomb proof" – far more secure than his own dungeons on the Liebichshöhe. They were also far more sumptuous. There were offices, a telephone exchange, radio room, galley, pantry, canteen, showers, bedrooms with fine curtains. The SS officers showed the general into a large room, dominated by a diplomat's writing table. Several people – some in SS uniforms, others in civilian clothes – rose. Hanke, in his brown *Gauleiter*'s suit adorned with red and gold braid, approached Niehoff and offered his hand. "So, my new commander is here," he said. "Thank God. A hearty welcome!" The general bowed gently before the two men sat down. Niehoff said nothing. The *Gauleiter* spoke endlessly. To date, every general had been a *Nichtskönner* – washout. They had done nothing right, opposed his every action. But he ended encouragingly. "Now I've got the right man in you."

Still Niehoff said nothing. Only when Hanke's staff departed did he open up. He had come determined to lay down the law. He was the fortress commander, not Karl Hanke. "From today I alone give orders in all military questions!" Hanke leapt out of his chair. "That means you want to neutralize me!" The general was unapologetic. "If you want to put it that way, yes." For a moment the *Gauleiter* looked at his belt lying on his desk – and his holstered pistol – before wearily directing his gaze back at Hermann Niehoff and offering the general his hand.[3]

Back in his headquarters beneath the Liebichshöhe, the forty-seven-year-old fortress commander began to contemplate the task ahead. "I was in no doubt that I had to lead the battle for Breslau, this piece of German soil, with inflexible ruthlessness," Niehoff wrote.[4] He told Breslauers as much in his first address to them as their general.

People of Breslau!

On the Führer's orders I have taken over command of *Festung* Breslau.

Since my arrival in the fortress I have seen the admirable bearing of the populace and observed that in all areas what needs to be done is being done and the right forces are committed at the right places.

The struggle has made you hard and has strengthened your powers of resistance.

I am firmly convinced that every warrior, every working man, every woman and, not least, the youth of Breslau have given their best in defence of their home.

Given our dogged powers of resistance and the proven courage of the fortress, powerfully supported by our great Fatherland, utterly convinced that we will be victorious in the end, we will hold the fortress until there is a change of fortune.

The eyes of the Führer and all of Germany are upon us.

Long live the Führer![5]

The front Hermann Niehoff inherited was some thirty miles long – fifteen miles shorter than when Breslau was encircled three weeks earlier. In the north and east, the perimeter had barely changed its course. But in the west and south, all the outlying villages – Goldschmieden, Schmiedefeld, Lohbrück, Opperau, Hartlieb, Brockau – had fallen to the Red Army. Fighting raged in Breslau's southern residential districts, while Soviet troops stood just a few hundred yards from the city's lifeline, the airfield at Gandau. But never again would *frontoviki* advance as rapidly as they had during those first days after the city was surrounded. The reason was obvious. "There's stubborn fighting for every house, usually for every floor, every cellar, every staircase," Sixth Army war correspondent Vassily Malinin wrote. "You have to use all your strength, all your skill as a soldier and cunning."[6] The Red Army had been introduced to the 'Breslau method'. It began with inhabitants being driven out of their homes. The battlefield, first von Ahlfen and later Niehoff determined, was no place for the ordinary Breslauer. Block by block, street by street, civilians living near the front were evicted. The methods used were brutal. "Party representatives come in the middle of the night and, using every possibly threat, bully people into leaving their homes," priest Paul Peikert wrote. There was no word of consolation, no word of comfort, no apology from the Nazi functionaries. "Their attitude was bossy," Ernst Hornig recalled. "They thought that they alone had the authority to give orders, something which the populace viewed as arrogance and ruthlessness."

Barely had people left their homes than the fire parties moved in to destroy the blocks. Hitler Youths were ordered to throw anything combustible out of the newly abandoned apartments: furniture, pictures, curtains, books, pianos. "We piled the items up in the street and set fire to then," recalled Hitler Youth Peter Bannert. "If residents had seen their expensive possessions going up in flames, they would have been in tears." Many did watch – and many did cry. Commercial properties fared no better. The boys carried files out of one bank and threw them on to a pyre. "Who knows whether we helped debtors or hurt creditors?" Bannert wondered half a century later.[7]

Now the buildings were ripe for demolition. "As soon as we cleared a house, we set it on fire," recalled Luftwaffe non-commissioned officer Herbert Richter. "Those were the orders – it prevented the Russians establishing themselves inside." The Soviets sent fire-fighters inside to extinguish the blaze. The Germans counter-attacked with the aim of rekindling the flames.[8] Corner houses would often be left standing as high as the first floor and turned into strongpoints, with the rubble from the rest of the block offering protection, while the houses opposite were flattened to create a field of fire. Communications trenches carved up Breslau's streets and open spaces, while cellar walls were knocked through so that troops, replacements, ammunition, food, the wounded could move around the city without ever having to set foot above ground.

This was the world paratrooper Rudi Christoph entered near Hindenburgplatz as the second week of March began. As the men took up their positions, Breslauers handed them chocolate and wine, overjoyed they had come to defend their district. The *Fallschirmjäger* had been in the fortress for nearly a fortnight now, but some had yet to receive their baptism of fire. "On quiet days we'd practised house-to-house fighting, so it didn't seem so bad," wrote Rudi Christoph. His mood changed when his unit was ordered to counter-attack.

> The sight which greeted us was depressing. Entire blocks were shot up and burned out and the ruins eerily towered into the heavens. Lighting wires, trees, pylons, street lamps, advertising pillars lay shot-up in the streets and several heaps of rubble, which had once been a house, blocked the road. We came ever closer to the front line. There was the dull rumble of artillery, and in between the mocking 'giggle' of machine-guns. A terrible fever seized us. So it looked like fighting in houses and the street! Houses burned brightly and lit up the streets despite darkness setting in. A beautifully tragic sight – had things not been so serious.

After an hour's fighting, two sister companies were exhausted. Christoph's, held in reserve until now, was thrown into the fray as night fell. The paratroopers moved down burning Körnerstrasse, one side occupied by German soldiers, the other by the Red Army. From barricaded cellar windows, the Soviets raked the street with "furious machine-gun and rifle fire". *Panzerfaust* and hand-grenades were repeatedly launched at the enemy-held cellars, but one machine-gun post doggedly held out until a self-propelled gun was called in to silence it. "One step closer to victory," thought Christoph – but still Körnerstrasse was not in German hands. There was one final assault by the paratroopers, this time using flamethrowers which, wrote Christoph, "lit the path to the 'eternal hunting ground' for the Ivans". With the foe eliminated, the *Fallschirmjäger* fell back to the opposite side of the street and rested in the cellars after a six-hour battle. "A solemn calm descended and we only heard the crackle of the burning houses," said Christoph. "Our heroic platoons looked suitably depleted – we finished the battle with one officer and fifteen men and retired for a short rest in the proud knowledge that they had carried out their orders to the last man. Sleep – that was our only wish after this battle because we had to be fresh for other days."[9]

Around the corner in Victoriastrasse, Reinhard Paffrath gathered his paratroopers on a pile of rubble in the entrance of a ruined home. Just five days before, the street had been relatively intact. Now, the homes were little more than façades with the occasional stairwell still standing. The first floor was propped up with beams and rubble, but every few minutes, enemy mortars landed on the ceiling. It was only a matter of time before the rubble gave way and the roof collapsed. But Paffrath was trapped. Sniper fire pinned his small group down. He held up a helmet and stuck out a boot to test the rifleman's accuracy. The sniper took the bait. When a Soviet ground-attack aircraft strafed Victoriastrasse, the officer convinced himself that the sniper – like the paratroopers – would be distracted. He was not. When Paffrath leaped across the street and jumped through the door of a sweet shop, a bullet just missed his backside and struck the doorway, shattering blue and white tiles. He used the near-miss to estimate the sniper's location, fired at every window and hole in the wall, and was never troubled by the Russian sharpshooter again.[10]

Back in Körnerstrasse, Rudi Christoph was still in the front line after thirty-six hours without rest, trying to drive the Soviets back to the next block in Neudorfstrasse. After a dawn attack, the paratroopers had seized one side of the street before running into an impenetrable wall of fire.

We took up defensive positions in the cellar of a burned-out house and waited for the Ivans to come at us. There was a tropical temperature of around 65°C thanks to the burnt coke and coal. Apart from the heat we noticed that the Ivans still occupied the opposite end of the house above our heads and dropped several hand-grenades right in front of us, or raised the temperature with their flamethrowers. Each one of us was seized by thirst and yet more thirst on the evening of this first day in our tropical paradise…

Thanks to the tremendous heat and dust we soon no longer looked like people. Our faces and hands were covered with a layer of dust and dirt. It stopped only around our mouths and eyes. We were soon overtaken by a sluggish tiredness as a result of the constant heat. Our only wish was to satiate our thirst and to be allowed to sleep. We had to wait three days for such luxuries. We waited day and night for Ivan to attack, but apart from his daily greetings, everything was quiet.[11]

Among the apartments Rudi Christoph was contesting in Neudorfstrasse was one owned by Lothar Reichel. "I don't know whether our house is still standing," the former teacher wrote to his mother. "I've not been there for a long time and there's been all sorts of damage and destruction in the city." The anti-tank gunner was committed in Lilienthal, a few miles north of his home, "up to our knees in water – storms and rain, cold nights." He had received no post from outside the fortress. "Our modest exchange of letters remains one-sided," he wrote a little despondently. "In three short weeks it will be Easter; will we be free by then?"[12]

Ferdinand Schörner believed so. "If you take the fight to the Bolsheviks," the general brashly declared, "they can be beaten under every circumstance." Ferdinand Schörner had taken the fight to the enemy. And he had beaten him – after a fashion. 1st Ukrainian Front intelligence officers had warned against dismissing the German Army out of hand: the Fritzes were not demoralized, they were not undisciplined and they were "still capable of fighting with great determination". The warning went unheeded. 'The iron Ferdinand' caught Third Guards Tank Army by surprise, smashing through its lines with two panzer corps on either side of the market town of Lauban, seventy-five miles west of Breslau. A few days after the breakthrough, the two corps linked up in the Queis valley, a handful of miles beyond Lauban. The town itself was liberated, as were a few square miles of Silesian soil, and more than 250 Soviet tanks, plus fifty guns and countless vehicles, were destroyed. Lauban barely merited the title 'battle' but was trumpeted by the Nazi propaganda machine with headlines proclaiming, 'Fighting spirit certain of victory in Silesia' and 'The hour of our victory will come.' Three days after Lauban's liberation, Joseph Goebbels visited the town, where he was welcomed like a conquering hero. Swastika flags had been hastily hung around the ruins of the main square, the walls of its houses burned black. A small platform had been erected next to a wrecked T34 to allow the propaganda minister to address the troops who had retaken Lauban. "You have succeeded in bringing our infernal foe to a standstill, in driving back the Bolshevik beast," Goebbels told them. "I know that this is only the beginning. It is the beginning of their end and downfall and the beginning of our mighty victory. The hour before sunrise is always the darkest; but soon the sun will shine brilliantly over Germany again." Goebbels drew his confidence from Ferdinand Schörner, "a born leader". In a few weeks, the general assured the propaganda minister, he would liberate Breslau.[13]

Schörner will come. It was the hope which sustained Breslauers – and it was a hope which quickly faded. "The eternal wait," FAMO employee Carl Völkel recorded in his journal on 10 March. "Death and ruins everywhere. Nowhere are we safe and we just wait." A week later: "Eight weeks have passed. We believed that the catastrophe would end, but we here in Breslau are in exactly the same spot as we were on day one." And on 4 April: "Always the same. We hope from day to day. Peace is tangibly close and yet nothing happens." Völkel's terse diary entries capture the bitter daily existence of Breslau's civilians as well as do any of the city's more erudite chroniclers. His fifteenth wedding anniversary passed with him besieged, his wife and children safely in Bavaria. Neither husband nor wife celebrated. Frau Völkel had no idea where her husband was, let alone whether he was dead or alive. "May God grant that he's healthy and alive for the sake of me and the children," she prayed. He was alive, but he was beginning to lose hope. "We face ruin," Carl Völkel wrote. "I am braced for anything."[14] Elderly electrician Hermann Nowack appreciated the irony that all the finest apartments and homes were empty, the tightly-packed workers' districts still heavily populated. He appreciated it until he was uprooted from his apartment in Bohrauer Strasse to a new 'home' on the right bank of the Oder in the first week of March.[15] In moving, Nowack joined Breslau's ever-growing underground community. In the basements of larger apartment blocks there was space for perhaps fifty beds. Stoves were set up, fed by coal since the city's gas supply had long since failed. It was basic, but as Ernst Hornig observed, "ordinary cellars with a little strength, heating and water connections were now more important and more desirable than the finest apartment because survival depended on them." The priest was a regular visitor to these cellar communities. All Breslau's clergy were. Basements became places of worship – the city's churches were no longer safe. "People asked for words to strengthen and lift them up," Hornig remembered. "There was silence as soon as the clergy spoke and even those who never attended church listened attentively." It reminded him of the earliest days of the Church when Christians also met underground, "for different reasons, persecution".[16] The Party leadership would celebrate the sense of community – *Volksgemeinschaft* – fostered in the bowels of Breslau, but Hermann Nowack saw little evidence of it. If he left his possessions in his suitcase in rooms above ground, they would be covered in ash and dust. If he left them in a cellar while he worked – cooking, chopping wood, sewing buttons, cleaning clothes – they would quickly be plundered. "I sometimes think I must be going mad," he wrote. "On the one hand, you fear for your life, and five minutes later the green-eyed monster has awoken in people."[17] For the most part, it was not valuable items which disappeared, *Volkssturm* man Willy Merkert realized. "We don't want to grab valuable furniture, silver, expensive radios, carpets, wardrobes from apartments because they're not worth anything any more. We look for what we can use, eat the finest stewed fruit and drag what we need to our cellar."[18] Despite the threat of execution, looting grew more and more prevalent. So too did orgies. Alcohol and sex were the roots of most transgressions. Where there was the one, there was invariably the other. Hermann Nowack found food and drinks lined up on the table of his local Party headquarters, transplanted to the basement of an electricity company. It was if "victory was being celebrated". [19] Each morning, junior officer Erich Schönfelder watched gaunt sixteen-year-old boys emerge from the cellars with young girls in tow. "A lost youth," he wrote. "Who would want to condemn them?"[20] There was less forgiveness for older women who succumbed to avarice and temptation, the *Bunkerliebchen* – 'bunker sweethearts' – driven to seek sexual gratification out of fear of death. Dressed brightly, with artificial flowers in their hair, these women forced their way to the front of cellars, sat longingly on window ledges singing popular tunes, talked of orgies, enjoyed brief flings with soldiers and batted their eyelashes at any passing male. Their lust grew stronger as Breslau's plight worsened.

Such women often ended up in the prison in Kletschkaustrasse, alongside political prisoners like Communist Maria Langner, imprisoned for four years for helping a deserter. Langner sneered at the bunker sweethearts – "the most repulsive vermin in the fortress and their numbers grow like flies around a rotting carcass" – who joined her in a 190-square-foot basement cell with twenty other women. The windows were smashed, so by night the women blocked the holes with mattresses which they aired during the day in the courtyard. For several days, however, the mattresses remained in place, the cell shrouded in darkness, as the legs of a dead British soldier – probably an escaped prisoner of war – lay in front of the window. "I met him during the final hours of his young life when he went for a walk," Langner recalled. "He was maybe twenty-three, extremely attractive, had a noble profile, neat dark hair, and in his eyes was a look of horror which no longer understood anything." His executioner was an SS officer "either already or still drunk" at 6am when he began his daily killings – as many as 250 prisoners were executed during the siege. "Once he's finished his quota of shootings for the day," Langner wrote, "he has breakfast then continues drinking until he falls asleep in his armchair." His men were sadistic. Sixteen-year-old shop assistant Cilli Steindörfer was left in the cells for three days with festering wounds, and only then was allowed to exercise in the prison garden. Cilli had been captured by the Russians when they overran her block. A veteran Red Army major took pity on the girl and looked after her – but not for long because the block was recaptured by German troops who wounded the girl during their counter-attack. They were convinced she was a spy and handed her over to the security service for interrogation. Now, as Cilli bent down to pick a couple of daisies, a guard shot her in the back of the neck.[21]

But not everyone in Kletschkau faced the executioner. Maria Langner would survive the siege. The bunker sweethearts would survive – their 'charms' worked as well on the guards as they had done on soldiers in the cellars. Fifty-nine-year-old Hermann Babisch had no charms to deploy, but he was released after just ten days. The grocer was arrested on spurious charges – a neighbour had reported him for giving her uncle a clean shirt in place of a sweaty one, and the shirt belonged to an evacuated Breslauer. Cäcilie Babisch watched her father being led away by the Gestapo. She realized immediately his arrest was political, not criminal. Herr Babisch had never attended any Party meetings, nor hung the swastika flag outside his store.[22]

The misery of Kletschkau prison paled compared with that of the labour camps for foreign workers. Some 3,000, two thirds of them Poles, were interned in a former girls' school in Clausewitzstrasse. The building was, wrote Paul Peikert, "like an anthill full of people". The Catholic priest was allowed inside the camp in March to lead its inmates in prayer. "Every passageway, every stairwell, every room is completely occupied," he wrote. "Young and old, young men and young girls, men and women next to one another." The atmosphere was dank, stuffy, suffocating. No efforts were made to provide adequate sanitation for the 3,000 prisoners. Peikert struggled up the stairs to the fourth floor. "In every corner on the stairwell, in the corridors, in the rooms lie people, homeless, haggard, separated from their loved ones, and have had to do without the solace of religion." The prison's commanders had done everything in their power to prevent inmates holding services, but finally relented. The fourth-floor hall was full. At one end a temporary altar had been built with a cross, a painting of the Sacred Heart and a small picture of the Black Madonna of Częstochowa, and adorned with flowers.

After Communion, Peikert married a dozen couples and baptised two children before heading into the basement which served as both air raid shelter and hospital. "Arms and legs were amputated on a narrow bench by candlelight and in the glow of a Davy lamp, faces, skulls, stomachs were patched up and a vast number of splinters removed," recalled Polish prisoner Irena Siwicka. On that same bench "festering bandages were changed, the injured were laid – their blood covered their rescuers and made them dirty. We were often so soaked in blood that our shirts stuck to our skin." Children suffered the worst injuries. For them, Fortress Breslau was a vast playground. "And then someone would bring us these terribly mutilated little ones with their arms torn as far as their armpits, with their stomachs ripped down to their legs, with their intestines hanging out, with head wounds through which you could see their brains," Siwicka recalled. It was, said Peikert, "a scene of misery and horror". He offered the camp's doctors – Hungarians, Bulgarians and Poles – his hands in gratitude. "Now I know what a camp for foreigners is."[23]

Conditions in hospitals for the city's German inhabitants and defenders were barely any better. The basements of convents, department stores, apartment blocks, city centre shops and public buildings served as first aid posts, treatment centres, hospitals. A red cross on a white flag hung above partially bricked-up windows often denoted their status, while patients – or, more accurately, casualties – were brought by 'ambulances': trucks, buses, even trams, their bodies painted white, red crosses in their windows. Martin Grunow was appointed chaplain for more than half a dozen hospitals by Hermann Niehoff. He did his best to visit each aid post at least once a week to care for the spiritual needs of the wounded. Of all the hospitals, none left as deep an impression as the one beneath the central station where only the most serious cases were treated. "There was a boy, not sixteen years old, whose open-mindedness and gratitude were touching," Grunow recalled. "He repeatedly asked: 'Herr chaplain, pray with me!' How could this child stricken by sorrow pray?" Hugo Hartung spent four weeks in a cellar hospital near the Ring recovering from exhaustion and fever. Every room of the vaulted cellar was filled with the sick and wounded, stacked in bunks three beds high. The air was filled with the smell of blood and pus. At night, Hartung was kept awake by the cries of dying comrades. In the morning nurses would administer some drugs and the patient would quietly die. A few minutes later a small, stooped non-commissioned officer – patients called him *Totenvogel*, the bird of the dead – would wander along and collect the man's personal effects. The empty bed was quickly filled. Occasionally, hospital staff would arrange a 'weekend dance': a keg of beer, a little music from a pianist and an accordion player. Even British and Russian prisoners joined in. "A funny world," thought Hartung. "Maybe in a couple of days we'll be the prisoners of our prisoners."

Wretched though these makeshift cellar hospitals were, their squalor was surpassed by Breslau's above-ground *Hochbunker* – tall bunkers – huge concrete structures dotted around the city. They served as gun platforms and command posts, their innards were used as air-raid shelters and, now, as hospitals. Hans Gottwald took cake, schnapps and cigarettes for comrades being treated in the five-storey Elbingstrasse bunker. "The air is hot and stuffy and almost takes my breath away. Thousands of wounded – mostly serious cases, amputees, head wounds and the like – lie packed tightly together. Like a maze inside. The passageways leading from the outside are like a snail's shell and you can't find your way." The higher Gottwald climbed, the worse the air in the bunker grew. Finally, he found a friend from Oels, a goalkeeper with the local football team, with a severe leg wound. A blue piece of paper was attached to his feather quilt: *Ju transport* – evacuation out of the city by aircraft. Gottwald wished him good luck and slipped a bottle of schnapps under his pillow. "Hopefully, he'll be lucky." He was. The footballer survived the war.

Georg Haas never forgot the horrific scenes he witnessed in the Striegauer Platz bunker. He passed the operating theatre where doctors cast amputated body parts into a large zinc bath sporadically emptied by the nurses. One brushed past the Waffen SS clerk carrying a bucket. Haas could hear the pail's contents sloshing around. A shiver ran down his spine. The "hopeless cases" were treated on the first floor – then it was not too far to carry the corpses when they died. Conditions were beyond basic. "Bare wooden beds, one on top of the other, hardly a mattress, straw sacks where a different poor devil croaked every day – sometimes even two or three in one shift. For most, musty blankets with dark, dried-up bloodstains." Only at night did the trucks come to take the dead away – and they did not come every night. Georg Haas stumbled past dozens of stiff bodies next to the walls of the gloomy foyer. "Since there's not enough space, the bodies of men who were ripped to shreds by battle and who died in the hands of overburdened doctors, have been piled up like sacks, one on top of the next, creating a gruesome barricade of stinking figures," he remembered. "Pale faces with pointed noses and open mouths; cramped hands stick out from this wall of the dead and seem to want to grab at those passing by."

For casualties being treated in the cellar hospitals there was at least the hope of fresh air. As he recovered, Hugo Hartung was allowed to stand at the door to the basement. The scene was almost serene. "It is wonderfully mild and the bushes have a green glimmer. Starlings build their home in a tree in the cloister courtyard. At this late hour, it is completely silent and the moon fills the sky. Only in the south do heavy black clouds of smoke rise." A couple of days later, he walked gingerly around the city centre, dodging into doorways every time low-flying Soviet aircraft passed. "How much Breslau's streets have changed already!" he wrote. "At every turn, shot-up and bombed-out houses."[24]

The bombing – or bombardment – was constant. Soviet artillery regularly sent its 'greetings' to the city. By day, Soviet bombers attacked the city with seeming impunity. By night, Russian Po2 biplanes – their stuttering engines earned them the nicknames 'sewing machines' or 'coffee grinders' – strafed and bombed Breslau at low height, "as if they have all the time in the world," fumed Georg Haas. Post official Conrad Bischof stuffed cotton wool in his ears each night to deaden the noise of the bombs and explosions. It normally worked, but one evening the crashing roused him from his bed. He cautiously shone a torch around his apartment – the boarding on one of the nailed-up windows had been blown away and he did not want to catch the eye of the Soviet aircraft flying no more than 300ft above the city. Air pressure had thrown a syrup drink around the room, plastering the walls with liquid. There was nothing he could do in the darkness. "I cleared the splinters from my bed and got in again, shoved cotton wool in my left ear and lay on my right side so that I didn't hear our batteries shooting barely 100 metres away." The bombardment was more ferocious on some days than others. Breslauers agree that Sunday, 11 March was particularly bad. Having been driven back from the edge of Gräbschen, and across Hindenburgplatz to the edge of Südpark, the Russians responded by subjecting the city's southern suburbs to a ferocious barrage. Pharmacist Kurt Donnerstag counted more than five hundred sorties by enemy bombers as he tried to deliver medical supplies. His cargo never reached its destination. One bomb landed near his car, turning it into a heap of metal in an instant, shattering the jars of medicine and scattering bandages and cotton wool all over the street. The bombardment left the Strasse der SA one "heap of rubble" for a mile-long stretch as far as Hindenburgplatz, *Volkssturm* man Alfred Hardlitschke wrote to his wife. "If you could see Breslau – how it looks already." [25]

It tore at the hearts of Breslauers to see their city destroyed. On his return from delivering a report, messenger Horst Gleiss passed the school he had attended just a few weeks earlier. "I stood in front of it, silent and full of mourning, and stepped over the ash, dust and ruins of the corridor to reach the first floor." He could go no further, for the staircase had collapsed. He could see the remnants of the stained-glass window dedicated to the fallen of the First World War. A keen scientist, Gleiss could not resist peering into the laboratory. "Reduced to nothing. Nothing, simply nothing is recognisable." Crestfallen, the schoolboy left in tears. His school had been reduced to a "desolate desert of ash and several brittle outer walls – so brittle they're almost falling down." What remained was "a sign of man's senseless, cruel destructive nature". Bitterly, Horst Gleiss was reminded of the Nazi slogan: 'our walls may break, but not our hearts'. "Oh, you beautiful Breslau, how you have changed, how you have turned into a field of ruins and all because you are no fortress, you were merely turned into one with words," Conrad Bischof lamented. To anti-tank gunner Lothar Reichel the city looked like "Sodom and Gomorrah before their downfall". [26]

It was man's, not God's, wrath destroying Breslau. God was powerless. Protestant clergyman Joachim Konrad protested that artillery observation posts and machine-gun nests were being installed in church towers. His protests were brushed aside by the fortress's blunt and uncompromising operations officer Albrecht Otto. "Every strategic point must be used in the interests of the defence." As far as Paul Peikert was concerned, this was war for war's sake. "This war has become the destruction of blood and worldly goods in the hands of a leadership for whom war is an end in itself and war now means the destruction of its own people," he wrote. "No government has used the word 'people' more than this one. And never have the rights of the people been trampled upon more than by these brutes, even here in Breslau. In their eyes, only they and the enemy exist. The people are like air. They are tortured and bullied. They have merely become objects." [27]

The "mania for destruction", as Peikert called it, was infectious. Explosive experts sized up the *Staatsbibliothek* – state library – on Sandinsel, then told librarians the 800-year-old institution was earmarked for demolition. Its ruins – books and all – would create a 'protective ceiling' for a new fortress command post when the Liebichshöhe became threatened. Staff protested. Many of the library's most precious items had been moved to safety before the siege, but there were still 550,000 volumes on its shelves. Niehoff eventually relented and allowed the books to be evacuated to the Annenkirche, across the Oder. At first 100, then 200 and finally 300 people began to empty the library, but so much activity on the otherwise quiet island attracted the attention of Soviet bombers. As the evacuation became ever more desperate, an overzealous junior officer piled up scores of books on the Oder embankment so they could simply be pushed into the river. They were saved, not out of any cultural sensitivity but to prevent the weirs being blocked.[28] Three streets near the Hauptbahnhof were singled out for demolition. "Every floor is cleared out, windows smashed, furniture, or what is left of it, thrown into the street, valuable and simple decorations, priceless ornaments, sacred family heirlooms and family souvenirs, holy pictures and religious statues, prayer books and crucifixes, it's all thrown into the street," the priest wrote. "On top of that, cupboards and drawers are emptied and clothes, pieces of washing and beds, they're all thrown into the street where they're set alight." For a day and night, the three streets burned. "Enormous clouds of smoke rise up into the sky and hang over the city like a sulphurous haze because of the mild weather," Peikert recorded. "In the evening, the moon still tries to cast its silvery light over the city, but the sky is red from the glow of flames from a street which is completely on fire. What a tragedy this act of self-destruction of a people is, how each person trembles and shakes because of this insane act and yet no one can find the strength to stop it." In this instance, the demolition served no purpose; the battle for Breslau would never reach the streets around the station.[29]

In fact, the Soviet assault on Breslau had miscarried. The ferocity of the fighting surprised even hardened campaigners such as Vassily Malinin. "The fighting doesn't pause even for one hour," he noted in his diary. While there was "joyful, victorious news" from every other front, in Breslau "the fighting's hard and stubborn. The enemy does not want to surrender. He doggedly occupies every street, every house." The war correspondent watched two Soviet machine-gunners haul their gun through water so they could bring it to bear on a German bunker guarding a factory. From behind a brick wall they directed their fire at the machine-gun nest and wiped it out. Their comrades took the works from the rear, standing firm in the face of a counter-attack by three dozen German troops. Anti-tank and field guns were called up to drive shells into houses until their walls collapsed, while self-propelled guns knocked out German guns hidden in barricades and provided cover for advancing infantry. After five days' fighting, Malinin and his comrades were given an hour's rest. "There's rarely an hour like this these days in this city. The men sort out their weapons and uniforms, wash, write letters home with the promise that they will soon return triumphantly."[30] Lieutenant Sergei Kravshenko could not fail to be impressed by the morale of his troops on the eve of battle. Some of his men had defended Odessa in the opening months of the war, although Kravshenko had only led them since the late summer of 1944. They did not need to be told an attack was imminent. "The soldiers had a nose for something," Kravshenko recalled. The signs were obvious. The regiment redeployed. Artillery observers moved up to the front line. Guns were camouflaged. Additional supplies of hand-grenades were brought up. In the final hours before an assault a few *frontoviki* wrote letters. More exchanged addresses with comrades. "If something happens to me, write to my . . ." One of Kravshenko's men picked up his accordion and played the popular folk song *Ogonek*. "How many of those men who had fought with me for the past seven months would see tomorrow?" the young officer wondered. "Dying is never pleasant – especially not now when the end of the war is within reach."[31] The proximity of the war's end was a common theme. It drove some men onwards. "We're all in a good mood," artillery commander Vitalij Babarykin, a major at just twenty-one, wrote to his family. "Now the entire world knows that the end of Fascism is near. Forever! We knew that this day would come from the very beginning. Understand, my love, what we feel, we veterans of this war, who have dealt the enemy a knockout blow, the enemy who began this war. There is justice yet."[32] For other *frontoviki* morale was sustained by the 1st Ukrainian Front newspaper, *Za chest' Rodiny* (*For the Honour of the Fatherland*), and Sixth Army's *Na rozgrom vraga* (*Down With The Enemy*), which were distributed every day among the troops. *For the Honour of the Fatherland* photographer Dmitri Baltermants was ordered to Breslau to capture images of combat. He joined a pioneer unit, took a handful of staged photographs, then heard the strains of Tchaikovsky coming from a ruined house. He quietly entered the room, whose outer wall had vanished, and found a handful of *frontoviki* gathered around a piano played by a second lieutenant. None of the men heard Baltermants come in, or noticed him taking his photograph. He took scores of images that day, hundreds more in the battle for the Silesian capital, but none possessed the power of a photograph Baltermants titled simply *Tchaikovsky, Germany 1945*.[33] It was not the task of front-line newspapers to capture the beauty of battle, but to carry men forward into battle, playing up the role of the Communist Party and its members in the vanguard of the struggle, of course. Political officers read out letters sent by strangers in the Motherland. Lectures were held on streetfighting, while *Down With The Enemy* produced a weekly sheet containing the latest advice on subjects as varied as the use of armour, night fighting, reconnaissance and smoke screens. "Move as quickly as possible!" one leaflet advised.

> Danger threatens with every step. It does no harm to toss a hand grenade around every corner, then advance! A burst from a machine pistol at the rest of the ceiling. And advance again! The next room, hand grenade! Turn around – another hand grenade! Spray the corners with your machine pistol! Do not hesitate! If you are already in the heart of the building, the enemy can try a counter-attack. Don't panic! You have already deprived him of the initiative – it is in your hands! Cling on to your hand grenade, your machine-pistol, your spade with even greater determination.[34]

Yet no amount of lectures, no article in a newspaper could prepare any man, *Landser* or *frontovik*, for the daily realities of the battle for Breslau. Otto Rothkugel was convinced he was prepared "for every eventuality". The *Volkssturm* man kept a second gun in reserve – his rifle frequently jammed because of the dust in the cellars – plus a hand-grenade. But there was one eventuality the *Volkssturm* man had not prepared for: fire in his cellar. Soviet mortar shells plastering his unit in Hohenzollernstrasse set fire to tinder-dry crates in the men's basement. "We were all but smoked out because we could not clear the growing smoke," he recalled. There was no water to extinguish the flames – or to wash away the dust and dirt of battle for that matter. The *Volkssturm* troops tore at the crates to break them up and throw them out of the cellar. Even so, many of the men, including the forty-seven-year-old Rothkugel, needed treatment for smoke inhalation. He slept for two solid days and nights. When he returned to his company, its original 150 men had been reduced to just 80. Fighting in a cellar while fires raged in the building above was commonplace. SS company commander Franz Budka continued to shoot at the enemy in the building of an insurance firm opposite his strongpoint in Augustastrasse. Bare-chested, he ordered a chain of helpers to pour buckets of water on him and his men so they could withstand the otherwise unbearable heat. Even when a house or a block finally fell to the Red Army it was not secure. Explosive charges, packed inside old bomb cases or empty acetylene and hydrogen bottles, were frequently buried under coal or junk in the cellars. When the Soviets occupied the building, the booby traps were detonated electrically. At least 200 such charges were laid. "The enemy was invariably completely surprised and the effect was considerable," one pioneer commander recalled. "One five-storey house went up in flames in a few seconds." It was not the only dirty trick the fortress engineers used. More than 5,000 'brick mines' – wooden boxes containing explosive and covered with red and white-yellow brick dust – were strewn amid the rubble. Indistinguishable from bricks, they were carefully laid at night by fishing lines from skylights, windows, balconies.[35]

Engineers from the former FAMO works fashioned all manner of makeshift weapons such as a machine-gun mounted on a three-wheel chassis protected by a steel-plate shield. Wheeled around a corner to fire a few short bursts, it was then hurriedly withdrawn to safety. Then there were 'sniper huts' – pyramid-shaped steel 'huts' dug into the railway embankment near Pöpelwitz to provide troops with protection.[36] FAMO's genius for improvisation reached its apotheosis in mid-March. On Tuesday the twentieth, the men of *Regiment Hanf* were being hard pressed by a Russian rifle regiment, supported by artillery, in Klein Mochbern on the western edge of the fortress. By nightfall, the Germans were undisputed masters of the village. The small victory was delivered by a new weapon – "the scourge of the Russians" – an armoured train.

For three weeks, some four hundred FAMO workers had toiled day and night in an abandoned railway depot to turn railway carriage chassis into an armoured train, mounting four 88mm flak guns, one 37mm flak, and four 20mm flak, plus a couple of machine-guns. It devoured men – six drivers and firemen, nearly three dozen railway workers to maintain the track, plus seventy troops to man the guns and a communications cabin. It was sluggish, pretty inflexible and presented a target to the enemy "as big as a barn door". But in the hands of a skilful commander – flak

Oberleutnant Paul Poersel – the *Panzerzug Poersel*, Armoured Train Poersel, bolstered the defence of the nearby airfield at Gandau "with brief, surprise attacks, suddenly opening fire with as many barrels as possible". It destroyed at least half a dozen enemy tanks and three aircraft before being withdrawn from the west of the city as Soviet troops closed in on the airfield. It was sent to the northern perimeter where it fought equally valiantly, but at a cost. For every three men who served in the armoured train, one became a casualty.[37]

Most of the weapons defending Breslau were far more rough and ready. Soviet troops attacking the junction of the Strasse der SA and Augustastrasse were convinced they were out of the range of German fire until hand-grenades began landing in their midst. Teenagers used schoolboy tricks to attack their foe, catapulting grenades into the Soviet positions at what became known as Hitler Youth Corner.[38] German paratroopers contesting the railway yard at Schmiedefeld went even further. They filled small fist-sized transparent bags with a yellow-green corrosive lye – the colour earned the 'weapon' the nickname 'piss bags'. These worked like tear gas – but longer exposure to the lye could destroy the lungs. Several bags were tossed into the cellar of a signal box, the last Soviet strongpoint which needed wiping out. "We could hear groans all night long," Reinhard Paffrath recalled. "The next morning it was quiet." The occupants of the cellar had been killed by the bags' contents.[39]

Some Soviet accounts claim the defenders of Breslau fired torpedoes mounted on wagons at strongpoints. The Red Army certainly used a rocket packed either with flammable liquid or explosives and fired these 'land torpedoes' along the ground or on rails towards German positions. The defenders responded with 'combat barricades': camouflaged 88mm flak – which also had a legendary reputation as anti-tank guns – built into several barriers. They were used sparingly, but to devastating effect. Whistling down a narrow street on a flat trajectory, the flak shells tore attacking infantry, guns or armour to pieces. A 15cm artillery piece in the heart of the city caused Russian armour advancing into the western suburbs "no end of trouble". Soviet bombers attacked every building around Matthiasplatz, but they never found the gun. After every firing, it was hauled back into the entrance of a large house and hidden from view.[40]

For Breslau's defenders, the Soviet sniper posed an ever-present threat. Luftwaffe *Stabsgefreiter* Herbert Richter and his comrades found themselves pinned down near Hindenburgplatz. "As soon as one of us moved, there was a bang," Richter recalled. A sixteen-year-old boy gingerly searched the kitchen of an apartment for food. It was still stocked. He crawled up to the cupboard, pushed the door open, using it for cover as he stood up to grab a jar from a shelf. One of the glasses slipped from his hand. The boy tried to catch it. For an instant he left the cover provided by the door. "There was an immediate bang from a window in the house opposite," Richter remembered. "The boy yelled out and fell down." He was killed instantly. The sniper's bullet had struck him in the forehead.[41]

The Soviet 76mm – the 'crash boom', nicknamed for the noise it made – "gnawed at the nerves" of German infantry, *Sturmgeschütz* commander Leo Hartmann recalled, thanks to the sharp whip-like crash of its shells between the rows of houses which suggested the 'crash booms' were much closer than they actually were. Rooting out these guns was never easy: their rapid firing rate meant the sound of the shell leaving the barrel could easily be confused with the simultaneous sound of it travelling through the air. And so Leo Hartmann climbed out of his gun, took a binocular periscope with him and hid behind a corner to observe his target, then showed his gunlayer precisely where to aim. "After that we prepared our gun to fire, drove like mad around the corner and just a few seconds later our first explosive shell was roaring down the street," Hartmann wrote. "No Russian dared to remain at his gun in the face of our fire-spewing *Sturmgeschütz* and we could coolly finish off the enemy anti-tank guns." Occasionally the Soviets built dummy positions, but to little effect. "The blast from our shells exploding blew the straw mat camouflage off the real gun," the *Sturmgeschütz* commander smiled.[42]

Leo Hartmann had learned to adapt to the fighting in Breslau. So too did his fellow defenders. They learned that the fighting would often subside at midday as the Russians stopped to eat. They learned that the fire extinguisher was often as important as a rifle. They learned that many enemy shells were duds – notes were often attached by the German prisoners forced to produce them: "We cannot do any more for you, comrades!" They learned that each evening they would receive food, ammunition, orders. "For a while we got used to this strange way of life," *Gefreiter* Gerhard Saches remembered. "We no longer thought about death or the devil. The same old shooting with rifles, machine pistols and machine-guns became the norm."[43] And they learned that eventually they would be pulled out of the line to recuperate.

Each afternoon, regimental commander Fritz Reinkorber ordered one of his men to the rear for two hours' rest in the company command post, where coffee, cakes, beer, cigars and cigarettes were provided. National Socialist Leadership Officers arranged entertainment courtesy of the fortress's film truck or the five-piece 'bunker band' which performed a mix of classical music and easy listening. On the other side of the front, the Vachtangov theatre and orchestra from Moscow staged numerous concerts and shows – sometimes just a few yards from the front line – entertaining as many as 10,000 troops during the siege. "The visits by these dear guests, these actors depicting art and beauty, was a signal of the end of the war for which we yearned," war correspondent Vassily Malinin wrote. For the most part, soldiers created their own entertainment. Albrecht Schulze van Loon and his company of paratroopers enjoyed a couple of days' rest in the vault of the Dresdner Bank in Tauentzienplatz, where there was a gramophone and a large record collection. Van Loon rifled through the discs, then invited his men to a concert. "Until deep into the night, we listen to Beethoven, Mozart, Brahms," he wrote. He picked out Tchaikovsky's *1812 Overture*. "We look at each other and understand that the music captures exactly what we're living through." And then the finale: Haydn's *Kaiserquartett*. "It is completely silent and we are not ashamed of our tears," the officer wrote. Hugo Hartung's company was sent to a restaurant on the edge of the city centre to recover after one month's fighting around Schöngarten airfield and Breslau's western suburbs. "In the evening we celebrate with a proper party," the theatre director wrote.

Each of us is handed a bottle of red wine and as one of Breslau's best-known sausage manufacturers lives in our guesthouse, we're given vast quantities of wonderful meat – including excellent warm sausages.

We drink and sing. Our medic, Pflanzl, the well known bass from Dresden's state opera, sings folk and homeland songs in his beautiful deep voice, which receives thunderous applause from the civilians present, including a pretty deaf-mute girl.

The party was interrupted on a couple of occasions by Russian air attacks. When the raids became too severe, the partygoers decamped to the cellar. "Even down in the narrow, damp, cold cellar passageways the loud merriment of our colourful, motley assortment does not die down."[44]

Occasionally, more formal events were arranged. The paratroopers staged a 'comradeship evening' in a tram depot. It was a black tie affair – and somehow the *Fallschirmjäger* found dinner suits, or rather black panzer uniforms to which were fixed Luftwaffe insignia: lapels, braid, the eagle and decorations. After a smart march, the regimental band reverted to sentimental tunes while their comrades "got stuck into the fire water," Rudi Christoph recalled. "Bottle after bottle was emptied and several comrades were convinced that the earth was spinning." The paratroops were allowed to sleep off their hangovers until noon the following day "and then the old routine began," Christoph bemoaned.[45]

More typically, life out of the line meant a good bath, a good meal and a good sleep. Sometimes it afforded a change of clothes. Reinhard Paffrath's company of *Fallschirmjäger* rested in the cellar of an abandoned apartment block. The men raided the closets of the empty homes, not for personal gain but for comfort on the battlefield. Fine silk scarves were particularly coveted, but any clothes could be cut into strips and wrapped around the throat beneath the paratrooper's camouflage jacket. The extra layer protected the men's skin from dust and dirt. "We had three days' rest," Paffrath recalled. "Eat and sleep. Eat and sleep . . ."[46]

Throughout the battle, the besiegers sought to undermine the morale of the besieged. The city's streets were littered with leaflets, some aimed at the civilian populace, others at the *Volkksturm* – "Hitler's last cannon fodder" – urging them to cast off their armbands, throw away their weapons and return home, and others still at soldiers:

Hitler is your enemy!
Get away from him!

Soldiers!

Hitler is your enemy
He began this war of plunder against the world and brought the hatred and wrath of all nations down upon Germany as a result of his crimes.

Hitler is your enemy
In this criminal war against the freedom-loving peoples of the world he has
senselessly killed or turned into cripples millions of Germans, he has made
millions of German women widows, millions of children orphans.

Hitler is your enemy
He has brought war to the heart of Germany, abandoned German towns and
villages to destruction from the air and on land and is now devastating all of
Germany.[47]

Written propaganda was complemented by a constant verbal barrage. At night Russian
loudspeakers urged the defenders of Breslau to desert, to give up the struggle. Music,
slogans, promises: peace, de-lousing, good food, sex: "Come over to us, one hundred
naked Caucasian women are waiting for you in a sky-blue bed"; "You will be free to go
home immediately after the end of the war"; "Comrades, we are not after your blood."
Sometimes, Soviet propaganda was quite specific. At the beginning of March, the
Russians hijacked the frequency used by the *Deutschlandsender*. At 9pm, just as German
state radio did every night, the news was broadcast in the same voice, in the same tone.
As the news ended, there was a special announcement: "And now we bring important
news for the brave soldiers and comrades in *Festung* Breslau. The hour of liberation
has come. Several panzer divisions, battle-hardened in the East, have smashed through
the enemy's encircling ring. Come to the south of the city to shake hands with your
liberators!"[48] Breslauers did not come.

There were some who *were* tempted by Soviet offers. Metalworker and *Volkssturm*
man Max Stock – fluent in Russian thanks to spending several years in a prison camp
during the Great War – encouraged six comrades to desert. Most of Klaus Franke's
comrades rejected calls to desert. Soviet promises sounded "awfully attractive," the
forward artillery observer wrote, but the men knew it was "too good to be true". Franke
watched a comrade grab a megaphone. "You over there, keep your mouth shut, come
here if you want it. We'll kick your arse!" Other troops were dissuaded by the increasing
repression in the fortress. Deserters had long since faced the death penalty. Now, the
fortress command ruled, their families would now also be punished, "forfeiting their
wealth, freedom or lives" for the sins of their husbands, brothers, fathers.[49]

The propaganda onslaught reached its climax ahead of a Soviet attack. "You'll hear
a Strauss waltz now – and tomorrow morning you'll hear Stalin's organ," a Russian voice
proclaimed. Over the loudspeakers, German classical music and folk songs: *Blue Danube*,
Donna Clara, *Wiener Blut*, the *Schwalbenlied*, *Als wir im August hinausgezogen sind*.
"When we sang these songs among comrades, in the bunker or in some tent in Corsica,
these melodies stirred a feeling of home and you felt an invisible ribbon and believed
you were close to those you love at home," Klaus Franke recalled. "Coming from over
there, they sound sad. The longer Ivan persists with his racket, the more rage and the will
for revenge grows within the assault troops. And so clever propaganda completely fails
in its objective and achieves the opposite of what is intended."[50]

Men on both sides could not escape the anniversaries which their respective regimes were so fond of celebrating. Russian troops commemorated the Red Army's twenty-seventh birthday on 23 February. Front-line commanders in Breslau celebrated with high-spirited banquets and toasts of vodka after reading out the words of Joseph Stalin to their men. "The nearer we are to victory," the generalissimo warned, "our vigilance must be even greater and our blows against the enemy even heavier."

The defenders of Breslau had already marked the anniversary of the Nazi assumption of power and the twenty-fifth birthday of the Nazi Party programme. The next date in their calendar was Sunday, 11 March, Heroes Memorial Day, when Germany paid tribute to her fallen. Before dawn, soldiers, *Volkssturm* and Hitler Youths left their units around the city and made for Karl Hanke's headquarters in the Oberpräsidium. Upwards of 150 men and boys were ushered into the ballroom, where the *Gauleiter* waited for them, accompanied by Hermann Niehoff. A Hitler Youth choir sang the soldiers' traditional lament, *Ich hatt' einen Kameraden*, before Hanke read out a brief speech. Hermann Niehoff's address was rather longer – but his words could have come straight out of the mouth of the *Gauleiter*. The men of Fortress Breslau would have to "stick it out", their commander told them, "even if in the end the city was nothing but a field of ruins". Fortunately, Niehoff assured his audience, Breslau would be relieved – although the date of the city's relief, Conrad Bischof noted, was vague. "It could be ten to fourteen days, but it could be even longer." Until that day, Hermann Niehoff concluded, "we pledge to the Führer that we in Breslau, that trusted old barrier in the East, will prove ourselves as fanatical warriors."[51]

As the speech ended and the men saluted the fallen, Hermann Niehoff pinned decorations to some of them – one incentive to keep the men fighting. The fortress commander was keen to reward *Volkssturm* men for their deeds with decorations which younger, more able men would have to strive much harder to attain. Karl Hanke liberally handed out decorations to FAMO workers for sustaining the war effort. The tank killer was the hero of Fortress Breslau, darling of the Nazi press, and he was richly rewarded. Peter Bannert remembered an arrogant seventeen-year-old who strutted around the city, a fresh Iron Cross pinned to his chest, a *Panzerfaust* on each shoulder. 'Panzer Karl', as the boys dubbed him, belonged to no unit. He enjoyed free range to hunt Soviet tanks anywhere in the fortress. For any man – or boy –who destroyed six enemy tanks with a *Panzerfaust* or other close-quarters anti-tank weapon, there was the promise of the Reich's highest military honour, the *Ritterkreuz* – Knight's Cross. The first *Ritterkreuz* recipient in the fortress destroyed no tanks, but he was a native Silesian, a veteran company commander, wounded seven times in battle. *Leutnant* Richard Wolf received his medal in hospital, where he gave an 'interview' to a *Schlesische Tageszeitung* correspondent; Wolf's words were most probably written by a propagandist. "If we hold on doggedly, then the enemy will not advance one metre," the *Ritterkreuz* winner proclaimed. "Despite the heavy burden we bear at present, I am convinced that we will be victorious!"[52]

It was a slogan repeated by the National Socialist Leadership Officers. "We must fight for victory, which Fate cannot deny us if there is a god above us in whom we believe," declared the fortress's senior military 'commissar' *Hauptmann* Herbert van Bürck, a thirty-five-year-old district lawyer, an urbane, educated man. He was also a committed Nazi. After being wounded on the opening day of the campaign in Russia, van Bürck had resumed his pre-war profession as a lawyer, this time on the staff of Hans Frank in the General Government. That service had come to an end in the summer of 1944 when he was thrown into prison, suspected of involvement in the 20 July attempt on Hitler's life. His experience at the hands of the Gestapo evidently did nothing to diminish his belief in National Socialism. Subsequently released and employed on the fortress's staff, van Bürck issued 'advice' to the Party activists in the ranks of the *Wehrmacht* and *Volkssturm* to maintain fighting spirit every few weeks. "A soldier cannot be left to his own thoughts," he warned. "Even the most stupid of soldiers will at least think about his fate or that of his family, consciously or unconsciously, in addition to thoughts about the fate of the entire German *Volk*." It was down to the Nazi commissars to "raise morale" and lead "in a deliberately-stirring manner". They told their comrades that the eyes of the Reich were upon them, that newspapers across Germany were filled with stories of heroism from Breslau, that barely a day went by when the fortress was not mentioned in the military communiqué, that even if letters from the city had not reached loved ones evacuated in January, they would know that Breslau stood firm. And if they gave up the struggle? Germany would go under. "Soldiers here in the East must understand that if we capitulate, we are lost," van Bürck warned. "Failing in battle means the end of our people and the end of the Reich. What poverty and torment we are suffering now is nothing compared with the fate which we will face if we capitulate." The Russians would deport "German slave workers to Siberia in their millions"; every family would be torn apart by "deportation and slavery"; children would be snatched from their parents, "deported and educated as Bolsheviks"; in a Bolshevik-run Germany "the shot in the neck will rule"; "German women will be raped, violated, murdered by beasts in human form." In short, if the Red Army triumphed on the soil of the Reich, "the German people as an organic, living community will be literally murdered. Germany will become nothing but a cemetery."[53]

Except that Breslau already was turning into nothing but a cemetery. The death toll in Paul Peikert's parish never fell below 63 every day in mid-March, and reached as high as 131. In a ten-day period, he counted more than 950 casualties, two-thirds of them soldiers. But where to lay them to rest? All the municipal burial grounds had either been captured by the Russians or lay too close to the front line to be used. Parks and green space took their place. Horst Gleiss watched as the grounds of the Odertorbahnhof, a stone's throw from his Benderplatz apartment, were dug up and turned into mass graves. There was nothing respectful about the process. Corpses, the fourteen-year-old wrote, were delivered. "*Ja*, delivered! The word is perfect for the method of transportation. During the night dead bodies arrived on trucks, most were unloaded in the dark and almost without exception were covered with earth before dawn." The first dead received coffins. When they ran out, wooden boxes were hurriedly built. They ran out too. Brown wrapping paper was laid over the layers of corpses. In the end, it too ran out. Horst Gleiss and fellow Hitler Youths were ordered to help with the burials, although in the darkness, the boys frequent failed to shovel a child's hand, fingers, an adult's arm or a piece of scalp into the grave. Often morning came before their work was complete, or before families could identify the dead. The bodies were simply left in the open. "The sight was terrible because hardly any of the bodies was intact," Gleiss recalled. Paul Peikert was asked to bury a housewife killed when the post office bank was hit. "Her body was torn to shreds. Her hair was there, a leg there, her bowels there, so that her remains cannot be recovered." What remained of this forty-seven-year-old woman was laid to rest in the coffin of a child. Former teacher and committed Nazi Hermann Krätzig was killed and buried within an hour. The sixty-one-year-old and other aged *Volkssturm* men took it in turns to supervise work details from the foreign labour camp in the Clausewitz school clearing rubble in Clausewitzstrasse. Soviet air attacks resumed. A bomb landed next to Krätzig, burying him beneath the rubble and killing nine foreign workers at the same time. Within twenty minutes, Hermann Krätzig's body had been recovered. Within an hour he had been laid to rest in the garden of a nearby home. A simple board was erected to mark his grave.[54]

Brief funeral services were held in the basements of the homes of the dead. Mass burials were blessed by the clergy. The dead were always laid to rest between 6.30 and 8am, a period most likely to be free from bombing and shelling – but not always. Paul Peikert buried two men from *Regiment Schulz*. "Because of the loud thunder of guns, the prayers were barely audible." Seven shells landed close to his church in the middle of the brief service. The final act of burial was invariably a desolate affair. Rarely were family members present. Rarely did the priest know anything about the body he was blessing. "I often stood there on my own with the gravediggers or graves officer," recalled Martin Grunow. "And yet I could still pray and bless these graves."[55]

A dedicated 'graves officer' on the fortress staff tried to collate details of fallen soldiers so news of their death could be passed on to their next of kin. That was why Hans Gottwald found himself crawling through a ditch in Lilienthal on Breslau's northern outskirts. After heavy fighting for the nearby *Infanterie Werk*, or *I-Werk*, 41 fortification, the dead were carried by night to Lilienthal. And there they were left, unburied. When the fighting relented, Gottwald was sent to check the dog tags of the dead. "It's an awful mission, but orders are orders." He inched his way for more than 300 yards through the trench until he reached a cluster of trees. And there he found the corpses of twenty-five men. "A shiver runs down my spine and I have to wait until I am capable of carrying out my task," he wrote. Having regained his nerve, he checked the bodies, each one "cold, waxen and covered in blood". He unbuttoned the collar of every man, found their dog tags and recorded the details on a slip of paper. Gottwald found half a dozen comrades, including one *Unteroffizier* with a splinter in his throat. He spent an hour among the dead, then slipped back towards the ditch to return to his unit. He washed, ate, slept. And then that night he was back in Lilienthal collecting the dead for burial in a cemetery. A horse and cart took the cadavers away. "They lie like cattle on top of each other and the cart jolts through the night," Gottwald recalled. "These men did not deserve that." And then a thought struck the young *Unteroffizier*. "Perhaps the day after tomorrow I too will be lying on such a vehicle."[56]

It was not merely experienced soldiers like Hans Gottwald who were dispatched to identify the dead. A *Volkssturm* commander ordered Horst Gleiss to help when two women staggered into his cellar covered in blood. In the street the schoolboy found that a shell had crashed into the stone pavement just a few feet from three people, killing them and a white horse grazing on the foliage on the opposite side of the road. The corpses were covered in dust, mutilated beyond all recognition.

> To judge from what's left of the clothes, it seems to be two women and a man. Blackish pools of blood seep across the granite pavement between the bits of bodies and the stone chunks of wall. The cranium of one of the two women has vanished as far as the bridge of her nose. Pieces of her scalp with strands of long black hair are scattered all around for many metres. Her limbs have been torn in several places and have similarly been scattered far and wide.
>
> My task now is to identify the mutilated dead. For me, as ever still a sensible young boy, that's not easy work. As I bend over the riddled male corpse to unbutton his jacket which is covered with plaster, I realize that it is the *feldgrau* tunic of a soldier. Beneath it a brown shirt appears. Only Party dignitaries wear this combination. But this isn't someone from our command post, is it? With my trembling hands I take the identification papers from the left breast pocket of the lifeless body. The leather wallet is strangely still undamaged and just as warm as if I'd taken it from my own coat pocket.

The body did indeed belong to a man Horst Gleiss knew: his local Party leader.[57]

The city's clergy tried as best they could to keep proper records of the burials. "If families of the dead return to Breslau one day, then we can at least tell them where their dead relatives are," said one priest. The Party took rather less care over the dead. Paul Peikert passed a small mound of earth covered by pussy-willow branches. He assumed an animal had been buried there. It was actually an elderly man whose body had been left for nearly a week in his apartment before the *Ortsgruppe* had come to collect it. "This irreverence towards the dead is exactly the same as the disregard for personal dignity, something which is fundamental to National Socialism," Peikert seethed. He ordered the badly decomposed body exhumed and laid to rest in a grave on hallowed ground.[58]

It was not so much irreverence for the dead as indifference. "We got used to the sight of corpses a long time ago," recalled sixteen-year-old Ursula Scholz. Former union official Otto Rothkugel saw a farmer's cart fully laden with corpses, frozen by the February frost. "All of them lay on the cart, completely naked." The *Volkssturm* soldier was unmoved. "This sight no longer arouses any particular horror in you because day in, day out, you have nothing but destruction and devastation around you. A human life counts for nothing here. On my travels through the city I encountered people who'd been killed by air raids, lying around in the streets like some rubbish tossed away, because no-one worried about it." There was only one rule in the fortress, wrote Rothkugel, "the instinct to survive". Every day, Horst Gleiss remembered being "constantly confronted with death". He walked past "soldiers sitting on a bank without heads because the blast of a shell had ripped off their skulls," or was ordered to "pick up a young, dear seventeen-year-old girl, torn into little pieces" by a bomb minutes after the two had sat side-by-side in an air-raid shelter. As a fourteen-year-old, Gleiss struggled to understand what was happening. "These are things you cannot forget," he shook his head sixty years later.[59]

Houses would often lie in ruins except for their chimneys; Breslauers huddling next to them at the moment of impact would often survive. But not always. Ursula Scholz passed a 'levitating' dinner table with a family sitting lifelessly around it. The bodies were unharmed, but the air pressure from the blast had shattered their lungs.[60] Being buried alive was far more common – living in the cellars offered little protection against a direct hit. The five-storey home occupied by the Grollmus family collapsed during one bombing raid. Five people were killed instantly, but rescuers could hear the faint cries of one of the Grollmus children, twelve-year-old Elisabeth. It took them nearly thirty hours to dig the girl, her legs crushed, from the rubble. A few days later Catholic priest Walter Lassmann visited her in Josef's Hospital. "Herr Minister, why don't my parents and Helmut and Eva Maria visit me?" she pleaded. "I took her small hand in mine and broke it to her that her papa and mama, little brother and sister were already in heaven," Lassmann wrote. "She looked at me with tears streaming down her face and didn't say a word. I had to leave her alone with this great heartache and I suspected then that she would soon follow them into eternity."[61]

It was hardly surprising that many Breslauers – soldiers and civilians – grew increasingly fatalistic as the siege dragged on. "We are all going under, no one will get out of here alive," one soldier from Brandenburg wrote to his wife. "The devil gets all those who began this game. We are the losers. Even an idiot knows that it's all over, but they still order us to continue dying." For many the burden became too great. "Where can we still go?" some asked. "Not this side of the Oder, not the other side of the Oder. The best thing to do is jump in the Oder." Some reports suggested as many as 120 Breslauers took their own lives each day, others that only a few committed suicide. The best estimate is that some two to three dozen people preferred death by their own hand than by other means *every day* the city was encircled – between 2,000 and 3,000 suicides during the eighty-two day siege. Alfred Hardlitschke, a Great War veteran and now the reluctant leader of a *Volkssturm* platoon, was determined to survive for the sake of his wife Kläre and their children Edwin and Erich, both serving at the front, but he doubted that he would ever see them again. "Death constantly passes me by," he wrote. "It's a miracle that I'm still alive." He penned farewell letters to all three. "If I do not have the opportunity in my hour of death to bid you a final farewell, then I want to do it like this," he told his wife. The strains and stresses of war had led to clashes and "harsh words" in the Hardlitschke household. Alfred told Kläre to forget all that. "Instead, let us think about how we loved each other when we were young, how happy we were watching our children grow up, how we looked after each other and went through joy and grief." To his elder son Edwin he pleaded forgiveness for treating him harshly as a child. "If you have children one day and have to do school work with them, then do not do it the way I did it with you. Teach them with love and kindness, so that you do not spend your whole life blaming yourself for being too hard on this child or that child." The younger Erich was a chip off the old block – "furious and hot-tempered". His father counselled: "You must try to control yourself. If you have children one day then what I've said to Edwin counts for you too." He ended his valedictory letter: "And now, my boys, thank you for the joy you have given me and a final farewell."[62] Alfred Hardlitschke was killed leading his *Volkssturm* platoon in battle on 19 April.

Hardlitschke survived two months longer than the idealistic former student Karl Oertel. He had begun the year convinced that 1945 would be the year of decision – in Germany's favour, of course. After ten days of battle, he was exhausted, unable to sleep, yet still "full of confidence". Another seven days and his mind was preoccupied with thoughts of home and heaven. A week later the machine-gunner's company was ordered to halt Russian armour which had penetrated the village of Wasserborn, five miles south-east of Breslau's city centre. "Are we going to make it again?" Oertel asked his friend. For the first ten minutes the counter-attack went well. "At that moment, there was very heavy shell fire directed at us, the first three men, one shell every metre," Oertel's friend recalled. The men were unable to move. The order remained: machine-gun to the front. "We carried out the order and suffered losses as a result," the soldier wrote to Oertel's family in Hamburg. Suddenly the philosophy student had cried: "Machine-gunner Oertel knocked out!" Those were his last words. Blood streamed down the left side of his face. Three fingers on his left hand were lacerated. "He knelt on his right foot, his head leaning over, his machine-gun in his right hand, as he entered eternity."[63]

Karl Oertel's passing sounded almost peaceful. But then it seemed that everyone killed in fortress Breslau died a peaceful death, died instantly, died without suffering. Post official and *Volkssturm* company commander Alfred Klose wrote a letter of condolence to the widow of one of his employees:

Dear Frau Rothe!

A sad event has made me write this letter to you.

On 11 April your husband was the victim of a Bolshevik bombing attack and gave his life for the Führer, people and Fatherland.

In the name of all my comrades, may I give you, dear Frau Rothe, and your children my heartfelt condolences for your painful loss.

In your husband, we have lost a good comrade who set an example by his constant willingness to act. His hero's death leaves a gaping hole in our ranks.

We laid the mortal remains of your husband to rest in the garden of the university library in Sandstrasse behind the Sandkirche. The grave was consecrated by a minister. We erected a simple wooden cross by his grave.

If it is any comfort, your husband did not suffer for long, for he died immediately.

We have kept your husband's personal effects safe here.
We are convinced that your husband's heroic death is not a pointless sacrifice.
God give you the strength to bear the loss of your husband.
With deepest sympathy.[64]

Georg Haas knew the lie behind such letters. The Waffen SS clerk kept records of the fallen in *Regiment Besslein*. "There are only shots to the head and shots through the heart in these stereotypical death notices, certainly no one dying an ugly death. And no one's left lying; they are all buried – a clean war! Is there anything more beautiful than to die on the field of honour? A shot through the heart, killed immediately – no pain, no grief." There was no mention of the cries of pain drifting across no man's land for hours on end, no mention between the lines of men bleeding to death, no mention of bodies torn apart by hand grenades or shells. "None of all that. The hero's death is a beautiful and clean affair: a smooth, round bullet hole; corpse buried."[65]

There was only one way to escape the hell of Breslau: evacuation by air – but only for the wounded. At night ambulances ferried casualties from the hospitals and aid stations to Gandau, then waited until the Junkers had departed. Some pilots would take twenty-eight, perhaps even thirty-two wounded. No Ju52 – or *Tante Ju* (Aunt Ju) as the men called them – ever left Gandau without injured troops aboard. But if the aircraft failed to turn up, the ambulances would return the men to their hospitals. Company commander Wolfgang Chutsch was taken to Gandau on three occasions. On the first, the Ju52 due to carry him out of Breslau was full. During take-off it careered into a crater, flipped on to its nose and exploded, killing or severely burning every occupant. On the second, the Russian barrage prevented any aircraft touching down. Finally, in the small hours of 3 March, a Ju52 took him to Dresden. The aircraft behind and in front of his Aunt Ju were both shot down. Chutsch's Junkers was hit eight times by flak and more than 120 times by small arms fire.[66]

More than 5,000 casualties were flown out of the city. The flights in brought food, mail, medicine, ammunition, light field guns, sometimes replacement troops. The 'air bridge' to airfields around Dresden and Breslau was the fortress's lifeline. "Without air supply," Hans von Ahlfen wrote, "Breslau's long struggle would have been unimaginable." Ahlfen and his successor Niehoff needed forty tons of supplies delivered every day. The three-engined Junkers 52, backbone of the Luftwaffe's transport fleet, was the favoured machine thanks to its two-ton payload. That was if the Aunt Ju landed. If it chose to drop its supplies by parachute, each aircraft could only deliver 1.3 tons. Worse still, fortress staff reckoned half the canisters parachuted into the city would fall over enemy lines, while those which did land on the German side were frequently plundered.[67] The Heinkel He111 could carry even less, and it could only drop supplies, not land at Gandau. While only twenty Ju52s were required to support Breslau each day, it would take forty-five Heinkels to deliver the forty tons of supplies.

And that was discounting the effects of the enemy and the weather. There were at least ninety medium and heavy Soviet anti-aircraft batteries ranged around the Silesian capital, plus a good hundred searchlights. The approach of an aircraft provoked "hundreds of tracer and flak shells racing skywards – an instant firework display to shoot down our aircraft," recalled chemist Hans Hoffmann. Vassily Malinin watched German aircraft "caught between the beams of searchlights" over Breslau. Seconds later they began "dragging trails of smoke and fire behind them" before crashing on the edge of the city. "Several enemy aircraft were shot down tonight," the war correspondent noted. "But some succeeded in fighting their way through to the city." On the ground at Gandau, small-arms fire and artillery added to the fliers' difficulties. As soon as the aircraft started their engines up again, mortar fire began from Red Army positions barely half a mile from the airfield. "Comrades who had flown supplies to Stalingrad said that the defences at Breslau were much stronger," one Ju52 radio operator recalled. On 17 March he and his Ju52 attempted to drop canisters of mail and medicines over the city. Low cloud thwarted any hope of landing at Gandau. The Junkers flew on to the sports fields of the Friesenwiese. Immediately Russian light and medium flak opened fire, then the searchlights captured the transporter. The pilot dived, climbed and banked to get out of them. The supply canisters were thrown out of their racks, smashing holes in the roof and scattering their contents around the fuselage. All thoughts of a drop were abandoned. The pilot turned for Dresden. It was nearly dawn when the Ju52 touched down. Its crew "found a hole the size of washbowl in the left tailplane, countless bullet holes in the elevator and fin as well as in the rear of the fuselage." They also learned that four other crews were missing. A fifth had nursed its badly damaged aircraft home.[68]

The air supply of Breslau had reached its turning point. Until mid-March, for every eight Junkers sent to Breslau, seven returned. But thereafter losses rose alarmingly. In the second half of the month, two in every five Aunt Jus never reached the city. It could not continue: if such losses persisted, the Luftwaffe warned, it would run out of aircraft by the first week in April.[69] The shortage of aircraft was compounded by the fact that Gandau was rapidly becoming untenable. By the end of the first week of April, it would be in Soviet hands. But by then, the Silesian capital had another airfield.

For half a century the red brick Lutherkirche had dominated the skyline of eastern Breslau. Built to celebrate the 400th anniversary of Martin Luther's birth, it took the city's Protestants ten years to raise the funds and three to erect their new house of worship, a near replica of Berlin's Lutheran church. More imposing than loved, the neo-Gothic Lutherkirche possessed the tallest spire in the city and excellent acoustics for its 1,400 worshippers. The latter lived in four-, five- and six-storey apartment blocks in the surrounding tree-lined boulevards which converged on one of Breslau's great intersections, the Scheitniger Stern. All would be flattened in the coming weeks as Karl Hanke bludgeoned a *Rollfeld* – runway – one mile long and at least 300 yards wide through the suburb.

Every day from 23 March until early April, Polish forced labourer Alexsander Szniolis was roused at 4am and marched through the streets to Scheitnig. There, Szniolis and his fellow prisoners – Poles, Italians, Frenchmen – found "an anthill of about 60,000 people from all the four corners of the earth and from all of Breslau". They also found every house "burning like a torch – the street was so hot that we could barely breathe". The prisoners tore down walls, usually still glowing from the heat, and piled the bricks up. An army of workers – most of those toiling on the *Rollfeld* were Germans, not foreign prisoners – carried the rubble away in carts and tipped it on the edge of the burgeoning runway, where it was levelled, while beams, planks, tram rails, even candelabras were used to reinforce barricades in nearby streets. This, according to the Party, was *Ehrendienst* – honorary service. "It was more slave labour than honorary service," Helga Schliepkorte, an evacuee from Düsseldorf, bitterly recalled. "Any delay, any slacking, any extended break, any non-compliance when it came to carrying out the work resulted in draconian punishments." Schoolgirl Ursula Scholz was lucky. She found an accommodating *Feldwebel* who realized the war was lost – and acted accordingly and allowed the women in his charge to work every other day.

The Red Army was not so forgiving. It would not allow work on the new runway to proceed unhindered. Shelling was regular, although those building the *Rollfeld* "soon became skilled in telling which of the shells whistling towards us would land nearby, so that we only took cover occasionally," Helga Schliepkorte remembered. Ursula Scholz heeded the advice of soldiers who told her to throw herself to the ground if caught in the open amid shellfire. "There's no need to walk upright when the air is full of iron." Soviet aircraft, especially fighter-bombers, also 'visited' the runway daily. Their bombs and cannon ploughed up the ground so painstakingly flattened and sent workers rushing to the side. Often they did not make it. The appearance of the enemy aircraft provoked panic and caused workers to group together out of fear, providing the airmen with "rich pickings". Six young women alongside Helga Schliepkorte, none older than eighteen, collapsed as a fighter-bomber strafed the flat red runway. Several of Schliepkorte's colleagues were buried alive during one bombing raid. The workers spent sixteen hours trying to dig them out. "We got there too late," wrote Schliepkorte. "They had all suffocated." Days, weeks of toil, of brutal treatment, of constant attacks, gnawed at the nerves of those building the *Rollfeld*. "We sleep like hares, our eyes open," former electrician Hermann Nowack recorded in his diary. "And we wait for death." Nowack survived. Not so an estimated 3,000 fellow workers. Their bodies were tossed into a mass grave in nearby Scheitniger Park. "No plaque records their names," Helga Schliepkorte bemoaned two decades later. "They died without names. Many of them are perhaps still sought by their relatives today." And yet at the time the housewife believed the sacrifices were worthwhile. She remembered how "everyone did their best, for no one wanted to admit that Breslau was lost".[70]

Their efforts were largely in vain. Records are vague, but very few transport aircraft ever set down on the *Rollfeld* after it was completed in early April. Twenty-three-year-old Werner Grund did use the new runway – on a one-way mission. Grund was towed to the edge of the city in a small DFS 230 glider. Six and a half thousand feet above Breslau, a crewman on the He111 towplane flashed a green torch and the glider was released. The bomber crew turned for home, relieved, for Soviet fighters were reported. Werner Grund looked for a place to land. He chose the new runway.

As I got lower, I saw bombs exploding and houses burning. The two-centimetre flak was too high. I pushed the sliding window back, threw my headphones out and put on my steel helmet. The searchlights hadn't got me. Below, I saw a burning house. The glow of fire illuminated a field as big as a children's playground. I selected it as an emergency landing ground. The houses were getting worryingly close as I lined up the approach. I steered the glider down. It dropped like a piano from the fifth storey. As I approached I saw six landing lights – Kaiserstrasse. Three metres above the ground I was ready to land. Tail wind and breathtaking speed prevented any mishap. I gently touched down but for some reason the undercarriage broke off and I landed on my runners, roughly twenty metres past the burning houses. I climbed out of the glider. Not a soul, just ruins and blazing houses. Then a figure appeared and called out: "Don't shoot!" – he'd heard me flicking my rifle's safety catch off. I was glad to have escaped once again. The glider was immediately unloaded and pushed into the burning house. I reported to a *Leutnant* in the shelter. The duty doctor was relieved that nothing had happened to me. The atmosphere was depressed. All of them wanted to know when the "relief" would come. What could I say to that?

Grund was offered a glass of schnapps and a plate of stewed fruit which he ate while bombs fell outside. After spending the night in the besieged city, he was flown out in a tiny Fieseler Storch reconnaissance aircraft.[71]

Airmen like Werner Grund saw Breslau as no man on the ground saw it. They saw the fires in the city burning on the horizon. They saw swathes of smoke carried across the Silesian capital by the wind. Aerial reconnaissance photographs show entire districts hidden beneath swirling grey and black smoke. But just occasionally, the hand of God shielded them from the horrors of war. After one hellish flight to Gandau to deliver paratroopers, a Junkers took off hurriedly under artillery fire. "The city was soon beneath us in the dark and gloomy night with all its war, fire and destruction covered up by blanket of white clouds," recalled a crew member. "The moon with its silver light shone brightly, turning the clouds into a sea of pure silver upon which our ship swam home. The heavens were blue, as blue as dark velvet. The stars in the heavens stood out and sparkled like jewels."[72]

Those inside the fortress were also struck by the contrast between the power of Nature and the battle raging about them. Sixteen-year-old Ursula Scholz struggled to understand "how life in Nature goes on, unfazed by the human misery". As soon as an air raid ended, the birds sang once more "as if nothing has happened", while in gardens which had still not been ploughed up by bombs and shells hyacinths, daffodils and narcissi were in bloom. "Life can be so beautiful!" Klaus Franke was entranced by the sight – and sound – of a blackbird which settled on a shot-up tree stump barely 100 feet from *I-Werk* 41. "The bird repeatedly opens its yellow beak, its larynx swells and jubilantly the bird sings its mating call to the approaching spring," the *Feldwebel* wrote.

"It is probably the only one which has not been scared away by the thunder of the cannons." Perhaps Ivan was similarly bewitched, for birdsong was the only sound carried across the battlefield. Franke continued:

> The blackbird repeatedly sings its call with drawn-out notes. The rain drips slowly from the splintered tree stumps on to the blood-soaked earth which is strewn with dead bodies. This innocent bird does not see the horror all around it, however. For it, it is spring, sunshine, mating time. It sits there without a care in the world, cleans its feathers and shakes the drops of rain off its plumage. It has no idea of the terrible slaughter all around it. It does not breathe in this pestilent air of decaying bodies. It does not see the mutilated human corpses. This little singer has no idea about the brutality and hypocrisy of human insanity. Only a shot could scare this small wonder of nature away and put an end to his wooing.

For many Breslauers, spring was synonymous with hope. "The sun is already wonderfully warm and there's the trickling and dripping of melting snow everywhere," wrote Hans Gottwald. "Only a few sporadic clumps of dirty snow still cover the earth. How good that is! But how wonderful it would be to be at home now. Peace, quiet." He paused. "*Ach*, no point thinking about that." Medic Gerhard Hauschild stared longingly at the first green shoots appearing. "It would be a godsend for us, too, if we had the hope and assurance that something was sprouting for us," he mused.[73]

Catholic priest Walter Lassmann saw few signs of hope in Breslau. "A strange spring approaches," he wrote. "All of us are filled with a melancholic foreboding of death." At midday on 25 March, Lassmann climbed one of the two cathedral towers which had dominated the right bank of the Oder for more than three centuries. From his vantage point 300ft above the city, the priest looked down upon "a scene of terrible reality": everywhere there were explosions, entire rows of houses and streets aflame beneath a grey sky.

> I have often envied the birds which fly around the two cathedral towers by day – all the time the way to freedom is open to them. We however cannot escape, nor may we.
>
> Reason could truly be brought to a standstill if you had to experience everything which evolution, toil, the arts and industry have created down the centuries was wiped out in a hail of bombs, a rain of shells, in firestorms, in a few blinks of an eye, when you witness the senseless destruction of your beloved homeland and thousands of dear fellow human beings suffering an often terrible death.

March 25 was Palm Sunday. "Holy week lies in front of us like a long street which we will have to go down, a street of tears and blood, of terrible desolation and destruction." Walter Lassmann's words were more prophetic than he could ever have imagined.[74]

Notes

1. Grieger, p.16 and Becker, p.126.
2. Hanke's speech is published in various forms, notably in the *Schlesische Tageszeitung*, 4/3/45, *Völkischer Beobachter*, Munich edition, 5/3/45, *Berliner Morgenpost*, 6/3/45 and *Deutsche Allgemeine Zeitung*, 6/3/45. It is difficult to know how many Breslauers heard the speech – or read it; the words were reproduced in full in the following day's *Schlesische Tageszeitung*. There are few references to it in the writings of the fortress's chroniclers. Priest Paul Peikert was appalled. He found Hanke "impossibly conceited", his speech "filled with a mania for destruction to the bitter end." See Peikert, pp.118-19. But medic Gerhard Hauschild was inspired. "He spoke for all of us," he gushed. "We do not make big, heroic speeches. Hold on, that's the watchword. Everyone here knows what's at stake. Most look to the west, wait and fight." See Gleiss, viii, p.309.
3. Gleiss, iii, pp.206-7.
4. Ibid., iii, p.202.
5. *Schlesische Tageszeitung*, 9/3/45.
6. Gleiss, iii, p.26.
7. Hornig, pp.118-20, Peikert, pp.112-13 and Bannert, p.68.
8. Van Aaken, pp.197-9.
9. Gleiss, iii, pp.298-300.
10. Ibid., iii, pp.446-7.
11. Ibid., iii, p.352.
12. Ibid., iii, p.421.
13. Lauban counterstroke is based on Scherstjanoi, p.115, *Deutsche Allgemeine Zeitung*, 11/3/45, Gleiss, viii, p.400, Hajo Knebel, *Jahrgang 1929*, pp.327-32 and TB Goebbels, 9/3/45.
14. Völkel, pp.51, 56, 62, 63, 66.
15. Becker, pp.135-6.
16. Hornig, pp.43, 118-20.
17. Becker, p.133.
18. Gleiss, iv, pp.450-1.
19. Becker, p.136.
20. Ibid., p.138.
21. Gleiss, iii, pp.797, 828 and Gleiss, vii, pp.1091-2.
22. Gleiss, iii, p.950.
23. Based on Peikert, pp.170-4 and Majewski, pp.86-7.
24. Life in Breslau's hospitals during the siege is based on Hartung, pp.72, 73, Martin Grunow, 'Erlbenisse und Erfahrungen eines Lazarettpfarrers und Pfarrers in Breslau 1945-1946' in *Jahrbuch für Schlesische Kirchengeschichte 1964*, p.159, Hans Gottwald's account in Gleiss, viii, p.327 and Haas, ii, pp.83-5.
25. Life under the bombs based on Haas, ii, p.145, Gleiss, iii, pp.362-3, Gleiss, viii, pp.532, 538.
26. Gleiss, iii, p.306, Gleiss, iv, p.748 and Gleiss, viii, p.561.
27. Konrad, p.16 and Peikert, pp.73-7, 240-1.
28. Grieger, pp.21-2.
29. Peikert, p.222.
30. Based on Malinin's diary in Gleiss, iii, pp.89, 172, 325, 853.
31. Majewski, p.104.
32. Gleiss, iii, p.636.
33. Majewski, pp.128-9.
34. Based on Gleiss, iii, p.639, I. I. Diebrin, 'In the Battle for Breslau' in *Wrocławska epopeja*, pp.132-3, and Majewski, p.55.
35. House fighting based on Gleiss, iii, pp.452-3 and *So Kämpfte Breslau*, pp.66-7, 68, 70.
36. *So Kämpfte Breslau*, pp.91-4.
37. Ibid., pp.74-5, 93-4 and Gleiss, ii, p.758.
38. Ibid., pp.66-7.
39. Gleiss, iii, p.910.
40. *So Kämpfte Breslau*, pp.63-4 and Gleiss, ii, pp.588-9.

41. Van Aaken, pp.197-9.
42. Gleiss, vii, pp.1648-9.
43. Ibid., vii, p.728.
44. Life out of the line from *So Kämpfte Breslau*, p.69, Documenty Nr.48, Nr.98, Majewski, p.128, Gleiss, viii, p.1344 and Hartung, pp.61-2.
45. Gleiss, iii, pp.916-17.
46. Ibid., iii, p.703.
47. Based on Peikert, pp.60-1 and Gleiss, ii, p.571.
48. *So Kämpfte Breslau*, p.53.
49. Documenty Nr.87.
50. Based on Franke, pp.44-5, Gleiss, vii, pp.1628-9 and Haas, ii, p.145.
51. Gleiss, viii, pp.467-9.
52. Decorations based on Documenty Nr.53 and Nr.88, Völkel, p.48, Bannert, p.83 and *Schlesische Tageszeitung*, 6/3/45.
53. Documenty Nr.155 and Gleiss, iii, pp.611-13.
54. Based on Peikert, pp.145, 198, 213, Gleiss, viii, p.347, Gleiss, *Pennäler, Pimpf und Volkssturmmann*, p.1 and *Die Grosse Flucht*, ZDF documentary, 2001, Episode 3, 'Festung Breslau'.
55. Peikert, p.112 and Grunow, 'Erlbenisse und Erfahrungen eines Lazarettpfarrers und Pfarrers in Breslau 1945-1946' in *Jahrbuch für Schlesische Kirchengeschichte 1964*, p.161.
56. Documenty Nr.41 and Gleiss, viii, pp.660-1.
57. Horst Gleiss, *Pennäler, Pimpf und Volkssturmmann*, p.9.
58. Hornig, pp.124-6 and Peikert, pp.215-17.
59. Gleiss, ii, pp.588-9 and *Die Grosse Flucht*, ZDF documentary, 2001, Episode 3, 'Festung Breslau'.
60. Waage, p.34.
61. Gleiss, iii, pp.627-8.
62. Morale based on *Izvestia*, 8/5/45, Kaps, *Tragödie Schlesiens 1945/46*, p.55, Hornig, pp.28-9, Gleiss, i, pp.25-6 and Gleiss, iii, pp.165-6, 911.
63. Bähr and Bähr, p.441.
64. Author's papers.
65. Haas, ii, pp.25-6.
66. Gleiss, viii, p.292.
67. *So Kämpfte Breslau*, pp.44-5 and Documenty Nr.227.
68. Gleiss, iii, p.839, Gleiss, iv, p.212 and Hornig, pp.128-30.
69. BA-MA RL 7/539/108-116.
70. *Rollfeld* construction based on Majewski, p.77, Van Aaken, pp.207-8, Jerrig, pp.30-1, Becker, p.140, Waage, pp.16, 27-8, Siebel, p.75 and *Microcosm*, p.29. Perhaps not quite did their best. "The Germans worked with unparalleled determination, while we only pretended to work," Alexsander Szniolis recalled.
71. Gleiss, iv, p.500 and Gleiss, viii, pp.754-5.
72. Gleiss, ii, p.644C.
73. For the effects of nature, see Waage, p.34, Franke, pp.82-3, and Gleiss, viii, pp.200, 309.
74. Gleiss, iii, p.799.

CHAPTER 7

The Old Breslau is No More

When the Oder flows with blood to the north and
the destroyed towers reach for the heavens
like scrawny fingers, Breslau will go under
Breslau proverb

There was a rumour swirling around Breslau in the final week of March. Rumours were banned – unless, of course, they were planted by the Nazis' 'whispering propaganda' campaign. The planted rumours – normally suggesting relief was imminent – came to naught. The latest rumour was not planted. It was carried from mouth to mouth: the Red Army would present Stalin with an Easter gift. That gift would be Breslau.

So far, however, this rumour too seemed to be just that. Saturday, 31 March – Easter Saturday – began quietly. Hugo Hartung admired the forsythias in bloom in Matthiasplatz. There was sporadic activity by the Red Air Force. Two German mortars in the square, heavily camouflaged under netting, only fired occasionally for lack of ammunition. "Towards evening, everything changes," wrote Hartung. Loudspeakers warned that 750 bombers would strike at Breslau incessantly on the holy day. It was no bluff. At dusk on Easter Saturday a barrage began "on a scale which surpasses anything experienced to date by us". It was the prelude to two days which would change the face of Breslau forever.[1]

Long before dawn on Easter Day, Paul Peikert hurried to take confession in St Mauritiuskirche on the eastern edge of the city centre. There were scores of soldiers, as well as parishioners, already waiting for him.[2]

Two miles to the west, Klaus Franke sat with his comrade Hans on the third floor of the clock tower in the Linke-Hofmann Werk. It was the fifth consecutive night the two forward artillery observers had spent in their perch, scanning Breslau's western approaches with field binoculars. Though not particularly high, their vantage point thirty feet up allowed them to see as far as Deutsch Lissa, four miles away, and Leuthen, nearly eight. By day they watched *panje* carts, trucks, carts, limbered artillery, tanks, columns of marching soldiers, cyclists, a continuous stream of traffic. By night, they could only hear the vehicles and the occasional shout from a driver. There was the occasional flash of a muzzle, the dull roar of a gun firing, the whistle of a shell. Otherwise, Franke recalled, the nights in the tower lasted an eternity. He smoked constantly and rummaged in the pockets of his camouflage jacket for his emergency rations. The night of 31 March/1 April was no different – until a thin strip of light in the east announced the coming day. At the same time, 4.45am, the western horizon also lit up, as if "one thousand fire-breathing throats" were being cleared at once. After the flashes came the thunder, an awful howling and hissing. "The ground shakes and the iron flying around in the air clinks and clanks," wrote Franke. "All hell has broken loose and the earth is like an inferno." His comrade reached for the field telephone. "The enemy barrage began at 4.45am on a scale never . . ." The line went dead. Franke reached for the wireless and tapped out a message to headquarters: *4.45am. Barrage of an intensity never known before. Continues. Observation impossible.* The response was almost immediate – and to the point: *Hold on till dawn.*

The barrage was intensifying. "It's as if a mighty volcano has erupted," Franke wrote. "Bubbling, caustic smoke and gunpowder fill the air. The hurricane with its crashing and exploding grows worse by the minute. It really is raining deadly iron." The clock tower shook and seemed to sway under the succession of explosions. Then a direct hit on the floor below the two observers. The men were stunned momentarily, their ears ringing, brick dust and smoke filling the observation post. Another shell caused the second floor to collapse, the stairs were ripped from their steel supports. The air was so thick it was almost impossible to breathe, but neither man left his post.[3]

Confession in St Mauritiuskirche lasted fifteen minutes longer than expected. There were simply too many soldiers for Paul Peikert to absolve. Mass finally got under way a little after 6am. It was far from a typical Easter Mass. There was no celebration of resurrection, to prevent the service dragging on too long. Nor was there the usual resurrection procession, because of the threat of air attack. It was the last service Peikert held in the church.

Outside Peikert's church, thirteen-year-old Eberhard 'Ebi' Hassenbach tenderly waved at his family. As long as he could still see his mother, father and sister, he waved. The Hassenbachs had risen at the crack of dawn to go to confession, then to take communion at St Mauritiuskirche's Easter service. As the service ended, Ebi Hassenbach bade his family farewell. A few weeks before, the lively, talkative teenager had been called up as a messenger by his *Ortsgruppe* in eastern Breslau. At first he returned home each night after his duties, but following promotion he no longer came home. He had briefly visited his family on Good Friday. His appearance shocked his mother Gertrud. "Before he was so trusting, how happily he chatted," she recalled. "Now he barely spoke a word, he was distracted, ate little and only wanted to sleep." When he did speak, Ebi's words were devastating. "*Mutti*", he simpered to his mother, "I am completely broken." Frau Hassenbach railed at the regime. "What have they turned our happy, carefree children into?" Enraged – and emboldened – she went to the *Ortsgruppe* and demanded her son's release from duties. A Party official brushed her away. "You too must make a sacrifice."[4]

Paul Peikert made his way to an overcrowded air raid shelter in Klosterstrasse where the occupants awaited high mass. As Peikert prepared himself next to a temporary altar, the first bombs began to fall from 340 Soviet aircraft. Within half an hour, five one-ton bombs landed around the shelter. One destroyed St Agnes seminary. The second landed in a mass grave, just thirty feet from the cellar, where a week before Peikert had buried ten victims of the bombing. Eight of those dead were vaporized – with their coffins to boot. The third bomb destroyed the neighbouring house, burying eight inhabitants alive. They were never recovered. The fourth ploughed up the church garden, gouging out a crater more than sixty feet across and more than twenty-five feet deep. The fifth struck the ill-fated seminary. Each time one of the bombs exploded, the cellar and the building above it shook. The candlesticks on the altar were knocked out. People jumped up, convinced they were about to be entombed.[5]

Wilhelm Saffe and his wife left their cellar in Rosenthaler Strasse to walk to mass at Bonifatiuskirche in nearby Benderplatz. Barely had the couple taken their seats when the first Soviet bombers appeared overhead. Mass continued. The walls of the small church shook, but its young priest remained calm. So too his choir, who "did not stop for a moment, not even when a hail of bombs seemed to herald the end and the congregation cried with terror in unison". A brief pause in the bombing allowed the worshippers to flee across the road, through the grove opposite – except that nothing remained of the small copse. "The fine trees lay strewn on the ground in every direction," Saffe remembered. The cadavers of horses lay next to their wrecked cart. It was, wrote Wilhelm Saffe, " a scene of misery". As the couple reached the edge of the desolate copse, the bombing resumed. "Aircraft. Get into the next house!" Saffe yelled at his wife. She disappeared into the nearest building, he went into the house next door then scurried down into the cellar as the first bombs fell. Another pause and the Saffes left their temporary shelter for their home. "Wheezing, dead tired, still bundles of nerves, we struggled down the stairs to our cellar – but we were home," a relieved Wilhelm Saffe wrote.[6]

Paul Peikert took advantage of a brief respite in the barrage to return to his vicarage, passing a smashed cart, its horses dead, its driver dead on the wagon, and two huge craters which had ripped up Klosterstrasse. As he grabbed breakfast in his home, the bombers returned. Peikert rushed into the vicarage's air raid shelter. "Waves of enemy aircraft passed over the city continuously, dropping their fatal payloads," he recorded in his diary. "The lights in the air raid shelter went out repeatedly. Everything went dark when the enemy bombs exploded and huge clouds of dust and gunpowder were whipped up so that it became completely black all around us. The walls of the cellar shook and we thought that the vicarage itself had been hit and it would soon collapse on top of us." After a few minutes, the clouds of dust dispersed and the occupants of the cellar realized a neighbouring building had been hit.[7]

Soldier Theo Klose was thrown off his motorcycle and immediately ran towards the nearest cellar. He stumbled down the stairs where he found distraught Breslauers sheltering from the barrage. The scenes, he remembered, were indescribable. "Children screamed, women cried. The cellar walls shook." The house above suffered a direct hit from a mortar and began to burn. Those in the cellar did not want to leave, but Theo Klose did. He felt his way up the cellar stairs and reached the street. It was aflame, his bicycle reduced to a pile of scrap. He ran down the road, throwing himself to the ground repeatedly as long tongues of flame licked out of blazing houses. "I don't know how often I did so," Klose recalled. "I only know that my whole face was battered and I eventually ended up in a public air raid shelter." It too was filled with screaming, crying Breslauers.[8]

During a pause in the bombing, Hugo Hartung and his company of convalescing troops were ordered to leave their posts near Matthiasplatz on the right bank of the Oder and head to Antonienstrasse in the old town, a journey of no more than a mile. Hartung and his comrades never reached the river. As they left the square, the barrage resumed. "It must be a joy for the Russian airmen to wander around in this endless, deep, bright blue sky," the theatre director wrote. "No German flak, no fighters pester them. The sky above Breslau is theirs." The soldiers hugged the walls of buildings, kept their heads down and rushed into cellars for cover every few minutes. After two and a half hours, the soldiers decided to return to their quarters. There was no hope of crossing Universitätsbrücke alive. The men returned to their basement in Matthiasplatz. Early in the afternoon, an elderly couple and a young woman tottered into the cellar; they were the family of Hartung's sergeant. His father tried to explain what had happened in halting sentences. "Just imagine a large shell," the aged gentleman stuttered, "landing in the very next cellar. It was a better cellar than ours. That's why there were more people in it. We were just about to move there ourselves, but my wife could not find the cake. And when she found it, it happened. Right in the neighbouring cellar. And there were at least twenty people inside." His wife put the rescued Easter cake, decorated with small red and green marzipan eggs, on the table, then offered to make coffee – not *Ersatz* coffee, but *real* coffee – for all the cellar dwellers. "At this hour, there are identical scenes in more than one Breslau cellar, sometimes with real coffee, sometimes with *Ersatz* coffee," Hartung observed. "There's not cake and gâteau everywhere, but in some places there's music from the radio or a gramophone if there's still electricity despite the bombardment." With or without music, there was a constant soundtrack: the drone of bombers, growing louder or fading, interspersed with the distinctive 'chug' of the 'sewing machines'. "Everywhere the ground moves, doors crack, lights goes out, ceilings and walls are torn," Hugo Hartung wrote, "yet this coffee hour at Easter remains one of the comforting illusions during our downfall."[9]

Waffen SS clerk Georg Haas took shelter in the cellar of a church on Klosterstrasse. Two girls with dirty faces beneath black helmets stood guard at the shelter's iron door. Occasionally, there was thumping from outside, but the basement was full. No one else was admitted.

With each impact, dust and mortar trickled from the ceiling, covering the shelter's occupants with a layer of grey. The heat grew worse by the minute. Children whimpered, mothers cried, some suffered hysterical screaming fits and tried to get out, trampling over other occupants to reach the door. They clawed at the iron door before finally giving up, their hands bleeding. Those at the back of the cellar began to inch away from the stone wall, now scorching hot from the fires raging outside. An old woman screamed: "We're all going to hell. The cellar. The house. The entire city. All to hell." She tried to reach the door, tripped and fell, smashing her head against a box. No one tried to help her up.[10]

Underground for years, Breslau's Communists chose Easter Sunday to reveal their true allegiances. As many as 125 white flags appeared across the city. If they were seen by Soviet aircrew – and there is no evidence they were – they were ignored.

The only thing most Breslauers could do this Sunday was remain in their cellars and pray as the entire city was "carpeted with bombs," as one anonymous chronicler wrote. His – or her – account continues:

> The air is filled with continual roaring, howling, bursting, there's the thunder of aircraft and the whistling of shells. On top of that, there's shelling from the south, east and west. Death has a rich harvest and celebrates with orgies of destruction. The bunker seems to rise up and fall back down with a crash. The building shakes like a mortally wounded animal. We are stunned by the air pressure and put our hands over our ears so we don't have to listen to this terrible, hellish symphony any more, and ram our fists into our mouths so we do not scream out of mad anxiety. Some fall to their knees and pray or mumble some incomprehensible noise to themselves. Some seem powerless out of horror. And everyone's face is ashen and looks very old. Hundreds of aircraft seem to be over our block alone, turning in circles continuously, and in the distance we can hear the endless, endless roaring, rising and falling, the melody of death.
>
> During the pauses, we rush out at the risk of our own lives and search for those buried alive in neighbouring houses. But we find no survivors among the ruins. They are all dead. And those who are able to save themselves crawling through the cracks. They are dirty, ragged, cut – more animal than human. The whites of their eyes, filled with terror, stand out in their blackened, scratched faces. They can still feel the breath of death and are mad with fear.[11]

It was 5pm when the bombing finally relented and Paul Peikert cautiously emerged from the air raid shelter in his vicarage. It was time for vespers, but there were no parishioners for Peikert to receive; none dared leave their cellars and shelters. The priest's only visitors were two officers, who talked at length about the day's events. They reckoned 5,000 bombs had fallen on Breslau on the holiest day in the Christian calendar.[12]

Night fell a little before 7pm, but there was no darkness in Breslau this Sunday, for aside from the full moon the sky glowed "red in the reflection of the flames," junior officer Erich Schönfelder observed. The sight was at once captivating and horrifying. After spending the day sheltering in a cellar, Peter Bannert and a comrade somehow felt drawn to the Ring and St Elisabethkirche. They climbed to the top of its 300ft tower and looked out silently over "a single sea of flames" before descending the steps depressed, while on the fortress's northern front, *Feldwebel* Gerhard Schwingel watched a comrade sit in his foxhole, his back to the enemy, "reading the newspaper and admiring the magnificent fireworks". Those still in the air raid shelters, bunkers and cellars had no concept of what was happening to their city, only that it was terrifying. In the church cellar in Klosterstrasse, the growing sense of panic was palpable. The acrid smell of burning penetrated gaps in the wall and the shelter's heavy iron door. Children coughed and began to cry. There was repeated hammering on the shelter entrance from outside. Those at the front of the shelter could hear a few broken sentences. "Fire! Out! The street's on fire! Save . . ." Until now, two girls had stoically guarded the door, allowing no one in or out. Now, one of them cracked. "We're burning! Get out of here! We're burning!" She threw herself against the door. Her actions sparked panic. Everyone in the shelter rushed for the door. Fists flew, bodies fell, a disabled veteran tried to clear a path to the exit with his crutch – until someone kicked his artificial leg away; he fell and was trampled by the crowd. The iron door was unbolted and the cellar's occupants rushed up the steps, down a hallway and into Klosterstrasse. Perhaps they wished they had not, for the street, Georg Haas recalled, was "just one huge sea of flames". Clothes caught fire; people threw themselves on to the torn-up pavement trying to put them out. "Shells roar over this place of horror and bring death and destruction to those who believed they had escaped the flames of hell," wrote Haas. "Embers threaten to suffocate your breath. The noise of howling shells, crackling flames, collapsing roof trusses, the constant explosions and shrill cries of people make your eardrums shake." He watched people thrown to the side of the street by the blast of a shell "like paper tossed in an autumn storm". A few of the more fortunate ones, like Georg Haas, escaped the fire, stumbling past the blackened façades of houses, deformed corpses and burned out vehicles, finally finding refuge in a shelter.[13]

Dawn on Easter Monday was hidden by swathes of smoke which the sun struggled to penetrate. In Niehoff's headquarters, a staff officer tapped an urgent plea to the Luftwaffe to shield the city from the Red Air Force. The fighters, he insisted, should come at 9.30am. The fighters did not come – and by 9.30 Soviet bombers had already been over Breslau for half an hour.[14] They heralded, priest Walter Lassmann wrote, "the worst day in the 1,000-year history of Breslau."

Librarian Friedrich Grieger arrived at the state library on Sandinsel at 8am, determined to rescue as many historic volumes as possible. He was surprised to see others had also turned up, "albeit in smaller numbers" than on Easter Day. The work was barely under way when the bombers approached. For the next few hours, library staff and soldiers stood shoulder-to-shoulder in the shelter as the small island was struck by "one bomb after another," Grieger wrote. "With each impact the women and girls cry out and cling to the soldiers." When the aircraft passed, the men opened the cellar hatches and climbed out into Sandstrasse. The first floor of the library had been completely burned out – 100,000 volumes consumed by the fire. Grieger headed home dejected. His apartment in Kreuzstrasse had till now escaped the inferno. But no longer. Kreuzstrasse was "a single sea of flames", the house next to the Griegers' already burning. With the help of three friends, the fifty-three-year-old hacked at the wooden fence separating the two buildings with pickaxes. It was too late. The tarred roof began to burn. The four rushed inside to save what they could. As the blaze spread, two bombs landed nearby devastating the rooms, causing shelves to collapse. Nevertheless, several suitcases and bundles were rescued and buried in the grounds of the neighbouring Botanic Gardens.[15]

The bombardment reached its peak in the early afternoon. It was not constant. The Soviet aircraft came in waves, each lasting up to three quarters of an hour. One doctor counted the bombers flying overhead: 100 aircraft in a thirty-minute period. The litany of destruction was never-ending. The 500-year-old Catholic St Maria auf dem Sande – known to every Breslauer simply as the Sandkirche – was burned out. On the other side of the Oder, the Vincenzkirche with its monument to thirteenth-century ruler Heinrich IV and the Klosterkirche of Ursuline next to it had been reduced to rubble. Its thirty remaining nuns knelt in front of it in disbelief. The famous organ in the Jahrhunderthalle, the largest in Europe after the one in Passau, Bavaria, played its final, awful notes as it was smashed by a Soviet shell. Twenty-five Party activists from an *Ortsgruppe* in Kreuzstrasse were buried alive by a bomb. The hand of God could not protect Dominsel – Cathedral Island – the spiritual and historic heart of Breslau. Besides the cathedral which gave the district its name, there were three more places of worship, plus seminaries, convents, numerous curiae – residences of the city's clergy – and the archbishop's palace. All fell victim to the inexorable conflagration. All bar one, that is. A sister stood on the roof of Our Lady of Sorrows, the cross in her hand. She turned to face every corner of the building, blessing and praying for each one in turn. Our Lady of Sorrows did not burn. The cathedral had no such guardian angel. Some time in the afternoon of Easter Monday, a terrible cry spread through the city: *Der Dom brennt*! The cathedral is on fire! And how it burned. The ceiling vaults on the south side and the nave collapsed under the heat, a mountain of ash had accumulated in the vestry as far as the vault. Rubble piled up "as high as a house". Only the building's north wing was spared.[16]

On the opposite bank of the Oder, around 150 employees were sheltering in the cellars of the central post office in Albrechtstrasse. They stayed there for the next forty-five minutes listening to the whistling when bombs fell, the roar when they exploded, the crash when walls gave way. It was perhaps 5.30pm when they dared to emerge from their shelter. They found the post office ablaze. Every pane of glass was broken and from every empty window frame licked tongues of flames. The postal workers turned around and saw "nothing but a sea of flames," according to senior telegraphist Kurt Hanke.[17]

Sea of flames. *Flammenmeer*. It is a description which appears frequently in Breslauers' accounts of that terrible afternoon and evening. There is another word they use repeatedly. *Feuersturm*. Firestorm. The weather throughout Easter Monday had been stormy. By evening, the winds had been whipped up to hurricane-like speeds; the conflagration heated the air around and above the city, causing it to rise. Cooler air rushed in at tremendous speed to feed the inferno, funnelled down Breslau's already burning streets. The result was a firestorm.

Friedrich Grieger took shelter in the Botanic Gardens as "a storm of millions of sparks and balls of fire" were carried over his head, setting buildings along Kreuzstrasse alight. He watched an elderly couple struggle against the firestorm, hauling a small cart. "The man falls suddenly, hit by a blow, the old woman moves on without even looking around once." In Röntgenstrasse, near the Scheitniger Stern, elderly electrician Hermann Nowack watched "gale-force" winds carry "embers the size of a fist" into abandoned apartments. "We run in, tear the curtains down, and tie the doors firmly shut somehow to prevent a draft, reducing the threat of a fire." Paul Peikert witnessed identical scenes in Klosterstrasse. "The hurricane-force storm drove thousands of sparks and balls of fire through the smashed windows into apartments," he wrote. "They found rich pickings in the bedding and cushions. The houses then went up in flames from top to bottom like furnaces." His vicarage succumbed at 5pm. It burned so swiftly, he was barely able to rescue any of his possessions. Paul Peikert fled to an air-raid shelter further down the road. First the building opposite, then Peikert's own church began to burn. The house above the shelter caught fire. The priest decided Klosterstrasse was no longer safe and ran to the next block, Alexanderstrasse, still not ablaze. He had been there barely an hour when that street too was devoured by the moloch of the firestorm. The occupants fled "through a corridor of fire" and a shower of a million sparks, past collapsed houses and mountains of rubble. The next street along, Herbert-Welkischstrasse, was also aflame. Only the Oder, a few yards away, offered salvation. But when they reached Kaiserbrücke, the ferocious winds almost hurled them on to the river. The bridge also offered the stragglers "the indescribably tragic sight of the burning city of Breslau, an unforgettable, blood-curdling drama". It was a sight as mesmerising as it was horrific. "We repeatedly turned around to see this tragic scene," Paul Peikert wrote. "Breslau burning on the evening and night of Easter Monday was an awful, gruesome sight, the downfall of this beautiful city and its most beautiful part. The dark, cloudy sky glowed red. Huge swathes of smoke hung over the entire city." The priest and his group fled down the right bank of the Oder, finally finding shelter in the technical high school, his fourth cellar of the evening.[18]

It was around 8pm when the Soviet onslaught ended. A disquieting silence descended upon Breslau when the bombing and shelling ceased and "one single fiery cloud" hung above the city, Friedrich Grieger observed. The towers of the cathedral still burned, their cupolas "glowing like a beacon in the night, announcing Breslau's destruction far and wide," according to Erich Schönfelder. "Like drops of blood, burned out, charred pieces of the tower fall down and the ravenous flames are reflected in the waters of the nearby Oder. The old Breslau is no more!" Several sisters from Our Lady of Sorrows stuffed essential items into rucksacks, wrapped themselves in damp clothes as shields from the rain of sparks, and set out to offer aid to the people of Carlowitz. "It was the worst journey of my life," Mother Superior Sigrid Negwer remembered. "The burning city behind us, a tragic, majestic sight. A world going under." Hugo Hartung's company spent the night trying to dowse the flames around Matthiasplatz. There was the distant chime of a church bell, moved by the heat – "Breslau's peal at Easter," Hartung observed. Soviet biplanes flew low over the city, through the clouds of smoke, strafing rooftops and streets, scattering bombs around Matthiasplatz. "The fire rages through our courtyard, burning pieces of wood and tumbling sparks are carried up by the infernal hurricane, deposited on the rooftops, kindling new fires," Hartung noted. His company was exhausted, dirty, the men's eyes smarting from the smoke. The pump no longer drew any water. "Everyone hopes that things will draw to a close quickly." On Dominsel, Walter Lassmann emerged from a cellar opposite the cathedral with numerous Breslauers taking refuge from the firestorm. "We faced an apocalyptic situation," he recalled. The entire street was burning: the cathedral, the archbishop's palace, at least two curiae. "The heat in the narrow Domstrasse was unbelievable. We protected ourselves from the flying sparks using wet cloths held over our faces." They ran to the end of the street and there, with other survivors, they resolved to make a stand. "We faced the supreme test but our courage and our will to live remained unbroken," wrote Lassmann. Thirty people formed a chain down to the Oder, where buckets were filled. "Each one of us used every ounce of our strength and our efforts were rewarded," Walter Lassmann remembered. While everything else around us was in flames, and the sweltering heat became ever more unbearable, while the wild fury of the unchecked fires turned the cathedral, the archbishop's palace, the remaining curiae of the cathedral's leading figures into burned-out ruins, our three curiae were spared."[19]

The Griegers returned to their apartment – "there's only the cellar left" – then wondered where they should spend the night. There was a large rabbit hutch in a corner of the botanic garden. The couple cleared it out, put on thick coats, and sat on two small chairs. It was so cold in the depths of night that the couple had to run around to keep warm. They remained there till dawn on the third, then climbed to the attic of what was left of the botanic institute. "We have a panoramic view of almost all of Breslau," Friedrich Grieger wrote. "It seems as if there's hardly any of the city left: jagged ruins everywhere."[20]

Horst Gleiss and his Hitler Youth unit were roused from their beds around 10pm. The fire they thought they had put out in the ruins of an apartment block in Belltafelstrasse had flared up again. Now it was raging out of control, threatening neighbouring buildings. A bucket chain was hastily formed, while a barricade of horse-drawn carts, tree trunks and sandbags so carefully built to stop the Soviets was quickly dismantled to halt the fire's spread. It took a good three hours to put the fire out. The boys were rewarded for their efforts by a local shopkeeper who brought out his remaining supply of schnapps and called a toast: down the hatch.[21]

Some time after 2am on the third, Walter Lassmann gave up his fire-fighting duties and wandered down to the Oder. There was "a magical unreality" about the sight with which he was presented.

> It was hard for me to believe that this was no dream, that the scenes before my eyes appeared to come from Hell. It is probably rare for the eyes of man to see what I saw here. I was amazed, bewildered, shaken to the depths of my soul. Behind me the huge flames of the cathedral towers, next to that the sea of flames that was the archbishop's palace, to the right the bright flames of the imposing Sandkirche, the entire Dominsel was a raging, roaring firestorm. In front of me, on the opposite bank of the Oder, the city burned. Five-storey houses were on fire, every window was lit up as if it were a festival of light. Every now and then a burned-out house collapsed, sending a magnificent shower of sparks high into the sky rather like wonderful fireworks.[22]

The people of Breslau woke to a light rain falling on their city as dawn broke on 3 April. They found their eyes smarted and stung thanks to the heavy, acrid air and smouldering smoke which hung over the Silesian capital, still ablaze in many places. The smell of burned flesh mixed with the foul stench emanating from the smashed sewer system. There was also an uncanny, discomforting silence this Tuesday morning. "What kind of a ghastly scene awaits us this morning?" wondered Hitler Youth Max Baselt as he woke. His question was soon answered. "Wherever we look, smoking ruins and burned-out houses. Where the firestorm raged there are only mountains of ash, a few stumps." It was enough, the fifteen-year-old remembered, "to leave even the most hardened person among us lost for words." The city, wrote *Stabsgefreiter* Theo Klose, "had turned into a blazing pyre. Corpses lay piled up in the streets." Hermann Nowack watched clearance parties move down Röntgenstrasse and three neighbouring streets. "They load corpses like wood to drive them to the pits." Hugo Hartung passed "large white parcels" – the dead were wrapped in paper – awaiting burial in the gardens of the Holteihöhe, just along the Oder from the university. The Oder embankment was lined with cadavers of horses and pools of blood. Almost every garden, every allotment had been dug up to accommodate the fallen, while the bombardment unearthed the dead as shells and bombs churned up cemeteries old and new. As for the flames, they had turned the yellow forsythia in the gardens of Matthiasplatz black, but the heat had also caused tulips and hyacinths to bloom.[23]

And so ended the blackest days in Breslau's history. The extent of the devastation was almost impossible to comprehend. Sandinsel – in ruins. Dominsel – burned-out; this day, the cupola of the cathedral's north tower finally gave way and crashed into the nave. It was symbolic, believed sixteen-year-old soldier Hans-Joachim Terp, who recalled an ancient Silesian proverb: "When the Oder flows with blood to the north and the destroyed towers reach for the heavens like scrawny fingers, Breslau will go under." The cathedral was not the only Breslau church to die that night. Paul Peikert surveyed the damage to his St Mauritiuskirche. The interior was largely untouched, but not its tower. The new clock was wrecked. A bell dating back to 1618 – spared when the Nazis raided Breslau's churches for metal – had melted. Doors and windows were blown out, the ceiling in the upper vestry had caved in and the tiled roof had been stripped, although the furnishings and decorations inside the church were all intact. The steep roof of the Dorotheenkirche had been stripped of most of its red slates, but the Elisabethkirche continued to tower over the city even if its baroque façade had been wrecked by shells. The list of devastation was almost endless: Neumarkt – burned out, not a single house spared; more than twenty bombs crashed into Hanke's headquarters in the Oberpräsidium; the city's principal shopping street, Schweidnitzer Strasse, was ruined; the central post office and the modern giro bank were ruins, so too the portrait gallery and the museum for antiquities and arts; the great market hall in Ritterplatz – wrecked, a huge hole in its roof; there were gaping holes in the west wing of the university, while the remnants of the legal department's reference library lay scattered along the bank of the Oder, tossed there by soldiers defending the bridge over the river; three Oder crossings now lay partially submerged; the Jahrhunderthalle still stood, but not two of its exhibition halls. And perhaps a few Breslauers raised a wry smile. The fires of Easter 1945 razed the SS headquarters in Sternstrasse.[24]

As for the human cost of Breslau's Easter apocalypse, there are no accurate figures. At least 130 soldiers and civilians were buried on 3 April alone, but days later the victims of the two-day Soviet onslaught were still being recovered. At dawn on the third, Gertrud Hassenbach had returned to Mauritiusplatz in search of her thirteen-year-old son Ebi, serving as a messenger with the local *Ortsgruppe*. The square was on fire. The *Ortsgruppe* building was on fire. Frau Hassenbach buttonholed anyone passing through Mauritiusplatz. No one knew anything about her son. It was the same story when she returned to the square that evening. The next morning, she and daughter were back, this time to begin clearing away the rubble. The bricks and stones were too hot. Thursday came and still no news of Ebi Hassenbach. The heat had subsided sufficiently for his mother to begin clearing the rubble away using hoes and spades. After struggling for several hours, the opening to a window had been created and Gertrud Hassenbach climbed inside with a friend. "We were faced by a wall of heat from the cellar," she remembered, but they pressed on regardless, and found the room where her son usually slept. "It was eerie in there," she said. "Everything was black with smoke. To me it seemed like an oven." Ebi's bed was made, his sheets folded, pillows stacked, just as he had left it. But Ebi himself was not there. His mother left the room and climbed out of the window.

> Suddenly a single thought weighed down on me: *You have not found your child and your angst, tormented by anxiety, will continue. Perhaps Ebi is still alive and urgently needs your help. Take heart and search the entire cellar.* I re-lit the lamp and climbed back into the cellar. When I reached the central passage – which was still glowing – I saw Ebi lying there. I recognised him immediately from his shoes and socks and saw his head. His hair was not burnt, but his head was completely black. I was so depressed yet grateful to God that I had found

him and that evidently he had been killed immediately by a bomb. I held up a sheet and laid it out next to him and tried to put him on it. His head fell to one side and when touching him I noticed that his ribs were broken. Now I called the man who had helped me with the digging to help again and we carried Ebi in the sheet to the window. The rescue was very difficult as the window was very high and there was still rubble in front of it. After many attempts, we succeeded. We borrowed a cart from the monastery and took Ebi home. His father made him a final bed, a small coffin.

Thirteen-year-old Ebi Hassenbach was laid to rest in the front garden of the family home on the evening of Saturday, 7 April under a birch tree which he had climbed just a few years before. Four soldiers carried the small coffin, while Walter Lassmann presided over the last act of the boy's short life. A volley resounded over the fresh grave as the sun dipped beneath the horizon with a blood-red hue. Gertrud Hassenbach remembered the last time she had seen her son alive, six days earlier. "In front of my eyes his face came alive once again as he said his goodbye and turned to us once more with a face which helplessly and sorrowfully seemed to formally plead for tenderness," she wrote. "Everything within me has been shaken up and turned upside down. Will a comforting light come to me in this dark time? I try to pray and to bow to divine will. But it is so unendingly difficult."[25]

Breslauers speak only of Easter 1945 in terms of horror and refer to the bombing almost exclusively as a 'Terrorangriff' – terror raid. But the attacks – at least those of Easter Sunday at any rate – were not intended merely to strike fear into the heart of every inhabitant of the city. They were intended to smash the fortress's western front. Hand-in-hand with the bombardment came a massed assault on German lines by three divisions, supported by motorized infantry and at least one regiment of tanks. The lunge into Breslau's western suburbs would seize the airfield at Gandau, the FAMO and Linke-Hofmann works, then smash through the inner defensive ring and reach the edge of the old town near the Freiburger Bahnhof.

And on Easter Sunday, Sixth Army advanced exactly as planned. The German front in the west of the city caved in. The main railway line, running north to south on an earthen embankment, was the last major obstacle barring the Red Army's progress into the heart of the city. Soviet troops established a toehold on the right side of the line in Mochbern, where there was particularly bitter fighting in the village cemetery, while a little over a mile away in Popelwitz, the Russians were swarming across the allotments and fields of the Viehweide. In the nearby Westend barracks, Hermann Niehoff conferred with the ashen-faced regimental commander, Walter-Peter Mohr, recently decorated with the Ritterkreuz for his leadership in Breslau. "Is this the end?" Niehoff asked. "There are no more reserves, just two Volkssturm battalions which consist of very young men," Mohr told him. Niehoff threw them into the battle. It was enough – for now – to tip the balance in the defenders' favour. By nightfall, German soldiers stood once more on the railway line in Popelwitz.[26]

There was no longer any distinction between boys as messengers and boys as soldiers. Hermann Niehoff may have ordered his commanders to treat the youths of Breslau "as if they were their own children"[27] and later claimed that he wrestled with his conscience daily about the struggle for the city, but by April 1945, boys of thirteen, fourteen, fifteen were simply *Menschenmaterial* – manpower – sorely needed to bolster the ever-thinning ranks of Breslau's defenders. And so it was that on the night of Easter Day, Peter Bannert and his comrades were ordered west to help defend Gandau. They spent the night digging foxholes in gardens and allotments near a guesthouse. By first light, they were convinced that, despite their makeshift positions, they were safe. The Soviet lines were just yards away. Enemy aircraft would surely not drop their bombs – except that the Russians had evacuated their trenches during the night. Only Germans remained dug in amid the allotments and gardens. For several hours, a hail of bombs shook the ground. When the barrage finally ended, messengers were sent out across what was now a field of ruins. The boys tried to haul a platoon leader out of his foxhole. They pulled only his upper body free; the rest remained in the hole.

The Hitler Youths fell back from the allotments and took up positions around the guesthouse. From its cellar, fifteen-year-old Bannert heard – and felt – a rattle which shook the earth. "We stared out of the cellar windows, *Panzerfaust* at the ready," Peter Bannert recalled. "But in the scrub, the iron monsters were hard to make out. They stopped at some range, fired at our position and turned around."

Brown figures dashed through the guesthouse's gardens. Bannert's comrades fired carbines and machine-pistols, while he fired his *Panzerfaust* – but not directly at the advancing Soviet troops. The head of the weapon had to strike something solid to explode. The schoolboy aimed the *Panzerfaust* at a corner wall so splinters would rip into the enemy soldiers. Next to the guesthouse, a flak gun directed its barrel groundwards and fired repeatedly. "With every shot my eardrum vibrated, the sweet smell of gunpowder smoke drifted up my nose," Bannert wrote. When the gun had expended its ammunition, the guesthouse was evacuated.[28]

The spirit of these boys impressed hardened campaigners like paratrooper Rudi Christoph, fighting alongside Hitler Youths for the first time. For three days Christoph's *Fallschirmjäger* had clung on to Gandau airfield. A nine-hour barrage on 4 April finally unseated them. Soon there were fifteen enemy tanks in the paratroopers' rear, opening fire on the German troops from a range of barely 200 yards. The *Fallschirmjäger* did the unexpected. They charged at the Soviet lines. "With machine-pistols under our arms, we fired at the Russians who were paralysed with fear," Christoph recalled. "Before they knew it, we were through them and away."

Their numbers depleted – several dead, some wounded and many missing – the companies of paratroopers regrouped. They occupied a new position which would be the focal point of the battle for the next three days and nights, the home for the blind.[29]

With the outward appearance of a school or college, Breslau's institute for the blind was a commanding four-storey structure which dominated the southern edge of the city's Westpark. From its fourth floor German artillery observers could – and did – watch the movement of Soviet troops now swarming over Gandau airfield. Max Baselt's Hitler Youth mortar unit was told wave after wave of enemy soldiers were moving across the airfield. It fired every round it had in response. The Soviets responded with overwhelming force, plastering the park, the institute, the public cemeteries opposite, forcing Baselt, like Christoph before him, to fall back towards the blind home. He spent the night listening to the sound of engines and rattling tank tracks.[30]

A few hundred yards away on the other side of the park, Leo Hartmann was enjoying the silence of the battlefield. That afternoon he'd been ordered to halt the Soviet armour bearing down on Westpark. But with what? Only his *Sturmgeschütz* was available. He set off anyway, heading down a dyke which ran along the Oder, past the open-air swimming baths, until he reached the edge of woods and could see the pioneer barracks beyond them. There he noticed the outline of a tank. "Given the situation, it can only be a Soviet one," he determined and fired several shells at it. The vehicle did not burn, but nor did it move again. Hartmann continued towards the village of Cosel, from where there was the unmistakable sound of engines and considerable movement. "Several high-explosive shells were sent in the direction of the noise," he wrote. "There was silence once more."

The wet dawn of 5 April found Max Baselt furiously digging a foxhole in the grounds of Westpark with his small infantryman's spade. His work was unfinished when Soviet artillery concentrated their effort on the park. It was a familiar story. When the barrage lifted, on came the Red infantry again. The German machine-guns had either been knocked out or run out of ammunition. Baselt's carbine jammed, so too did many of his comrades'. Hauling their wounded, the company of Hitler Youths withdrew towards the blind institute.

Leo Hartmann was summoned to the cellar of the institute to receive fresh orders. During the night, his *Sturmgeschütz* had been joined by a second. A junior officer told the bespectacled gun commander that Soviet armour was bearing down on the blind home through the park and had to be stopped. Hartmann agreed, although his reasons for offering a spirited defence of the Gandau district were not entirely altruistic. All *Sturmgeschütze* ammunition had to be flown into Breslau. It could be dropped by parachute, of course, but three out of four canisters invariably ended up in Soviet hands. The longer the airfield could be used, the longer the guns could fight.

Max Baselt's Hitler Youths joined a platoon of paratroopers in a water-filled ditch 250 yards from the blind home. There was a brief respite, but then Soviet infantry attacked head-on. Soviet bombers and ground-attack aircraft circled overhead before aiming for the German lines. Baselt watched "a carpet of bombs" dropped above the heads of his comrades: the enemy aircraft released their payloads too late. The bombs landed among the attacking troops.

After Soviet infantry came Soviet armour. Two tanks nosed into a copse in Westpark, one a self-propelled howitzer with a long barrel. The paratroopers at Baselt's side readied their *Panzerfaust*. "Suddenly a double bang, the assault howitzer is hit and burns," the surprised teenager wrote in his diary. "Now it's the second tank's turn." Max Baselt turned around to see two *Sturmgeschütze*.

Leo Hartmann had left his assault gun behind and crawled up to an uprooted tree from where he could see an enemy self-propelled gun moving through a cutting. Hartmann returned to his gun and made immediately for the hollow. "The Russian had already spotted us and began to lower his barrel, which had been aimed at the trees," Hartmann later wrote. "He was too late. With the crash of our gun – almost painful to the ears yet always somehow reassuring – I saw a fiery red flash just to the left of the barrel. The first shot had hit home." Some Hitler Youths guided him to the second enemy tank. Hartmann directed several shells at it.

Despite the loss of their armoured support, the Russian infantry resumed their assault. "Anyone who still has a working gun fires for all it's worth," Max Baselt wrote. His squad leader jumped on to the edge of the ditch with his assault rifle, firing short bursts in rapid succession, while a comrade took carefully aimed shots, loudly reporting each successful kill: six, seven, eight. It was enough to halt the Soviet advance.

Two desperately-needed *Sturmgeschütze* and a ragtag bunch of paratroopers and Hitler Youths could not hold the blind institute indefinitely. Thanks to flanking fire from heavy machine-guns, Soviet infantry finally penetrated the ground floor. Their foe continued to occupy the other storeys. "We fought bitterly for each stairway, each room," Major M M Gordiyenko remembered. More than thirty years later he could still picture the institute – "a large building with spacious cellars" – when he closed his eyes. In one room he found fifteen German troops. He called on them to surrender. They responded with machine-pistol fire. A *frontovik* squeezed into a pantry, found a hole in the wall and tossed in several grenades. When the smoke settled, just one German staggered out, dazed but somehow unscathed. All his comrades were dead or gravely wounded. The institute fell. And with it Gandau was finally lost.[31]

As Breslau's western front collapsed, so too its northern front began to crumble. But there was one final substantial obstacle to sweeping Soviet gains: *Infanterie Werk* 41. For six weeks, the fort had served as a cornerstone of the northern front and command post of the local Party leader. He had fled, but not the garrison, whose domain grew ever smaller. Built as part of a chain of defences to protect Breslau a generation earlier, *I-Werk* 41, as the men knew it, was a partially buried concrete fort in the middle of a copse four miles from the city centre. Five smaller strongpoints were spread around it in a semi-circle. But by April 1945 they had fallen to the Russians. Only the main fort was still held by the Germans, led by a hoarse fifty-nine-year-old *Hauptmann*. The aged officer was idolized by his men – probably because he did not mince his words. "As men in danger we are now dependent on one another," he declared. "Death wandering around like a ghost on the battlefield doesn't ask about either your background or your rank."

It was to *I-Werk* 41 that forward artillery observer Klaus Franke was sent after escaping the maelstrom enveloping the clock tower at the Linke-Hofmann factory on Easter Day. His initial impressions were unfavourable. "The terrain looks desolate," he wrote. "Trees now tower above the ground only as stumps. Destroyed weapons lie around everywhere, between them the dead of friend and foe who cannot be buried."

Two Soviet *shtraf* battalions were sent to storm *I-Werk* 41. Three attacks were cut down by the defenders, leaving the approaches to the fortification littered with Soviet corpses. "The dead are tightly packed in front of the entrance – even one on top of the other," Klaus Franke recalled. Inside the bunker he could hear the groans and the death rattles of Soviet troops outside. The defenders had been reduced to two officers and forty men, armed with a handful of *Panzerfaust* and a couple of magazines each. "The passages are full of men sleeping," wrote Franke. "They lean against the walls, their machine-pistols between their knees, steel helmets hanging around their necks, sitting, dozing." There was no food. The men shared a can of water, which tasted of petrol, and divided their last emergency rations. There was no hope of relief. The fort had no communications beyond its walls. Its sole medic could not cope with more than fifty wounded men. "There is only the slightest hope for most of them," Klaus Franke continued. "There's no medicine or expert treatment by a doctor to keep them alive. The mood is desolate as the men suspect that they will never see their homes again. Blood, blood everywhere, and by day no one dares set one foot outside."

Eventually they did dare set foot outside. After nearly a week of fighting, the defenders of *I-Werk* 41 decided it was time to break out. Just eight men – among them Klaus Franke – were fit enough to slip away from the fortification. When they did, they moved across a battlefield where the Soviet penal units had been cut down in swathes. "The effects of our artillery are terrible," the artilleryman observed. He continued:

> The men sink to their ankles in the soft ground. One foot steps in the stinking entrails of a man. Among the dead in the earth bunker you can already see some bleached bones. Limbs, separated from the torso, lie all around among pieces of equipment and smashed weapons.
>
> Often they are kicked up to the surface by soldiers' boots or else trampled further down into the dirt. You can't go more than three metres without your feet striking one of these ghastly finds which weren't visible at all initially. Even the puddles have been turned red a little by blood. The stench of pus and decomposition hangs over everything.

Nevertheless, this was the first 'fresh' air the men had smelled in a week. Anything, Klaus Franke believed, was better than the "pestilent stench, the eternal darkness of the bunker".[32]

Hans Gottwald had already pulled out of Breslau's northern front. His company had orders to regroup in the city for a fresh assignment. It was now ten days since Breslau's black Easter and still the fires raged. Surely, thought the *Unteroffizier*, this was not the city he marched out of just a few weeks before.

> I do not know Breslau any more. The bombardment at Easter was a terrible rampage. Entire streets have been swept away. Fires rage in the streets, charred window frames look at us dishearteningly. Civilians with clothes and faces blackened by soot stand amid the ruins and give us blank looks as we head for the front. Two dead *Landsers* lie at the entrance to a burning cellar. The wind which blows the smoke through the streets plays with their camouflage jackets which have been torn to shreds. No one worries about them, no one can worry about them. Each man has his own burden to bear.

Gottwald's company was billeted in a former police barracks, home to "all kinds of scattered remnants from every possible unit", comprising "bearded, ragged figures" who stood silently next to the walls and barely responded when anyone asked them a question. But then Hans Gottwald realized he too had become one of those bearded, ragged figures.

> My tunic, my boots, my trousers are encrusted with dirt. Somewhere I find a brush, a knife and a flat piece of wood. Then some 'cleaning'. After an hour I at least look like a soldier again. There's something else I must put right. On my face there's a bristly stubble. I barely recognize myself when I look in a fragment of a mirror. 'I look like a tramp,' goes through my head. Am I actually any different? I manage to do something akin to shaving on the bottommost cellar step. In the distance, artillery, bombers and ground-attack aircraft rumble in the clear sky. There's no sight of German aircraft far and wide. The Soviets can drop their bombs without any problems. In between you can hear the rat-a-tat-tat of the guns of Russian ground-attack aircraft. Our flak does not shoot any more. A fortnight ago you could still see little clouds of exploding flak shells in the sky occasionally. But the gunners have long since used up all their ammunition. Not too far from here house-to-house fighting rages. You can clearly hear the rattle of small arms fire.

There had been talk amongst the men of a breakout attempt to reach German lines south of Breslau on the slopes of the Zobten. No such luck. The company was being committed to the workers' district of Pöpelwitz. They had left the northern front imbued with "a tiny glimmer of hope". Some men had even begun to sing. Now, they were demoralized. House fighting. "If I had known all that was still waiting for me, I don't know if I'd have had the strength to take one more step forwards," Gottwald wrote later. "You get the feeling that everything is slowly, but surely, coming apart. We are moving towards a certain end. No *Landser* doubts that any more."[33]

Gottwald's feelings were shared by many of Breslau's defenders in the aftermath of the Easter onslaught. They fought on, but they realized no one would come to rescue them, despite the promises and assertions of their leaders. Easter 1945 did not merely change the face of Breslau, it extinguished the faint hopes, however improbable, to which men clung. The diaries and letters of the city's defenders in April 1945 are filled with nothing but despair. "My love, I will never forget these Easter days," one *Gefreiter* wrote to his wife. "I hardly believe any longer that we'll see each other again; we must leave that to the kind fate of heaven. The Russians are already in my beloved home. I only hope that you, my dear, are not in danger. I can tell you, my dear wife, that I am utterly desperate. It really would be for the best if all of us heard and saw nothing more of this world." *Volkssturm* man Willy Merkert was similarly pessimistic. "We no longer believe in relief any more," he told his family. "We can still hold out for a few more weeks, but sooner or later the decision will occur in the Reich before we surrender. At worst, we'll scrape through, if all else fails. Half of us will go under. We expect only death or captivity."[34]

When he wrote home, Merkert and the rest of his company were contesting the huge grounds of the abattoir on the eastern edge of Pöpelwitz. The fighting was as dogged as any house-to-house encounter, as one veteran Waffen SS officer tried to explain in a letter to his son, serving with the *Volkssturm*:

> We manoeuvred the *Sturmgeschütz* into position behind a wall thirty metres from the Russians. Pioneers blew a hole in the wall and nine shots smashed into the Ivans' position on the first floor of three houses. We couldn't go into the cellars to root them out as the buildings were still on fire. As the storm troops advanced I had to go with them. Ivan had been driven from two houses by shelling, but he continued to shoot from one. We threw our hand-grenades through the windows, but the Russians threw them out again. We suffered one casualty (wounded) as a result. I suffered a small wound on my right hand (only a flesh wound) and a large splinter bounced off a hand-grenade in my right trouser pocket, thank God. Something like that only makes you more angry. As we were unable to get those swine out of the rear rooms even with our *Panzerfaust*, the *Sturmgeschütz* fired six more rounds and I stormed the ground-floor rooms with my men wielding hand-grenades and revolvers. The Ivans not dealt with – there were still seven of them – skedaddled down the street. Two were knocked out by a flanking machine-gun.[35]

Despite the ferocity of the struggle for the abattoir, the men could still find something to raise a smile. "Willy, here in the slaughterhouse is the right place for us," a comrade told Merkert. "All that's left to do is turn us into mince and send it to our women in cans – the herd of sheep is right here." The 'herd' had begun the battle for the abattoir 120 men strong. Now Willy Merkert's company numbered just forty-five men. The remnants were exhausted, so tired that they could sleep in their foxholes despite Russian shells impacting a few yards away. It drove some of them mad, but not Merkert. "I merely thank God that I have a certain couldn't-care-less attitude and am unflappable," he assured his wife. He was killed by a shot to the head a few days later.[36]

Hans Gottwald was holed up in a cellar a couple of blocks away in Pöpelwitz, dragged into the house fighting he had so feared. It was every bit as horrific as he had imagined it to be:

> I'm woken around 8am. Every bone in my body hurts and shivers go right through me. I quickly come to my senses, however. My first glance is at the cellar window. We worked well last night. We neatly cleared away all the bricks. I am nervously waiting for 10am. Will it be like yesterday and the day before? I can hardly wait until 10am. My nerves are extremely taut. I pull my last packet of cigarettes from my jacket pocket and smoke nervously. Dirty and unshaved, we look like pigs. Our faces, out of which peer bleary, reddened eyes, are almost black. 10am at last. Nervously I scan the ground in front of us. There! Like yesterday. A mass of men again storm across the gardens towards us, accompanied by a hail of machine-gun fire. They evidently believe we have cracked under the strain of the hand-grenade barrage, because today they're attacking rather boldly and swiftly, without lying down. From a range of 100 metres, our machine-gun rattles away. In an instant, 200 rounds are fired. Devastating effect! Many fall down, others run away. Murder, plain murder, flashes through my mind. And for what? Deep down I feel sorry for those chaps there who are rolling around in their own blood. I cannot stand this any more. Every day murder! Dreadful. But where's the end to it?

The men enjoyed an eight-hour reprieve until late in the afternoon there was a distant rumble. Gottwald stared out of the cellar window and saw a Soviet tank no more than 150 yards away. It ploughed through the wall of a house, then turned its barrel towards the German troops' hideout. Gottwald yelled: "Take cover!" and the men threw themselves on to the cellar floor. "There's the devastating crash of a tank shell – the awful bang almost leaves us deaf." When the initial shock of the impact passed, the men realized they were unharmed. Thanks to an incline in the street, the tank's shells either struck the ground fifty yards from the cellar, or the façade of the house above. "We've been spared," thought Gottwald as a thick cloud of dust filled the cellar. For half an hour the Soviet tank sent shells into the earth or into the house wall. The men in the cellar held cloths and rags to their mouths as they struggled to breath. Then the tank gave up, turned on its heels and drove away. "Once again, we can breathe a sigh of relief."[37]

One mile away, Leo Hartmann manoeuvred his ugly *Sturmpanzer* IV, armed with a high-velocity 75mm cannon from a Panther tank, towards the allotments of north-west Breslau. Soviet armour had smashed its way across the railway embankment under a heavy artillery barrage. Through his binoculars the young *Leutnant* could see several green-brown self-propelled guns armed with powerful 152mm cannons. Outgunned, Hartmann used the element of surprise. A flash, a bang, a thunderous crash and the first Soviet gun exploded. "Right next to the tank was another one, and one more a little further on," he recalled. "Ever more steel monsters came into view. I couldn't collect my thoughts at all. When I'd fired all my ammunition, several Russian tanks burned like torches – five of them at the hands of my gun." A second *Sturmgeschütz* joined battle, knocking out a Soviet tank on the railway embankment, thirty feet above the battlefield. After restocking his ammunition, Hartmann returned to find yet more enemy tanks had appeared. He saw off two of them, his comrade destroyed five pieces of armour. "In the heat of battle, I hadn't realized that the Russians were also shooting," Hartmann wrote later. "It was a really mad day." Their aim was poor, for they destroyed no German tanks. They did, however, wreck the *Sturmpanzer*'s radio antenna.

The mad day was far from over. In mid-afternoon the German armour was ordered to support a counter-attack by Hitler Youths to drive the Russians back to the railway embankment. They did. By nightfall, the allotments and marshes in north-west Breslau were in German hands. But that did not mean that the battlefield was silent. Towards dusk, the troops found a Soviet tank which had fallen into a bomb crater "as deep as a house". It could not climb out again. Hartmann decided to salvage it with the aid of thirty *Volkssturm* men, leaving his deputy in charge. A few minutes later, his deputy staggered into his command post "black with smoke". The tank's crew were still inside – they had even fired the gun; the muzzle flash burned Hartmann's deputy. The commander immediately returned to the scene. The tank crew refused to surrender. Grenades were tossed inside and finally a *Panzerfaust* was used. It was the thirteenth and final victory of the day for Hartmann's men. They called it the day of the *Panzersterben* – tank slaughter. Leo Hartmann was mentioned in the daily communiqué and received the *Ritterkreuz* for his actions. Yet he was troubled by his thirteenth kill of the day.

> Later I often wondered why the tank's crew had not climbed out but had defended themselves so stubbornly to the end. I assume that the unit commander was in the tank. He had blundered into the crater early in the morning as this armoured formation had crossed the railway embankment in preparation for the true assault. At that moment – when the unit was leaderless – I arrived with my guns and began to clear things up. The Russian commander probably realized the scale of the catastrophe, no longer dared to go back and preferred to let himself be blown into the air.[38]

Leo Hartmann was not the only officer to question the Soviet troops' lacklustre performance. Fortress commander Hermann Niehoff was equally puzzled. The general had transferred his headquarters from the Liebichshöhe – deserters had revealed its location to the Russians, who promptly turned it into a "smoking volcano" – to the cellars of the Staatsbibliothek on the Sandinsel. With sufficient will, the Red Army could have carried the day, it could have presented Breslau as an Easter gift for Stalin. It had not. Weeks later, in captivity, Niehoff asked his captors why they had not crushed the defenders at Easter. "We had a different plan," a Soviet staff officer told him.[39]

The 'different plan' was the seizure of Berlin. On the day Vladimir Gluzdovski's army smashed through Niehoff's western front, Ivan Konev had been summoned to Moscow to draw up plans for the fall of Berlin. Thereafter, Breslau was merely a sideshow. The bulk of 1st Ukrainian Front regrouped for an assault on the capital of the Reich.

It was a decision which did not please everyone, not least Gluzdovski. Breslau could wait until after Berlin had fallen, Konev told him. The Sixth Army commander protested, convinced his forces were weaker than those inside the encircled fortress and convinced that the Germans would attempt a breakout. At all hours of the day he called his marshal, pleading for permission to take the Silesian capital. "We're almost at the war's end," Konev told him. "There's no need to storm the fortress." All Gluzdovski needed to do was to keep the defenders of the fortress in check and remind them from time to time that their position was hopeless.[40]

Gluzdovski's frustration was shared by the 90,000 men of Polish Second Army, fighting alongside Soviet troops. After combat in Pomerania, the Poles regrouped in mid-March 1945 and were sent south to take part in the final battle for Breslau. "In our imagination," wrote Lieutenant Waldemar Kotowicz, Breslau "was a panorama of church steeples, a strip of white buildings, with a network of streets, hundreds of squares and the broad waters of the Oder passing through it." And the reality? "We saw a huge cloud of dust and smoke hanging over the entire city, a swirl of raging chaos, then a mushroom shooting up into the sky, spreading out sideways and obscuring the afternoon sun," he recalled. "We saw a gigantic sea of flames, fires side by side, the brief glow of fire from explosions which turned what had once been a house, school or church into dust." Kotowicz scanned the horizon with his binoculars. "Nowhere was there a lofty Gothic tower, nowhere were there white buildings, no greens, no free streets, or the outline of the Oder." It was a scene, the Polish officer remembered, "whose scale and impression bordered on madness". Lieutenant Ryszard Skala found a street map of the city in an abandoned apartment. He spread it out on a large oak table and studied it with his comrades: "I memorised the names of the streets and districts, the location of crossroads and bridges," he recalled. "We all tested our knowledge of the city: Matthiasstrasse, Gartenstrasse, Palmstrasse, Strasse der SA. We knew this city would be ours."[41]

It would. But in April 1945, Polish Second Army got no closer than the outskirts of the city. It was ordered west to take Dresden instead.

There was only one man in Breslau who was happy in April 1945 and that man was Karl Hanke. The *Gauleiter* was basking in fulsome adoration from other senior Nazis for his leadership. There was praise from another besieged city in the East, Königsberg. "Just as in 1813, when the torch of freedom was lit in East Prussia and Silesia, so it will be lit in this decisive struggle," *Kreisleiter* Ernst Wagner radioed.

Germany, Europe, the world are looking at us. Raise Hitler's flags on barricades!
Heroic and loyal, proud and defiant, we will turn our fortresses into mass graves for the Soviet hordes. These dogs will come a cropper.

Like you, we know that the hour before sunrise is always the darkest. Remember that when the blood runs into your eyes during battle and there is darkness all around you. Whatever happens, victory will be ours.

Death to the Bolsheviks! Long live the Führer![42]

There was praise from Hanke's long-standing friend, Albert Speer. "You have already given Germany a great deal through your achievement as the defender of Breslau," Hitler's armament minister gushed. "Your example – whose greatness has not yet been appreciated – will have inestimable importance for the *Volk*, like many heroes in German history." Speer's fawning continued:

At a time when the nation's entire leadership strata is collapsing and giving up, you set an example – a witness against many!

Germany will not go under! It has been badly hurt by Fate. It will live on and one day regain its old respectability. We must not give up hope in these bitter hours.

The *Volk* have been heroic, loyal, unique. The *Volk* have not failed.

Anyone who attacks this *Volk* and its destiny will be severely punished by Fate.

God protect Germany.

I, dear Hanke, thank you once more with all my heart for everything which you have done for me. You brought me my first decisive successes and later, as a friend, you have stood loyally by my side.

You have nothing to feel sorry about. You are approaching a beautiful and worthy end to your life.[43]

And there was praise from Adolf Hitler for the city in one of his final public pronouncements – "an example to the entire German people"– and for its *Gauleiter*, the highest honour the Party could bestow, the Golden Cross of the German Order, "in grateful recognition of your great achievement in the struggle for the future of our people".[44]

In turn, the fortress would honour its leader on his fifty-sixth birthday. In years gone by, 20 April had been a public holiday, Breslau's streets adorned with flags, garlands, banners. But not in 1945. In 1945, front-line commanders were urged to gather their men, their workers, their staff around them and explain that the best way to honour Adolf Hitler would be to continue the struggle "with an iron will and unbroken strength" and "do more than one's duty until a German victory". Breslau's leaders obliged. "On the Führer's birthday, we remember with gratitude and respect the man who held high the banners of the Reich and its honour against a world of enemies amid the storms and tempests of this mighty, fateful struggle," declared the fortress's artillery commander Hermann Hartl. "We pledge to him that we will fight to the last man. He can rely on us." As for fortress commander Hermann Niehoff, he praised the Führer's "unique greatness" in an order of the day which plumbed new depths of obsequiousness.

His life is Germany's life, his struggle is the struggle of the German soldier, his goal is the freedom of the German worker and the German citizen. Because he is one of us, he has the love and the complete faith of the entire nation.

Today, in this fateful hour, the German people look to the Führer and withstand the hardest days in this war. We in Fortress Breslau also look to the Führer. Our confidence is based upon him and becomes all the stronger the longer we defend ourselves. For Adolf Hitler is with the brave, his strength will be our strength![45]

Such words were meant to steel the defenders of Breslau. They did not. Hugo Hartung listened to his commander proclaim his faith in ultimate victory. "Most of his officers look extremely sceptical," he observed. A National Socialist Leadership Officer addressed Emil Heinze and his *Volkssturm* comrades. "I have spoken with an expert," the officer declared. "A destroyed street like Albrechtsstrasse can be rebuilt in four weeks." The company fell about laughing. For most Breslauers, 20 April was remarkable only because it was an excuse to celebrate and forget about the horrors of life in the fortress. Girls from the *Bund Deutscher Mädel* serenaded convalescing soldiers in the bunker hospitals. Hugo Hartung enjoyed a fine lunch washed down with a bottle of wine. Hermann Niehoff handed out chocolate and champagne to his staff. After spending the day piling up 3,000 empty shell cases, Horst Gleiss returned to his cellar to find a party in full swing. There was gingerbread, raspberry juice, schnapps, red wine and cigarettes. A gramophone, radio and accordion provided the music, young girls provided the distraction. They sang the wistful *Es geht alles vorüber* – it's all over – and danced long into the night. Only when the wine ran out did the party end.[46]

With or without Polish Second Army, with or without Ivan Konev's approval, Vladimir Gluzdovski continued to gnaw at Breslau. Never was there a day without bombing, without an artillery barrage, without some house, some bunker, some building being contested. Soviet historians reckoned sixty-four *Landsers* and forty-nine *frontoviki* died every day in Breslau in April 1945; both figures are conservative. The focal point was the city's western suburbs and one obstinate nest of German resistance in particular, the *Hochbunker* in Striegauer Platz. The wounded had already been evacuated, distributed among the city's remaining bunker and basement hospitals. Eighty soldiers and pioneers took their place. The latter hid explosive charges in the centre of the bunker as a booby trap in case it fell to the Soviets. By the third week of April Russian troops had reached the outside of the bunker. They set charges on the ventilation ducts. One set fire to the bunker's fuel reserves, igniting more than 400 gallons of oil which raced down the concrete ducts inside, setting fire to everything it touched. The defenders retreated to the only safe room: the airlock. Some eighty men squeezed into a room of barely 100 square feet. The final hours there, recalled master plumber Gustav Paneck, were hellish.

Concrete dust and clouds of smoke filled the lobby. On top of that, the charges placed by the pioneers exploded in the burning bunker. The steel door between the interior and the air lock opened around ten centimetres because of the enormous heat in the shelter. I dared to look inside and saw nothing but fire. Enemy shells now hit the wall of the air lock constantly. Concrete dust, powdery smoke and the flames carried by the blast of air billowed over our heads through the bunker. The young soldiers bravely defended our air lock with machine-guns. But some were hurt by enemy shells. Some suffered serious arm and leg injuries. The medic was also wounded while administering first aid. Remaining in the air lock became ever more dangerous.

The men pleaded with the pioneer commander to give up the struggle. He refused, convinced his family would be executed if he surrendered the bunker. One of his soldiers was prepared to take such a risk, fixing a white handkerchief to his rifle and pushing it through a metal grate. The handkerchief was shot off. "So we had to wait as our plight grew more and more threatening," Paneck remembered.

There was another enormous explosion. Another of the charges placed by our pioneers had exploded. We felt as if our clothes, our faces, our hair were covered with oil. A small chink of light appeared at the airlock entrance and grew larger and larger. Overcome by panic, everyone tried to reach the exit, stretching their hands towards this gleam of light. Those escaping stepped on the injured lying on the ground, who cried for help. At that moment, everyone was trying to save their own skin. Those who escaped through the main exit fell into Russian hands. I was able to escape through the metal lattice which had now been ripped out and was slightly bent.

Behind Paneck, someone inside the airlock cried: "Open the door. Leave the bunker!" A non-commissioned officer struggled through the flames of burning oil to prise the door open. He was struck by a bullet and fell back into the flames. A comrade followed him, leapt through the flames and scurried across the square. It was only later that he realized his clothes and hair were on fire. No more men escaped the bunker. As they forced their way out of the exit, they fell almost immediately into Soviet hands – as did the bunker.[47]

The *Hochbunker* in Elbingstrasse was still in German hands, and still treating casualties, as Hans Gottwald learned. Conditions had deteriorated immeasurably since he visited comrades a month earlier. Except that now he was a patient, not a visitor, shot in the left arm. "A wall of heat and stench hits me," he wrote. "I can hardly breathe. There's groaning and crying everywhere." He was shown to a small concrete room lit by candles where he found "bloody canvas sheets lying around. There are wounded everywhere as well, waiting for things to happen. No one speaks. Every now and then two medics come and haul a wounded man out, depending on the seriousness of his wounds. Apparently, I'm 'lightly wounded', so I have to wait a long time." Gottwald waited several hours until he was operated on, then he was taken to the top floor of the bunker to convalesce.

"The heat and stench become more and more unbearable," he recalled.

> There's very little oxygen in the air. There's the most terrible misery everywhere.
> The gravely injured groan and hallucinate thanks to the fever. There's still a
> place on top of a bunk bed. Here and there one space is created as dead bodies
> are carried out repeatedly.
>   I'm lifted up into the upper bed. Right next to me is the concrete roof of the
> shelter. 'No one can recover here' I think to myself. 'Just be grateful that you're
> still alive and that you're cared for to some degree.' I'm given another painkiller
> and then I'm left to my fate. Drinking water has to be brought all the time – the
> thirst of the wounded men is tremendous. I fall into a state of semi-
> consciousness. The syringe and the pill have had an effect.[48]

For Gottwald and fellow sufferers in the Elbingstrasse bunker, or in any of Breslau's
cellar hospitals and first-aid posts, there was no longer any hope of evacuation. Despite
all the exertions, despite the 3,000 killed in its construction, no aircraft were landing on
the runway Karl Hanke had needlessly driven through Scheitnig. The last wounded had
been flown out of Breslau on 7 April, the final flight into the fortress by an 'Aunt Ju'
occurred the following night. Only Heinkel 111s, Me109 fighters and gliders still carried
supplies to the beleaguered city. On a good night, they might deliver sixty tons of
ammunition. But good nights were the exception. Some nights barely one ton of supplies
was landed or dropped. And after the night of 29/30 April, nothing. The last glider to
touch down in Breslau did so shortly after 3am on the thirtieth. Struck by flak, it crashed
in a cemetery, its cargo wrecked, but its pilot, one Erwin Thies, safe.[49]

By now, Breslau was in the full grip of a Silesian spring. By day, temperatures topped 25°C.
The cherry trees were in bloom, so too the small almond trees; young birches were a vibrant
green, lilacs were starting to bloom. The first blossom had already fallen, blanketing parts
of the city, adding colour to an otherwise desolate scene. In the suburbs, the trees buzzed
with life. Every branch was filled with singing or whistling birds, while in the city centre
some Breslauers picked posies to adorn their cellars. Others gathered spring flowers and
laid them on the mounds marked with small wooden crosses which littered the city's
promenades, lawns, parks, church grounds, roadsides – they could even be found amid the
ruins of houses. Mail was delivered sporadically – at least until the final week of April –
although it took upwards of forty days to reach the fortress. The cinema truck still showed
films and newsreels to troops enjoying a few hours out of the line. Some women hung
eiderdowns out of windows in the morning to air them, others clambered over the rubble
with shopping bags in search of food. Sometimes they found it. A store in Posener Strasse,
a short distance from the fortress's western front, opened at the end of the week, although
it could offer patrons nothing but *Ersatz* food on ration coupons. Soviet artillery fired into
the city sporadically. It was rarely aimed but rarely did it not demand sacrifices. "The sun
draws people out of the damp cellars into the open," Waffen SS clerk Georg Haas observed.
"Children play by the roadside or search out plants coming into bloom. A smouldering shell

crater often shows where just a few moments earlier the cheerful laughter of children rang out." The wildest rumours were seized upon. Haas's comrades were sent to find a spy, a Russian artillery observer believed to be directing Soviet guns on to targets in the heart of the Breslau. The Waffen SS troops found no spy, despite wasting an afternoon searching lofts and abandoned apartments. They did find a deserter, a half-starved *Volkssturm* man who asked hesitantly whether Stalin had entered the city. "Only one rumour can make us hold firm," wrote Haas, "the rumour of imminent liberation." From some of the city's spires, soldiers could make out the distant peak of the Zobten on clear days. "Over there, do you see, there on the Zobten, is Schörner's army," a comrade assured Haas. "Soon, perhaps as early as tomorrow, it will advance to liberate us. Until then, we have to hold out . . ."[50]

The same rumour swept through the cellar hospital in Reusche Strasse in the old town where Hans Gottwald was now convalescing. Some men even claimed they could already hear the distant thunder of cannon. Others rejoiced at the news of the death of President Roosevelt, convinced that it changed everything. Gottwald preferred to chat with a young nurse, Nora, who used to sit on the end of his bed. Occasionally, he would climb the cellar steps to sample the fresh spring air. A bomb landed in a building several yards away – evidently one of the fortress warehouses, because hundreds of packets of Casino brand cigarettes were strewn around the street. Lightly-wounded men rushed out of the cellar to collect as many packs as they could hold. "Who knows what's going to happen?" thought Gottwald. "We can always use cigarettes."[51]

Seizing those cigarettes was plundering, of course, but Breslauers were beginning to test the limits of Nazi authority. People openly distrusted the daily military communiqué. They listened to German-language broadcasts from the BBC – the cellars of the opera house positively echoed to the sound of news from London. They heard that Berlin was encircled, that American and Soviet troops had shaken hands on the Elbe at Torgau. In Zimpel and Bischofswalde, at the eastern end of the pocket, scores of women openly challenged their masters, demonstrating outside the *Ortsgruppe* headquarters. "*Wir wollen keinen Krieg!*" they chanted – we don't want war – or "*Unsere Männer hier!*" – bring our men here. The deputy Party leader appeared, demanded the women disperse, said they were stabbing the soldiers in the back. The crowd laughed and waved strips of cloth and handkerchiefs at the Soviet bombers circling overhead. The authority of the Party had been challenged – and the Party responded. Troops were ordered into Zimpel to break up the demonstration. Several women were arrested. Some accounts say eight were subsequently shot, others seventeen, others still around one hundred.[52]

Nor was any clemency shown to deserters. One was brought to Hugo Hartung's company command post: a worker, a father who had decided his family needed him more than the fortress did. Hartung's commander asked the man why he fled. The deserter was silent. "The man has a good face and a decent bearing," Hartung noted. "He knows that his fate is sealed." There was only one topic of conversation in the dramatist's cellar: 'afterwards'. After the war was over, after the Nazis were gone. "But what will become of us?" Hugo Hartung wondered.[53] It was a question asked repeatedly in the ruins of Breslau. "We felt the impending end, but deep down we were torn violently between fear and hope," priest Konrad Büchsel recalled.[54] Horst Gleiss saw signs of hope. "Everyone knows it but no one dares say it," he recorded in his diary. "The Second World War can only last a few more days. We have survived so far and the chances of getting through the final days as well aren't bad."[55] Other defenders saw nothing but ruin ahead. "Forgive me, Erich, if as your youngest brother I've done anything shitty in your life and, if you still can, then pray for me, the heroic defender of the infamous fortress Breslau," one soldier, Heinz Liedtke, pleaded in a last letter to his sibling.

> We sit in Breslau like rats in a trap and wait for the end. I've already lost hope that I'll get out of this shit sometime. We fight, drink out of despair (if we manage to organize something to drink) and lead a debauched life with whores of various nationalities – there's no shortage of them here. Yesterday I received a pass for a couple of hours and went to find Aunt Trude. All that's left of her house in Königsplatz is a burnt wall. Our fire parties probably did that. No one knows what happened to our aunt and the rest of the tenants but it seems to me that we'll never see her again. I'll probably meet the same fate in this [damned] fortress.[56]

There is no record of Heinz Liedtke after the end of April 1945. Within a week most of his comrades would be in captivity and the Hammer and Sickle would fly above the ruins of Fortress Breslau.

Notes

1. Hartung, pp.76-7 and Gleiss, iii, p.985.
2. Peikert, pp.281-2.
3. Franke, pp.5-21.
4. Gleiss, iv, pp.201-3.
5. Peikert, pp.282-4.
6. Gleiss, iv, p.26.
7. Peikert, pp.282-4.
8. Van Aaken, pp.208-9.
9. Based on Hartung, p.77 and Hugo Hartung, 'Ostern 1945', in Hupka, Hubert (ed), *Breslau: Geliebt und unvergessen*, pp.73-4.
10. Haas, ii, pp.128-31.
11. Gleiss, iv, p.58.
12. Peikert, pp.282-4.
13. Based on Gleiss, iv, p.55, Gleiss, viii, p.869, Bannert, p.81 and Haas, ii, pp.128-31.
14. Gleiss, iv, p.109.
15. Ibid., iv, pp.172-3.
16. Based on Gleiss, iv, pp.55, 119, Gleiss, iii, p.991 and Hornig, pp.160-1.
17. Gleiss, iv, p.158.
18. Based on Gleiss, iv, p.173, Becker, p.143 and Peikert, pp.284-7.
19. See Gleiss, iv, pp.55, 165, Hartung, pp.77-8 and Gleiss, iv, pp.121-2.
20. Gleiss, iv, p.173.
21. Ibid., iv, p.118.

22. Ibid., iv, pp.121-2.
23. Gleiss, iv, p.243, Van Aaken, pp.208-9, Becker, p.143 and Hartung, pp.78, 79.
24. *Die Grosse Flucht*, ZDF documentary, 2001, Episode 3, 'Festung Breslau', Peikert, pp.284-7 and Grieger, pp.23-7.
25. Gleiss, iv, pp.201-3.
26. Ibid., iv, p.113.
27. Documenty Nr.227.
28. Bannert, pp.81-4.
29. Gleiss, iv, p.296.
30. Ibid., iv, p.297.
31. The battle for the blind institute is based on Gleiss, iv, pp.297-8, 323, *So Kämpfte Breslau*, pp.77-8 and Majewski, pp.109-10.
32. Franke, pp.61-2, 65-6, 95-6.
33. Gleiss, viii, pp.988, 1055.
34. Gleiss, viii, p.963 and Gleiss, iv, pp.450-1.
35. Gleiss, iv, p.651.
36. Ibid., iv, pp.631-3.
37. Gleiss, viii, pp.1034-5.
38. *So Kämpfte Breslau*, pp.80-2.
39. Ibid., p.77.
40. Konev, p.124, 162 and Gleiss iv, p.980.
41. Majewski, pp.98-9.
42. Gleiss, viii, pp.827-8.
43. Ibid., viii, pp.1032-3.
44. BA-MA RH2/1914/31 and *Völkischer Beobachter*, 13/4/45.
45. Documenty Nr.200, 239 and Nr.241.
46. Gleiss, iv, pp.860, 883, 886-7 and Hartung, p.85.
47. Hornig, pp.188-91 and Gleiss, iv, pp.1019-21.
48. Gleiss, viii, pp.1088-89.
49. Gleiss, iv, p.1171.
50. Gleiss, iv, pp.998-9, 1063 and Haas, ii, pp.144-5.
51. Gleiss, viii, p.1153.
52. Ibid., viii, p.1188. The revolt was deemed serious enough by Niehoff to report it to the German High Command – a report which was intercepted by British intelligence. See also NA HW1/3744.
53. Hartung, pp.86-7, 89.
54. Hornig, p.203.
55. Gleiss, iv, p.887.
56. Gleiss, ix, p.178.

CHAPTER 8

Any Further Sacrifice is a Crime

Now it's all over. My ideals are destroyed, Germany lies in ruins.
What will the Russians do with us?

Horst Gleiss

The first day of May in Breslau was traditionally one of celebration, a celebration of Nature and, in more recent years, a celebration of the National Socialist 'people's community'. "Today we have no time or opportunity to celebrate our May 1," the fortress newspaper lamented. "Today, for us, it is predominantly a memory and a hope." Some Breslauers celebrated anyway. "Our doctor, Dr Franz, is plastered and unable to work," wrote priest Walter Lassmann. Drunken soldiers staggered through the streets yelling, "Enjoy life." From somewhere the sound of an accordion. Soldiers in uniform danced with each other. One pranced around in his uniform like a horse, barefooted, but also wearing a top hat. "It all gave the impression of a last dance after a wild feast," Lassmann observed.[1]

There was a strange mood in Breslau as May 1945 began, an unreal feeling, a feeling that the city was trapped between peace and war. There were signs that the great German war machine and the apparatus of Nazi rule were disintegrating. For the last time, during the night the Luftwaffe had dropped supplies over Breslau – seven tons of ammunition. There would be no more; there was no fuel for the aircraft. The guards of Kletschkau prison could also read the writing on the wall. This day they released fifty of the two hundred inmates and kept their rucksacks packed, ready to flee at a moment's notice.

As for the attackers, a joke was doing the rounds of the Sixth Army which captured the mood of the *frontoviki* perfectly:

Victorious Soviet troops are on the way from Berlin to Moscow for the victory parade. Suddenly they hear explosions and the machine-gun fire.

"Is that our welcoming salute?" asks one soldier.

"No," says his comrade. "It's just Sixth Army. It's still busy conquering Breslau!"[2]

Except that Sixth Army wasn't busy. It had not been busy for several days now. The loudspeakers continued to drone their promises and Soviet aircraft dropped leaflets – "It is madness to continue to fight now," pleaded the former commander of 16th Panzer

Division, captured a few days earlier in Czechoslovakia. There was little actual fighting, but that did not mean zero casualties. At least forty-four *Landsers* died in the fortress on 1 May, among them footballer Hermann Heinzel, a popular defender with Hertha Breslau during the 1930s and '40s. Six Soviet officers were also laid to rest this day. There are no comparative figures for the ordinary *frontoviki*.

It was at least quiet in Lilienthal on the northern flank. Battalion commander *Major* Adolf Graf von Seidlitz-Sandreczki left his command post to rally his troops in the bunkers and trenches. "Hold out men," he urged. "We're all sitting all in the same boat – we don't want to sink into chaos but to survive. The Lord has protected us from death until now and he will continue to protect us."[3]

In a cellar which served as a temporary hospital near the ruins of the cathedral, Walter Lassmann conducted his first service of the new month as the sun dipped beneath the western horizon. So many people – surgeons, medics, patients – wished to attend that they spilled out of the small room which served as Lassmann's chapel, and filled the passageways. Whether they believed or not, they prayed and sang. "We beseeched the May Queen to intercede on behalf of all of us and finally bring an end to all the misery and agonising fear," the priest recalled. "Rarely did we pray with such ardour and sing with such faith as during the May worship in 1945."[4] The May Queen was listening.

There were few radio stations still in German hands as May 1945 dawned. Prague was still broadcasting. So too Bremen. But it was the *Hamburgsender* which was the last major station used by the propaganda machine of the ever-shrinking Reich. Tonight, despite the gravity of Germany's situation, the programme was unchanged: Wagner's *Tannhauser* followed by a piano concerto from Weber. As the music ended, the announcer broke into the evening's entertainment with a warning to listeners to await important news. There was more Wagner, *Götterdämmerung*, but only for three minutes, as the announcer broke in once more. "*Achtung! Achtung!* German radio will broadcast an important announcement for the German people from the German Government." Wagner again, *Das Rheingold*, before another interruption, then finally the adagio from Bruckner's *Symphony No.7*. At 10.25pm, the music stopped. There were three drum rolls, then the ominous voice of the announcer once again. "It is reported from the Führer's headquarters that our Führer, Adolf Hitler, fell for Germany this afternoon in his command post in the Reich Chancellery, fighting to his last breath against Bolshevism."

The news was described variously by Breslauers who heard it as a thunderclap, a bolt of lightning, an electric shock. Their reactions, however, differed vastly. In Klaus Franke's cellar, men stopped playing chess or tossed playing cards to one side. Those who had been asleep threw off their blankets and got up. The artillerymen gathered around their company commander. "*Ja*, men, and now?" the officer looked at them. There was silence in the cellar, save for the ticking of wristwatches. "Now more than ever, *Herr Oberleutnant*," the men told him in unison. Hans Gottwald, recovering from a bullet wound in a makeshift hospital in Reuschstrasse, observed mixed reactions. "Most of us are paralysed by horror initially, but some comrades also openly show their delight," he wrote. His comrade Meier beamed. "Thank God the swine's no longer alive." Others shared Meier's relief. "There was an indescribable joyous mood when we heard that," priest Helmut Richter recalled. "Now we have the fundamental pre-condition for peace." And in a command post on the fortress's northern front, there was silence. *Major* Adolf Graf von Seidlitz-Sandreczki's turned to his men. His question was brief, simple. "What now?"[5]

The answer – from Ferdinand Schörner and Karl Hanke – was the same: the struggle would continue. From Schörner, recently promoted field marshal and now named Commander-in-Chief of the German Army by Hitler in his will, the assurance that "the struggle for Germany's freedom and her future goes on". From Hanke, named Himmler's successor as head of the SS in the Führer's testament, a call to Germans "to do everything in our power to save as many people from Bolshevism as possible". The *Schlesische Tageszeitung* urged Breslauers to hold out "as long as we have to so that our time in the fortress comes to a happy ending, a reward for all our effort and sacrifices", while placards quickly appeared around the city – *He lives among us, he fights with us, he fell for us*. The fortress's senior National Socialist Leadership Officer, Herbert van Bürck, remained committed to the cause. "History teaches us that ideas which have a decisive role in shaping the world often only come to the fore when the original torchbearer of the idea has proven himself through his death," he explained. "The revolution, for which the Führer has fallen and to which we all belong, must be won." There would be no surrender. "We must never put our heads on the Bolsheviks' block as long as we can still challenge them," van Bürck continued. "In our situation there is only one choice: to be deported to Siberia or, by fighting on, to create the basis for a political change which ensures that the struggle of the German people has not been in vain."[6]

Few people rose to Herbert van Bürck's clarion call. Elderly electrician Hermann Nowack had had his fill of Nazi slogans. As May began, the seventy-one-year-old struggled through the ruins of his city:

> Crossed the piles of rubble to Kaiserbrücke. Utter desert. Garvestrasse to Stanitzkistrasse: ruins. Mauritiusplatz: ruins. Brothers' convent: badly damaged. Brüderstrasse: a lot burned out. Tauentzienstrasse: totally burned out: My son's house, No.101, razed down to the cellars. Not one slat, only the blackened walls. Goebbels said: "We must be hard." Now I stand here. Turned to stone, like a rock.[7]

Postal official Conrad Bischof shared Hermann Nowack's disgust:

> Now Adolf Hitler is dead and he has taken all of us and our beautiful Germany with him. I have been proved right that these fellows are our knights of death. His thousand-year Reich, like everything else, was a complete sham. Three years ago I wrote that not only Germans but the entire world would curse him one day. Now he's like a gambler at Monte Carlo who's simply left the game because of

his death. That they still call it a hero's death is neither here nor there; he has plunged 100 million people into misery and left them without jobs and homes.[8]

Still the dying regime persisted with its lies. The whispering propaganda campaign continued to the bitter end. Panzer divisions were coming from Schweidnitz – some men claimed they could already hear the clatter of tank tracks, or had seen the relief columns on the edge of the fortress – or a 'panzer corridor' two dozen miles long would be carved through Lower Silesia, allowing the besieged garrison and civilians to flow out. The lies were not merely spread by Party functionaries, or by junior officers such as Herbert van Bürck. They also came from the upper echelons of the military. As he had done two months before, Ferdinand Schörner assured the fortress commander he would come to his aid. "Niehoff, we will liberate the fortress," he promised. "Fight to the last round and to the last man." Hermann Niehoff did not believe him. His staff had chewed over the idea of breaking out – and quickly dismissed it. A breakout would have been "an irresponsible, unworkable and senseless undertaking which would have drowned a terrible death in its own blood". In the wake of Hitler's death, the fortress commander had pleaded with the people of Breslau. "Have faith in me in this most difficult hour. Be assured that I shall do what is best for you." With Hitler dead, with Berlin about to fall, with the full force of the Red Army about to be unleashed against his fortress, Hermann Niehoff could see only one course of action. "*Herr Feldmarschall*," he told Schörner, "I intend to end the struggle and surrender the city." As ever, 'iron Ferdinand' was inflexible. "Niehoff, I expect you to be loyal to our dead Führer." Breslau's commander did not respond. He put the telephone down. And he revealed his decision to no one.[9]

Shortly after 1pm on 4 May, Niehoff's staff car pulled up outside the entrance to Staatsbibliothek on the Sandinsel. Four clergy – Catholic bishop Joseph Ferche, in full regalia, and his canon, Joseph Kramer, and Protestants Joachim Konrad and Ernst Hornig – climbed out and were led past numerous guard posts into the bowels of the library cellars. Seated at a table waiting for them were Hermann Niehoff and two of his staff officers. The white-haired Ferche introduced his colleagues, then addressed the fortress commander, calmly but firmly. "*Herr General*, we do not have the right to intervene in your decisions. But we regard it as our duty, before God and before our people, to ask you whether you can still take responsibility for continuing the struggle." Ernst Hornig now took up the cause. The plight of the city's civilian populace was pitiful, he told Niehoff. Every day people asked him "Will all of us die beneath the bombs and in fires?" Every day faith in the Party, faith in the leadership declined. People no longer saw any sense in defending Breslau. Perhaps in a few days they would no longer follow orders. "Under these circumstances, can you answer to God for continuing the defence of the city?" the priest asked the general. There was silence in the bunker. Niehoff lowered his head for a good minute, then looked once more at the men of God. "Your concerns are my concerns. Now tell me what I should do."

The clergymen answered in unison.

"Surrender."

"*Meine Herren*, you can be certain that I will consider your suggestion very seriously," Niehoff told them. "You will hear from me shortly."

Three hours later, the guns on both sides fell silent. Two German officers stood at the corner of the Strasse der SA and Viktoriastrasse under a white flag. They wanted to discuss surrender terms.[10]

Karl Hanke had been involved neither in the discussions with Breslau's clergy nor in Hermann Niehoff's decision to send negotiators across the lines – but he heard about them. Late on the fourth he stormed into the cellars of the Staatsbibliothek.

"General, I've just learned that you want to surrender!"

"You heard correctly, *Gauleiter*, I am preparing to surrender."

"Then I must have you arrested, general!"

"If anyone is doing the arresting, *Gauleiter*, then it's probably me!"

There was an awkward silence before Hanke spoke once more.

"Forgive my threat, it was not meant as such. But what should I do?"

Niehoff suggested Hanke take his own life. "I can't do that," the *Gauleiter* insisted. "I'm still so young. I must live. If I have to wander around the world like a tramp . . ." The sentence trailed off. "General, help me!"

Niehoff offered to disguise Hanke as a front-line soldier, a *Grenadier* Meier. The *Gauleiter* shook his head. "I'd be recognised and betrayed in half an hour." Niehoff offered bandages, perhaps some plasters. Again Hanke declined. "That's no use either. I'll be betrayed just as quickly."

"Then there's only one thing left for you," the general said. "When it's dark tonight, I'll clear a path for you through the minefields. You can sneak out of the city. Behind the Russian lines you will be on your own."

As Hanke considered the general's proposal, Niehoff added bluntly: "That's the only choice you have left." But Karl Hanke had other plans.[11]

With Berlin subdued, the Red Army and Red Air Force could devote their full wrath to Hitler's last fortress. Soviet loudspeakers declared they would level Breslau with the earth. Mid-morning on Saturday 5 May, there was a portent of the impending onslaught. Despite the previous afternoon's tentative surrender negotiations, the bombers were unleashed once more: countless twin-engined aircraft escorted by fighters. The raid caught many Breslauers by surprise. Several bombs straddled Benderplatz, killing at least ten people, including a soldier who was decapitated by the force of the blast. The bombs this day badly damaged two churches in Zimpel, a suburb largely untouched by the war. In the city centre, the Matthias school was destroyed, houses in the narrow streets around the university collapsed, burying inhabitants alive. After the attack there was another tense cease-fire, this time for three hours – one last attempt to persuade the fortress to surrender before the final onslaught. Under a white flag, Soviet negotiators crossed the lines, accompanied by prisoners captured at Stalingrad – proof of fair treatment for German soldiers in Russian hands. In Viktoriastrasse, Hitler Youth Max

Baselt watched a few Ivans tentatively emerge from their trenches and beckon the Germans over. Some *Landsers* heeded the call. In no-man's land they exchanged cigarettes, a few even played football. For a while friend and foe fraternized, until a German officer appeared and ordered the men back to their positions. The Russians also sheepishly returned to their lines.[12]

As the Soviet envoys crossed the lines, Hermann Niehoff summoned his officers in his headquarters beneath the Staatsbibliothek. While the men gathered, a brief signal from Seventeenth Army was handed to the fortress commander: "Germany's flags are lowered in proud sorrow in tribute of the resolve of the garrison and the self-sacrifice of the populace of Breslau."[13] The Reich expected Breslau to surrender – and that was what Hermann Niehoff intended to do. "The clouds of an impending storm, which the city would no longer be able to withstand, were gathering over Breslau," he wrote later. It was time to end the struggle, as he explained to his staff.

> *Meine Herren*, I have called you together for a final roll-call. What has been achieved by you, by our men and the civilian population, needs no words. One day history will pass judgment.
> Hitler is dead. Berlin has fallen. The Eastern and Western Allies have shaken hands in the heart of Germany. There is no longer any reason to continue the struggle for Breslau. Any further sacrifice is a crime. I have decided to end the fighting and to offer to surrender the city and the garrison to the enemy under honourable terms. We have fired our last round. We have done our duty as the law dictated.

Every man agreed except Otto Herzog, an inveterate Nazi who had been rewarded with the *Ritterkreuz* for his leadership of Breslau's *Volkssturm*. In a few weeks, the Western Allies and the Soviet Union would be at war and the German Army would once again be marching, he told Niehoff as he left the command bunker. Herzog's fate is unclear. Some reports say he shot himself, others that he tried to escape the fortress and was killed when his car struck a mine.[14]

Saturday night was warm and languid. On the Russian side of the lines, loudspeakers repeatedly broadcast the surrender terms interspersed with music, while the *frontoviki* fired star shells, tracer and rockets in celebration. And behind the German front, Breslau burned – as on every night for the past three months. The flames 'cooked off' some infantry ammunition which roared skywards. And yet, every Breslauer, every defender knew that peace was at hand. "There's a feeling that the end of a three-month struggle – waged with such fury on both sides – is in the air," Max Baselt wrote. In these final hours, the defenders of Breslau became wistful. Now was no time to die. "Thoughts drift far, far away," one *Landser* wrote. "We dream of bygone days, scenes appear before our eyes which seem to have been long since forgotten. We long for our mothers, the maidens whom we love, the people who are dear to us. We see them in front of us, they speak to us, we caress them, speak to them. Everything is so clear." From FAMO employee Carl Völkel, a simple prayer: "May we still get through these final hours in the fortress."[15]

In western Breslau, battalion commander Captain Vasiliya Grigorievich Kostielniuka was directing one more raid by the men of 135th Rifle Division. Five times his division had been singled out for praise by the Red Army's command for its performance on Polish soil, culminating in its receiving the Order of the Red Banner. The battles of 1945 had cost it 4,000 men. And now, on the eve of victory, a bullet fired by a German sniper in one of Breslau's church towers struck down Vasiliya Kostielniuka. He was probably the division's final casualty of the Great Patriotic War.[16]

Saturday was turning to Sunday as a column of Red Army trucks headed down Frankfurter Strasse, past the ruins of Gandau airfield, under the railway underpass and into the western suburbs of Breslau. The vehicles halted and three platoons of soldiers, some eighty men in all, jumped out. From here it was perhaps 1,000 yards to the front line in Friedrich Karl Strasse, the men's objectives. This night, for the first time during the siege of Breslau, for the *only* time during the siege of Breslau, German would face German as the anti-Fascists of the *Nationalkomitee Freies Deutschland* – National Committee for Free Germany – tried to infiltrate the defenders' lines with the aim of seizing the former offices of a pensions company, now the headquarters of an SS battalion. After struggling to orient themselves amid the ruins of the West End, the three platoons crawled their way through fences and rubble as far as Friedrich Karl Strasse. Some of the men were spotted and snipers open fired. One of the platoon leaders stepped into the light and yelled out: "You moron, if you don't stop shooting, I'll bash your head in." The shooting stopped. Three SS guards were taken prisoner in a house and led back through Soviet lines, but it proved impossible to sneak inside the battalion command post, defended by at least one machine-gun. Instead, the anti-Fascists learned the meaning of street fighting as *Panzerfaust* and machine-guns were brought to bear against them. The operation's commander, *Leutnant* Horst Vieth, was mortally wounded by a burst from a machine-pistol during a skirmish for rooms in one apartment block. Shortly afterwards, as the first signs of dawn began to appear in the East, the mission was abandoned. The NKFD troops and their Soviet radiomen were ordered back to Russian lines. They had captured perhaps a dozen German soldiers. Otherwise, the raid had been a complete failure.[17]

The inmates of Kletschkau prison awoke on Sunday, 6 May to find the three cells of condemned inmates empty, the doors wide open. Some time during the night, eighteen men and one woman had been ordered into the field behind the prison where each one was dispatched by a shot to the back of the neck. Their corpses were tossed into a pit next to barracks for foreign workers, where soil, ash, jars of food and other rubbish was thrown on top of them. At least one of the prisoners struggled to the very end. His face was swollen, his eyes were battered, his right hand still clasped a tuft of hair.[18]

The typesetters on the *Schlesische Tageszeitung* finished composing the copy of the day's edition, the 122nd of the sixteenth year of publication. It did not take them long; the 'fortress newspaper' had been reduced not merely to a single sheet of paper, but a single side. *Widerstand gegen die Sowjets geht weiter!* – Resistance against the Soviets continues – screamed the headline next to a eulogy to the defenders of Breslau – "a shining example to the entire German people". Rather less prominence was given to the surrender of Berlin, the capture of Hamburg or the fact that the British had seized Kiel. And there was no mention of Breslau's imminent capitulation.[19]

It was light by the time Karl Hanke arrived in the grounds of the Jahrhunderthalle where a young *Leutnant* was waiting for him. Helmut Alsleben had wheeled a small Fieseler Storch reconnaissance aircraft out of one of the hall's side buildings and unfolded its wings. The Storch was the only airworthy aircraft in the fortress, held in storage for Hermann Niehoff to use at his discretion. He never did.

The Storch's only passenger was the *Gauleiter* of Breslau, dressed in the ill-fitting uniform of an ordinary soldier. Karl Hanke had commandeered Niehoff's aircraft to reach Hirschberg, sixty miles to the southwest, before crossing the border to join German forces in Bohemia and Moravia. Around 5.30am, Alsleben and Hanke took off, flying south, low over the ruins of Breslau. For the first ten miles, the flight passed without incident. But then the Storch was struck by machine-gun fire. The engine stuttered on for another mile before Alsleben set the aircraft down on the slopes of the Zobten to effect emergency repairs. With the fuel tank patched up, the Storch was airborne again for a flight of no more than a dozen miles to the airfield at Schweidnitz, where a panzer officer was waiting for Breslau's *Gauleiter*.[20]

Breslauers were waking to a beautiful spring morning. "A peaceful calm ruled," recalled chemist Hanns Hoffmann. "No shell fire, no bombs exploding, and Nature had put on her Sunday best." Pale figures crawled out of cellars and filled their lungs with the fresh May air.[21]

In the basement of the Staatsbibliothek, Hermann Niehoff was feeling harassed. "Have you any idea where the *Gauleiter* is?" his officers asked him. Then came the telephone calls, finally a visit from one of Karl Hanke's staff. As officers, soldiers and Party officials searched the fortress for Karl Hanke, a breathless soldier reported to his commander. "*Herr General*, your Fieseler Storch has gone." There was further confirmation in the form of a terse signal from Hirschberg handed to Niehoff: Gauleiter *Hanke, lightly wounded, has just landed here with faulty machine*.[22]

Leo Hartmann drove his *Sturmgeschütz* through the city for the final time. The guns on both sides were silent, the only noise came from the civilian populace who had spilled into the streets. "You poor soldiers!" an elderly woman called out at the gun commander. "Now you must go into captivity!"[23]

Throughout the siege, the brutal Party leader of Breslau *Mitte* – central – liked nothing better than a roast on a Sunday, usually rabbit. Today was no different for *Ortsgruppenleiter* Hass in the house he had occupied when its Jewish owners had been deported. The family's elderly tomcat had stayed behind where he was pampered by Hass's housekeepers – until the day when they had nothing more to give him. Today was that day. The cat was killed, cooked and served to the Nazi. It was his last meal. Satiated, Hass shot himself.[24]

The fate of more than 100,000 men and women, warriors and civilians, young and old, weighed more heavily on the mind of Hermann Niehoff than the fate of one Nazi overlord. "Never in the two world wars did I struggle with my conscience – daily and hourly – as much as I did during the struggle for Breslau," the general recounted later. Today, for the final time, he would try to influence the fates of the Breslauers entrusted to him. At 3pm, two Soviet negotiators – the Chief of Staff of XXII Infantry Corps, Colonel Tchitschin, and interpreter Major Omar Jachjavev – were ushered into Niehoff's command post. Jachjavev eyed up the maps and charts on the walls of the fortress commander's office while his colonel pulled a letter from his pocket. One of Niehoff's staff began to translate – "Proposal for an honourable surrender of the city and garrison of Fortress Breslau . . ." – as Omar Jachjavev gathered up all the useful documents and maps he could find and put them in a trunk. To Hermann Niehoff, the terms sounded "unusually magnanimous". There was one snag, however. Neither Tchitschin nor Jachjavev had any authority. Negotiations with them, however correct, even cordial, were useless. The fortress commander resolved to sit down with his opposite number. As he left his bunker with the two Soviet officers, he turned to his operations officer Albrecht Otto. "If I don't come back, continue the fight."[25]

Near the Hauptbahnhof, Peter Bannert was waiting for the two Soviet emissaries to return. Two hours earlier, the Hitler Youth and his comrades had guided the blindfolded Tchitschin and Jachjavev from the front line to the central station where a car took them to Niehoff's headquarters. Now the Soviet officers returned, minus blindfolds. Trailing behind them was the fortress commander, the red stripes on his trousers, denoting he was a member of Germany's lauded General Staff, clearly visible. "We were speechless," Bannert recalled. "Never had I seen a proper general so close up." The boys hurriedly presented arms. Niehoff stopped and put his hands on the helmet of one of Bannert's comrades. "Young men, thank you!" he said softly. "You won't understand the walk I'm making now. But later you'll realize that it was right." With tears in their eyes, the Hitler Youths accompanied the group until it had safely reached Soviet lines.[26]

In the north of the city, Soviet troops had already taken advantage of the cease-fire to row across the Oder. All afternoon inflatable boats, dinghies and motor launches moved to and fro between the Russian- and German-held banks. The Ivans played folk songs on their accordions, talked with the few Breslauers who emerged from their cellars, even chatted with their foe. "Perhaps everything won't turn out as badly as National

Socialist propaganda reported," wondered Horst Gleiss, sent by his commander to investigate the reports of fraternisation. "The Russians are not inhuman barbarians, murdering beasts, are they?"[27]

Hermann Niehoff was driven to the south-western edge of the city and a smart detached house in Kaiser Friedrich Strasse in the suburb of Krietern. Here, in the Villa Colonia, Vladimir Gluzdovski had made his headquarters. Staff officers stood smartly to attention in the garden as the German general passed them. The fortress commander was shown into a room where a good dozen Soviet generals, among them Gluzdovski, were standing around a large table. An orderly brought in a tray of glasses and schnapps. Gluzdovski invited the German officer to drink and passed him a glass. Niehoff declined. The Sixth Army commander grabbed the glass and quickly downed the contents. Niehoff nodded and emptied the fresh glass handed to him. Smiles flashed around the room.

Now Gluzdovski's deputy, General Panov, handed the German a document, the terms of surrender. The conditions were far more lenient than Niehoff could have dared hope. The sick and wounded would receive medical assistance from the Soviets; the security of Breslau's civilians was "assured"; soldiers would be fed, treated well and be allowed to keep decorations and personal possessions. They would also be permitted "to return home at the end of the war". At 6pm Hermann Niehoff put his name to the document of surrender. "It was my fault that I, as an honourable soldier, believed the word solemnly given by our enemy," he said ruefully a decade later.

The last act of Hermann Niehoff's leadership was to issue an order of the day:

Comrades!
Citizens of Breslau!

For three months in the encircled fortress you have done your heavy duty and achieved 'the miracle of Breslau', unparalleled in the history of this war!

Loyal to the order the Führer gave me and believing in salvation from outside, I demanded you take up the defensive struggle. Now I no longer expect help from outside , and I can no longer bear responsibility for further bloodshed and continuing our heroic fight! With a heavy heart, but with a feeling of loyalty towards you, I have asked the enemy for a cease-fire. Negotiations are now under way. Continue to show your confidence in me by maintaining your iron discipline and calm. Only in this way can I direct your fate for the best. I remain at your side as I have promised you!

Niehoff, Fortress Commander[28]

Until now, one man in the room had remained silent, Vassily Klokov, the army's commissar. He turned to Niehoff. The chatter stopped. "The Soviet Sixth Army will move into Breslau around 9pm," he said icily. The German general was aghast. There was no way his troops could be disarmed in an orderly fashion in little more than two hours. There would be chaos, clashes, men needlessly killed. Niehoff protested. The commissar cut him off. "Marshal Konev has orders from Moscow to announce the occupation of Breslau tonight."[29]

The *Schlesische Tageszeitung* had already passed into history. Now the city's wire radio station broadcast for the last time. At 6.45pm the loudspeaker columns around Breslau spoke for the last time: "I am finishing my work, I am finishing my work."[30]

In the *Volkssturm* bunker on the Benderplatz, the men of *Ortsgruppe Schiesswerder* gathered for the final time. The commander told the men and boys that the fortress had surrendered and the Party and all its apparatus were being disbanded. The courtyard became a bonfire as files, documents, membership books, certificates went up in flames, while Party badges, medals and decorations were cast into a small stove. Horst Gleiss burned his *Jungvolk* uniform, his *Hitlerjugend* badge and a portrait of Hitler. Only his precious diaries did not go on to the pyre.

> I was neither a soldier nor did I belong to the *Volkssturm*. I take off my *feldgrau* tunic which I've worn for sixty-eight days and throw it away in Benderplatz. Under my uniform I have always worn a shirt. For a long time I stare at the grey-green jacket which has accompanied me for almost ten weeks on my dangerous journeys. I know it's not a long time but to me it seemed like an eternity . . .
>
> 'Now it's all over', I think on my way home to my mother. 'My ideals are destroyed, Germany lies in ruins. What will the Russians do with us? Will they kill us all in revenge because we defended ourselves for so long? Will they deport us to Siberia? Even if they let us live and leave us in our homes, will we ever escape the misery if all the nations who were involved in the war with us demand reparations? How will things turn out?' For me a world has collapsed, a world in which – and for which – I lived, a world which made me happy and proud. I feel like a defenceless sacrifice, delivered, for better or worse, into the hands of our mortal foe.
>
> These fears torment me as I pass by the graves of 2,000 soldiers and civilians in Benderplatz. When I get home I am once again a schoolboy in a checked shirt, short trousers and knee-length socks. No-one in our household wonders why I've taken off my *feldgrau* jacket. To everyone, I had always been the schoolboy, to some I was also an abused child or the caricature of a soldier. And I really was that as well.[31]

Artillery observer Klaus Franke was one of four hundred men – gunners, mortar troops, *Landsers*, *Fallschirmjäger* gathered in a large cellar. The soldiers were in defiant mood. "Betrayed and sold out," one veteran *Unteroffizier* snarled. "We're not thinking about chopping wood in Siberia." A paratroop officer climbed on to a stool to address the men:

> Men! Comrades! I've been a soldier now for ten years, six years of those in action. I've known many of you for a long time. I came to know many more

good comrades who are no longer among us. They made the supreme sacrifice in this struggle, believing in a better future, believing in our common idea. It is not our fault that this will never come true. We have done what we could. I thank you for your constant readiness to act in fighting which was often hard. I have nothing more to say now. Do what you can reconcile with your honour towards your fallen comrades and your consciences.

There was silence in the cellar. The officer raised his voice. "Germany is lost, Europe is going under and there's no longer a place on this earth for an old *Fallschirmjäger* captain." He reached at his hip, withdrew his pistol, aimed it at his head and pulled the trigger. His body toppled off the stool and landed at the feet of the men he had commanded just seconds before.[32]

"Don't let your heads drop now," *Leutnant* Erich Schönfelder's company commander urged his troops. "You've survived the period of the fortress, you will survive captivity too. We're all in the same boat." Some of the men interjected. "We don't trust the Ivans," "We didn't fight for this," or "It'll be years before we return from Siberia – if we return at all."[33]

After firing their last shell, *Oberleutnant* Albrecht Schulze van Loon's paratroopers mustered around their company commander. "Whoever wants to go his own way is free to do so," van Loon told them. No more than one third of his men did. The rest gathered at the rallying point, minus their weapons, and marched off. It had been a sultry day. Now the rain began to fall. "We move through the rain, over anti-tank ditches, past ruins and burning houses," van Loon wrote. "The heavens weep – it rains cats and dogs and no one can tell what is rain and what is tears."[34]

Leo Hartmann's commander addressed his men in the courtyard of a prison and told them the fortress had surrendered. The *Sturmgeschütze* crews had no intention of letting their guns fall into Soviet hands. They drove the vehicles repeatedly around the block in first gear until the pistons seized up through overheating. With their weapons rendered useless, the men marched down Frankfurter Strasse into captivity, past a burned out Stalin tank, the last victim of the *Panzerjäger Abteilung Breslau*.[35]

Some men headed into captivity singing the old marching song, *Die blauen Dragoner, sie reiten* – the blue dragoons, they ride. Rarely had the refrain – "The way back to our homeland is long, so long, so long" – held such meaning. Max Baselt's heavy company marched down the Strasse der SA, where Soviet soldiers formed a guard of honour. "*Gitler kaputt*," they yelled at the troops marching into captivity. "*Breslau kaputt. Woina* (war) *kaputt*." The Germans stared at the rubble of this once fine boulevard. They passed Südpark on their left, stripped bare. Only now did the ruins give way to opulent villas, still intact. Finally, some five miles from the city centre, the column halted in front of the gates of an old sugar factory in Klettendorf, now a makeshift prison camp. "Captivity: a bitter fate after 83 days encircled, after being in the fortress 105 days and nights during which we worried – and hoped," Baselt thought. "Grit your teeth and get on with it. We are prisoners." *Volkssturm* soldier Otto Rothkugel was struck by the sudden silence which had descended over the city – "something strange, because for weeks it had thundered continuously". He stood outside his house in the northern suburb of Rosenthal and watched lines of German soldiers heading out of the city towards Trebnitz. It was a ragged, disorganized, endless column. Hitler Youths played the accordion and sang while men without weapons marched or rode on horse-drawn carts "in a never-ending column".[36]

Like the rest of his comrades in 135th Rifle Division, commissar Aleksander Parszynki waited impatiently for the Germans to appear. All evening long, the men had stared into Breslau's western suburbs, but the rain and darkness were impenetrable. "Finally we heard a commotion coming from the city centre," Parszynki recalled. "Out of the darkness a German column emerges in several large lorries – an infantry battalion, disarmed."[37]

Elsewhere, there were uneasy encounters between victor and vanquished. A column of German artillerymen marching out of the city passed a column of Soviet soldiers marching into Breslau. A Russian leapt out of his column and wrestled with the artillery commander, *Major* Frohnert, determined to rip the German Cross in Gold from the left breast of his jacket. Suddenly a Russian officer grabbed his man by the collar, punched him in the face and shoulder, thrust him back into the column and apologized to the German major.[38]

The first Soviet troops began to filter into the west of the city shortly after nightfall. They were, Ernst Hornig remembered, as cautious as Breslau's civilian inhabitants. "They were evidently looking to make contact with the populace, were friendly and affable in conversation with civilians as far as they could make themselves understood."[39]

In the Ring, Party leaders stripped off their uniforms and drove off in over-loaded cars. The dissolution of the Party meant the dissolution of order. Soldiers and Hitler Youths smashed their way into the storerooms of Breslau's merchants and helped themselves to vast quantities of wine, schnapps, tobacco, cigars, flour and sugar. Civilians joined in the looting. With his master gone, an apprentice butcher handed out sausage, smoked meat and ham to customers for free – better that than let them fall into the hands of the Russians. Otherwise, supplies of alcohol were emptied to prevent Soviet troops drinking themselves into a stupor. The gutters of Breslau flowed with wine. "There was a strange mood that night," recalled teacher Klemens Lorenz, "a mixture of fear and gallows humour."[40]

By late Sunday evening the atmosphere in the Villa Colonia had completely changed. Now Sixth Army's commissar had departed, the generals and staff officers talked openly. They buttonholed Hermann Niehoff with every possible question: was Hitler really dead? Could the fortress still resist? Was Hanke still in the city? The Russians ushered their guest into the dining room and to a candle-lit table filled with cold dishes, seafood, meat pies, appetisers and bottles of vodka. *"Gospodin [Herr]* general, please have the best seat!" Gluzdovski insisted. A glass filled to the rim with vodka was handed to Niehoff as his Soviet counterpart toasted the defender of Breslau: "Heroic garrison . . . The fight is over . . . Yesterday's enemy, tomorrow's friend. No hatred but a policy of alliances . . . I drink to the health of the commander of Breslau!" The evening grew more lively, Niehoff more subdued. In the end it became too much for the German general, who asked to retire to bed.[41]

Ernst Hornig had also retired. Monday, 7 May was one hour old when he was woken by footsteps and loud chatter. From his front door he watched Soviet troops swarming across Königsplatz and along Nikolaistrasse towards the Ring. It reminded Hornig of New Year's Eves of old, when every street was filled with revellers converging on the city's historic heart. "How different the crowd looked now," the priest recalled. "How different was the night which followed."[42]

At first light on Monday one Breslauer left her cellar on the edge of Schlossplatz to go to mass in St Antoniuskirche. It was the first time in weeks she'd been able to cross the huge parade ground without crawling, ducking, jumping from house to house, taking shelter from bombs, shells and mortars. The first Soviet troops were milling around the city centre, calmly, quietly. A few saluted the cross over the small church, some peered inside, others sat quietly in the pews. "It was all so peaceful that we really didn't need to be worried about the Russians," the woman recalled.[43]

The residents of the 'garden city' of Zimpel in the east of the city hurriedly hung out red flags – the outlines of a black swastika on a white background still visible on many – to greet the Red Army, while banners were stretched across the main road: *Welcome to the liberators from Hitler's Fascism.* Banners were also erected across Jahnstrasse on the western edge of the old town: *We greet the brave heroes of the Red Army*! and *We thank our liberators from Nazi terror*! Women handed the Soviet soldiers bottles of wine and posies. German troops shuffled in the opposite direction. A woman stepped out from the side of the road and spat at a veteran *Landser*. "Be off with you!" she yelled. "You're to blame for everything! Why didn't you end it sooner?" An enraged *Volkssturm* soldier broke ranks and punched the woman in the face. He continued down the road, muttering to himself. "Poor people, they're completely out of their minds. For us men, the war is over. For them everything is only just beginning . . ."[44]

To priest Joachim Konrad, the Ring this Monday morning "resembled an army camp", filled with "*panje* carts pulled by small horses" and echoing to the "din of loudspeakers which blared out Strauss's waltz" and "bawling and shrieking" Russian soldiers.[45] There were similar scenes a couple of streets away in Schlossplatz. The Breslauer who had attended mass at St Antonius early that morning returned to find the scene in the square had changed completely. It was filled with carts and wagons laden with wine and liquor – there were rumours that 80,000 bottles had been found in the cellars of the Liebichshöhe alone. "Crouching and lying down between the barrels and wagons lay the victors in their thousands, bellowing and roaring," the Breslauer recalled. She ran to the Antonius convent to warn the women and girls sheltering there.[46]

Dutch Waffen SS volunteer Hendrik Verton was enjoying a beautiful spring day in the courtyard of the Christian Hansen wine bar in Schweidnitzer Strasse. The courtyard acted as a suntrap for men being treated in the wine bar's cellar, now First Aid Post No.5. A well-built Russian junior officer with short red hair suddenly appeared in the yard, muttering to himself in his native tongue. He suddenly grabbed Verton by the shoulder, kissed him on both cheeks and laughed: "*Woina kapuut, Hitler kapuut, guut!*" The officer pointed at the decorations on his uniform, and those on Verton's. "*Guut Soldat, woina nix guut!*" The convalescing Germans managed to stop the Russian entering the cellar. Instead, he dragged three of them to the nearby Hotel Monopol, kicked open the tradesmen's door and searched every room for alcohol. Finally, the Soviet officer and his new-found 'friends' stumbled into the hotel kitchen. The cooks and maids fled screaming. The Russian drew his pistol and began shooting wildly. He hit nothing but the white wall tiles which fell off and shattered. After the three Germans calmed him down, he took them out into the street, handed them a few cigarettes and urged "*Davai!*" – keep going.[47]

Klaus Franke had spent the day in hiding. He had no intention of entering Soviet captivity. He and half a dozen comrades skulked in the ruins of a church near the Rosenthaler Brücke waiting for an opportunity to slip out of the city. Suddenly, footsteps. Then voices. "Ursel, come quickly behind the hedge, to the large bush!" Someone sobbed. "I think they've seen us. Go, quickly!"

There was the sound of branches snapping, followed by the thud of boots and the voices of Russians. "Come, drink vodka, vodka's good, very good." There was the sound of rustling coming from the bushes, then screams from the German girls. "No, I do not want to. No! No!" The shrieks became hysterical. "Leave me. No. Go away!"

In the church's ruined crypt, Klaus Franke wanted to act but could not. He heard the bodies fall to the ground. The women's cries turned to sobbing and whimpering. "The *Landsers* shake with powerless rage, bite their teeth – they cannot help," Franke wrote. The two girls were the first victims of the day in the churchyard. Throughout the seventh, as the soldiers hid, they listened to "weeping, groaning, tormented German voices, cursing, joking and very loud Russian voices," the artillery observer recalled. "Sometimes they come close, at others you can hear them in the distance, and always the word 'vodka'. It doesn't end – all day long."[48]

Soviet war correspondent Vassily Malinin found nothing but "an unnatural calm" over Breslau this day. "Silence rules in the streets. No barking of machine-guns, no explosions of mines and artillery shells. Houses set on fire during the fighting still burn." At every road junction, weapons, military kit and ammunition were piled high, while white flags hung from every window and balcony in the city centre. German soldiers, their heads bowed, filed past. Some tried to fraternize with their new masters "like chattering parrots," Malinin observed. *"Hitler kaputt, Breslau kaputt, Krieg kaputt,"* they smiled.[49]

As night fell on the seventh, the *frontoviki* fired their weapons into the sky in celebration. "All manner of weapons can be heard," Major Pjotr Savchenko remembered. "Victory! The war is over! This night, no one closed their eyes." Or perhaps some did. Not every Russian soldier celebrated. "The others went on a trophy hunt, searching for machine-pistols, binoculars and medals," seventeen-year-old Alexander Fedotov wrote to his mother. "It may sound strange, mama, but what I have longed for most of all these past few months was quiet – quiet without the cry of machine-guns, without the noise of shells. I went down to the river and stared at the water running past for two hours. And in the evening, for the first time in my life I heard nightingales singing in the bushes."[50]

There was little peace for Breslauers this Monday evening. They called it *Schreckensnacht* – the night of terror. Russian troops burst into the cellars of the Schlosskirche, an air raid shelter which had become home mostly to women and children. The handful of men were dragged outside, beaten senseless, gagged, then tossed into the corner of one of the cellars. Now the soldiers turned their attention to the women, forcing them to undress and take to their beds. "Then they jumped on top of their victims, beat them, cut them with scissors, stabbed them with knives until, submissive and powerless, they resigned themselves to their fate," one eyewitness recalled. "It didn't matter whether they were old women aged seventy or children aged thirteen or fourteen. They spared no one. Finally they set the beds alight and shot the electric lamps with their pistols. The ravaged women fled to the ruins of the nearby Schloss where they waited for this night to end, their clothes torn, their bodies and souls broken." Twenty Russian soldiers kicked down the door of a convent near Karl Hanke's runway. They ransacked every room, seizing food, suitcases, anything upon which they could lay their hands and tossed it into a waiting truck. Next they turned their attention to the nuns and the womenfolk of Breslau who believed the house of God would afford them protection. It did not, for the soldiers now scoured the cellars, shining torches into the corners and crevices. "A Russian grabbed hold of my wrists and dragged me to the cellar door," one nun recalled. "I put up fierce resistance. In the end he tried to grab my veil, but seized my shawl instead and so I escaped into the darkness. Unfortunately, he grabbed one of the girls who tried to protect me and she was unable to escape. Six Russians pounced on her." The poor girl was raped for the next two hours.[51]

The peoples of the Soviet Union learned none of this. They learned only that a great fortress had fallen. They learned that their foe had used every ruse, every conceivable weapon, defended every house, every room of every house. They learned that the Russian soldier displayed an iron will and brought up heavy mortars capable of "destroying a building several storeys high". They learned that Breslau was surrounded by the wreckage of downed German aircraft, its streets littered with "hundreds of destroyed German guns, mortars and tanks". They learned that Breslau burned: by day "grey clouds of smoke hung over the roofs"; by night there was a "dark red glow over the city". They learned that Breslau had died. "Where once there was a great, beautiful city, there is a shapeless scene of devastation," the special correspondent of the government organ *Izvestia* reported. "Thousands of German soldiers are buried beneath the rubble of houses, in deep communication trenches, in the vaults of cellars, and beneath heaps of ash." For the conquerors of Breslau, there was "eternal glory" and twenty salvoes each from 224 guns lined up in Moscow after dark on 7 May. Ceremonies in Breslau itself were rather more modest. The wrecks of Ju52s and other detritus of three months of battle were cleared out of the way at Gandau airfield and a dais hurriedly erected in front of the remains of the terminal. Next to a banner of a *frontovik* brandishing the Red Army standard hung an inscription: *Long live the Party of the Bolsheviks, leader of the victory over the German Fascist yoke*. Regiments from every division which invested the city filed past Vladimir Gluzdovski and his staff on the platform.[52]

If he attended the victory parade, Vassily Malinin did not mention it in his diary. He did, however, head to the southern outskirts of the city and a Red Army cemetery where two guns stood mounted on plinths. After reading numerous terse inscriptions, he placed a few spring flowers on one of the graves. "We remember the names," he recorded in his journal. "Glory to you, fallen comrades! Eternal glory!"[53]

As for the "once-so-mighty German Wehrmacht", it had turned into "an endless column of misery" passing through the streets and squares of Breslau. For three quarters of an hour, Horst Gleiss and his mother watched captive German soldiers, six rows deep, march across Benderplatz. Women handed out bread and water, while Horst tossed packets of tobacco and cigarettes out of his apartment window at the marching prisoners. A delighted *Landser* picked them up and was promptly struck in the ribs with a rifle butt by his guard. "Tears filled our eyes at the sight of our warriors, young and old, ragged, shattered, worn out," the fourteen-year-old recalled. "Shaken and still thinking about it, we stood at the window for a long time long after the column had gone past." A mile to the south, thousands of German soldiers passed through the Ring, heading north. Most wore no shoes or boots, some were barefoot, others wrapped rags around their feet. All were hungry and thirsty. It was, thought travel agent Conrad Schumacher, "the perfect picture of human misery and the total collapse of the Wehrmacht". Some of the prisoners asked for water. Pails, buckets and cans were quickly fetched from cellars, and water distributed among several hundred men "before our actions were suddenly stopped by a lot of screaming, pistol shots and cracking of whips by the Russian guards".[54]

Peter Bannert had left the city behind and was marching, aimlessly it seemed, through the Lower Silesian countryside. By day the heat was unbearable – he cast his helmet aside. By night, the boys shivered. Bannert fell asleep even as he marched. "My legs moved mechanically," he remembered. "When the column stopped, I pushed against the man in front of me." The column of Hitler Youths, *Volkssturm* and soldiers passed Ohlau, eighteen miles south-east of Breslau. "Dead cattle, giving off an evil smell, lay everywhere. Here and there, a shot-up tank or a battered gun. The lane was muddy, we followed deep tank tracks," the fifteen-year-old recalled. "My head sank when I saw the caterpillar tracks in the mud and the boots of the man in front. A face suddenly stared back at me – bloated and jet black from the morass. His white eyes seemed to look at me sadly. Tanks had rolled over him in the mud." To raise morale, Hitler Youth leader Herbert Hirsch told his boys to sing:

> Frail bones in the world tremble in the face of the great war!
> We will continue to march until everything falls to pieces!

Silent, anxious people stood by the roadside. Some of them wiped tears from their eyes. Behind one window, someone raised their right arm to give the *Hitlergruss*. Poles with red-white armbands and rifles stood on the pavement, forcing back any Ohlau inhabitant who tried to hand the boys bread or water. "It was a grotesque scene," Bannert recalled. "Thousands of beaten German soldiers moved wearily through a town occupied by the enemy, yet echoing off the walls 'for today Germany belongs to us and tomorrow the entire world!'"[55]

Hans Gottwald was struck by Nature's orgy in the gardens on the north-western outskirts of Breslau. "Everything's sprouting and growing," he wrote. "The fruit trees are in full bloom and a blackbird occasionally sings." Such beauty and signs of spring merely made the prisoners' fate "even more tragic". There was no time to admire the wonders of Nature. The guards spurred the men on. Beyond Hundsfeld, the prisoners were ordered down a track until they came to a vast camp surrounded by barbed wire with watchtowers every hundred metres. Prisoners milled around between the wooden barrack blocks or dozed on the small patches of grass in the grounds: soldiers, Party officials, police, SS. Just a few weeks earlier, the last had guarded forced labourers in the same camp.[56]

Upon entering, a soldier's rucksack was searched by the camp police – Germans – who were overseen by Russian officers. Weapons, ammunition, maps, compasses, candles, all were seized, as well as "other items which caught the guards' eyes". Watches were surrendered in a "special ceremony". A large table covered with the Red Flag was set up in the middle of the camp. Prisoners handed over their watches to Russian officers and women in uniform before being presented with a receipt. Watches would be returned upon a prisoner's release, the officials explained. "Marshal Stalin does not want to profit from your watches." The receipts were meaningless. A few days later the German guards searched the prisoners' possessions once more. They seized the receipts. Life in Hundsfeld was repetitive rather than brutal. It was the food, or lack of it, which prisoners complained about most. Breakfast and evening 'meal' consisted of a slice of toast, sometimes burned, and a drink of something the guards called tea or coffee. Lunch was the principal meal – a watery soup, occasionally flavoured with cabbage, potato skins or sauerkraut, accompanied by bread which, if it tasted of anything, tasted of lubricating oil. A few prisoners supplemented their meagre food with the iron rations they had kept from the fighting. Many men went hungry, some died of exhaustion.[57]

Hundsfeld was not the only concentration camp filled with prisoners once more.

Breslau's defenders were also held at Fünfteichen, once the labour camp for Krupp's Berthawerk. It had been liberated nearly four months earlier, but there were still the corpses of forced workers littering its grounds. Fünfteichen's new occupants began to learn about the horrors of Nazi rule. They found the barracks infested with lice. They slept in the same bunks as concentration camp inmates had once used – bunks just twenty inches apart. And they found the kitchens simply could not cope with an influx of between 12,000 and 15,000 prisoners; there were pots and pans to cook for barely 1,000 inmates.[58]

Just as Fünfteichen had been brought back into use, so there was soon traffic along the railway line which ran past it. Every day sixteen-year-old Christian Lüdke watched trains roll past the camp heading east, packed with all manner of loot, from pianos to bicycles. He also saw trains carrying German prisoners "with anxious faces".[59] They came from Breslau.

In all, 1,135 officers and 43,728 men marched into captivity. They left behind more than 250 field guns and mortars, 1,750 machine-guns, 30,000 rifles, plus twenty armoured vehicles and nearly 350 cars and trucks. Some 50 panzers and *Sturmgeschütze* had been destroyed during the three-month siege, plus well over 120 mortars, guns and batteries, while Red Army anti-aircraft gunners reckoned they shot down in excess of 130 German aircraft and gliders.

As for the human cost of battle, a tally of dog tags suggests 5,663 men were killed defending Fortress Breslau. In March, seventy *Landsers* died every day. In April, sixty-five. An estimated 23,000 soldiers were wounded – 6,000 were being treated in the cellar hospitals on the day of capitulation alone. In short, more than half the soldiers and *Volkssturm* in Breslau became casualties. Soviet dead numbered fewer than 8,000: 763 officers buried on the southern edge of the city, 7,121 men in a large cemetery not far from Südpark.

There is little agreement on civilian losses. At least sixty-four soldiers and civilians were hanged or shot by fortress authorities, mostly for desertion or plundering, although the true figure is thought to be four times higher. Some 3,000 Breslauers committed suicide. A similar number were killed building Hanke's runway, although some estimates believe the figure was as high as 13,000. Total civilian dead numbered anywhere between 10,000 and 80,000 – the latter figure was provided by the senior doctor on the fortress's staff, Paul Mehling; he told his captors that 50,000 civilians died in the first six weeks of encirclement, 30,000 between Easter and the city's surrender. Thousands more died before the siege: 18,000 people froze during the Kanth death march while the corpses of 90,000 people were revealed in the ditches and fields of Lower Silesia when the ice and snow melted.[60]

The city they inhabited or defended suffered destruction greater than Berlin, greater even than Dresden – the byword for devastation in the popular memory of World War II. In twelve weeks of encirclement, the perimeter had been halved to around two dozen miles. Most of northern and eastern Breslau and the outlying villages were still in German hands – and largely intact. The same could not be said for the city's southern and western suburbs. The latter were all lost – Mochbern, Gandau, Gräbschen, and with them the airfield and Linke Hofmann works. In the south, the front line ran down the middle of Augustastrasse, cutting the city's finest boulevard, Strasse der SA, in two. Soviet troops stood less than half a mile from the central station and were contesting the yards of the Freiburger Bahnhof, barely half a mile from the Ring. Two-thirds of Breslau were in ruins, two-thirds of its industry damaged or destroyed. Two in every three homes or apartment blocks were no longer habitable. Seven out of ten high schools were in ruins. Almost the entire tram and rail network was wrecked, while every electricity line and three quarters of telephone wires were down. The water mains had been damaged or destroyed in 3,000 locations while the sewage system was broken in 7,000 places. Of the 400 miles of roads and streets in Breslau, nearly 200 were impassable, buried beneath 600 million cubic feet of rubble and ash. The Botanic Gardens had been ploughed up for ammunition bunkers, the Scheitniger Park scarred by trenches, bomb craters and mass graves. Four hundred of the six hundred memorials and monuments scattered around the city were gone. Other treasures fared no better. Most of the city's museums had been destroyed – although at least most of their collections had been evacuated. Little was left of Karl Hanke's former seat of power. The Oberpräsidium in the Palais Hatzfeld was hit by twenty-one bombs on Easter Monday alone. That other bastion of authority for much of the siege, the Liebichshöhe, had largely survived despite the pounding it received, with the exception of its ornate tower. The Jahrhunderthalle was mainly intact, so too the technical college and central station. The university was not so fortunate. Its southern wing and music hall were wrecked, its library badly damaged; only a fraction of the volumes it once held were not destroyed. At least the university's magnificent eighteenth-century baroque hall, the Aula Leopoldina, lived on. So too did the Rathaus, apart from several shell hits to its southern gable. Only one wing of the Schloss was still standing, while Neumarkt and Königsplatz were in ruins, as was most of the Dominsel. Breslau's many churches had suffered terribly during the siege: the Canisius and Luther had been flattened to make way for Hanke's runway, the Begräbnis, Bernhardin, Hedwig, Georg, Erlöser, Paulus, Savaltor, Trinitatis were all destroyed, the Adalbert, Annen, Barbara, Holz, Kreuz, Konrad, Mauritius, Michaelis, Nikolaus, Sand, Vincenz burned out, and the cathedral was seventy per cent destroyed.[61]

Such a scale of devastation was inevitable. Breslau lay under siege for more than eighty days, longer than every other fortress in the East: Danzig, Königsberg, Schneidemühl, Kolberg, Poznań and, of course, Berlin. Nazi propaganda talked about *Das Wunder von Breslau* – the miracle of Breslau. The fifteen-week defence of the city was no miracle. It was the result of a resolute, nay ruthless, German leadership, redoubtable defenders with a remarkable propensity for improvisation, but above all a lack of will on the part of the Soviets to crush the fortress on the Oder. Lack of will was compounded by less than inspired Soviet conduct of the battle. To be sure, Vladimir Gluzdovski was hampered by a lack of resources and reined in by Ivan Konev – especially after Easter. But the attacks Sixth Army did launch were poorly co-ordinated. Never did the Soviets attempt to squeeze the pocket from every side simultaneously; a concerted assault on the city – particularly on 1 or 2 April – would probably have caused Breslau's fall. Instead, Hans von Ahlfen and his successor Hermann Niehoff continued to tie down Soviet troops, slowing their westward advance, thus allowing thousands of civilians to reach safety before their towns and villages were captured. It is an argument which is only partly valid. Tie down the Red Army Breslau did – the fortress commanders believed the city was invested by a force three times the size of their garrison, 150,000 men in all (Soviet sources claim there were never more than 65,000 troops surrounding Breslau). But by Easter, the Soviet leadership had become quite content to leave barely 50,000 troops around Breslau, unleashing a force of more than two million men against Berlin. Fortress Breslau had become little more than an irritant to the Red Army.[62]

Three days after the Red Army marched into the capital of Silesia, posters began to appear on the city's walls – in many cases the remains of walls:

To the German populace

The criminal war begun by Hitler is over!
    Nazi propaganda terrified you with 'atrocities' which reportedly accompany the Red Army's march into Germany. The Nazis deliberately deceived you and slandered the Red Army when they claimed that it was the goal of the Red Army to wipe out the German people.
    The Red Army never had the task of wiping out the German people . . .
    No danger threatens the civilian populace in the area occupied by the Red Army.
    Only those who try to fight against the Red Army will be severely and brutally punished according to the laws of war . . .
    The Red Army brings peace for every German who has broken away from the Hitler clique and returned to peaceful work.[63]

A Russian major claimed the Red Army was bringing order to Breslau, while the *Izvestia* special correspondent assured his readers in the Motherland that "after the bitter, bloody fighting in Breslau, the great calm began".[64] There was no great calm in Breslau, no peace, no order. Not in the first few days after the surrender at any rate. Plunder, pillage and rape were the orders of the day.
    The occupier sought money, schnapps and women – "the latter were especially coveted" – recalled pharmacist Hanns Hoffmann (he might have added watches and bicycles to his list). Hoffmann had dismissed stories of assault and rape as Nazi propaganda. Now he realized they were not untrue. Women frequently came to him for medicine and recounted their horrific experiences. "Russians in groups of up to ten hunted down twelve-year-old girls, women were assaulted in such numbers that they were driven to the clinics because they were no longer able to walk, even seventy or eighty-year-old women were not spared by these fiends who apparently had no understanding of beauty or humanity," the chemist wrote. Many Breslauers were

convinced the Russians had been given free rein to rape and pillage. Some said for a few days, others a week, others still longer. At the very least, it seemed the people of Breslau were "considered fair game" by their new masters, former *Volkssturm* soldier Otto Rothkugel observed. To Rothkugel, the Russians were never Russians, never Soviets, never Ukrainians, never Mongols, Georgians, Uzbeks. They were always *Bestien* – beasts, a word which appears frequently in Breslauers' descriptions of the days following the surrender. "The Russians rooted out women from the cellars of bombed-out houses," Rothkugel wrote. "Cries of fear rang out when they arrived. They fell upon their defenceless victims like madmen." Whenever a Russian forced his way into houses in Conrad Schumacher's suburb of Wilhelmsruh in the north-east of the city, the occupant would rush into the street and cry for help. Neighbours would join them in the street and the shouting grew louder. "The entire district echoed with these cries," Schumacher remembered. "They were horrific to listen to, especially at night." Hendrik Verton watched as the Red Cross sister who had tended to his gunshot wound for the past ten days was raped by "several drunken Russians". The woman's fiancée, a medic in the same first aid post in Schweidnitzer Strasse, tried to stop them. He was beaten furiously. Not every woman of Breslau was a victim of the Red Army, however. As they had done during the siege, some women willingly slept with the soldiers to satisfy their lust or for personal gain. The uniforms of the masters had changed, but not human desires. And a handful of Breslauers simply resigned themselves to their fate. "It's always like this when victors enter a city," post official Conrad Bischof wrote. "Our soldiers have not and do not behave any differently in enemy territory."[65]

The city's underground communist, socialist and anti-fascist movements, who had welcomed the Red Army's arrival "in the warmest possible manner" quickly became disillusioned. "It did not matter whether someone had been a Fascist or anti-Fascist; all that mattered was that they were German!" decorator Georg Fritsch recalled bitterly. Fritsch had been an opponent of the Nazi regime and hoped the fact would curry favour with the city's new masters. It did not. Another Breslau communist was struck by the contradictory nature of the occupiers. A Russian soldier could "share his last piece of bread with German children" or a Russian truck driver could "pick up an old woman and her half-broken handcarts on a country lane and bring her home". But this was perhaps the same Russian who "lay in wait at a cemetery to attack women and young girls, to rob and rape them".[66]

The orgy was largely fuelled by alcohol. "So long as he is sober, one has almost never anything to fear," one report stated. "Only under the influence of alcohol and also when several are drunk together do the excesses begin." A Russian pilot touring the city encountered "shooting and general drunkenness" everywhere. Kegs of beer and wine were rolled into the street from cellars. Soldiers fired their pistols into the air, drinking their booty from pots and pails. "At every step there was the staggering body of a drunk." The flier regretted visiting Breslau. "It would have been better not to go," he sighed. Thirty soldiers were taken to hospital suffering from severe stomach cramps and blindness after drinking "a sweetish liquid". The sweetish liquid was methanol – anti-freeze – and the men had drunk between ten and thirty times the lethal dose. Each one died in agony.

More typically, the victims were Breslauers. A drunken tank commander picked up a boy and threw him into a burning building.

"Why did you do that? Of what was the child guilty?" an officer asked him.

"You just shut up captain!! Do you have children?"

"Yes."

"Well, they killed mine." [67]

Such crimes did not always go unpunished. In Zimpel, three Soviet soldiers were shot after being caught plundering or assaulting women. At dusk each night the Soviet commandant and two of his staff patrolled the streets to maintain order. And raiding Breslau's vast supplies of alcohol did not always lead to violence. One night the sick and wounded in First Aid Post No.5 in Schweidnitzer Strasse were ordered to gather in a cellar room, irrespective of their condition. The patients feared the worse. Instead, a drunken Russian soldier climbed on to a box and preached to the wounded soldiers and civilians about the achievements of communism for several hours. A *Landser* from Upper Silesia, fluent in Russian, was drafted in as translator – but he deliberately mistranslated the orator's words. "This drunken swine wants to teach us about culture," the translator explained. After each sentence, the 'audience' applauded enthusiastically. The speaker "was as happy as a child," unaware his words were being twisted. Finally he fell off the box and collapsed into a drunken sleep. His audience crept out of the room and back to their beds. [68]

Drunkenness, raping, pillaging, plundering. Arson was a natural progression. Official reports blamed German 'saboteurs' or Polish bandits for the fires. Neither was responsible. Accidently or wantonly, Soviet soldiers set what was left of Breslau aflame. "They entered closets with burning candles, tore everything out, and what they didn't take with them, they trampled on and set it ablaze," recalled Joachim Konrad. "If you didn't have the courage to act immediately your house burned."

It wasn't just Breslau's houses which burned. Librarian Friedrich Grieger had still not recovered from the shock of the Easter firestorm. He sat in the Botanical Gardens, in front of the ruins of his home – one of the countless victims of the conflagration a month before – "waiting for things to happen". He had grown accustomed to the smell of burning and the sight of towers of smoke rising above the city each day. Today, 11 May, the Sandkirche burned once more – it was ravaged by fire for three days which left ninety-five per cent of it destroyed. Huge dark clouds enveloped the church's blackened steeple while the May breeze carried small scraps of singed paper. Sometimes, larger pieces fell from the heavens. One landed at Friedrich Grieger's feet. Although partially burned, he immediately recognised it as a page from a university library catalogue, a catalogue which lay at the bottom of a pile of books in the Annenkirche. More than half a million volumes were destroyed. A few days later, the Oder bridges were reopened. Grieger headed straight for the Annenkirche. The church was a hollow ruin. Inside there was nothing but "one gigantic pile of waste paper".

The fire brigade was powerless to help. There were no modern engines; the men relied on three relics wheeled out of the fire service museum. Nor was there enough water to douse the flames, for the city's hydrants had collapsed. But then the sheer scale of the problem would have tested a fire brigade in peacetime. As late as one month after Breslau's surrender, Joachim Konrad counted up to thirty blazes a day. A voluntary fire watch saved his beloved Elisabethkirche – they barricaded the iron doors to the tower and found rags soaked in petrol before they could be set alight. The St Barbarakirche was not so fortunate. It fell victim to the flames on 11 May. The Church of St Maria Magdalena, two decades older than Cologne's great cathedral, survived until the seventeenth. Soviet troops emptied a barrel of petrol in the towers and set them alight. Both towers were burned out, so too the western side of the church and its magnificent organ. In the heat, the 550-year-old Armesünderglocke – poor sinner's bell – melted in its steel bellcage. Of the 113 hundredweight of bronze, just twenty-two hundredweight of almost worthless slag were found in the ruins.

Three days later, St Maria Magdalena's priest Ulrich Bunzel led the Whitsun service in the smoke-blackened vestry of his ruined church. He began with a prayer:

Now our Father's work goes under in rubble and horror.
What our ancestors achieved through many years of toil
Suddenly turns to ruins overnight,
And will only appear to our grandchildren in their dreams.[69]

Breslau *would* rise again. The grandchildren of Breslauers *would* see its towers and spires restored and rebuilt. But they would see the new Breslau as visitors, not as its inhabitants.

Notes

1. *Schlesische Tageszeitung*, 1/5/45 and Gleiss, v, p.24.
2. Majewski, p.115.
3. Gleiss, v, p.57.
4. Ibid., v, p.65.
5. News of Hitler's death in Franke, pp.132-3, Gleiss, viii, p.1227, Gleiss, v, p.51 and Gleiss, v, p.54.
6. *Schlesische Tageszeitung*, 3/5/45 and Documenty Nr.274, 276.
7. Becker, p.149.
8. Gleiss, viii, p.1236.
9. Gleiss, v, pp.91, 94, 161, 238, *Schlesische Tageszeitung*, 2/5/45, and *So Kämpfte Breslau*, pp.107-8.
10. Based on Hornig, pp.214-16, 218, Konrad, p.17, *So Kämpfte Breslau*, p.108 and Gleiss, v, p.185.
11. Gleiss, v, p.204.
12. Ibid., v, pp.222-5, 231.
13. Ibid., v, p.236.
14. Ibid., v, pp.233-4, 236 and *So Kämpfte Breslau*, p.107.
15. Based on Gleiss, v, pp.243, 245, Hartung, p.90 and Völkel, p.83.
16. *Wrocławska epopeja*, p.87.
17. Gleiss, v, pp.246-61, 685.
18. Gleiss, v, p.482 and Gleiss, viii, p.1432.
19. *Schlesische Tageszeitung*, 6/5/45.
20. Gleiss, v, p.289.
21. Ibid., v, pp.326, 327.

22. Ibid., v, pp.289, 301.
23. *So Kämpfte Breslau*, p.111.
24. Terp, pp.76-7; Gleiss, v, p.626.
25. Gleiss, iii, p.202 and Gleiss, v, pp.385-7.
26. Bannert, p.93.
27. Gleiss, v, pp.394, 395-6.
28. Ibid., v, p.393.
29. Based on Gleiss, v, pp.416, 424 and *So Kämpfte Breslau*, pp.109-10.
30. *Izvestia*, 8/5/45.
31. Gleiss, v, pp.394, 395-6.
32. Franke, pp.140-1, 145.
33. Gleiss, v, p.453.
34. Ibid., v, p.447.
35. *So Kämpfte Breslau*, p.111.
36. Jerrig, p.59, Gleiss, v, pp.432, 468.
37. *Wrocławska epopeja*, p.86.
38. Gleiss, viii, p.1307.
39. Hornig, p.231.
40. Gleiss, v, p.493 and Hornig, p.231.
41. Gleiss, v, p.433.
42. Hornig, pp.231-2.
43. Kaps, *Martyrium und Heldentum ostdeutscher Frauen*, pp.37-8.
44. Waage, p.47 and Haas, ii, pp.244-5.
45. Konrad, p.19; see also Gleiss, iv, plates 42-4.
46. Kaps, *Martyrium und Heldentum ostdeutscher Frauen*, pp.37-8.
47. Gleiss, v, pp.564-5.
48. Franke, pp.168-70.
49. Gleiss, v, pp.542, 570.
50. Majewski, pp.135-6.
51. Kaps, *Martyrium und Heldentum ostdeutscher Frauen*, pp.37-8, 39-40.
52. *Izvestia*, 8/5/45, Majewski, p.136 and *Microcosm*, p.408.
53. Gleiss, v, p.785.
54. Ibid., v, pp.810, 966.
55. Bannert, pp.96-7.
56. Gleiss, viii, p.1473.
57. Gleiss, v, pp. 680, 837, 839.
58. Gleiss, viii, pp.1317-18.
59. Gleiss, v, p.779.
60. Casualties based on Gleiss, v, pp.1088-1101, Gleiss, ix, pp.400-03, Peikert, p.272 and *So Kämpfte Breslau*, p.118.
61. Level of destruction based on Gleiss, v, pp.1103-29, Gleiss, viii, pp.1527-8 and Thum, p.180.
62. *So Kämpfte Breslau*, p.112, 118-19 and Majewski, pp.131, 133.
63. Becker, pp.158-9.
64. Gleiss, v, p.571 and *Izvestia*, 8/5/45.
65. Russian actions based on Gleiss, v, pp.565, 582, 734, 944, Vertreibung, ii, pp.344-5, and Gleiss, viii, pp.1417, 1452.
66. Gleiss, viii, p.1423 and Vertreibung, ii, pp.327, 344-5.
67. Naimark, pp.112, 113 and Gleiss, v, p.1003.
68. Gleiss, v, pp.566, 742.
69. Fires based on Gleiss, v, pp.799, 911, 941, Konrad, p.19 and Thum, pp.173-5.

CHAPTER 9

The Land of the Dead

The future of our people appears to be an unparalleled
life of suffering and sacrifice
Paul Peikert

On the afternoon of Wednesday, 9 May, a truck made its way along the lanes and highways of Silesia. It had pulled out of Krakow early that morning carrying thirteen men, supplies for several days and the Polish standard. In the coming days more lorries would make the 160-mile journey carrying a hundred volunteers in all – hoteliers, clergy, journalists, filmmakers, academics, university lecturers, teachers, doctors, experts from utility companies, builders, electricians – a 'Noah's Ark' of pioneers who would lay the foundations for the city's rebirth. A dozen miles from their destination, the passengers spied columns of black smoke rising on the horizon to the south. As they drew closer, the clouds rose higher, fires were also visible now. "All of Breslau seemed to be in flames," Kazimierz Kuligowski recalled uneasily. In the suburbs, the vehicle edged its way around barricades. Soviet troops warned the driver not to stray on to the pavements – they were probably mined. The truck followed Oppelner Strasse and Tauentzienstrasse while the passengers stared at the city in disbelief. "Breslau burned, the streets were buried beneath the ruins of houses still on fire," wrote Kuligowski. "We heard the exploding of ammunition, set off by the fires. We got lost in the burning streets, weaving our way until we could no longer go any further." The men continued on foot. After several hours of wandering through smoke and fire, they eventually reached the headquarters of the city's Soviet commandant, Colonel Lapunov, in Ritterplatz. There they were advised to find quarters in the relatively undamaged district around Waterlooplatz, near the Dominsel. The visitors located three apartment blocks in Blücherstrasse, numbers 23, 25 and 27. They were occupied by Breslauers, but no matter. In twenty minutes, all but one of the inhabitants – a baker who would provide fresh bread in the days to come – had been evicted. At around 6pm, the Polish standard was fixed to the outside of the building and the red-white flag raised. It was the first act of a terrible drama which would turn German Breslau into Polish Wrocław.[1]

Few of Breslau's German inhabitants noticed this *pièce de théâtre*. They were preoccupied with preventing their possessions being stolen by drunken Red Army soldiers, preventing their properties, their churches, their convents being set alight, preventing their daughters, sisters, mothers being raped. They registered their belongings – pianos, bicycles, radios, typewriters, sewing machines – with their new masters. It soon became apparent why. Trucks pulled up outside blocks and apartments stripped of their possessions, which were carried on the wagons to waiting goods trains. This looting was sanctioned. But there was unofficial looting as well. Kalmucks, Tartars, and Kirghiz were particularly skilled in locating some of the valuables Breslau's citizens had hidden. They were rather less skilled in hiding them. They smashed their way into the vaults of Pohlanowitz cemetery, tossed out the decaying cadavers, and filled the now-empty mausoleums with their booty.

Besides registering their possessions with headquarters established on every block, Breslauers registered their personal details. Each morning, some days at 5am, others at 6.30, they reported in their hundreds for work details. They replaced sleepers and filled in bomb craters on the railway lines; two thousand men women and children were sent to the Linke-Hofmann works to dismantle equipment; they were sent to the Oder to salvage barges which had been sunk by German troops to block the channel. Everyone aged between fourteen and sixty had to work. Work meant food; payment for ten days' labour was one pound of bread.

There had been plenty of food in Breslau when the city fell – enough to feed the 130,000 or so Germans estimated to be living amid the ruins. But in the chaos of the days following the city's surrender the warehouses were emptied. Migrants, prisoners, thieves, forced labourers, soldiers, all plundered the stores.[2] Every day, scores of Germans returned to Breslau – refugees from the winter evacuations, displaced civilians, soldiers. They came from the rest of Silesia, the Sudetenland, sometimes Poland. There was no one to cater for these *Rückwanderer* – returning travellers – no one to organize accommodation. The consequences were chaotic. "Everyone gets what they need from apartments which are still standing empty," wrote twenty-five-year-old Annelies Matuszczyk. "One cart after the next rolls through the streets, old prams, bicycle trailers, carts, trolleys and panel vans. It's an organization like you'd find in an anthill. Everyone digs, burrows and looks for something useful. There's no authority."[3]

There *was* authority in Breslau. It was Polish. And in many cases it would treat Breslau's Germans as the Nazis had once treated Poles.

Barely a fortnight after the low-key Soviet victory parade on Gandau airfield, the city's pioneering Polish settlers were urged to converge on Schlossplatz, now renamed Plac Wolności – Freedom Square. After marching on Berlin and defeating the "Hitlerist hydra", the men of 10th Infantry Division were returning to Wrocław to stand guard on the Oder. "Fulfil your civic duty," posters urged. "Come in great numbers to the festive square to demonstrate your respect for our army returning from Berlin, Dresden and other German cities with the flags of victory." It was an eclectic group which gathered in front of the ruins of Frederick the Great's palace: academics, railway workers, militia. "My eyes well up," the city's 'president' of two weeks, Bolesław Drobner, told his audience. "I can hardly believe that Polish forces are standing on the old Schlossplatz and that we can sing *Jeszcze Polska nie zginęła* ['Poland is not yet lost' – the national anthem] and that I can speak in the name of the Polish Government; and yet this is real."[4]

More Russians than Poles heard Bolesław Drobner speak that Saturday. And 'real' though the moment was, the Polish foothold in Wrocław – pronounced *vrots-waf*; the name, like Breslau, traces its roots back to Vratislav I – was precarious. The borders of Europe would be re-drawn in the aftermath of Hitler's war, to be sure, Poland's chief among them. Indeed, long before the war's end, Stalin had insisted Poland's boundaries would be shifted. At Teheran in 1943, the marshal had demanded that eastern Poland – the lands annexed when the Red Army invaded in 1939 – become a permanent part of the Soviet Union: the western Ukraine, Byelorussia, the lands around Wilno. Poland would be compensated with German soil: Danzig, much of East and West Prussia, and Upper and Lower Silesia. In short, the new Poland would 'shuffle' westwards, its frontier coming to a rest along the Oder and Neisse rivers. But none of this was set in stone. None of this had been formally agreed by the Allied powers. The task of Bolesław Drobner and his pioneers was to 'Polonize' the city as quickly as possible so that when the Allies did meet, Breslau would already be Wrocław.

Posters began to appear in railway stations across Poland with promises of an Eldorado in the West, a land where the farmer "lives like a prince". One appeal declared:

Fellow countrymen!

The might of the Third Reich lies in ruins. Lands first stolen from us by Crusaders, then Bismarck and Hitler, are returning to the mother country. The [former] conqueror has fled across the Oder and has left behind villages and towns, estates and factories, well-tilled fields, ponds and gardens. These depopulated lands are waiting for us – the rightful inhabitants.

Farmers!
    There's no need to emigrate overseas any more. The new Poland has land enough for you, your property for eternity.
    Do you want bread? There's bread in the West!
    Do you want land? There's land in the West!
    The urban population will find workshops and business abandoned by the Germans in the West, professionals will find work in offices and bureaux.
    Fellow countrymen!
    Go west![5]

Thousands did. As in January, the lanes of Silesia were filled with people on the move, carts and wagons, but this time it was Poles not Germans heading west, in hope not out of fear. They found no Eldorado. "The closer we got, the more our fear worsened," one settler remembered. "All around us were fires, mountains of rubble and towering ruins. This city is almost dead!" He was filled with "consternation and growing dejection". Above all, one question raced through his mind: Why have we come here?[6]

Other settlers came by train – but not directly to Breslau; the bridge over the Weide was still not repaired. Instead, the trains halted in a marshy field outside Hundsfeld. The journey was often tortuous. The carriages were overcrowded – some people even tried to sit on the roof. Compartments had no floors. Passengers swung their feet on the benches, staring at the track and sleepers passing beneath them. When the train came to a halt outside Hundsfeld, the settlers stepped out into a field littered with carts, prams, bicycles. As they got off, other Poles got in, stuffing the carriages with pictures, carpets, bedding, anything which they had been able to plunder. The Konopińska family grabbed a blue pram, filled it with their possessions and made for the eastern suburb of Bischofswalde; the father of the family had 'reserved' a semi-detached property there on his first visit to the city. Tadeusz Konopińska had predicted this day since 1942. One day, he told friends, he would teach agriculture in Breslau's university. "In Breslau?" his friends laughed. "Do you know how the war will turn out? You view things too optimistically, professor!" Tadeusz Konopińska relished a return to Breslau, where he had studied and lectured before the war, rather more than his twenty-year-old daughter Joanna. She would have preferred to remain in Poznań and continue her history studies. Joanna's first impressions of Breslau did nothing to dull such feelings. "A huge cloud of dust hung over the city," she recalled. "The air was filled with the smell of burning." The family passed cherry trees and roses in full bloom, a sofa abandoned in a garden, three upturned military vehicles, apartments with all their windows blown out, fresh graves marked by simple wooden crosses. Despite the slaughter of many of the creatures in February, there were still animals in the zoo. A couple of zebras trotted behind the fence and there was an awful bellowing coming from somewhere in the zoo grounds. In the middle of the road, a wrecked yellow tram, the tracks twisted and reaching for the sky. There were rags, paper, a handbag, photographs scattered across the road. A little further on, an emaciated horse pulled a cart. The driver kicked a corpse off it into a mass grave. "The awful stench drifted towards us. I wanted to get away from all this evil and that very moment I wanted to return."

Finally, the Konopińskas reached Heinzelmännchenweg and their new home. There was no gas, no electricity. Every window was boarded up. When the boards were removed, Joanna recalled, "the decay and chaos throughout the apartment became apparent". She continued in her diary:

> In the kitchen there were still dirty dishes in the sink, clothes and towels covered in dust hung on a line, over the back of a chair hung a white-and-blue-striped apron. The flowers on the windowsill had dried up, only the cacti flourished – one was even in bloom...
>
> After supper, which consisted of bread baked in oil, we sat on the balcony. It was already dark, a light wind blew, catching the branches of the trees, and lifting up the scent of the roses in the garden. It was very quiet and it seemed to us as if we were completely alone in this dead city.[7]

Bolesław Drobner would argue that this was not a dead city. The city president used the inaugural edition of the first Polish newspaper, *Nasz Wrocław* – Our Wrocław – to outline the achievements of one month of Polish rule: the first bus service was operating, there was a limited supply of electricity and fresh water; the cinemas would soon open – the first film, *Majdanek*, a documentary about the liberation of the death camp near Lublin, was shown on 16 June; the trams would be running imminently (in fact, early August); schools would re-open for the new academic year on 1 September, followed later in the autumn by the university (they did). The city president praised the 2,000 or so Poles who had already settled in the city – "you can call them pioneers of Polishness". He continued: "We, people from the Vistula, came to these ruins to build a new Polish Wrocław in keeping with the tradition of the Silesian piasts."[8]

Despite Drobner's high ideals and grandiose words, life in his city was chaotic. "The traditional sounds in Breslau" during the first weeks of Polish rule, recalled settler Andrzej Jochelson, were "shooting, the thunder of exploding mines and in between the songs of nightingales, the cries of swallows and the twitter of sparrows". Jochelson passed the corpse of a German railway worker, lying in the street. The only dignity permitted the man was a curtain wrapped around his head. No one took the body away. "People were busy clearing artillery shells from the thoroughfare, throwing them into the ruins of houses. Perhaps a shell exploded. Perhaps it was a mine. Or perhaps this person had simply been shot dead." It was likely the latter, for Breslau was quickly earning a reputation for lawlessness. The streets beyond the main railway station were regarded as particularly unruly. Gangs lived in the ruins. Not a night passed without nearby homes being raided and someone being shot. "Our people were dragged into the ruins and robbed by the hundreds," one German priest protested. "If they tried to defend themselves or called for help, they were simply beaten to a pulp or shot." Night after night, the streets resounded to cries for help or the hellish sound of cooking pot lids being banged to drive the plunderers away. Even the dead were afforded no rest. Graves were dug up and gold teeth pulled out of corpses. The plunder was sent east, on trains – as Joanna Konopińska discovered at Hundsfeld – or on the highways and lanes of Silesia. The road from Breslau to Oels – barely eighteen miles away – was, remembered Alfred Görny on the staff of the civic administration, "one long chain of people. People with wagons and on foot, some heading for Breslau, some for Oels. Gas-powered bathroom boilers, bathtubs, kitchenware and the devil knows what other things were the plunderer's booty." Poles soon branded Breslau *Dziki Zachód* – the Wild West – as Joanna Konopińska learned. "Can we live here?" a Ukrainian settler asked the student. "Isn't it too dangerous?" Joanna said nothing. "So it's true then," she recorded in her diary. "Lower Silesia is regarded as the Wild West or Mexico by central Poland. Not entirely without justification."[9]

   There were, of course, law enforcers in Breslau, militiamen, but they brought little order to the city. When a sixty-year-old German inhabitant failed to return from laying flowers on his daughter's grave, his family set off in search. At the cemetery they found a large pile of leaves next to the grave. They frantically brushed the leaves away to find the man, stripped of his suit and shoes and shot. The police showed no interest. "We have several such cases every day," an official told them. That week alone, some twenty Germans were killed. To most Breslauers, it seemed the militia – "rowdy louts dressed in leather or military jackets with rifles and revolvers," in the words of one observer – were more interested in joining in the plunder than maintaining order. Four militia barged into St Heinrichkirche, ostensibly looking for hidden weapons and radios. They found neither. They did, however, deprive the Catholic priest of all his clothes, even his handkerchiefs. When he reported the theft to the authorities, they merely sneered. "You're a German so you don't have any possessions any more. We'll take what we need." It was not an uncommon response. Whenever Breslauers protested, they heard: "German soldiers took everything away like this in Poland", or "Quiet, German pig." Poles forced their way into Friedrich Mondwurf's apartment "more than once" and took his mother and older sister away. "Powerless and full of horror I had to watch as they were taken away from us under the threat of force," the schoolboy remembered. "And always the anxious question: will they come back unharmed?" To protect themselves, the city's German populace barricaded themselves in their homes at night, placing boards under front-door handles so they could not be forced open. Frequently, Soviet troops intervened on the Germans' behalf. But occasionally, Breslauers took matters into their own hands. When a young woman was dragged out of her apartment in Benderplatz and raped by Poles, the entire district rose up. "We Germans are not fair game," a spokesman declared. "We want protection and help! We need food! Otherwise the people will stop working."[10]

The demand for food was a common one. Those who worked earned food, but the rations were minimal – barely one-third of what Poles were given. Very small children received less than one pint of milk every two days, but otherwise Germans rummaged in the rubble and in cellars for old potatoes, picked corn from the fields and tried to find food in any way they could. "Those who don't want to starve are forced to hunt for food, that is to say, from cellar to cellar, from ruin to ruin, often with the threat of collapse. We look, hoping to find something edible," Annelies Matuszczyk recalled. She was successful. Beneath the ash in several collapsed cellars, she found some old potatoes. "At the moment they're our only source of food." Twelve-year-old Friedhelm Mondwurf was entranced by the sight of Russian soldiers with their horses camped on the few green spaces in the city not scarred by war. "I soon began to mingle with them," he recalled. "Depending on their mood they'd curse and chase me, or embrace me – perhaps I reminded them of their own children." Friedhelm would sing songs for them. The Soviet troops swigged vodka and spurred him on. Soon he was "spinning around like a dancing bear". After each song, he held out his hand and the soldiers offered some of their rations – black bread, a few ounces of sugar wrapped in strips of newspaper, a piece of bacon. After a couple of draws on strong Russian cigarettes, the boy collapsed exhausted. "With my last ounce of strength, I made my way home, full of pride, and couldn't understand why my mother burst into tears," he wrote. "But we survived." While Germans begged, stole or rummaged for food, in Breslau's Polish-run shops, one report noted, "there's everything the heart desires – meat, butter, bacon, eggs, bread etc." There was one snag. Only Polish currency, Złoty, was accepted. Germans could convert their Reichsmarks into Złoty, but the exchange rate was punishing. The Reichsmark was devalued 120-, 150-, sometimes even 200-fold. Before the war, Breslauers could buy one kilo of butter for 4 marks; in June 1945, the price ranged anywhere from 320 to 880 marks. Bread, once 30 Pfennigs, would cost at least 60 marks. Medicines were similarly expensive – a single aspirin tablet cost perhaps 15 marks, a bottle of child's cough mixture 50 marks – while doctors charged up to 30 Złoty for each consultation.[11]

Germans resorted to selling what possessions they still had on the thriving black market. The wasteland in Kaiserstrasse, now renamed Plac Grunwaldzki, became the unofficial heart of the city. Germans and Poles, civic officials and militia, all jostled for bargains in what they dubbed *Szaberplac* – Plunderers' square. "A painter could take inspiration for all his work here: there are so many different characters and races here," Annelies Matuszczyk wrote. "There's haggling, bartering for every Złoty and cheating." The square was littered with scrap iron, old cars, bicycles, smashed glassware and ornaments. The Polish settler could find anything in *Szaberplac*: dinner sets, individual plates, cups, pots, quilts, duvets, cutlery, pictures, typewriters, sewing machines, cameras, shoes, clothes, vases, crystal, vacuum cleaners. Bacon, sausage, ham, meat, cakes, butter, cigarettes and tobacco were laid out on stalls, while Polish women squatted on the ground offering fruit, vegetables, chickens and geese. No one bought goods with money, they merely bartered. Sugar was particularly valuable, so too tea and coffee, and alcohol – vodka and cognac especially – even more so. Joanna Konopińksa went in search of a meat grinder, taking two bottles of cooking oil and a bag of sugar as barter. She found no grinder, but she did swap her oil for a set of bed linen, while the sugar was exchanged for a pair of winter shoes. "I then cursed myself for that deal because right in front of me a woman got a fur jacket for the same amount of sugar." At night, the square emptied, leaving behind mountains of rubbish. Next morning, the traders gathered once more and the bartering resumed.[12]

Bartering and the black market could not save Breslauers for long. By the end of July 1945, the city was gripped by what priest Johannes Kaps called "a hunger catastrophe". The old and the very young were particularly affected; Kaps estimated nine out of ten babies died from starvation. Schoolboy Horst Gleiss regularly passed elderly – and sometimes young – people sitting by the roadside; they had fallen asleep through hunger or exhaustion. "Children, who are normally so wild and noisy, sit in the midday sun, hungry and sluggish, far too weak for frivolous playing," he wrote. Those who did not succumb to hunger, succumbed to typhus, dysentery and diphtheria. Scraps of yellow cloth were hung outside cellars or houses where disease struck – a warning to other Breslauers: do not enter. At least three dozen Germans were dying daily. Paul Peikert reckoned the figure was closer to three or four hundred. "Old people and children are dying like flies," the priest told a friend. Newborn babies were all but condemned to death. "Mothers could not silence them since they had no food," a former estate agent recalled. There was no bathing water, no clean laundry, no way of caring for a child since most of their mothers had to work." Young or old, there were no coffins. The corpses were wrapped in blankets – but even these were stolen during the night by bandits. Mortuary attendants arrived in the morning to find the bodies naked. "Almost every day completely naked, battered, skeletal corpses were delivered to the cemetery," one priest remembered. Funeral services at one of the two cemeteries in use – the rest were still mined – were often interrupted by marauders who fired their guns indiscriminately and even raped female mourners. In many cases, Breslauers simply buried the dead next to their properties – as they had done during the siege. It wasn't the only phenomenon from the days of encirclement which was repeated. "The number of suicides rises alarmingly," Johannes Kaps observed in August 1945. "It would be even higher if there was cooking gas."

The city's leaders – Polish and Soviet – were not oblivious to the plight of the German populace. Around 1,500 Germans demonstrated outside one labour office on the edge of the city centre, refusing to work without adequate food. The arrival of the militia merely inflamed the situation – they wanted to open fire on the demonstrators. It took Soviet troops and the mollifying words of a Polish official to quieten the unrest. "As they have nothing with which to pay, the Germans are dying without medical assistance, their children especially," a civic official reported. To labour the point, one woman laid her child on the desk of the city's commandant, Colonel Lapunov; it died in front of him. Another Breslauer even wrote to Stalin. The city's German inhabitants were being starved by the Poles, she protested. The death-rate was rising alarmingly. These were valid points, but the letter was laced with traditional German contempt for the Pole. Breslauers, she claimed, were possessed by a single wish – "to be free of the Poles", so much so they would rather have the Russians in charge. "Reconstruction can never be carried out by the Poles with the energy it requires," the letter's author complained. "Silesia is not a suitable land for the Polish nation. To whom is reconstruction dearer than the Silesian himself?" Her letter never got beyond the city's Polish administration. "The same methods of extermination which we used against other peoples are being used against us," Paul Peikert commented, "only with the outward appearance of humanity that the Russians and Poles do not murder senselessly, as our Waffen SS and Gestapo did in the occupied territory to the horror of the entire world. But the outcome is still the same."[13]

And the war continued to claim its victims, too. Walter Lassmann was asked to consecrate a grave on the railway embankment in Ohlewiesen on the south-eastern edge of the city. Three children found a *Panzerfaust* while playing and set it off. All three were killed instantly. The two German dead were buried in the cemetery, the third child – the ten-year-old son of a Russian officer stationed in Breslau – was laid to rest where the accident occurred, according to Russian custom. At least two hundred people were killed or injured after stepping on mines around Steinstrasse, where there had been particularly bitter fighting. The room which served as a hospital for SS trooper Hendrik Verton and other wounded prisoners near Universitätsbrücke was severely shaken by a tremendous series of explosions. The makeshift ward was turned upside down. Plaster fell off the walls. The water level of the nearby Oder had fallen, exposing shells, grenades and *Panzerfaust* tossed into the river after surrender. In the summer heat, they had detonated.[14]

Death by starvation. Death by disease. Death by suicide. Plundered and pillaged. Raped. Beaten. Murdered. Forced to pawn their possessions. It was hardly surprising, as one observer noted in the summer of 1945, that "emotionally, the Germans in Breslau are slowly dying."[15] To Paul Peikert, it seemed that the Almighty was passing judgment:

> The future of our people appears to be an unparalleled life of suffering and sacrifice. What has the despicable Nazi regime done to the German people? Now we must atone for the atrocities and crimes which this regime committed as it smashed and trampled on God's laws.[16]

At the end of June, Hugo Hartung was led with a group of prisoners towards the city centre, across Hindenburgbrücke then along Matthiasstrasse where "smashed apartments lie open like dolls houses. The family portraits are still on the walls, there are tidy kitchens, high up and inaccessible, a polished black piano, exposed to downpours and the cool nights, out of tune and silent". Hartung crossed Universitätsbrücke and glanced at the Sandinsel where there were "only the bleak remains of once-perfect beauty", then he walked past the partially ruined university and its wrecked music hall. "Where once an organ sounded, where a Viennese string quartet played its sweet yet melancholic melody, death and Fate have prevailed and destroyed beauty which seemed created for eternity." He stared at the ruins of the Matthiaskirche where just six months earlier his children had looked in wonder at the mangers. Then a blanket of snow had covered the city. Now Breslau was buried beneath a layer of dust and ash and the streets were filled with a sweet smell of burning. The Ring no longer pulsed with life. The streets running off it were dead too. A handful of people moved down Schweidnitzer Strasse, once Breslau's principal shopping street. "Shop windows have just one thing on display to passers-by: ashes and the remains of charred beams." His beloved opera house still stood. Only slightly damaged. "They'll perform in it one day," Hartung convinced himself.[17]

The former chief dramatist at the opera house had spent the eight weeks since surrender in a prison camp-cum-hospital in the northern suburb of Karlowitz. He had still not recovered from the exhaustion and fever which had dogged his later days in the fortress. For that reason, he was released – a fate shared by fewer than one in twenty of Breslau's defenders, mainly the elderly and infirm. The rest spent several weeks at Fünfteichen and Hundsfeld – in all some 300,000 prisoners passed through the two transit camps, 15,000 at any one time – before being moved on. Food was meagre. Sanitary conditions were dreadful. Yet otherwise life in Fünfteichen and Hundsfeld was basic, not inhuman. Former Hitler Youths received schooling from their former teachers, minus text books. Choirs were formed, performing everything from hymns and opera to popular tunes from films. In one of the barracks at Fünfteichen, there was political instruction in the ways of the new Europe from members of the National Committee for Free Germany; portraits of Paulus and Seydlitz – two generals captured at Stalingrad who had subsequently turned against the Nazi regime – hung on the wall. But at the end of July, rumours began to circulate through both transit camps. The barracks began to empty. In Hundsfeld, Hans Gottwald watched groups of 400 or 500 men at a time form up, then march out of the gate every few days and be loaded on to trains. "There's a rumour that they're going to East Prussia to gather the harvest," wrote Gottwald. "We don't believe it." Prisoners were never told where the trains were heading. They knew only that they "went east, not west for the reconstruction of our homeland," Erich Schönfelder observed. They were sent to the Caucasus, to Karelia, to the Ukraine, to the Don and the Volga. The method of transport was almost always the cattle truck. The journey might last eleven days or in some cases eight weeks. A fortunate few were released, like *Volkssturm* man Otto Pohl, whose weight had dropped seventy-two pounds in captivity. He did not relish his new-found freedom. "I am one of the poorest of the poor because the Russians took everything from us," he wrote to a friend. "I possess only what I have on me. It is very bitter at the age of fifty to start all over again."[18]

As Hundsfeld and Fünfteichen emptied, Kletschkau prison in the heart of Breslau was filling up once more, under new ownership. Ex-Nazis, saboteurs, dissenters and dissidents and criminals were locked up – in most cases without trial. As many as 8,000 people were held in a jail intended for 500 prisoners. Perhaps as many as one in three never saw their families again. There were six men in each cell measuring eight square yards. On the floor were three straw mattresses – two prisoners had to share each one. A bucket sufficed for calls of nature; it was emptied each night through the barred window. There was no heating. In the winter, numerous inmates suffered, or died from, frostbite. Hundreds more went hungry, for the only food was a watery broth which was so weak the prisoners did not need to use the spoons the guards gave them. Whenever the cart brought fodder for the prison horses, the inmates would rush it and eat what raw potatoes they could grab before the driver's whip forced them away. It was not the only beating the prisoners suffered. Inmates were forced to call out their names and numbers in Polish; any man who did not received thirty strokes to the face. "Not a day passed without a cell door being flung open and someone being kicked out," one recalled. "Every day we asked ourselves if we'd get out of this house of torture alive." Eighteen-year-old Hubertus Kindler remembered how the guards "beat the soles of my feet with sticks. The pain was terrible. At first I cried, but then I could not feel anything any more. My feet were so swollen that I could not run any more. I crawled around the cellar on my hands and knees and was still trodden upon." Kindler was thrown in Kletschkau prison for laying a mine – he claimed it was a slab of beeswax. A military court sentenced him to execution as a saboteur. He awaited his fate in Wing 2a – death row. "Shots repeatedly echoed along the corridors," he wrote.

> What saved me this whole time were the many prayers which my mother had taught me. I was no longer very religious, of course, that had been driven out of us in the *Hitlerjugend*, but I composed prayers in my own way. I asked the Lord to give me a sign if I still had any chance of a sign. I did not know what kind of sign it would be. Suddenly a great tit went for the bars in front of the window. It sat there for a long time and looked straight at me – as if it was the sign, as if

it wanted to say: I bring you the news you've been longing for.

After several months in Kletschkau prison, Kindler's sentence was commuted to fifteen years' hard labour in Pomerania. He was finally released in 1956. By then, Breslau had long since been cleansed of Germans.[19]

To thousands of Germans, Breslau and Silesia still offered sanctuary. Displaced and evacuated by the war, sent west in the face of the Red Army, by mid-summer 1945 they were streaming eastwards, driven by a single thought: *Heimat* – home. Most got no further than the Oder or the Neisse. The small city of Görlitz, which straddles the Neisse ninety miles west of Breslau, was the centre of the maelstrom. Each day, an estimated 20,000 people arrived in the city. And there they stayed – they were not permitted to cross the river. Görlitz could not cope. The authorities erected signs on the edge of the city, urging people to turn back. "If you do not heed this warning, you are at risk of death from starvation."[20] People did not heed the warning, among them Richard Süssmuth, trying to reach Penzig, a few miles downstream from Görlitz on the right bank of the Neisse. Conditions in the city were every bit as black as the posters warned. "The inhabitants of Görlitz look like walking corpses – waxen, gaunt and emaciated like skeletons," Süssmuth wrote. Every day carts collected the corpses of people who had starved. Süssmuth counted 46 coffins on one passing wagon, 114 in Görlitz's Nikolaikirche – the dead from just two days. Notices were fixed to every tree, every front door:

> *Residents of Wohlau! Richard Höhne and family have moved on in the direction of Niesky. Whoever finds our daughter Marianne Höhne, give her this message.*

> *Residents of Güntersdorf! We have found Hans and Joachim from the family of Willi Einer found, taken them with us and are heading and are heading towards Bautzen and Saxony.*

An endless column of "ragged, starved and robbed people" streamed westwards through the city, pushing what meagre possessions they had left on hand carts or hauling them on horse-drawn carts – minus the horses. "This rope is all I have left," one man muttered. "They took everything away from me but they left me this rope with which I shall surely hang myself today." Those coming from the east bank of the Neisse urged Silesians hoping to return home to go no further. "Turn around – there's no point continuing," they insisted. "You cannot cross the Neisse. The Poles will take everything from you. They will steal from you as they stole from us and throw you out of Silesia. Go back to where you've come from." People did not listen. Scenes on the banks of the Oder were chaotic and horrific. The columns of carts stretched back for miles on both sides of the river. Polish militia shot anyone trying to force their way across to the east bank. Süssmuth watched six women from his home town shot in the river. And on the right bank he observed Polish soldiers plundering carts, unharnessing horses, stealing luggage.[21]

Those who did manage to slip across the Neisse entered "the land without security, the land without laws, the land of the outlaws, the *Totenland* – land of the dead," wrote journalist Robert Jungk. Beyond the river lay "ransacked towns, villages ravaged by epidemics, concentration camps, barren untended fields, streets littered with corpses where robbers lurk and deprive refugees of their last possessions". The deeper he went into Silesia, the more common "the huge posters at the edge of villages with warnings in Latin and Cyrillic characters: TYPHUS". Jungk, a German émigré who had fled Berlin when the Nazis seized power in 1933, wrote of "a veritable wave of suicides sweeping the land," "girls, women and old women raped in public by members of the Polish militia," of vast swathes of Silesia with not a single child aged under twelve months "because they all starved or were beaten to death". This was not atrocity propaganda, he told readers of the Zürich *Weltwoche*. "We have rightly condemned Germans for closing their eyes to the atrocities of the Nazis for so long because of their belief in the mission of their Fatherland. Will the champions of democracy be blamed for the very same thing one day?"[22]

Richard Süssmuth never entered the land of the dead. He spent seven weeks following the course of the Neisse, trying without success to find a way across. And yet he did not despair. These chaotic conditions were only temporary, he reasoned. "No one thought that the line of the border was the definitive one, that all of Silesia, above all purely German Lower Silesia, as far as the Neisse would be surrendered to the Poles," he wrote. "Everyone clings to the hope that a reasonable solution must be found and that we will be able to return one day."[23]

There would be no return. The frontier along the Neisse and Oder was the definitive one. Breslauers learned as much from a British radio report on 2 August "which specifically made Breslau a Polish city," fourteen-year-old Horst Gleiss recorded in his diary. Throughout the summer, "one big, terrifying question" had dominated conversation: Breslau or Wrocław?[24] There was no news, only rumours. Radios had been confiscated – although a few Breslauers hid sets and listened in secret to foreign broadcasts. The postal service had resumed as early as 16 May, but only for Poles. Not until 24 June, seven weeks after the city's surrender, did the first German-language newspaper appear, the *Deutsche Zeitung* – German newspaper. It told Breslau's inhabitants little of substance. They learned that their country had been partitioned by the four Allied powers, that the Red Army had been partially demobilized, that the peoples of Czechoslovakia had sent a gushing greeting to their brothers in the Soviet Union and their liberator, Stalin. They learned nothing about their fate, or the future of their city.[25] Only on 5 August – three days after the British radio report Horst Gleiss had overheard – did the *Deutsche Zeitung* publish details of the agreement reached in Potsdam by the governments of the Soviet Union, Great Britain and the United States. The three powers re-drew the border of Poland along the lower Oder and western Neisse: henceforth Breslau and Lower Silesia belonged to Warsaw. It meant the greatest human migration in history, upwards of seven million Germans expelled from their homes in lands now under Polish, Czech and Hungarian control. The governments of all three countries promised the transportation of Germans would be carried out "in an orderly and humane manner". In Breslau it was orderly, but rarely was it humane.

It began in earnest in October 1945. Breslau, declared its new president Aleksander Wachniewski – the first mayor, Bolesław Drobner had quickly fallen out of favour with his communist masters – "must be cleansed of Germans as soon as possible"; Germans outnumbered Poles ten to one in the city.[26] Wachniewski's staff talked of *Aussiedlung* – resettlement. "The Germans should feel they are being expelled as little as possible," one senior administrator in Lower Silesia wrote. "As a result, a repatriation of Germans shall begin."[27] Germans know it only as *Vertreibung* – expulsion. It began at 6am on 1 October. Guards stood at the door of every house in the village of Friedewalde on the north-eastern edge of Breslau. The 800 or so inhabitants were given half an hour to leave their properties, then were marched to barracks in the city, while Poles moved into the homes the Germans had been forced to abandon. The next day 1,157 Germans were evicted from the suburb of Rosenthal.[28] It went on like this for two months. "Entire districts were evacuated in a few hours," decorator Georg Fritsch remembered. "We could take forty-four pounds of luggage, but the guards took what they liked. To protest would have meant death."[29] Four policemen thumped on the door to Horst Gleiss's apartment in Benderplatz. The flat was being commandeered. A Polish officer would move in that afternoon. The Gleiss family could take with them only what they could carry. "We packed everything jumbled together in blankets, sheets, bags, even cushion covers, at top speed," the teenager recalled. What he could never take was his beloved chemistry set and a collection of more than a hundred jars.[30] Ursula Scholz, now turned seventeen, was given just ten minutes to leave her apartment. She was not unprepared. "For weeks, we'd hidden a rucksack as well as two suitcases with things behind piles of wood in the cellar as a precaution."[31]

The expulsion of the Germans evoked memories of the German invasion of Poland seven years before for Joanna Konopińska. Her family had been given fifteen minutes to pack their belongings when they were driven out of their village near Poznań. "When I think back to 1939, I believe we're fussing too much over the Germans."[32] Senior officials concurred. The commander of 5th Infantry Division called on his men "to throw the German *plugastwo* [filth] from these eternal Polish lands," while his counterpart in the 10th Infantry told his soldiers they had "been given the honourable task of clearing ancient Polish soil of German vermin. Expel the Germans from Polish soil without any chance of them returning." As for the general in charge of Second Army, he urged his troops to "deal with the Germans as they dealt with us". He continued:

> We must carry out our mission in such a harsh and decisive manner that the Germanic vermin do not hide in their houses but flee from us of their own accord. Once they're in their own land they'll thank God they were lucky enough to save their skin.[33]

Nor were civic officials against stoking anti-German hatred. "Us or them," declared the senior government representative in Silesia, Aleksander Zawadzki. "Now is not the time for any sentimental weakness and sympathy for Germans. The Germans are our mortal foes and we must fight them with all means at our disposal."[34]

The expellees spent several days in a transit camp – usually an abandoned school or barracks – before they were sent west. After a transitory existence lasting three months – they spent a couple of days living in a laundry room, ten days in a coal cellar, and finally ten weeks in an apartment in Gräbschen – the Gleiss family were driven out of Breslau in a Red Army truck at the end of October. The column stopped for the night on the Autobahn. The refugees climbed out and lit a campfire. "We all sat down around and sang melancholy songs about our homeland and the golden stars in the firmament," wrote Horst Gleiss, now turned fifteen. "Many tears welled up in our eyes. Several drops crept down their cheeks and dampened the native soil which is so dear to and beloved by all of us." The column entered the 'rump' of Germany, as the refugees called it, near Cottbus, eighty miles south-east of Berlin. "For the first time in many days we felt we were safe again and free of the Polish yoke among our German brothers and sisters," wrote Horst.[35]

Most Breslauers were 'repatriated' by train, not bus, in locked cattle trucks and goods wagons from the Freiburger Bahnhof. "I left my home town of Breslau, a dead city, full of ruins, graves, starving, pale, dejected and broken people, leaving the misery behind," wrote one expellee. "A torrent of indescribable misery crashes into the border day after day – women, old men, babies, the sick and invalids." Many crossed the border at Görlitz, where refugee camps were established to receive the influx of refugees – and where the carriages were often opened for the first time since the train had departed. "Out of one wagon alone ten corpses were taken and thrown into coffins," Catholic priest Conrad Gröber remembered. As for the living, some had been driven insane. The rest "were covered in excrement, which led me to believe that they were squeezed together so tightly that there was no longer any possibility for them to relieve themselves at a designated place". At the beginning of December a train of anti-Fascists left Breslau. Their opposition to the Nazis afforded the passengers no protection. After a seemingly uneventful journey as far as Sagan, militia and railway workers began to unload luggage at gunpoint in the middle of the night at an unscheduled stop. When the train finally reached the German border, the passengers were ordered out into a field on the Polish side of the line. Drunken militia searched the refugees, depriving them of most of the luggage which remained. At the border post there were more surly Poles who refused to let them pass unless they paid a toll in złoty. Those who still had some handed it over and were allowed to pass, others were searched yet again, surrendering candles, batteries, even shoes. A few refused and were beaten, some were even thrown into the Neisse. Soviet troops came to the Germans' aid and helped them collect the corpses. There were fifty-seven dead in all.[36]

The trains passing through Görlitz and Sagan were not the only ones pulling west through Silesia carrying expellees in the autumn and winter of 1945. Coming from the east were hundreds of thousands of Poles displaced as Stalin drove the borders of his Soviet empire on to Polish soil. One in ten of Wrocław's new inhabitants came from the capital of the western Ukraine, Lwów. The fate of these expellees – Poland's communist rulers preferred the term 'repatriates' – mirrored that of Germans driven from the Silesian capital. They too were transported in cattle trucks. There was no food for them. They had little idea where they were going. The trains stopped frequently on Polish soil. They were told to continue on their journey; the settlers from the east were not wanted. "Everywhere we heard the same thing," one woman lamented. "There's no more space. They moved us from place to place for six weeks." During the spring and summer, the passengers jumped out and foraged for food for their animals. Farmers repeatedly drove them back on to the trains. "We asked them to give us some grass for the cattle because we'd come a long way," one woman remembered. "They did not even listen. We returned to the trucks and cursed their heartlessness and miserly attitude." All that kept the refugees from slaughtering their cows was the need for milk by mothers and children on the train. "We all learned to steal," one Ukrainian Pole admitted. "As soon as the train stopped, everyone pounced upon the fields and ripped up what they could. Grass, clover, even raw grain. The cows wanted to eat! People and the children needed milk!"[37] Poles who had already settled in Wrocław showed the repatriates little sympathy. They cared little for this largely rural population who kept rabbits in their bathrooms, chickens in kitchens, cows, pigs and goats in garages and cellars.[38] Nor did they wish to turn their city into "a second Lwów"; instead, they were forging "a Polish Wrocław which is not a replica of a city in eastern Poland".[39]

Joanna Konopińska spent the summer in her native Poland. The history student returned to Breslau at the beginning of October. She found the trams were now running – minus seats and windows – but little else had changed. The city was still scarred by rubble, ruins, houses without windowpanes, uprooted street lamps. She could not settle in her home in Bischofswalde – now given a Polish name, Biskupin. The house was still "terribly foreign and German. At every turn I come up against objects which belong to somebody else, are witnesses of a foreign life which I know nothing about, which remind me of people who built this house, lived here and now, perhaps, are no longer alive. How could I feel at home here? I cannot imagine that I could ever say: this is my home." Six weeks later, she changed her mind after a trip to the city centre. "What struck me were the Polish signs above shops and in houses where the authorities are housed," Konopińska wrote. There were the most primitive signposts and advertisements on trams and on the walls of bombed-out houses for restaurants, cafés and nightclubs. They were far from attractive, or professional, but it was proof, the student noted, of "Polish presence in a city which is still so thoroughly German".[40]

What Joanna Konopińska had witnessed was the growing *Polonisierung* and *Entdeutschung* – 'Polonization' and 'de-Germanization' – of Breslau. Some things could be easily Polonized. The streets of Breslau had undergone radical name changes in the past twenty-five years. The Weimar Republic had erased traces of the Imperial era. The Nazis in turn had erased all traces of the Republic. Some streets had even changed their titles twice during the Nazis' reign as acolytes such as the first *Gauleiter* Helmuth Brückner and SA leader Edmund Heines fell out of favour. And now new titles were applied once more. Schlossplatz had been renamed Plac Wolności on the orders of Bolesław Drobner, but otherwise the *Komisja do Zmian Nazw Ulic* – Committee for the

Changing of Street Names – determined the new names of 1,500 streets, alleys and districts. In many instances, the committee simply translated German names into Polish: Sandbrücke remained faithful to its old name as Most Piaskowski (sand bridge), the Ring became the Rynek (market), Neumarkt was turned into Nowy Targ (new market). Adolf Hitler Strasse had to go, of course; it now bore the name of the poet Adam Mickiewicza. Hitler was not the only German leader to be erased from Breslau's streets. Bismarck – regarded by many as an oppressor of Poles – was replaced by Bolesław Chrobry (Bolesław the Brave), who forged a Polish empire in the eleventh century. The wasteland created by Karl Hanke's runway around Kaiserstrasse was renamed after the iconic triumph of Slav over Teuton, the Battle of Grunwald in 1410, while Kaiserbrücke became the Most Grunwaldzki. The names of German cities and towns disappeared from the street map – unless they had become part of post-war Poland, such as Stettin (Szczecin) or Danzig (Gdańsk). There was a nod to the liberator of Breslau: not Vladimir Gluzdovski, but the Soviet leader, honoured with Ulica Marszalka Stalina (Marshal Stalin Street) – previously Matthiasstrasse. In time, more Soviet-inspired street names would appear: Ulica Stalingradzka (Stalingrad Street), Ulica Przyjazni Polsko-Radzieckiej (Street of Polish-Soviet Friendship) and roads and squares named after the doyens of communism – Marx, Engels, Rosa Luxemburg and Karl Liebknecht.[41]

De-Germanization did not end with eradicating German names. "All traces of German culture are to be removed," Silesia's communist leadership ordered. The Polish authorities demanded German ashtrays and beer mats in bars and restaurants be thrown out, inscriptions on chapels removed, even gravestone headings removed. German music – popular or classical – was banned. German books were burned by the dozen – it was less about the contents than the simple fact that the words within were in German. "Everything which bore a German inscription had to be removed from our house," recalled truck driver Hans Gora. The authorities tried to take away his mother's bread bin and cups with gold Germanic lettering. "We had to paint or tape over German lettering. After that the items could remain in the household." Breslau's sixteenth-century coat of arms with its double-tailed Bohemian lion and 'W' (for Wratislavia, the city's Latin name, rather than Wrocław) was retained. But German monuments were demolished, statues melted down, their foundations used to rebuild the city or to serve as pedestals for Polish monuments. For the most part, the removal of German symbols and symbolism was carried out discreetly, but not that of the fifty-year-old monument to Wilhelm I in Schweidnitzer Strasse. The statue was removed with great ceremony in October 1945. An orchestra played, the street was bedecked with banners, Polish flags and standards. A large crowd listened to speeches, cheered and applauded as the statue was toppled. "The fall of this little Fritz is a symbol for the fall of the entire Nazi-Prussian regime," rejoiced the city's socialist newspaper, *Naprzód Dolnośląski* (Forward Lower Silesia). There was no place for Frederick the Great's Palace in Polish Wrocław. Burned-out and left in ruins by the fighting for the city, civic authorities determined not to rebuild it. The palace was "a German reminder of a political nature. To preserve it could feed German revisionist desires," the city's curator decided. Besides, the palace possessed little architectural value. "You find buildings like this all over Europe." The ruins of the Palais Hatzfeldt, the seat of German government in Breslau for nearly 150 years and Karl Hanke's former headquarters, lasted rather longer. They were only pulled down in the 1960s, leaving behind just an entrance and lobby.[42]

Just as the city's physical past was erased, so Poland's leadership re-wrote its history. They talked of living *w odzyskanym Wrocławiu* – in regained Wrocław. At its core, they argued, Silesia was Polish, not German. Silesia was one of the *ziemie odzyskane* – regained territories – and the Germans who had lived there for centuries were *okupanci* – occupiers. As late as the nineteenth century, its capital – "Germanized outwardly" – was a "half-Polish city surrounded by a Slavic sea," the Polish tongue "the language heard everyday in Breslau's streets". Only with the advent of Wilhelmine Germany and the Third Reich was Breslau's 'Polishness' eclipsed. This was "the soil of our grandfathers," Poland's communist leader Władysław Gomułka proclaimed in a speech in Psie Pole (Hundsfeld). For centuries, the land had been "Germanized by force and oppression". There was, Gomułka told his audience, "no way of Germanizing history," however. Silesia – Wrocław and Głogów (Glogau) especially – had been bastions of Polish culture which had eventually succumbed to the "overwhelming might of the Germanic invaders. After many centuries without freedom, this land has been liberated."[43]

As 1945 drew to a close, Wrocław was still far from being 'liberated'. Despite the changes to street names, despite the removal of German statues, it was still not a Polish city. Germans still outnumbered Polish settlers and repatriates five to one. Plans to brand Breslauers, as Jews had once been branded with the yellow star, using armbands marked with the letter 'N' for *Niemiec* – German – were finally dismissed by the city's leadership, but not on moral grounds; it would merely reinforce Breslau's "German character".[44]

In truth, neither German nor Pole felt at home in the city at the year's end. The new settlers deserted Wrocław in their droves, determined to rejoin their families who still lived in central Poland. There was little celebration of the festive season among Breslauers left behind. "It's bleak and tragic," wrote former post official Conrad Bischof. "You sit alone and abandoned, as poor as a beggar in Breslau, city of ruins."[45] The turn of the year was no less bitter. "We awaken in the New Year to one long horror," tailor's daughter Charlotte Pösel noted. "The general mood is lousy."[46] Another of the city's German inhabitants recorded despondently:

> The situation is desperate, the nights are restless, hundreds of thousands destitute, homeless, without a roof over their head. The responsible authorities are helpless and heartless. Discussions are futile, complaints useless. Young people are hopeless, women are unstable, men are disloyal. The hunt for calories is unrestrained, the meals fat-free. After the currency reform, hope of things getting better is pointless. They have made us despondent and unemployed, deprived us of all rights, deprived us of our future. That's what is happening to us. It is our sad, central German fate.[47]

The sad daily fate of Breslauers was to serve in Polish work details, clearing the ruins. By January 1946 much of the rubble had been removed from the streets and pavements. But walls and ledges, balconies, the entire façades of properties were still falling into the street and killing pedestrians on a regular basis.

There was no new city rising in the place of the ruins. The bricks which built Breslau and could build a new Wrocław were being dispatched to Warsaw to rebuild the Polish capital. A miniature railway was laid down the middle of Ulica Oławska (Ohlauer Strasse); carts carried away bricks in their thousands. The wholesale dismantling of Wrocław continued well into the 1950s. Nor did the city's factories fare any better. In his first interview with the communist-run press in June 1945, Bolesław Drobner praised the Soviets for providing Polish settlers with working sewage plants, a power station and gas works, as well as "various extremely valuable industrial items in a relatively good state". In fact, Wrocław's factories had been stripped bare, their contents shipped east. Not half the machines in the two dozen textile factories remained – and most of those were damaged. More than 3,700 pieces of equipment were sent east from metalwork plants – 1,000 each from the FAMO and Rheinmetall works. Every tool was removed from the Linke-Hofmann works, now renamed *Państwowa Fabryka Wagonów* – National Railway Carriage Factory – while barely one in four machines the Soviets left behind after removing hundreds of lathes, engines and motors, worked. And what was not sent to the Soviet Union was sent to the Polish capital. Joanna Konopińska watched trucks carrying printing presses, teletypes, telephone exchanges and other machines to Warsaw. "It's probably my local patriotism speaking," the student fumed. "but I'm angry at the way Wrocław is being impoverished." In short, the city possessed just two-fifths of its industrial potential. It would take more than a decade for Wrocław's factories to recover from the ravages of war and Stalinism.[48]

The same counted for some of Breslau's defenders. Most would not see Germany again until the end of the 1940s. Some, such as Hermann Niehoff, would not see Germany again until ten years after the end of the war. And some – one in ten prisoners – would never see their country or their families again. This first winter of captivity was the worst. The men fell victim to the cold, to disease, to maltreatment, to starvation. "Death moves around the camp, he's our constant, invisible companion," wrote former *Leutnant* Erich Schönfelder in a camp in Karelia, where temperatures dropped to forty degrees below zero. Many of Schönfelder's fellow inmates simply gave up. "It's not the workload, but the despondency of their situation, the sapping of all energy, their inner instability." After watching the dead carried out of the camp hospital day after day, one of the prisoners turned to poetry:

A flat sledge, a white horse in front,
Moved each night through the camp gate
A dark, rigid, horrible cargo:
Our dead from last night.

We stand at the wire, the snow is deep,
The storm drives ice crystals into our faces
And in the snowstorm around the gate
The sledge of the dead slowly disappears.

The Russian guards called to us:
"*Davai, davai*, all men back!"
The storm devoured our faint cry
The gate was only open for the dead.

The burden of these days was soon so great
That many could not stand it any more
A flat sledge, a white horse in front
Only move through the camp gate at night.

You will not see your homeland again
The mounds will blow away in the snowstorm
But you won, you died in agony
You unforgotten on the sledges of the dead.[49]

In the Ukraine, dead prisoners were carried out of camp on a wheelbarrow. "They are just skeletons, so light that even we emaciated men can lift one body in pairs comfortably," one inmate recalled. The burial details – always German prisoners – struggled to dig even a shallow grave in the frozen ground. Finally, they had removed earth for the dead to be buried. "The stretchers are moved to the edge, one man pulls the tarpaulin away, the other tips the stretcher up and lets the naked, frozen-stiff bodies, slip down," the prisoner wrote. "Frozen clods of earth are already slapping against the dead bodies, followed by snow, the wind takes care of the rest. By tomorrow it will have rounded off the uneven edges of the flat hill and covered it up with a cold, white shroud. Lord, what a misery."[50] There was little dignity shown the dead even when the snow melted. They were buried in mass graves and covered with a layer of pine branches before earth was thrown on top. If there was time, a brief prayer was said.

And for the living? In a camp north-east of Gorki, prisoners were woken at 4.30am. Breakfast – "a blob of porridge, some bread and a spoonful of sugar" – was served an hour later. Then the work began. The men were marched out of camp to begin a day's hard labour, usually construction. "'*Davai davai*' – get a move on – the cry hounds us constantly, at every opportunity, even when we have to relieve ourselves, this '*davai, davai*' was ever-present," former SS *Sturmmann* Werner Zillich recalled. Eventually, even the guards tired of their constant exhortations and marched the prisoners back to the camp at the double. After a wash and perhaps a brief doze – the men always kept one eye open so as not to miss supper – the evening meal was served at 7pm. The prisoners rushed for the serving hatch, then took their food back to the barracks, guarding it covetously, eating every crumb. For the next two hours there was political instruction from a commissar, occasionally a film. "If you were to draw comparisons, it was the same system as under the National Socialists. Informants, threats and the like are the order of the day," wrote Zillich. At 10pm the *Last Post* sounded across the camp and quiet descended. By then, most prisoners were already asleep.[51]

For the first year in captivity, a handful of Breslau's defenders enjoyed privileged status. Camp guards and officials respected any man who possessed a copy of the surrender terms. It had "a magical effect," operations officer *Major* Albrecht Otto recalled. Any officer who showed them the document "was certain to be spared any inconvenience, especially the searching of baggage". An irate German communist finally tore up Otto's copy, while fortress commander Hermann Niehoff held on to his copy until the summer of 1946 when a camp official demanded he hand it over. "Comrade general, we urgently need your original copy for the archives!" Niehoff refused. He was frisked, his possessions thoroughly searched before the document was recovered. "These so-called conditions for an honourable surrender of Breslau are no contract," a commissar scoffed. "They're nothing more than *ruse de guerre* which succeeded."[52]

Not least among the surrender terms ignored was clause number five – "The entire civilian populace is guaranteed security and normal living conditions." The expulsions resumed in mid-February 1946. "Only ten per cent of Germans can stay," tailor's daughter Charlotte Pösel wrote. "The tumult is real now. Most people lose their nerves and sell their possessions at bargain prices." Once again Annelies Matuszczyk watched "rivers of people with their meagre possessions on their backs or on handcarts head for the station. It's a tragic sight." Schoolboy Friedhelm Mondwurf and his family were ordered to wait at their collection point, the Clausewitz school on the western edge of the old town. Mondwurf's family had nothing left, but other expellees clung on to their worldly goods. "Using hand carts, worn-out prams, old bicycles or simply tied-up blankets, everyone tried to save their last possessions," he wrote. "The entire column repeatedly came to a halt because the wagons could not withstand the load or people simply collapsed under the burden." They waited for a day and a half in the school. "Hunger and illness took people to the brink of exhaustion," Mondwurf remembered. It was "like a lunatic asylum – there was everything from a violent clash to complete apathy." Finally the expellees were escorted to the nearby Freiburger Bahnhof. "We were loaded into goods wagons like cattle prepared for slaughter," the schoolboy wrote. "Packed tightly together, we squatted on the bare floor. The door was closed. Today I can still hear the click of the heavy iron lock which not only locked the door but also drew a line under an entire chapter in our lives. A dramatic journey to freedom began." The Rothkugel family were transported in a cattle truck to Rabber in Lower Saxony in early March. Strangely, leaving Breslau after twenty-two years was a relief. "The fear which had constantly hung over us for the past year suddenly evaporated," Otto Rothkugel remembered. "Like a heavy burden it fell from us and a joyful feeling of being free came over us." It was not a typical feeling of joy, of course. "We had left everything which was dear to us, which we valued, had been left behind – forever. One chapter of our lives had come to an end and an uncertain future lay before us." The Rothkugels put their faith in God. "The good thing which arose from the misery we had to endure was that our faith became even stronger, even more unshakeable," Otto Rothkugel wrote. "They have taken everything away from us, but they could not deprive us of our faith. We took it with us."[53]

They left behind a city still hideously scarred by war. "I will remember my stay in Breslau for a long time," wrote one expellee from Upper Silesia who spent several days there in May 1946 waiting for a transport west. "From the window of our spartan attic we were presented with a view which you only see today in horror films: a sea of burned-out houses without windows where only horror lived, a forest of towering chimneys, blackened by soot, as far as the eye could see." He killed time waiting by wandering around Breslau, especially its southern suburbs where the fighting had been its fiercest. The town houses in Ulica Ślężna (Lohestrasse) were still empty. "You could wander through deserted, plundered apartments – linked to each other by holes in the wall – for hours on end," the refugee recalled. The names of the apartments' former occupants were still legible on the doors. There were handwritten details of missing people, addresses, remarks, often scribbled in chalk on the walls. In one room there was even a field gun buried beneath brick dust and rubble.[54] On a spring walk around the Holteihöhe by the Oder, Annelies Matuszczyk found steel helmets, gun parts and gas masks, the lawns still carved up by half-collapsed communication trenches and positions and uprooted trees hanging over craters. The park had been dug up twelve months earlier and turned into a makeshift cemetery. Breslauers were still leaving fresh flowers on graves; "We read the inscriptions on the wooden crosses, some of which have already weathered badly. There's an eleven-year-old messenger next to a sixty-one-year-old *Volkssturm* man." Most of the dead were born in 1927 – seventeen- and eighteen-year-olds – and on one side of the hill, two dozen men from one battalion all killed on the same day.[55] Joanna Konopińska passed a German woman digging up graves near the Most Zwierzyniecki (Passbrücke). "My seventeen-year-old son is buried here somewhere," she explained. "I would certainly recognise him – he has a small, initialled silver chain on his wrist." The boy had stayed behind to build Karl Hanke's runway while the rest of his family fled to Schweidnitz. "I will soon go across the Oder but the grave of my son gives me no peace."[56] She probably never found him; the bodies were soon reinterred in a mass grave.

Nature was proving more successful than man at eradicating the traces of war. Each spring morning Breslau was filled with life. The ruins had become home to thousands of birds who burst into song as the sun rose. "Wherever you look you see trees and hedges covered with small leaves, the lawns are green, the streets and environs are clean," Joanna Konopińska wrote. Returning home from her studies at the university, Konopińska felt she was "riding into a different world" as her tram crossed the Most Zwierzyniecki and entered Biskupin (Bischofswalde). The suburb had been less ravaged than most in the city during the siege, but nevertheless staring out of the tram windows every day brought fresh changes.

The bomb craters in the street have been flattened out and, although there's no asphalt or pavement, cars can already drive without the threat of their suspension breaking. There are so few cars driving in our city, however, that the streets have turned green like the Oder meadows in the spring sun.

An elderly woman buttonholed Joanna as she walked home from the tram stop. "Yesterday there were still two graves next to this house and there were three crosses on the pile of rubble," she explained. "Today they're no longer there. It's a little more pleasant to pass through the city because you don't run into graves everywhere. Don't you think so?"[57]

The graves were disappearing and so were the Germans. By the summer of 1946, they were outnumbered six to one by Wrocław's Polish settlers as the rate of 'repatriation' was accelerated. Sometimes daily, sometimes two or three times a week, sometimes only weekly, trains of Germans expelled from Silesia headed west, with anywhere between 1,480 and 1,750 men, women and children on board. Some trains headed for the Soviet-occupied zone of Germany, others for the sector occupied by the British under Operation *Swallow*, among the latter one carrying priest Joachim Konrad. As the train pulled out of the Freiburger Bahnhof, the youth group of Konrad's St Elisabethkirche burst into hymn: *Ein feste Burg ist unser Gott* – A mighty fortress is our God. "With tears in our eyes, we saw the towering spires fade into the distance – and with them our beloved Breslau home," he recalled. "Would we see it again?" A week beforehand, Konrad had given his final sermon in his church, a bulwark of Breslau's Protestant community since 1525. Quoting the Book of Genesis – "And the Lord said to Abraham: 'Go forth from your country, and from your relatives and from your father's house, to the land which I will show you'" – the priest told his dwindling congregation: "When you see these trains of misery leaving Breslau, your heart stops. God has passed a harsh judgement on the German East."[58]

The 'trains of misery' – each one with a number – continued throughout the summer and autumn of 1946. By the year's end, more than 500 transports had rolled westwards. The last train of the year, number 514, pulled out of the Freiburger Bahnhof with 1,543 expellees aboard on the morning of 17 December. Only 1,511 passengers would reach the train's destination in Lower Saxony. Its passengers – Germans evicted from across Lower Silesia as well as Breslau – had spent several days waiting in an unheated school building before being ordered to the Freiburger Bahnhof on 16 December where a train would take them to Germany. Of the fifty-five cattle trucks allocated to train 514, only sixteen were waiting. A few hundred refugees boarded, most spent the night on the open platform. The temperature dropped to -18°C. It was 8am on the seventeenth before the remaining carriages – again cattle wagons – arrived, and several more hours before the train was ready to depart. For the next five days, the train sluggishly made its way through Lower Silesia and Lower Saxony. There was no heating – except in the carriage reserved for the Polish guards – no straw, no lighting, no stoves, no medicine, and the rubbish and human waste from the previous transport covered the floor of each truck.

Temperatures fluctuated between -15°C and -20°C. A layer of ice formed on blankets and on the sides of the carriages from the refugees' breath. When the expellees woke in the mornings, they found their hair had frozen. Some found their feet had turned black during the night through frostbite. During the day, the ice on the roof melted and dripped on passengers. On only four occasions during the journey did the refugees enjoy a warm drink, or alight from the train for a call of nature; the rest of the time they used buckets provided in every wagon. In one truck, an elderly man kept spirits up, leading Christmas songs. By the second day of the journey, he was dead. His was one of nineteen corpses unloaded at the first halt, Maltsch on the Oder, just two dozen miles from Breslau. Seven more dead were carried off the train in Kohlfurt, a dozen in Marienthal. The only medical assistance was provided by one Dr Loch, previously the senior doctor at Breslau's St Joseph's Hospital. Besides being overburdened, his wife was gravely ill (she died three days after the train arrived in the British zone), while Loch himself suffered a heart attack and frostbite to his legs. In other carriages, the expellees were left to their own devices. "I was called to help deliver a baby," one woman recalled "I climbed over bundles and piles of luggage and found a woman. I moved towards her – nothing happened. I touched her. Nothing. Dead. I approached the woman who'd given birth. She was bleeding badly – it was a miscarriage. When I tried to make her more comfortable, I noticed that she had frozen to the floor in her own blood."

By the time the train arrived in Hameln and Bückeburg in the British-occupied sector of Germany, thirty-two people were dead. Nearly 300 were admitted to hospital, where another twenty-six died. The transport quickly earned a name: *Todeszug 514* – death train 514. "Only after reaching the English zone did we feel that we were human beings," one of the refugees recalled. "We got something warm for the first time in a fortnight. This was most welcome, but for those with frostbitten limbs, the suffering was only beginning." Another – evidently oblivious to the horrors of Auschwitz, Gross Rosen, Fünfteichen – protested: "There's not a single example in German history of such bestial treatment." There was more measured condemnation from the local press:

> In the past twenty months, many words have been used to convince the German people that this last war was waged and won by our adversaries to re-establish humane laws. In dozen of trials for crimes against humanity, insofar as they were committed by Germans, they have condemned to death or given strict prison sentences. Not least, they defamed the entire German people because, out of ignorance or a lack of principles, it allowed a degenerate caste to commit these crimes. The German people have willingly submitted to the just verdict of world opinion and entrusted themselves to the hands of the upholders of humanity.

Nothing came of the protests. But there was, at least, no repeat of death train 514.[59]

By September 1947, Polish authorities could claim the 'repatriation' of Breslau's Germans complete. There were some left, of course, but the large-scale transports were over.[60] Breslau had become Wrocław. Now, wrote student Joanna Konopińska, "a new chapter in our lives has begun". She had been among the city's first settlers. Back then "in the streets, on the trams, in businesses, everywhere you heard the German tongue, reminding us of the war and all the terrible things connected with it." But no longer. "Wrocław becomes more familiar and more likeable by the day," Konopińska recorded in her diary. "I have learned to love this city and cannot imagine that I could ever leave it again. I have a home, a job, studies and many new friends. I don't know why Wrocław has grown on me so quickly. I only know that my fate is bound with it."[61]

Notes

1. Thum, pp.69-70.
2. Ibid., p.189.
3. Gleiss, vi, p.138.
4. Gleiss, v, p.1007 and Gleiss, viii, p.1507.
5. Thum, p.120.
6. Ibid., p.254.
7. Thum, pp.248-51 and Höntsch, pp.298-302.
8. Bolesław Drobner, 'Bilans miesica', *Nasz Wrocław* 10-16/6/45. Cited in Gleiss, vi, p.115; and *Dziennik Polski* 16/6/45, cited in Gleiss, vi, p.113.
9. Based on Thum, pp.187, 261, Kaps, *Tragödie Schlesiens*, p.347, and Höntsch, p.303.
10. Based on *Vertreibung und Vertreibungsverbrechen 1945-1948: Bericht des Bundesarchivs vom 28 Mai 1974*, p.261, Gleiss, v, p.827, Gleiss, vi, pp.82, 151, Kaps, *Tragödie Schlesiens*, pp.346-7 and Mondwurf, Friedhelm, 'Als Bettelmann in Breslau' in Hupka, Herbert (ed), *Letzte Tage in Schlesien*, p.178.
11. Food shortages based on Gleiss, vi, pp.138, 470, 562, 583-4, Gleiss, *Breslauer Exodus*, p.37, Vertreibung, ii, p.330, DDRZW 10/2, pp.617-18, Mondwurf, Friedhelm, 'Als Bettelmann in Breslau' in Hupka, Herbert (ed), *Letzte Tage in Schlesien*, p.179.
12. Black market based on Gleiss, vi, p.1018, *Breslauer Exodus*, pp.94-5, Thum, pp.190-3.
13. Starvation and deaths based on Gleiss, vi, pp.631, 668, 583-4, Gleiss, viii, pp.1553-54, Kaps, *Tragödie Schlesiens*, p.355, Böddeker, *Die Flüchtlinge*, p.241, and Borodziej, Docs.181, 192, 197.
14. Gleiss, vi, pp.249, 494 and Kaps, *Tragödie Schlesiens*, p.347.
15. Gleiss, vi, pp.584.
16. Peikert, p.20.
17. Hartung, pp.100-2.
18. Life as PoWs based on Bannert, pp.98-108, Gleiss, vi, pp.527-8, 789 and Gleiss, viii, p.1681.
19. Kaps, *Tragödie Schlesiens*, pp.497-9 and Knopp, *Grosse Flucht*, pp.196-7.
20. Gleiss, vi, p.172.
21. Ibid., vi, pp.173-6.
22. *Weltwoche*, Zürich, November 1945. Reprinted in Aust, Stefan and Burgdorff, Stephan (eds), *Die Flucht: Über die Vertreibung der Deutschen aus dem Osten*, pp.149-54.
23. Gleiss, vi, pp.173-6.
24. Ibid., vi, p.515.
25. Ibid., vi, pp.194-6.
26. Hofmann, pp.215-16.
27. Borodziej, Doc.188.
28. Borodziej, Doc.203.
29. Vertreibung, ii, pp.344-5.
30. Gleiss, vi, p.432.
31. Waage, p.68.
32. Höntsch, pp.308-10, Gleiss, *Breslauer Exodus*, pp.396-7.

33. Scholz, p.61, Borodziej, Doc.168 and Thum, pp.115-16.
34. DDRZW, 10/2, p.609.
35. Gleiss, vi, pp.895-900.
36. Based on Gleiss, vi, p.950, *Microcosm*, p.422 and Borodziej, Doc.211.
37. Hofmann, pp.113-14.
38. Thum, p.164.
39. Ibid., p.155.
40. Höntsch, pp.302-04.
41. Thum, pp.350-9 and Jerrig, pp.49-50.
42. De-Germanisation based on *Als die Deutschen weg waren*, pp.55, 97, 98 and Thum, pp.380-1, 482-4.
43. Thum, pp.279-80, 327-8 and *Wrocław 1945 1965*, p.20.
44. Thum, p.136.
45. Gleiss, vi, p.1067.
46. Gleiss, *Breslauer Exodus*, p.53.
47. Ibid., p.1.
48. Gleiss, *Breslauer Exodus*, pp.120, 176, Gleiss, vi, p.113 and Thum, pp.182-3.
49. Gleiss, *Breslauer Exodus*, p.45.
50. Böddeker, *Die Gefangenen*, p.296.
51. Gleiss, *Breslauer Exodus*, pp.30-1.
52. *So Kämpfte Breslau*, p.111 and Gleiss, *Breslauer Exodus*, pp.13-14.
53. Gleiss, *Breslauer Exodus*, pp.225, 266, 269, Mondwurf, Friedhelm, 'Als Bettelmann in Breslau' in Hupka, Herbert (ed), *Letzte Tage in Schlesien*, pp.182-3.
54. Gleiss, *Breslauer Exodus*, pp.478-9.
55. Ibid., pp.344-5.
56. Gleiss, ix, p.277.
57. Gleiss, *Breslauer Exodus*, pp.377-8, 478-9.
58. Konrad, pp.35, 43.
59. Borodziej, Doc.261, Gleiss, *Breslauer Exodus*, pp.857-88 and *Hannoversche Presse*, 3/1/47 and 7/1/47.
60. Borodziej, Doc.286.
61. Höntsch, pp.308-10, Gleiss, *Breslauer Exodus*, pp.396-7.

CHAPTER 10

Quiet Flows the Oder

For old Breslauers who visit the former capital of Silesia,
it is a journey into the past which becomes present only in the memory
Hans Eberhard Henkel

On a late summer's evening there is a buzz around the bars and restaurants which run all around the Rynek. There is lively chatter at the tables beneath the awnings in a Babel of languages, not just Polish, as diners enjoy a *piwo* (beer). The Babel of tongues is complemented by the food of every imaginable nation offered by the hostelries – Greek, Mexican, Italian, German, Indian, and Polish, of course – plus the ubiquitous global fast food chains – KFC, Pizza Hut, McDonald's. As darkness falls, the *Ratusz* (city hall) is bathed in gold from the lights which surround it. The 700-year-old building looks much as it did seven decades ago. The baroque and art nouveau houses which surround the huge square have changed little too, and the the imposing structure of the modernist Bank Zachodni (Western Bank – formerly the *Sparkasse*); survived the siege largely intact. Fire eaters move among the restaurants, while the strains of guitars and accordions – playing less-than-authentic Polish tunes such as *Que sera sera* – struggle to be heard above the conversations. At the end of their performances they pass plates around, hoping for a tip.

As it ever was, the Rynek (Ring) is the heart of Wrocław. Vratislavians realized it as soon as they settled in the city. It was here that they focused their efforts to rebuild the shattered city after the apocalypse of 1945. The reconstruction was sympathetic. Planners tried to restore the pre-war appearance of Wrocław's historic heart – the Rynek, the old town, the cathedral district. But the rest of the city took decades to rise from the rubble. Hundreds of buildings were pulled down; the salvaged bricks and other raw materials were sent to rebuild Poland's other ruined cities. This new rape of Wrocław reached its climax in the early 1950s. As many as 165 million bricks a year were sent from the city to central Poland. "Every Vratislavian gives fifty bricks for Warsaw – we are helping to build the capital," the *Gazeta Robotnicza* declared proudly at the end of August 1953.[1]

It was hardly surprising that the city still had not shaken off its 'wild west' label. *Wrocław jest brudny* – Wrocław is dirty – Poles complained. "Yardsticks which apply to other Polish towns, even for the newly-acquired Szczecin, do not count in Wrocław," a

246

German visitor observed in 1949. But it was not all bad. There were now a dozen hospitals with more than 3,000 beds catering for Wrocław's sick, while three dozen schools educated the city's youth. As Hugo Hartung had predicted, performances had resumed in the opera house – now renamed Teatr Miejski (municipal theatre). They had resumed as early as September 1945 with the Polish national opera *Halka*, performed by a German orchestra and ballet – all Breslauers –and a Polish choir and soloists. Some of the cinemas were back in service. For wealthier visitors, the Hotel Monopol had re-opened, although it possessed little of its former grandeur. "Our room is by no means clean," one guest complained. "Several light switches don't work, the beds are extremely bad." Ordinary Vratislavians liked nothing more than relaxing in one of the city's 400-plus restaurants and bars, as the editor of the newspaper *Pionier*, Wiesław Glogowski, wrote:

> Where the low Silesian sun blazes,
> Oder and Neisse roar in the distance,
> The settlers have come
> And opened pubs and bars.[2]

Wrocław needed bars. It needed restaurants. Schools. Hospitals. But in the early 1950s, what it needed most was homes. As the *Gazeta Robotnicza* was trumpeting Wrocław's sacrifice of bricks, the decision was finally taken to concentrate on rebuilding the city. New apartment blocks, shops and offices were erected around Plac Kościuszki (Tauentzienplatz) in keeping with the surviving buildings. But this was a slow – and expensive – process. The pressing need for housing saw flagship projects such as Plac Kościuszki abandoned in favour of utilitarian tower blocks which began to spring up across the city in the late 1950s and early 1960s, at the central railway station, on the edge of Nowy Targ (Neumarkt), in Gajowice (Gabitz) and Grabiszyńska (Gräbschen), and especially on the western outskirts of Muchobór Mały (Mochbern). "When there are tens of thousands of people who need a roof over their heads, you can't spend ages discussing it," a builder told Vienna-born journalist Charles Wassermann. "You have to build with what you've got."[3]

Wassermann visited Wrocław in the summer of 1957, one of scores of towns and cities in the former German East he toured with his wife. By then, the Rynek had largely been restored, so too the cathedral – minus its twin spires. But for the most part Wassermann found a city which was part building site, part rubble. Nowy Targ was a wasteland, framed by ruined buildings. In some places weeds and bushes devoured the rubble, in others there were still large gaps in rows of houses. Wrocław was slowly being rebuilt "with primitive means," he observed, but it would probably remain the same for some years to come. "The overall impression remains that of a very badly destroyed city."[4]

Poland's Communist leadership would champion the new Wrocław which arose in the late 1950s and 1960s. It scoffed at the "old, crowded, monotonous buildings" which once lined the Oder. They were gone. In their place, new apartment blocks surrounded by green space which "let air and sunshine into all apartments". As for the eleven- and twelve-storey tower blocks which rose in Gajowice, they "harmonize well with the slender spires of the Gothic churches of old Wrocław". No one was fooled.[5]

Former Breslauers sought to forge new lives in a Germany they no longer recognized. "At times you envy the many who fell back then for they did not experience what happened to Germany and to us," sighed former company commander Wolfgang Chutsch who settled in Nuremberg. Many Silesians led a transitory life after being driven from their homes on the Oder. "After the war, we lived in Seidmannsdorf near Coburg, in Coburg, in Cologne, in Aachen, in Mannheim, in Hamburg, in Oldenburg, in Hamburg, in Hanover, and in Hamburg again," one expellee recalled. As many as twelve million eastern Germans had been displaced by the war and expulsions. West Germans took them under their wing: various cities 'adopted' communities from the former German East – in Breslau's case, Cologne. Today it is home to the *Breslauer Sammlung* – Breslau collection: paintings, coins, medals, books, the papers of Breslau poet and artist Karl von Holtei salvaged from the Silesian capital. But Cologne was not Breslau. It was not *home*. "Home is more than a piece of land on a map," explained Horst Gleiss, who eventually settled near Hamburg. "It's where I grew up, where I lived with my parents, where grew up, where I spoke my Breslau or Silesian dialect, from where I was torn. Such a wound never completely heals."[6]

The expellees formed numerous groups, organizations and associations to help establish themselves – and to lobby for the return of their homeland and their possessions. Each year, members of the *Landsmannschaft Schlesien* – Silesian cultural association – gathered in their thousands for a reunion, but also a political rally. Some 150,000 Silesians attended the 1971 event over three days in Munich. They heard their chairman, the journalist, author and politician, Herbert Hupka, declare: "Breslau is called Breslau, not Wrocław. We will not abandon Silesia." Mimicking the words of the Polish national anthem, Hupka closed his address: "Silesia is not yet lost."[7]

Except that Silesia *was* lost. *German* Silesia at any rate. Communist East Germany – on instructions from Moscow – had been quick to recognise the new border along the Oder and Neisse. Bonn had not. Only with Willy Brandt's policy of *Ostpolitik* did West Germany finally accept the re-drawn frontier in 1970. That was reaffirmed two decades later with a formal treaty between a reunified Germany and democratic Poland.

With changing political realities and the passing of the expellees' generation, the cries of *Schlesien bleibt unser* – Silesia is still ours – are growing ever more faint. Some Silesians accept it. "The older I become, the more I think back to the home of my youth wistfully. I want to yet cannot forget it," wrote one Breslauer who left the city at the age of fourteen. But he has no desire to return. "The family of my childhood and youth has long since gone, my Breslau, the home town, died an agonising death in the Easter fires of 1945 and its corpse was given away to foreign hands on 6 May."[8]

Most Breslauers, however, have felt drawn to the city of their birth – a journey possible for most only from the 1970s onwards. Only with the fall of Communism did Hans Eberhard Henkel entertain thoughts of going back. There was little in the southern suburbs he remembered or recognized. He made immediately for the Ring on foot, down

the once-elegant 'Schwo', Schweidnitzer Strasse, now Ulica Świdnicka. He was surprised
by how many German streets names had simply been translated into Polish: Ohlauer
Strasse now Oławska, Liegnitzer (Legnicka), and the Ring (Rynek). "It seemed as if the
new inhabitants wanted to link the German past with the Polish present, because otherwise
Breslau could not be Wrocław." Henkel was impressed by the "wonderfully restored"
Ring, a sight to "stir the memory of any former Breslauer". How often he had dreamed
of seeing it once more. Now walking through it, it did not feel real for it was "no longer
filled with Silesian life" – not *German* Silesian life at any rate. Wherever he went in the
city, he was left with "an unsettling feeling of home". He believed the Poles had failed
to treat the city they had inherited in the manner it deserved. "For old Breslauers who
visit the former capital of Silesia, it is a journey into the past which becomes present only
in the memory, a dream of distant days between walls which have become foreign."[9]

To many, returning to the city was a cathartic experience. "It had always been my
great wish to return to a land which was my first and therefore my true home, to a land
with which I was never able to form a proper relationship, yet which remained alive
through snippets of memory and chiefly through the stories of my parents," wrote one
woman who was driven from the city at the age of eight. "But there was something else:
repeatedly before my eyes I saw moments when I was suddenly torn from places and
people and – at the same time – from a happy and safe childhood. Thinking about it
through the decades had caused me the same pain. Perhaps if I could revive wonderful
memories in places from my childhood, I might escape the bad events I experienced to
some degree." The Ksoll family returned to Wrocław in the mid-1970s. The children
barely remembered the city; they had been able to adjust to life in West Germany. But
not Herr Ksoll. For three decades he had been unable to accept the loss of his home.
"Only after we visited Breslau for the first time and my father said unequivocally that
it was no longer 'his' Breslau, but was Polish Wrocław, did he feel at ease," his children
wrote.[10]

Some of Wrocław's Polish inhabitants also longed to return to their homes. "Of
course I mourned my Lwów," said Tadeusz Myczkowski. "For a long time I headed the
Association of the Friends of Lwów. How often we longed to return. But now Silesia is
my home, this is where I grew up, this is where my sons were born." A fellow settler
from the western Ukraine, Krzeslawa Maliszewska, added: "We understood what the
Germans were going through because we were being resettled and they were being
resettled. They did not deserve it and we too did not deserve it. But that's the fate of
history."[11]

Fate overtook some of the men and women of 1945 and smiled on others.

Ferdinand Schörner's army group was the last major formation to surrender in the
war in Europe – three days after the rest of the Wehrmacht. Hitler's last field marshal fell
into American hands, but was subsequently handed over to the Russians. They imprisoned
him for twenty-five years for waging war on Soviet soil, a sentence later halved. He was
released in 1958 and handed over to the West German authorities, who subsequently
charged him with war crimes for executing soldiers without trial in the latter months of

the war. Schörner spent more than four years behind bars once more, before living out his later years in Munich where he died in 1973.

Despite his dismissal as fortress commander, **Hans von Ahlfen** was re-employed almost immediately as the pioneer commander of *Heeresgruppe* B on the Western Front. He served less than three weeks; the army group was surrounded in the Ruhr pocket and surrendered in mid-March. Ahlfen spent two years in American captivity. Upon release, he turned to writing military history, including the story of the struggle for Silesia, until his death from a heart attack in 1966.

His successor **Hermann Niehoff** was not released from Soviet captivity until October 1955. Besides working as a consultant for the Düsseldorf chemical firm Henkel, he wrote numerous articles on the siege and, with his predecessor, the standard work on the city's fall, *So Kämpfte Breslau* – How Breslau Fought. He died in the Rhineland in 1980 at the age of eighty-three.

Their adversary **Vladimir Gluzdovski** served at the prestigious Frunze Military Academy, the Red Army's staff college before joining the staffs of various military districts in the USSR. He died in Moscow aged sixty-four in 1967.

At the war's end, **Ivan Konev** was appointed the senior Soviet commander in Germany, then replaced his great rival Zhukov as defence minister. It was a post he held for four years until he fell foul of Stalin's jealousy and was moved to command of a military district. Stalin's death and Khruschev's rise saw Konev back in favour. He was appointed defence minister once more, then Commander-in-Chief of the Warsaw Pact forces; he used the latter to crush the Hungarian uprising in 1956. He retired four years later, only to be recalled briefly as the commander of Soviet forces in East Germany. Upon his death in 1973 aged seventy-five, he was afforded the highest honour by the Soviet Union, burial in the Kremlin's wall. His body is still there.

Journalist **Boris Polevoy** became one of the Soviet Union's most celebrated writers and novelists. Sixth Army's faithful diarist **Vassily Malinin** remained in the military after the war, rising to the rank of colonel.

Ulrich Frodien became a journalist for the *Süddeutsche Zeitung* and *Münchner Illustrierte* before founding the photographic archive of the Süddeutscher Verlag publishing house in Munich which he ran for nearly forty years.

Hugo Hartung spent a dozen days wandering through Silesia and Saxony on foot before being reunited with his family in Neustadt an der Orla, more than 250 miles west of Breslau.[12] He eventually settled in Munich where he became a theatre critic and novelist until his death in 1972.

Following four weeks recuperating from his bitter trek between the Vistula and Oder, **Paul Arnhold** returned to duty, fighting with a scratch German unit in Czechoslovakia. At the war's end, he was about to be handed over by American troops to Czech partisans. He jumped from a moving car and, "after another adventure-filled march" fled Czech soil. In the chaos of post-war Germany, he spent two decades trying to track down the loyal comrades from his odyssey in January and February 1945 – without success. Arnhold was not disheartened. "A voice inside me tells me that I will see them again one day," he wrote.[13]

Waffen SS clerk **Georg Haas** became a probation officer. He also wrote a fictionalized account of the siege, which featured one Hendrik Velthove – a pseudonym for Dutch volunteer **Hendrik Verton**. Verton was freed on account of his wounds in September 1945. He lived in the ruined city, where he met his future wife Brigitte, until fleeing in 1946. In the west, he eventually established a floor-laying firm which thrives to this day. A return to his native Netherlands was impossible until the early 1960s, but Verton remained true to his ideological roots; he attended Waffen SS reunions, met former luminaries such as Kurt Meyer and Paul Hausser and even enjoyed a week in Madrid as a guest of Mussolini's liberator, Otto Skorzeny.

Leo Hartmann ended the war with an estimated forty-five tank 'kills' to his name. He spent more than four years in Soviet prison camps before being released. He joined the newly-formed Bundeswehr in the mid-1950s, finally retiring with the rank of *Hauptmann*. That allowed him to resume his original trade: law. He died in Würzburg in 1995 at the age of eighty-two.

Artillery observer **Klaus Franke** evaded capture at the war's end and slipped out of Breslau. He finally made it back to his home on the Lüneberg Heath, via the Sudeten Mountains and Saxony, and became a fire-fighter.

Paul Peikert was 'repatriated' from Breslau in 1946. He lived for just three years in Westphalia before dying in 1949. His diary was discovered by Communist authorities in the early 1960s. An edited version – removing any criticism of the post-war regime – has been published in numerous editions. Fellow Catholic priest **Walter Lassmann** was among the last of Breslau's Germans to be expelled. He lived in East Germany until the mid-1960s before moving to the west, latterly serving the Catholic community of Paderborn. Once resettled in Görlitz, **Ernst Hornig** became Bishop of Silesia – the province was gone, but the title remained, serving what little of Silesia was left within Germany's new borders. He supported repeatedly the rights of his worshippers under the Communist regime until he retired in 1964. His later years were spent compiling one of the great chronicles of the battle for Breslau.

Former union leader and *Volkssturm* man **Otto Rothkugel** settled with his family in Bad Essen in Lower Saxony where he lived beyond the age of 100.

As a former Party member, **Conrad Bischof** went through a 'de-Nazification' court in the British zone. He resumed his postal duties, but in Hanover, where he died from heart failure in 1961 aged sixty-seven. Another faithful chronicler of the siege, **Conrad Schumacher**, also resumed his pre-war career as a travel agent, this time in Hamburg. He too died in 1961.

Of Breslau's young diarists, **Max Baselt** spent two years in prison camps near Voronezh and Gorki before he was released through ill health in early 1948. He became a customs official and, in retirement in Düsseldorf, a regular contributor to the expatriates' newsletter, *Der Schlesier*. **Peter Bannert** was not released from Soviet captivity until the end of 1949. He became a history and geography teacher in Mecklenburg. **Horst Gleiss** became an expert zoologist, botanist and geographer in Wedel near Hamburg. He wrote more than 1,000 articles and, in 1975, founded the archive for memories, documents and photographs of the fortress. Those formed the basis of his ten-volume history, *Breslauer Apokalypse* – Breslau's Apocalypse – which in turn has provided much of the material for this book.

As for the conscientious chronicler of the fledgling Polish city, **Joanna Konopińska** completed her studies and became a writer. Four decades later two volumes of her diaries were published. They provide a unique record of Wrocław's 'pioneer days'.

National Socialist Leadership Officer **Herbert van Bürck** spent the few remaining months of his short life in the Polish city. Van Bürck had been wounded by a mine as he returned from surrender negotiations on 6 May 1945. Once he recovered from his wounds, he was thrown into Kletschkau prison where he was mistreated for four months. His health and nerves broken, he was released and sent home by train. He died at the end of the five-day journey on 1 February 1946, aged just thirty-six. Van Bürck was not the only one of the fortress's trusted staff officers to die in captivity. **Kurt 'Papa' Tiesler** was among a group of officers condemned to twenty-five years' hard labour in the Urals. He died of a heart attack while peeling potatoes in a basement in early 1953.

And then there is **Karl Hanke**. Little is certain about his fate. The circumstances of his flight from Breslau on the morning of 6 May have become myth and legend – his friend Albert Speer (who was not there, of course) claimed he fled by prototype helicopter, for example. Some accounts say the *Gauleiter* took off from the Kaiserstrasse runway, others from the grounds of the Jahrhunderthalle. He landed in Hirschberg. He landed on the slopes of the Zobten. He landed in Schweidnitz, where he spent the day with Party leaders before a car took him to Hirschberg. Reports generally agree that Karl Hanke reached the Sudeten Mountains, but thereafter the trail runs in every possible direction. He was shot by Czech partisans some time in July 1945. He was shot by Soviet troops as he tried to swim the River Eger, close to the Bavarian border. He was living in Spain courtesy of misappropriated funds he had sent to his wife. British and American war crimes investigators were certainly still looking for him in February 1946, while authorities in Cologne were making inquiries into Karl Hanke's whereabouts in the late 1950s. By then, most people believed the *Gauleiter* dead, not least his widow Freda who had him declared legally dead in the early 1950s. Karl Hanke's most likely fate, however, is one which befits the shabby nature of his flight from Breslau. Dressed as an ordinary SS trooper, he mingled with stragglers from the 18th SS Panzer Grenadier Division in Komotau (today Chomutov) in the Sudetenland. Before he could leave the farm where he was hiding, Hanke and several other fugitives, including the local Party functionary, were seized by Czech partisans and taken a short distance up the road to Görkau (Jirkov) where he was held in a cellar for several weeks with other German prisoners. In early June, the Czechs decided to move the prisoners – 65 men in all – on foot. When a train passed the march route, Hanke and several prisoners made a break for it and clung on to the train. The guards opened fire. Karl Hanke fell first. Two other prisoners slumped on to the track. The Czechs then beat the three men repeatedly with rifle butts until there were no more signs of life. They returned to their prisoners laughing: "*Vse v poradku* – everything's okay." They had no idea they had killed the last *Reichsführer* SS and former *Gauleiter* of Breslau.[14]

New homes, new careers, new lives. But there was no way of creating new minds. "In the silence of the night, when the memory of all these events deprives us of our sleep, the scenes of terror and the hours of mortal fear come to life once more," priest Walter Lassmann wrote twenty-five years later. It was the flight of Breslauers in the snow, rather than the inferno of Easter, which came to life when he closed his eyes. "The faces of so many dead appear in front of me repeatedly as if out of one hundred fogs; I see them again and again, the thousands who had lost their lives on country lanes, fleeing before the approaching enemy in the icy winter. An endless column, all the misery in the world seemed to be on the road."[15] Former Hitler Youth Peter Bannert was haunted by the face of the corpse he had seen when marching into captivity, staring back at him from the mud into which a tank had crushed it. For years, Bannert was hounded by a single question: "Which mother might be waiting for this man, her son, who was trampled on by thousands of feet?"[16] Other Breslauers were reminded of the horrors of 1945 by the seemingly innocuous. Holidaying in Copenhagen two decades later with her husband and three children, Vera Eckle visited a waxworks. "Suddenly there was a display case with wax heads, about the size of a child's head," she remembered. "They were pale and had eye sockets with rigid glass eyes." Eckle began screaming. "Just take these dead children away. Take the children away!" In an instant, she had been taken back to the Kanth road in January 1945. It took sedatives to finally calm her down.[17]

Wrocław's buildings and structures still bear the scars of 1945 too. Concrete bunkers still pepper the city. You will find them in the suburbs on Ulica Grabiszynska (Gräbschener Strasse) and on Ulica Ladna (Selenka Strasse). They are still pockmarked. At least two of the huge round *Hochbunker* survive. The Ulica Ołbińska (Elbingstrasse) bunker remains grey and forbidding. That in Ulica Legnicka (Striegauer Platz) is a brilliant white. For years it served as a warehouse, then as a shopping arcade. Today it is being turned into a museum of modern art. Less obvious are the subterranean bunkers. The one beneath Nowy Targ is likely to be turned into an underground car park. The former hospital under Plac Solny (Blücherplatz) is due to become a puppet museum, of all things, whilst there are plans to create a Fortress Breslau museum under Plac Strzegomski (Striegauerplatz).

Other fortifications crumble. Those on the Promenada Staromiejska (Holteihöhe) are smashed. Much of *I-Werk* 41 lies in ruins in fields not far from the route of a new motorway. On the reverse slope of the Wzgórze Partyznatów (Liebichshöhe) there is another crumbling concrete structure, its entrance bricked up, its walls daubed with graffiti. As for the one-time headquarters of the fortress command, they are now a rather run-down restaurant with a Russian-themed nightclub – Provocation – on the ground floor. After dark a thumping bass-line reverberates across Ulica Piotra Skagi (Taschenstrasse) and down Ulica Teatralna (Zwingerstrasse) into the park opposite. Perhaps it was this which caused the sorry statue of Mother Russia, her eyes closed, to crumble and decay. She forlornly faces east. There are no inscriptions, no plaques. A handful of students sit on the chipped marble base, perusing their notes and enjoying a coffee.

It is not the only Soviet monument to suffer. On the southern edge of the city, two anti-tank guns and a couple of T34 tanks mounted on plinths stand guard at the entrance to the resting place of 763 officers. Regular visitors to military cemeteries in Western Europe will be surprised by the poor state of the grounds. It has at least fared better than Skowronia Góra cemetery a mile and a half away, where more than 7,000 *frontoviki* are buried. Most of the Soviet dead were interred here in mass graves between 1947 and 1953 as the temporary burial grounds of 1945 were cleared. Skowronia Góra is dominated by a huge slab of marble which promises "eternal glory to the fallen heroes of the struggle for freedom and the independence of the Soviet motherland." There is little eternal glory to be found here. The mass graves are overgrown. Individual monuments to the fallen have faded over time, been chipped or cracked, and photographs prised off many of the headstones.

But at least the Soviet cemeteries, however run-down, still exist. Not so the city's German cemeteries. For a quarter of a century they lay untouched, overgrown. But in 1970 the civic authorities began clearing them – no burials for twenty-five years provided the official pretext. Over the next two years, all were cleared, flattened, bulldozed. The gravestones and sculptures were used as rubble to strengthen the gullies in the city moat, or served as the foundation for a stand in a sports stadium. Some were incorporated into a new animal run in Wrocław's zoo. "Only the animals can stare at the epitaphs of German citizens," city historian Maciej Łagiewski wryly observed. Other headstones ended up on the site of the former cemetery in Osobowice (Oswitz). Stonemasons wandered among them with pots of white paint, daubing the ones they wished to recycle as headstones for Wrocław's Polish dead. No one protested. Most Vratislavians turned a blind eye, objecting only when there were plans to erect memorial stones explaining the German past of a cemetery or park.[18]

Other traces of the city's German past have been erased. In the immediate aftermath of the war, the *Entdeutschung* – de-Germanization – of Breslau was waged almost fanatically. You will find few, if any, pre-1945 buildings with the inscription '*Erbaut*' – built – or '*im Jahre*' – in the year. The Kaiserbrücke still spans the Oder, but as on the Most Grunwaldzki all traces of Kaiser and Reich have been removed. The motifs on the imposing stone towers celebrate the Slavic heroes of 1410. If you look closely, however, you will see a few traces of a more recent battle.

On the other side of the bridge, Karl Hanke's Kaiserstrasse wasteland has been replaced by a mish-mash of bleak Communist-era tower blocks and the more sympathetic stone structures of the polytechnic. Plac Grunwaldzki (Scheitniger Stern) is now a celebration of capitalism. A glass skyscraper office block and one of Wrocław's many shopping malls – *galeria* – which have sprung up since the fall of Communism dominate this once vast space.

Walk east along Ulica Marie Curie Sklodowskiej (Tiergartenstrasse) and cross the Most Zwierzyniecki (Passbrücke) which spans the Stara Odra (Alte Oder). The inscription on the bridge reads 1895–1897, but the plaque above has been erased. Another couple of hundred yards and you will come to the Jahrhunderthalle – far larger and more imposing than any photograph can convey. It survived the war largely intact and resumed its pre-war role as a venue for exhibitions, conferences, rallies and concerts under two names, *Hala Ludowa* – People's Hall – and *Hala Stulecia* – Century Hall, a direct translation of its original title. The broad boulevard which leads up to the imposing structure is dominated by a 315ft spike, the *Iglica* – needle – erected for an exhibition celebrating the 'regained territories' in 1948. And on the left is the now partially empty four-domed pavilion with its fading memorials to the Soviet and Polish soldiers who drove the Wehrmacht from Moscow to Berlin.

Whilst monuments to the Red Army and Poles who fought side-by-side decay, more recent memorials are visited on a daily or weekly basis by Vratislavians. In a park on the north-eastern edge of the old town, a mother holds her son to her bosom as she looks upwards forlornly at an angel – the memorial to the victims of the Katyn massacre. A short distance away on the former Holteihöhe, now a rather run-down green space, there is the statue of a crucified man torn in two – the monument to the people of Lwów, driven from their homes at the war's end.

Although Wrocław's leaders strove not to make it "a second Lwów", the city is inextricably bound with the capital of the Western Ukraine. Lwów's world-famous Ossolineum, one of the finest collections of Polish art and literature in existence, found a new home in Wrocław. The city's academics helped re-start Wrocław University. And Lwów's greatest treasure of all became one of Wrocław's most popular tourist attractions. Eventually. The *Racławice Panorama* depicts the victory of a Polish peasant army against the Russians in 1793 – a military triumph ranked by Poles almost as highly as the defeat of the Teutons at Grunwald in 1410. It was transported west with the rest of the Ossolineum, but for four decades the enormous painting – 375 feet long and 50 high – remained in storage, the rotunda built to house it during the mid-1960s remaining empty until 1985 when the panorama was finally unveiled to the public once more.

Not five minutes' walk from the rotunda is the Odra (Oder) promenade. Directly opposite, the cathedral continues to dominate the skyline of the right bank of the Oder. For nearly half a century its twin towers lacked their spires. They were only replaced at the beginning of the 1990s. The view from the top – if you pay a few złoty to ride the lift – is as commanding as it ever was. Below, the sun dances over the Oder as the gentle September breeze catches the river. Pleasure cruisers carry tourists, while rowers paddle hurriedly out of their way. To the east, the four floodlights of the Olympic Stadium – which has never hosted an Olympic event – lean inwards, towering above the woods and parks below. It has changed remarkably little since the *Sportfest* of 1938, although the principal sporting activity enjoyed here these days is speedway. In the south, almost hidden by the haze, lies the distinctive outline of the 2,350ft Mount Ślęża (Zobten). Sixty-five years ago, observers in Breslau's spires and towers looked at German positions on its slopes and prayed that Schörner would come.

The immediate skyline to the west is dominated by the green copper spire of the Kolegiata Świętego Krzyża (Kreuzkirche). From this height the cross shape which gave the church its German name is obvious. Beyond that, the Oder is channelled around half a dozen islands. Wyspa Piasek is much as it was when it was known as Sandinsel. The warehouses and mills on the Vorderbleiche, today Wyspa Słodowa, have long gone. A single tenement block remains from the city's German era, its rear walls dominated by gigantic paintings. The rest of the island has been turned into a park. On an early September evening you will find couples, young people, perhaps a few older ones, sitting on the wooden benches here. They look across at the magnificent façade of the university, like the town hall, wonderfully lit up by night; so too is the cathedral; one spire is silver, the other a drab grey. An elderly fisherman rests his rod over the side of the steep bank and chews away at a sandwich as he waits for a bite. All that passes on the water is a family of ducks, making its way downstream. The Oder is at peace.

Notes

1. Thum, p.197
2. Life in the city in the late 1940s/early 1950s is based on Jerrig, pp.46, 48-9, Gleiss, vi,pp.10-Wassermann, p.226.
3. Rebuilding of Wrocław is based on Thum, pp.197-8, 229-243 and Wassermann, p.230.
4. Wassermann, pp.228-31.
5. See *Wrocław 1945 1965*, pp.39-49.
6. Gleiss, viii, p.292, Reuth, p.155, and Knopp, *Grosse Flucht*, p.215.
7. Author's papers.
8. Dörr, pp.529-30.
9. Henkel, pp.59-60, 77-9.
10. Dörr, pp.528-9 and Reuth, p.155.
11. Knopp, *Die Grosse Flucht*, p.213.
12. Hartung, pp.157-8.
13. Arnhold, pp.260-2.
14. Fate of Karl Hanke based on NA WO309/140 and *Hamburger Allgemeine Zeitung*, 11/5/49.
15. Gleiss, v, p.480.
16. Bannert, p.86.
17. Knopp, *Grosse Flucht*, p.160.
18. Kalicki, Włodzimierz, 'Als es hiess: Jeder Pole hat seinen Deutschen', *Frankfurter Allgemeine Zeitung*, 23/11/93.

Equivalent Military Ranks

German Army	Waffen SS	British Army
Generalfeldmarschall	Reichsführer-SS	Field Marshal
Generaloberst	SS Oberstgruppenführer	General
General	SS Obergruppenführer	Lieutenant General
Generalleutnant	SS Gruppenführer	Major General
Generalmajor	SS Brigadeführer	Brigadier
Oberst	SS Standartenführer	Colonel
	SS Oberführer	
Oberstleutnant	SS Obersturmbannführer	Lieutenant Colonel
Major	SS Sturmbannführer	Major
Hauptmann	SS Hauptsturmführer	Captain
Oberleutnant	SS Obersturmführer	Lieutenant
Leutnant	SS Untersturmführer	2nd Lieutenant
Stabsfeldwebel	SS Sturmsharführer	Sergeant Major
Hauptfeldwebel	SS Stabsscharführer	
Oberfeldwebel	SS Hauptscharführer	
Feldwebel	SS Oberscharführer	Colour Sergeant
Unterfeldwebel	SS Scharführer	Sergeant
Unteroffizier	SS Unterscharführer	
Stabsgefreiter		
Obergefreiter	SS Rottenführer	Corporal
Gefreiter	SS Sturmmann	Lance Corporal
Oberschütz/Oberjäger	SS Oberschutz	
Schütze/Jäger/Grenadier	SS Schütze	Private

Bibliography

UNPUBLISHED SOURCES

Bundesarchiv-Militärarchiv, Freiburg im Breisgau

RH 2 Files of Oberkommando des Heeres/Generalstab des Heeres
RH2/2470 Papers of Fremde Heere Ost
RH2/2681 Papers of Fremde Heere Ost
RH2/2683 Papers of Fremde Heere Ost
RH2/2685 Papers of Fremde Heere Ost

RH13 Files of General z. b. V. beim OKH
RH13/48 Feldpostberichte August 1944
RH13/49 Feldpostberichte September 1944

RH 20 Files of Eighth Army
RH20-8/1 Tagebuch Hans Felber, Polenfeldzug

RH 26 Infantry Division papers
RH26-6/112 6 Infanterie Division im Warka Brückenkopf-Lauban

Imperial War Museum, London
02/23/1 Herbert Rühlemann, 'Father Tells Daughter'
95/4/1 Fritz Neugebauer, 'Tatsachenbericht unserer Erlebnisse während der letzten Kriegszeit, 1945'
07/15/1 Memoirs of Ursel Dittman

NATIONAL ARCHIVES, KEW

FO898 Political Warfare Executive and Foreign Office, Political Intelligence Department
FO898/186 Summary of and comments on German Propaganda Ministry broadcasts 1943-1944
FO898/187 Summary of and comments on German Propaganda Ministry broadcasts 1943-1945

HW1 Government Code and Cypher School
HW1/3744 Signals intelligence passed to the Prime Minister, messages and correspondence

WO 204 Allied Forces, Mediterranean Theatre: Military Headquarters Papers
WO204/985 Allied Forces Headquarters (Mediterranean) G-2 Intelligence Notes
WO204/987 Allied Forces Headquarters (Mediterranean) G-2 Intelligence Notes

WO 309 Judge Advocate General's Office, British Army of the Rhine War Crimes Group
WO309/140 Alleged war crimes committed by Karl Hanke, *Gauleiter* of Breslau

PUBLISHED WORKS

Television documentaries
Die Große Flucht, ZDF, 2001, Episode 5, 'Festung Breslau'

Newspapers
Deutsche Allgemeine Zeitung, Berlin, 1945
Gross Wartenberger Heimatblatt, Nr.1, 1995
Oberschlesische Zeitung, Kattowitz, 1944-45
Schlesische Tageszeitung, Breslau, 1938-1945
Völkischer Beobachter, Berlin edition, 1938, 1944-1945
Völkischer Beobachter, Munich edition, 1944-1945

258

PRIMARY SOURCES

Adamczyk, Werner, *Feuer! An Artilleryman's Life on the Eastern Front*, Broadfoot, Wilmington, 1992

Arnhold, Paul, *Der gnadenlose Weg: Von der Weichsel nach Breslau 12 Januar bis 15 Februar 1945*, Blick & Bild Verlag, 1966

Axmann, Artur, *Das kann doch nicht das Ende sein: Hitlers letzter Reichsjugendführer erinnert sich*, Verlag S Bublies, Koblenz, 1995

Baedeker, Karl, *Schlesien. Riesengerbirge. Grafschaft Glatz. Reisehandbuch*, 2nd ed, Baedeker, Leipzig, 1938

Bähr, Walter and Bähr, Hans (eds) *Kriegsbriefe Gefallener Studenten 1939-1945*, Rainer Wunderlich Verlag, Tübingen, 1952

Bannert, Peter, *Meine Jugend in Sowjetlagern 1945-1949*, Zeitgut Verlag, Berlin, 2006

Boberach, Heinz, *Meldungen aus dem Reich: Die geheimen Lageberichte des Sicherheitsdienstes der SS 1938-1945*, Pawlak Verlag, Herrsching, 1984

Borodziej, Wlodzimierz and Lemberg, Hans (eds), *Unsere Heimat ist uns ein fremdes Land geworden: Die Deutschen östlich von Oder und Neiße 1945-1950. Dokumente aus polnischen Archiven*, Band 4, *Wojewodschaft Pommerellen und Danzig (Westpreußen), Wojewodschaft Breslau (Niederschlesien)*, Herder Institut, Marburg, 2004

Cohn, Willi, *Kein Recht, nirgends: Tagebuch vom Untergang des Breslauer Judentums 1933-1941*, Böhlau, Cologne, 2007

Dippel, Ernst, *Erinnerungen: Krieg und Gefangenschaft*, Selbstverlag, 2002

Dollinger, Hans, *Kain, wo ist dein Bruder?* Fischer Verlag, Frankfurt am Main, 1987

Dokumentation der Vertreibung der Deutschen aus Ost-Mitteleuropa I, *Die Vertreibung der deutschen Bevölkerung aus den Gebieten östlich der Oder-Neisse*, three volumes, DTV, Munich, 1984

Dragunski, David Abramovich, *Jahre im Panzer*, Militärverlag der Deutschen Demokratischen Republik, Berlin, 1980

Elliger, Katharina, *Und tief in der Seele des Ferne: Die Geschichte einer Vertreibung aus Schlesien*, Rowohlt Taschenbuch Verlag, Hamburg, 2004

Franke, Klaus, *Hölle Breslau 1945: Ein Erinnerungsbericht*, Druffel Verlag, Berg am Starnberger See, 1998

Freytag von Loringhoven, Bernd, *In the Bunker with Hitler: The Last Witness Speaks*, Weidenfeld & Nicolson, London, 2006

Fritze, Eugen, *Unter dem Zeichen des Aeskulap 1940-1945: Das Tagebuch eines Soldaten Arztes bei der 6 Panzer Division*, Selbstverlag, 2003

Frodien, Ulrich, *Bleib übrig: Eine Kriegsjugend in Deutschland*, DTV, Munich, 2004

Gelfand, Wladimir, *Deutschland Tagebuch 1945-1946*, Aufbau Verlag, Berlin, 2005

Gleiss, Horst, *Breslauer Apokalypse 1945: Dokumentarchronik vom Todeskampf und Untergang einer Deutschen Stadt und Festung am Ende des zweiten Weltkrieges*, ten volumes, Natura et Patria Verlag, Wedel, 1986-1997

Gleiss, Horst, *Breslauer Exodus 1946: Beiträge zur Dokumentarchronik einer Stadt und ihrer Menschen*, Natura et Patria Verlag, Rosenheim, 2003

Gleiss, Horst, *Pennäler, Pimpf und Volkssturmmann*, Verlag Der Schlesier, Recklinghausen, 1982

Goebbels, Joseph, *Die Tagebücher von Joseph Goebbels 1923-1945*, twenty-four volumes, K G Saur, Munich, 1993-1996

Grunow, Martin, 'Erlbenisse und Erfahrungen eines Lazarettpfarrers und Pfarrers in Breslau 1945-1946' in *Jahrbuch für Schlesische Kirchengeschichte 1964*

Guderian, Heinz, *Panzer Leader*, Michael Joseph, London, 1952

Haas, Georg, *Brände an der Oder*, Helmut Cramer Verlag, Lohmar, 1977

Haas, Georg, *Und gaben die Hoffnung nicht auf*, Helmut Cramer Verlag, Lohmar, 1977

Hartmann, Hans Jürgen, *Zwischen Nichts und Niemandsland*, Machtwortverlag, Dessau, 2006

Hartung, Hugo, *Schlesien 1944-45*, DTV, Munich, 1976

Henkel, Hans Eberhard, *Breslau: Flucht und Wiederbegegnung*, Freiling, Berlin, 1996

Höntsch, Ursula, (ed) *Mir bleibt mein lied: Schlesisches Lesebuch*, Piper Verlag, Munich, 1995

Höss, Rudolf, *Commandant of Auschwitz*, Pan, London, 1961

Hupka, Herbert (ed), *Breslau: Geliebt und unvergessen*, Verlag Gerhard Rautenberg, Leer, 1990

Hupka, Herbert (ed), *Letzte Tage in Schlesien*, Bertelsmann, Gütersloh, 1985

Hupka, Herbert (ed), *Meine Heimat Schlesien: Errinerungen*, Weltbild Verlag, Augsburg, 1989

Hupka, Herbert (ed), *Meine Heimat Schlesien:Städte und Landschaften,* Weltbild Verlag, Augsburg, 1990

International Military Tribunal, *The Trial of German Major War Criminals*, twenty-three volumes, HMSO, London, 1946

Jakubowski, Iwan Ignatjewitsch, *Erde im Feuer*, Militärverlag der Deutschen Demokratischen Republik, Berlin, 1977

Jonca, Karol and Konieczny, Alfred (eds), *Festung Breslau: Documenty Oblezenia 16/2-6/5/45*, Państwowe Wydawnictwo Naukowe, Wrocław, 1962

Kempowski, Walter (ed), *Das Echolot: Abgesang '45 – Ein Kollektives Tagebuch*, btb Verlag, Munich, 2007

Kempowski, Walter (ed), *Das Echolot: Fuga furiosa – Ein kollektives Tagebuch Winter 1945*, four volumes, btb Verlag, Munich, 2004

Knappe, Siegfried, *Soldat*, Dell, New York, 1993

Knebel, Hajo, *Jahrgang 1929*, Bergstadtverlag Korn, Würzburg, 1962

Konev, Ivan, *Year of Victory*, Progress, Moscow, 1969

Konopińska, Joanna, *Tamten wrocławski rok 1945-1946: dziennik*, Wydawnictwo Dolnośląskie, Wrocław, 1987

Konrad, Joachim, *Als letzter Stadtdekan von Breslau*, Verlag Unser Weg, Ulm, 1963

Koriakov, Mikhail, *I'll Never Go Back: A Red Army Officer Talks*, George Harrap, London, 1948

Litvin, Nikolai, *800 Days on the Eastern Front: A Russian Soldier Remembers World War II*, University Press of Kansas, Kansas, 2007

Mondwurf, Friedhelm, 'Als Bettelmann in Breslau' in Hupka, Herbert (ed), *Letzte Tage in Schlesien*, Bertelsmann, Gütersloh, 1985

Nuremberg Military Tribunal, *Trials of War Criminals Before the Nuremberg Military Tribunals, Case 10: United States against Alfred Krupp, et al*, USGPO, Washington DC, 1949

Oven, Wilfred von, *Finale Furioso: Mit Goebbels bis zum Ende*, Grabert Verlag, Tübingen, 1974

Ozanna, Josef Georg, 'Aus den Tagebuchaufzeichnungen eines schlesischen Pfarrers 1945-46' in *Jahrbuch für Schlesische Kirchengeschichte 1964*

Peikert, Paul, *Festung Breslau in den Berichten eines Pfarrers*, Union Verlag, Berlin, c.1968

Polewoi, Boris, *Berlin 896km: Aufzeichnungen eines Frontkorrespondenten*, Verlag Volk und Welt, Berlin, 1975

Rogall, Joachim (ed), *Die Räumung des Reichsgaus Wartheland vom 16 bis 26 Januar 1945 im Spiegel amtlicher Berichte*, Jan Thorbecke Verlag, Sigmaringen, 1995

Rudel, Hans-Ulrich, *Stuka Pilot*, George Mann, Maidstone, 1973

Schleicher, Karl-Theodor and Walle, Heinrich (eds), *Aus Feldpostbriefen junger Christen 1939-1945*, Franz Steiner Verlag, Stuttgart, 2005

Scholz, Franz, *Görlitzer Tagebuch: Chronik einer Vertreibung, 1945/46*, Zentralstelle Grafschaft Glatz/Schlesien, Lüdenscheid, 1995

Speer, Albert, *Inside the Third Reich*, Sphere, London, 1988

Steinmann an Haack, Edith, *Schlesisches Tagebuch: Tagebuchnotizen 1945/46*, Projekte-Verlag, Halle, 2007

Tausk, Walter, *Breslauer Tagebuch 1933-1940*, Rütten & Loening, Berlin, 1975

Terp, Hans-Joachim, *Für'n Sechser Fett auf zwei Semmeln*, Neisse Verlag, Görlitz, 2005

Verton, Hendrik, *In the Fire of the Eastern Front: The Experiences of a Dutch Waffen-SS Volunteer on the Eastern Front 1941-45*, Helion, Solihull, 2006

Vertreibung und Vertreibungsverbrechen 1945-1948: Bericht des Bundesarchivs vom 28 Mai 1974, Kulturstiftung der deutschen Vertriebenen, Bonn, 1989

Völkel, Hans, *Breslauer – Evakuierte in Bayern: Zwei Tagebücher aus der Kriegs- und Nachkriegszeit 1945-1946*, Bochumer Universität Verlag, Bochum, 2005

Waage, Ursula, *Bleib übrig*, Projekte Verlag, Halle, 2004

Wassermann, Charles, *Unter Polnischer Verwaltung*, Bertelsmann Verlag, Lesering, 1958

SECONDARY SOURCES

Ahlfen, Hans von, *Der Kampf um Schlesien*, Motorbuch Verlag, Stuttgart, 1998

Ahlfen, Hans von, and Niehoff, Hermann, *So kämpfte Breslau*, Gräfe und Unzer Verlag, Munich, 1960

Alexijewitsch, Swetlana, *Der Krieg hat kein weibliches Gesicht*, Berliner Taschenbuch Verlag, Berlin, 2004

Als die Deutschen weg waren: Was nach der Vertreibung geschah: Ostpreussen, Schlesien, Sudetenland, Rowohlt, Hamburg, 2007

Ascher, Abraham, *A Community under Siege: The Jews of Breslau under Nazism*, Stanford University Press, 2007

Asmus, Dietwart, *20.Inf.Div.(mot) Chronik und Geschichte*, 9 Teil, VI. Abschnitt 1945, Selbstverlag, 2009

Aust, Stefan and Burgdorff, Stephan (eds), *Die Flucht: Über die Vertreibung der Deutschen aus dem Osten*, Deutsche Verlags-Anstalt, Stuttgart, 2002

Becker, Rolf, *Niederschlesien 1945: Die Flucht, die Besetzung*, Aufstieg Verlag, Munich, 1974

Böddeker, Günter, *Die Flüchtlinge: die Verteibung der Deutschen im Osten*, Gustav Lübbe Verlag, 1982

Carell, Paul, and Böddeker, Günter, *Die Gefangenen: Leben und Überleben deutscher Soldaten hinter Stacheldraht*, Ullstein, Frankfurt am Main, 1980

Davies, Norman, and Moorhouse, Roger, *Microcosm: Portrait of a Central European City*, Pimlico, London, 2003

Dörr, Margarete, *Der Krieg hat uns geprägt: Wie Kinder den Zweiten Weltkrieg erlebten*, Campus Verlag, Frankfurt, 2007

Duffy, Christopher, *Red Storm on the Reich*, Atheneum, London, 1992

Ferencz, Benjamin B, *Less than Slaves: Jewish Forced Labor and the Quest for Compensation*, Indiana University Press, 2002

Führer durch das Deutsches Turn- und Sportfest Breslau 1938

Glantz, David (ed), *From the Vistula to the Oder: Soviet Offensive Operations October 1944-March 1945: 1986 Art of War Symposium*, Center for Land Warfare, US Army War College, 1986

Glantz, David, and House, Jonathan, *When Titans Clashed: How the Red Army Stopped Hitler*, University Press of Kansas, Kansas, 1995

Grau, Karl Friedrich, *Schlesische Inferno: Kriegsverbrechen der Roten Armee beim Einbruch in Schlesien 1945*, Seewald Verlag, Stuttgart, 1966

Grieger, Friedrich, *Wie Breslau fiel*, Verlag Die Zukunft, Metzingen, 1948

Gunter, Georg, *Letzter Lorbeer: Vorgeschichte und Geschichte der Kämpfe in Oberschlesien von Januar bis Mai 1945*, Oberschlesischer Heimatverlag, Augsburg, 2006

Hargreaves, Richard, *Blitzkrieg Unleashed: The German Invasion of Poland*, Pen and Sword, Barnsley, 2008

Hartmann, Christian, *Wehrmacht im Ostkrieg: Front und militärisches Hinterland 1941/42*, Oldenbourg Verlag, Munich, 2009

Hastings, Max, *Armageddon: The Battle for Germany 1944-45*, Macmillan, London, 2004

Heiss, Friedrich, *Das Schlesienbuch. Ein Zeugnis ostdeutschen Schicksals*, Volk und Reich Verlag, Berlin, 1938

Hinze, Rolf, *19 Infanterie und Panzer Division: Divisiongeschichte aus der Sicht eines Artilleristen*, Verlag Dr Rolf Hinze, Meerbusch, 1994

Hinze, Rolf, *Hitze, Frost und Pulverdampf: Der Schicksalsweg der 20 Panzer Division*, 5th Ed, Selbstverlag, Meerbusch, 1994

Hofmann, Andreas R, *Nachkriegszeit in Schlesien*, Böhlau Verlag, Köln, 2000

Hornig, Ernst, *Breslau 1945: Erlebnisse in der eingeschlossenen Stadt*, Bergstadtverlag, München, 1975

Irving, David, *Goebbels*, Focal Point, London, 1996

Irving, David, *Hitler's War*, Hodder and Stoughton, London, 1977

Irving, David, *Trail of the Fox*, Book Club Associates, London, 1977

Jahnke, Karl Heinz, *Hitlers letztes Aufgebot: Deutsche Jugend im sechsten Kriegsjahr 1944-45*, Klartext, Koblenz, 1993

Jerrig, F O, *Aus Breslau wurde Wrocław*, Verlag Wolfgang Kwiecinski, Hannover, 1949

Kalicki, Włodzimierz, 'Als es hiess: Jeder Pole hat seinen Deutschen', *Frankfurter Allgemeine Zeitung*, 23/11/93

Kaltenegger, Roland, *Schörner – Feldmarschall der letzten Stunde*, Herbig Verlag, Munich, 1994

Kaps, Johannes, *Die Tragödie Schlesiens 1945/1946 in Dokumenten*, Christ Unterwegs Verlag, Munich, 1952

Kaps, Johannes, *Martyrium und Heldentum ostdeutscher Frauen: Ein Ausschnitt aus der schlesischen Passion 1945/46*, Niedermayer & Miesgang, Neuötting am Inn, n.d.

Kaps, Johannes, *Vom Sterben schlesischer Priester 1945/46: Ein Ausschnitt aus der schlesischen Passion 1945/46*, Wienand, Cologne, 1960

Klabunde, Anja, *Magda Goebbels*, Sphere, London, 2003

Knopp, Guido, *Der Sturm: Kriegsende im Osten*, Ullstein, Berlin, 2006

Knopp, Guido, *Der Verdammte Krieg*, three volumes, Orbis Verlag, Munich, 1998

Knopp, Guido, *Die Grosse Flucht*, Ullstein, Munich, 2002

Kunz, Andreas, *Wehrmacht und Niederlage*, Oldenbourg Verlag, Munich, 2007

Lukas, Oskar (ed) Breslau: *Bekenntnis zu Deutschland: Ein Bildbericht vom 1 Deutschen Turn– und Sportfest 1938*, Cam Schneider Verlag, Selb/Asch, 1938

Magenheimer, Heinz, *Abwehrschlacht an der Weichsel 1945: Vorbereitung, Ablauf, Erfahrungen*, Rombach Verlag, Freiburg, 1976

Mammach, Klaus, *Der Volkssturm: Das letzte Aufgebot 1944-45*, Akademie Verlag, Berlin, 1981

Majewski, Rysard and Sozanska, Teresa, *Die Schlacht um Breslau Januar-Mai 1945*, Union Verlag, Berlin, 1979

Majewski, Ryszard (ed), *Wrocławska epopeja: Wspomnienia z walk o wyzwolenie miasta w 1945r*, Ossolineum, 1975

Manchester, William, *The Arms of Krupp*, Michael Joseph, London, 1969

Manteuffel, Hasso von, *Die 7. Panzer-Division im Zweiten Weltkrieg: Einsatz und Kampf der Gespenster-Division 1939-1945*, Traditionsverband ehem. 7 Panzer Division Kameradenhilfe, Ürdigen, 1965

Merridale, Catherine, *Ivan's War*, Faber and Faber, London, 2005

Messerschmidt, Manfred, *Die Wehrmacht im NS-Staat*, R V Decker Verlag, Hamburg, 1969

Müller, Rolf-Dieter (ed), *Das Deutsche Reich und der Zweite Weltkrieg*, Band 10/1, *Der Zusammenbruch des Deutschen Reiches 1945*, Deutsche Verlags-Anstalt, Munich, 2008

Müller, Rolf-Dieter (ed), *Das Deutsche Reich und der Zweite Weltkrieg, Band 10/2, Der Zusammenbruch des Deutschen Reiches 1945: Die Folgen des Zweiten Weltkrieges*, Deutsche Verlags-Anstalt, Munich, 2008

Naimark, Norman, *The Russians in Germany: A History of the Soviet Zone of Occupation 1945-49*, Harvard University Press, 1997

Noble, Alastair, *Nazi Rule and the Soviet Offensive in Eastern Germany, 1944-1945: The Darkest Hour*, Sussex University Press, 2008

Olszewski, Tomasz, and Rutkiewicz, Ignacy, *Wrocław 1945-1965*, Polonia, Warsaw, 1966

Paul, Wolfgang, *Der Endkampf um Deutschland 1945*, second edition, Esslingen, 1978

Rada, Uwe, *Die Oder: Lebenslauf eines Flusses*, Siedler, Munich, 2009

Ramm, Gerald, *Gott Mit Uns: Kriegserlebnisse aus Brandenburg und Berlin*, Verlag Gerald Ramm, Woltersdorf/Schleuse, 2005

Rees, Laurence, *Auschwitz: The Nazis and the Final Solution*, BBC Books, London, 2005

Reuth, Ralf Georg, *Deutsche auf der Flucht. Zeitzeugen-Berichte über die Vertreibung aus dem Osten*, Weltbild Verlag, Augsburg, 2007

Römhild, Helmut, *Geschichte der 269. Infanterie-Division*, Podzun Verlag, Bad Nauheim, 1967

Schenk, Dieter, *Hans Frank: Hitlers Kronjurist und Generalgouverneur*, S Fischer Verlag, Frankfurt am Main, 2006

Scherstjanoi, Elke (ed), *Rotarmisten schreiben aus Deutschland: Briefe von der Front 1945*, K G Saur, Munich, 2004

Schimmel-Falkenau, Walter, *Breslau: Vom Herzog zum Gauleiter*, Verlag Weidlich, Frankfurt am Main, 1965

Schwarz, Wolfgang, *Die Flucht und Vertreibung Oberschlesien 1945-46*, Podzun Verlag, Bad Nauheim, 1965

Seidler, Franz W, *Deutscher Volkssturm: Das letzte Aufgebot 1944-1945*, Bechtermünz Verlag, Augsburg, 1999

Seidler, Franz W, *Die Militärgerichtsbarkeit der Deutschen Wehrmacht 1939-1945*, Herbig, Munich, 1991

Seidler, Franz W, *Fahnenflucht: Der Soldat zwischen Eid und Gewissen*, Herbig, Munich, 1993

Siebel-Achenbach, Sebastian, *Lower Silesia from Nazi Germany to Communist Poland, 1942-49*, St Martin's Press, London, 1994

Shulman, Milton, *Defeat in the West*, 2nd edition, Coronet, London, 1973

Thorwald, Jürgen, *Es begann an der Weichsel*, Steingrüben Verlag, Stuttgart, n.d

Thum, Gregor, *Die fremde Stadt: Breslau nach 1945*, Pantheon, Munich, 2006

Van Aaken, Wolf, *Hexenkessel Ostfront: Von Smolensk nach Breslau*, Erich Pabel Verlag, Rastatt, 1964

Werth, Alexander, *Russia at War*, Pan, London, 1965

Werthen, Wolfgang, *Geschichte der 16 Panzer Division*, Podzun Verlag, Bad Nauheim, 1958

Wette, Bremer and Vogel, *Das letzte halbe Jahr: Stimmungsberichte der Wehrmachtpropaganda*, Klartext, Essen, 2001

Wette, Wolfram (ed), *Der Krieg des kleinen Mannes. Eine Militärgeschichte von unten*, Piper Verlag, Munich, 1998

Wette, Wolfram (ed), *Was damals Recht war: NS Militär und Strafjustiz im Vernichtungskrieg*, Klartext, Essen, 1996

Zeidler, Manfred, *Kriegsende im Osten: Die Rote Armee und die Besetzung Deutschlands östlich von Oder und Neisse 1944-45*, Oldenbourg, Munich, 1996

Zoepf, Arne W G, *Wehrmacht zwischen Tradition und Ideologie der NS-Führungsoffizier im Zweiten Weltkrieg*, Peter Lang, Frankfurt am Main, 1988

Index

Stackpole Military History Series

Real battles. Real soldiers. Real stories.

Stackpole Military History Series

Real battles. Real soldiers. Real stories.

Stackpole Military History Series

Real battles. Real soldiers. Real stories.

Stackpole Military History Series

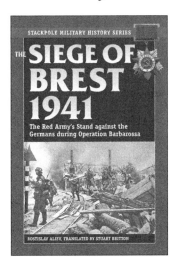

THE SIEGE OF BREST 1941
THE RED ARMY'S STAND AGAINST THE GERMANS
DURING OPERATION BARBAROSSA
Rostislav Aliev

On 22 June 1941, the first German shells smashed into the
Soviet frontier fortress of Brest, marking the start of Hitler's
Operation Barbarossa. As the *Wehrmacht* advanced, taking
the Red Army by surprise, the isolated stronghold of Brest
held out in one of the most legendary defenses of World War
II. This graphic account reconstructs in vivid, hour-by-hour
detail the siege of Brest by the German 45th Infantry
Division and the resistance of the isolated groups of Red
Army soldiers who carried out doomed counterattacks under
a storm of German firepower and fought to the bitter end.

Paperback • 6 x 9 • 272 pages • 45 b/w photos, 5 maps

WWW.STACKPOLEBOOKS.COM
1-800-732-3669

Stackpole Military History Series

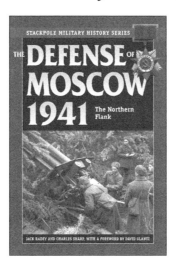

THE DEFENSE OF MOSCOW 1941
THE NORTHERN FLANK
Jack Radey and Charles Sharp; Foreword by David Glantz

Nazi Germany's best chance of winning World War II on the Eastern Front came in October 1941. Most of the Red Army's forces around Moscow had been smashed or encircled, and no reserves were available for the capital's defense. All that stood in Germany's way was a handful of Soviet rifle divisions, tank brigades, and militia. When their attack ground to a halt, the Germans blamed the mud, but close examination reveals it was the scraped together and poorly coordinated resistance of the Red Army that stopped the Germans. Radey and Sharp tell this dramatic story in their study of a pivotal battle in the struggle for supremacy in the East.

Paperback • 6 x 9 • 304 pages • 31 b/w photos

WWW.STACKPOLEBOOKS.COM
1-800-732-3669

Stackpole Military History Series

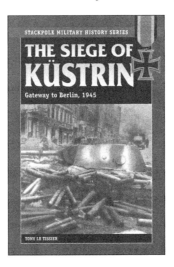

THE SIEGE OF KÜSTRIN

GATEWAY TO BERLIN, 1945

Tony Le Tissier

Only fifty miles from Berlin, the ancient fortress of Küstrin was one of the final roadblocks standing between the Red Army and the Third Reich's capital in the closing months of World War II. When the Soviets reached the town in January 1945, Hitler ordered it defended to the last bullet. Taking advantage of flooding and Soviet blunders and relying largely on high-school students and old men to do the fighting, the Germans turned the battle into a costly sixty-day siege. Tony Le Tissier's graphic account brings these harrowing two months to life through the stories of soldiers and civilians who survived the ordeal.

Paperback • 6 x 9 • 336 pages • 16 b/w photos

WWW.STACKPOLEBOOKS.COM
1-800-732-3669

Stackpole Military History Series

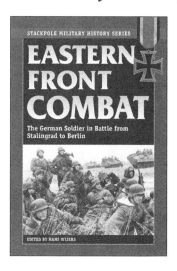

EASTERN FRONT COMBAT
THE GERMAN SOLDIER IN BATTLE FROM
STALINGRAD TO BERLIN
Edited by Hans Wijers

In these firsthand accounts—never before published in English—German soldiers describe the horrors of combat on the Eastern Front during World War II. A panzer crewman holds out to the bitter end at Stalingrad, fighting the Soviets as well as cold and hunger. An assault gun commander seeks out and destroys enemy tanks in Poland. Along the Oder River, a ragtag antiaircraft battery turns its guns against Russian infantry. And in Berlin a paratrooper makes a last, desperate stand in the war's closing days.

Paperback • 6 x 9 • 336 pages • 109 photos, 4 maps

WWW.STACKPOLEBOOKS.COM
1-800-732-3669

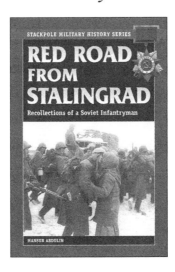

Stackpole Military History Series

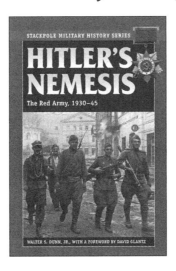

HITLER'S NEMESIS
THE RED ARMY, 1930–45
Walter S. Dunn, Jr.

Hitler's Nemesis "fills a major gap in our understanding of the Red Army at war. . . . By adding flesh and sinew to what had formerly seemed a gaunt skeleton, he has placed recognizable faces on that great gray mass of men whom the German Army fought against. . . . Here, laid out in detail for the reader, are the infantry, armor, artillery, and cavalry formations which enabled the Red Army to survive and emerge victorious after four years of struggle." —from the foreword by David Glantz

Paperback • 6 x 9 • 288 pages • 23 b/w photos

WWW.STACKPOLEBOOKS.COM
1-800-732-3669

Stackpole Military History Series

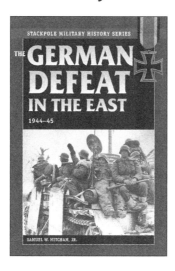

THE GERMAN DEFEAT IN THE EAST
1944–45
Samuel W. Mitcham, Jr.

The last place a German soldier wanted to be in 1944 was the Eastern Front. That summer, Stalin hurled millions of men and thousands of tanks and planes against German forces across a broad front. In a series of massive, devastating battles, the Red Army decimated Hitler's Army Group Center in Belorussia, annihilated Army Group South in the Ukraine, and inflicted crushing casualties while taking Rumania and Hungary. By the time Budapest fell to the Soviets in February 1945, the German Army had been slaughtered—and the Third Reich was in its death throes.

Paperback • 6 x 9 • 336 pages • 35 photos, 21 maps

WWW.STACKPOLEBOOKS.COM
1-800-732-3669

Stackpole Military History Series

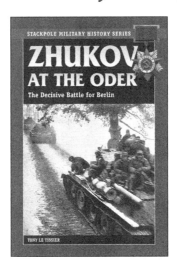

ZHUKOV AT THE ODER
THE DECISIVE BATTLE FOR BERLIN
Tony Le Tissier

On January 31, 1945, the Red Army stood on a line along the Oder River, about thirty-five miles east of Berlin. The fall of the Third Reich seemed imminent, especially with Marshal Georgi Zhukov leading the offensive, but the Soviets would not reach the German capital for more than two months, after a bloody campaign to establish bridgeheads across the Oder, seize the fortress of Küstrin, and take the Seelow Heights. While many historians have tended to focus on the final battle in Berlin, Tony Le Tissier provides a detailed account of how the Soviets fought their way to the city.

Paperback • 6 x 9 • 384 pages • 29 maps, 30 b/w photos

WWW.STACKPOLEBOOKS.COM
1-800-732-3669